## Financing Real Estate

### principles and practices

# Financing Real Estate

## principles and practices

**Sherman J. Maisel**

*Professor*
*University of California*
*Berkeley*

*McGraw-Hill Book Company*

*New York    St. Louis    San Francisco*
*Toronto    London    Sydney*

# Preface

This book presents the necessary background and techniques for making sound decisions in the financing of real estate. It also serves to introduce interested students to this major financial market by showing how analytic tools required by brokers, developers, financers, and users of real estate are developed. Attention is given to how lending occurs, what forces make it risky, why the market fluctuates, and how these elements can be evaluated to aid owners and lenders in making proper choices.

Most previous books in the field have tended to emphasize the institutional aspects of the financing process. They fail to give the potential lender, borrower, or observer of the real estate and construction markets a concrete analysis of what happens, why, and how to take advantage of various situations. In this book, in contrast, I have attempted to blend the necessary institutional and operational information into a sounder analytic approach. Information has been gathered on the best current practices from a variety of ably managed firms of both investors and lenders. The forces which create extensive opportunities, as well as dangers, are made clear here. Stress is placed on the need to analyze all transactions, so that they can be judged profitable or only seemingly profitable.

Acquired experience is distilled for students and practitioners who are eager to profit from better operations. In addition to lessons from mortgage lending, techniques developed in other areas of finance and portfolio management are discussed. As a result, many concepts are included that are not yet used by the average firm. This seems to me a minimum requirement of a new study. The time and effort required for understanding real estate financing should result in future insights, not merely in repeating a past which is rapidly becoming outmoded.

The successful decision-maker requires, first, considerable knowledge of facts and principles; second, a clear view of his goals; and finally, logical, organized procedures to help him toward his objectives. The book is divided into three corresponding parts. Chapters 2 to 5 deal with the environment and institutions within which real estate financing occurs. Chapters 6 to 11 approach the problem from the point of view of the lender and discuss the decisions he must make and the procedures he must adopt to aid him in reaching wise decisions. Chapters 12 to 16 consider the techniques needed in analyzing property financing from the home buyer's, developer's, and investor's viewpoints.

Clearly any such division is arbitrary. The one proposed is followed only in the interest of a logical presentation. The knowledge required by the borrower and the lender cannot really be separated. They are operating in the same market, which is dominated by identical legal and institutional constraints. Both have to be aware of the factors which may make one financing agreement successful and another disastrous. Each should understand the logic of the other's position so that better bargains can be made.

The reader is referred to the special Glossary of Real Estate Financing Terms at the end of the book. Every field has many unique usages of language. Although readers who approach this book with an industry background may find detailed explanations of such terms superfluous, they are useful and necessary for students and for others new to the field. In addition to defining the terms for those to whom they are new, the Glossary can serve in the future as a convenient professional reference.

I am grateful to the Center for Real Estate and Urban Economics, University of California, Berkeley, which over the years has contributed to much of the research which has been distilled into this volume. I also want to thank particularly the Capital Markets Research Project, Harvard University, and its directors, Professors James Duesenberry and Lawrence Thompson. It was at their urging and with their support that I initially investigated in detail some of the many problems in the field of real estate financing.

The list of those who aid in formulating or criticizing ideas that go into a book is always long. I should like to thank John Denton, James Mao, Richard Ratcliff, and Albert Schaaf for their careful reading of the initial draft of this volume and for their valuable suggestions, many of which have been incorporated into this final product. Valuable research aid was rendered by John Mendel and Michael Soper. My wife, Lucy Maisel, performed a yeoman's task in helping me develop the final form of presentation in this book as well as in all my previous works. Mrs. Helen Way did an extremely able job in the typing of this volume.

Sherman J. Maisel

# Contents

# Tables

# Figures

# Introduction_____1

The purchase, sale, and financing of real property play an extremely important role in the economy. More people own real estate equities than own any other type of equity. Many fortunes, both large and small, have arisen from the development and ownership of real estate. The financing of real property constitutes by far the largest use of all the net savings and funds that flow into our financial institutions and money markets.

Real estate values are affected by growth of the population, by expanding income, and by general price movements. Through most of the postwar period, all these causes combined to increase real estate values rapidly. In such circumstances the need for accurate analysis was slight. Rapid growth of the market and ever-rising prices were sufficient to bail out all except the poorest of developments and the most mistaken of investments. When markets shifted to a condition of stability or of only slightly rising values, however, the situation changed radically. Investments and loans entered into without proper analysis turned out to contain all the risks traditional in this market.

## THE SCOPE OF THE INDUSTRY

Real estate financing has become one of the most fascinating and most rapidly expanding sectors of the United States economy. That real estate financing is a major American business is obvious from the number of borrowers and the amounts they borrow. In an average recent year, more than 17 million American firms and families owed over $280 billion on debts secured by mortgages. Newly written mortgages exceeded 4 million per year. In a typical year, more than $55 billion was transferred to borrowers on their freshly created mortgage debts.

To supply this vast demand for credit, over 20,000 institutions—including commercial, savings, and mortgage banks, together with insurance companies and savings and loans—actively engage in mortgage lending. Because many of these institutions have numerous branches, the number of actual lending offices is close to 40,000.

For most financial institutions, mortgages rank among the most significant sources for investments and income. In many recent years, more than half the net flow of funds from financial institutions to the capital markets has taken the form of mortgages. Net mortgage investment recently has been more than five times the net investment in corporations through bonds and stock combined. It far exceeded lenders' portfolio additions of all types of government obligations.

This concentration on mortgages for investments has been closely related to the fact that they have traditionally paid among the highest rates of return of all major assets. For financial institutions, there is a clear correlation between the number of mortgages held and average earnings. For most classes of financial institutions, the higher the percentage of mortgages they hold, the higher their returns.

The profitability and safety of the more than 20,000 mortgage lenders are directly related to their adroitness in this kind of lending. As the ability of their managers and employees to understand the possibilities and problems in the mortgage market expands, our entire financial structure and our economy become more efficient.

## SOME CONSEQUENCES OF REAL ESTATE FINANCING

The availability of mortgage credit is a primary determinant of many facets of our economic life. It influences property values, construction and income, the efficiency and operation of financial institutions, the amount and yield of savings, and the standards and costs of homeownership.

### A Key Factor in the Sale and Purchase of Real Estate

One major group of borrowers includes the purchasers and owners of nonresidential property. They require funds either to enable them to invest in income properties or for the normal operations of their industrial or commercial businesses.

Income property investments have ranked among both the most profitable and the most risky individual ventures. Potential hazards and gains are a direct consequence of the terms of the mortgage financing. Only rarely do those seeking property have sufficient money of their own for the purchase. For most, the amount paid, as well as the likelihood of continued ownership and successful sale, is completely tied to the size and type of mortgage they can raise.

Successful investing or lending on income properties requires a careful balance of the owners' equities, the lenders' contributions and payment requirements, and the cash flow. Sales prices and potential risks and yields are closely related to the amount of debt leverage. In past booms, both borrowers and lenders have tended to overestimate the potential income of many properties. This led to higher loans and inflationary values, followed by collapse and catastrophe when the mortgage payments could not be met.

Lending conditions are equally, or perhaps more, significant for the much larger number of individual borrowers who engage in mortgage transactions to purchase their own homes. Their standard of housing, their type of house, and their chances of concluding a successful purchase are all closely related to available terms.

Because most families find it difficult to accumulate large savings, their ability to become homeowners depends directly on the equity required above whatever mortgage loan they can negotiate. For the past 20 years, the required down payment on all types of loans has steadily decreased. As a result, the number of potential owners has risen at a rapid rate.

Monthly payments play an equally important role. A family whose income becomes overcommitted either will suffer through lower expenditures on other consumption or will risk default. If income fluctuates or decreases sharply, many borrowers unable to maintain their mortgage payments may lose their homes. In addition, the interest charges on a mortgage are a direct cost to the family. The less it need pay to lenders, the more it has available for other purposes.

### Fluctuations in Construction and Property Values

One of the outstanding characteristics of the American economy has been the extreme instability in the prices of real property and in the amount of spending on construction activity. Building cycles, a major problem in the past, are still dangerous. Periods of high demand for real property, with rising values, have been followed by stagnant markets, diving prices, and numerous foreclosures.

While changing mortgage availability is not the only cause and perhaps not even the principal cause of these fluctuations, it is generally agreed that financing does play an important role in generating them. When mortgages are available easily and on liberal terms, building and property purchases are stimulated. If the market shifts to a tighter condition, activity is curtailed. While other offsetting forces intrude, financing shifts are major generators of movements in the real estate world.

### Standards of Urban Life

High loan-to-value ratios in single-family lending are made possible by the ability of the lender to look on the property securing the mortgage as a major part of his protection. Even if the individual fails in his obligation, the property remains a potential source of repayment of the loan. Consequently, the lender must carefully analyze the property to determine its prospects as a satisfactory security. In this process, the lending analysis becomes a major force affecting the design of properties built, what they look like, where they are, and what purposes they serve.

Through its influences on houses and on income property, mortgage lending affects the manner in which cities are built, as well as their form and maintenance. A lender who disagrees with the design or location of a shopping center, for instance, will refuse to lend on it. One who believes that modern-style houses have less resale value will demand conservative styling and oppose innovations. The lack of dynamic progress in building has frequently been attributed to the conservatism prevailing among lenders.

While the advance in individual housing standards since World War II has been spectacular, our total living standards may not have kept pace. The general deterioration of the urban scene has been the subject of universal comment and debate. The fact that large groups in our cities are finding it difficult not to fall far behind the average rate of improvement is also cause for continuous concern. The mortgage market has a significant part to play in assuring a better future for urban dwellers and in promoting the renewal and rehabilitation of our cities.

The extreme complexity of urban conservation or renewal is rapidly being realized. The practitioners of this new art put more and more emphasis on the great significance of financing in determining what we renew, what we conserve, and what we tear down. The metropolitan area is the investment frontier of the future. Real estate financiers will determine how well we solve our existing problems and how successfully we meet our new challenges.

### Efficiency and Productivity

A major goal of our economy is to increase the efficiency with which we use our resources. The costs of operating our credit system are far from inconsequential. Fortunately, the postwar period has seen a decided improvement in this situation. It now costs less money and resources to make funds available on real property than it did in the past.

Even more spectacular has been our improved ability to transfer funds, and therefore resources, from one state or region of the country to another. Major divergences have existed in the rates of growth and savings of the individual states. Some states have had money requirements which far outran their capacity to save. Without a smoothly operating mortgage market, the areas of rapid growth would be severely penalized by high interest rates and general shortages of funds. The total standard of living would be lowered. A successful national mortgage market minimizes regional differences and improves the lot of both borrowers and lenders.

Another prime need—that for increased rates of growth and productivity—can also be influenced by the allocation of funds. The potential in this area remains great because the past record has been so poor. Increases of productivity in the real estate markets have not kept up with the rest of the economy. Losses have also been incurred through instability. There is general agreement that lower costs of production, greater stability, and more efficiency in the construction process are urgently needed.

## Mortgages and Saving

How well our saving system operates is also highly dependent on the mortgage market.

During periods when financial institutions have been racked by significant losses on their mortgage portfolios, individuals become much less willing to entrust money to them. Our whole financial structure depends on the faith of individuals in the ability of lending institutions to protect the funds deposited with them.

The level of earnings on mortgages also has a significant influence on the amount of savings. Two forces are at work. Most importantly, a great deal of money earned from mortgages by lenders is saved automatically or semiautomatically. Life insurance companies build reserves. Saving institutions find that much of the interest credited to accounts remains on deposit.

Also, apparently, families increase their willingness to save when the reward offered for depositing money in savings institutions rises. While the relation between the amount of reward and the sums saved may not be as direct as some believe, at least in recent years those institutions which could offer higher interest because of the large yields they received from their mortgage portfolios did attract more savings.

## LENDERS AND BORROWERS

The skill with which real estate financing activities are conducted determines the profitability of most real estate transactions and the income level of a majority of our financial institutions. This also influences the general standard of living of most American families.

The knowledge and skills required of those actively engaged in real estate financing have been steadily increasing. Today the mortgage lender or borrower needs more than an ability to fill out forms correctly. He must understand the complex relationships that determine the ultimate profitability of intricate transactions. Upon what do yields and safety depend? Are scarce funds and high rates the result of temporary factors or are they likely to prevail over long periods?

Lenders must assume many risks. Many lending decisions are still based upon hunches, intuition, or rough rules of thumb, but performance levels which once would have been thought adequate are no longer acceptable to the best-managed, most successful firms. Firms that examine carefully the logic of their operations are often able to surpass their competition; careful planning reduces the number of common errors they commit. While the knowledge and training of both borrowers' representatives and lenders have improved steadily, vast areas for progress remain.

It is impossible to find and describe the typical person concerned with real estate financing. The number of lenders and borrowers runs into the millions. Each operates somewhat uniquely. What we can do is to picture their variety and then determine what basic knowledge is required of each if he is to do his job successfully.

The following brief descriptions of some typical positions which utilize mortgage knowledge show the types of jobs requiring the making of critical decisions. They may give the uninitiated reader some idea of the diversity of mortgage lending. The general pattern is clear. In a small unit, the mortgage man is a jack-of-all-trades. He performs all the myriad tasks of the mortgage market along with savings, brokerage, lending, or other functions. As size increases, mortgage work first absorbs all of one person's time. Then with growth, each lending or borrowing task becomes the function of a separate individual.

## Small-sized Lenders

Joe Johnson is manager, savings officer, and chief loan officer of the Home Savings and Loan Association, a firm with assets of $6 million. Although most of his time is occupied in being manager and savings officer, the firm's income and safety depend primarily on his skills as a mortgage officer. Home is close to the middle range of savings and loans. Joe has a staff of five people and an operating budget in the vicinity of $100,000. On the average, one or two customers come in every day to talk seriously about the possibility of a loan. In the course of the interview, Joe must learn enough about the property, the amount of money needed, and the customer's income and asset situation to decide whether Home is interested in the particular case.

If there is a mutual interest and an informal agreement, a loan application will be filled out. It lists the proposed amount of the mortgage and its terms, the property description, and the customer's personal credit information. Joe then has to get a credit check and see that the property is appraised, either by himself with part of his management committee or by an independent appraiser; finally, on the basis of his report, recommendation, and discussion, the loan or management committee may approve the loan.

The money will be paid out only after numerous forms, documents, and ledgers have been prepared and after a formal closing procedure has taken place to ensure that all legal and administrative requirements are met. Then the loan is added to the 500 to 600 already existing loans which Home is servicing. Johnson, with the aid of his clerk, has to check carefully the papers and the entire procedure. As each loan is completed, he hopes that it will fall into the routine category which requires only his minimal attention.

Unfortunately, though, this is frequently not the case. Payments slow up and the account becomes delinquent. Now extra time and special efforts are required. Mail communications, interviews, working out of new payment agreements, or a decision to ask for transfer of title or start of foreclosure may be necessary. Johnson may even have to manage the rental and eventual sale of the foreclosed property.

If Joe worked for the considerably larger commercial bank across the street, he would probably be a loan officer. He might find himself spending about the same or not quite as much time handling mortgage problems, but the rest of his work would be concerned with other types of lending. Many of the customers who approached him for money for their businesses would end up with their loans secured by a mortgage.

If the business were not a savings and loan but the Johnson Mortgage Company, the size of operation would be about the same. Instead of spending time in attracting savers, Joe would have to spend an equivalent amount of time in finding and negotiating correspondent and lending agreements with out-of-town lenders. Travel to the main insurance capitals would be necessary to line up commitments to purchase the mortgages his firm would originate. He would need to negotiate a line of credit with his local bank. Very frequent contacts would be required as he borrowed on his loans in progress (warehousing). He would also be far more active in calling on builders and real estate brokers so that they would come to him when their clients needed money to finance purchases.

### Middle-sized Lenders

In its 80 years of existence, the Provident Mutual Savings Bank has accumulated about $40 million in assets. It is one of the smaller mutual banks, with an operating budget of around $½ million. Like most of these institutions, it is in a Northeastern state. Its mortgage department makes between 400 and 600 new loans a year and services over 3,000. There are eight people in the mortgage loan department.

Jack Roberts might hold any of four or five different jobs in this unit. If he were head, he might carry the title of vice-president and might even have a carpet on his floor. In general charge of all mortgage activity, he would spend less time with borrowers for individual homes but more time on specialized loans such as store or apartment loans. Recently, Provident Mutual has had some abrupt shifts in its inflow of savings and over-all demand for funds. It has bought and sold mortgages in the secondary market and has varied considerably its ratio of bond investments to other assets. All these activities require greater skill, a constant reexamination and determination of policy, and negotiations with other lenders, borrowers, and officers. Roberts is so occupied by these negotiations, committees, and over-all supervision that in the normal course of events he handles only individual loans that are problems or exceptional for some other reason.

If Jack had not reached the top of the mortgage department, he might spend most of his time in making appraisals; or he might be in charge of loan servicing and particularly of attempting to clear up delinquencies. Provident has an active construction-loan program. One man spends almost full time on builders' sales and contacts. Another loan officer does most of the interviewing and qualifying of customers coming in for individual loans. Still another officer specializes in government-underwritten loans and in negotiations with the Federal Housing Administration or Veterans Administration.

The mortgage unit of Provident could be transplanted in size and general functions to a large commercial bank or a slightly smaller savings and loan. In the savings and loan field, units of this size or larger account for more than half the lending. If this unit were an independent mortgage company, it would be above the average size.

Some but not many functions would differ if this were a unit in one of the other institutions. Depending on what type of lender the unit serviced, more or less time might have to be spent on problems of the general money market, the demand for loans, and competitive terms and interest rates. Actually, functions would probably vary more with the geographical area and size of city that the mortgage unit was in than they would vary by type of lender.

## Larger Lenders

In 1948, Paul Mosher founded Urban Mortgage Company, and it has grown steadily since. Urban now has five offices and 150 employees, places over $125 million in loans annually, and services over $400 million in outstanding mortgages.

As president of Urban, Mosher spends almost all his time and effort concentrating on over-all problems of policy and management and in meetings with lenders, large-scale builders, and industry and community groups. He attributes his company's success and rapid growth to its willingness and ability to follow the market carefully and to some of its successful innovations that have helped to shape the patterns of the mortgage industry. Servicing contracts, prices, commitments, and interim financing—all have changed constantly. Mosher has had to improvise and find new lenders as major sources of funds dropped out of the market. Shifting interest rates have given him sizable profits and losses on his inventory of loans.

Urban has built up a fairly large management staff. Most now specialize in very specific tasks even though, as a rule, they have had experience in many of the other functions performed by the firm. One group of officers is charged with producing the customers for loans by working with builders, large-sized real estate firms, and land developers. At the other end, several executives handle relationships with final lenders, traveling to their home offices, placing mortgages, obtaining commitments, and smoothing out servicing problems.

In between are the numerous officers who handle individual loans. These include appraisers, loan processors, and men who interview loan applicants. A firm of this size requires accountants, treasurers, and even computer specialists. There is a section for loan closings and a legal division. Another unit handles construction supervision and lending and the obtaining of interim financing. The actual servicing of the loans, for routine and for delinquent cases, requires both large clerical staffs and skilled management.

While some of these functions of a large-scale mortgage company are unique, similar-sized staffs, having many of the same skills and performing related duties, are found in large commercial and mutual savings banks, in the largest savings and loan associations, and, with somewhat curtailed size and duties, in large life insurance companies.

### Borrowers

Robert Rice is a real estate broker who for many years did not pay much attention to the mortgage market. His customers did most of their borrowing through the local savings and loan. Suddenly, in one 3-month period, he found that 20 per cent of his office's sales had fallen through because the customers whose deposits had been obtained after much backbreaking effort had not been able to qualify for the necessary mortgage.

At this point Rice realized that financing was nearly as important a part of his business as selling. He began to spend more time in following and analyzing mortgage markets. By dealing with five different types of lenders, he found it possible to increase considerably his services to his clients. Each lender had somewhat different mortgage needs, and while their terms and conditions overlapped somewhat, at any given time one would be more likely than another to accept a particular type of loan. At times, also, one lender might find himself overcommitted or cautious and as a result would be far more stringent in his handling of applicants.

Upon analysis, Rice was able to see that these changes in policies were not haphazard or unique. They depended on what was happening in the economy, in the money market, and to the over-all demand for mortgages. Rice found he could anticipate changing situations and through care could make certain that his clients approached the most logical lender in any period. The percentage of the sales he lost because of lack of financing dropped drastically.

Edward Brewster is a large-scale builder and land developer. Almost from the start, he recognized the importance of financing, and this was a major factor in his success. Initially he specialized in tract building based on FHA-VA mortgages. To protect his operations, he carefully cultivated several lenders as sources for both construction and final take-out loans. When the money markets shifted, his costs in fees and discounts (explained in Chapter 5) rose sharply, but because of his previous efforts with lenders, he was able to continue sales. In contrast, some of his competitors had to curtail their production sharply. Others saw most of their profits disappear into financing charges. The cost and availability of credit dominate much of the action of firms of this size.

Brewster continues to spend a great deal of his time on financing. When he has entered into a shopping center or apartment development, he has found that the negotiation of lending terms is a major determinant of possible success. In addition to his own time, Brewster Development Company has a vice-president who spends full time on financing matters. He handles day-to-day negotiations with the bank, the mortgage company, and the FHA and VA.

If we examine the previous group and hundreds of other successful mortgage men, what underlying skills and knowledge can be observed, abstracted, and transmitted to those who want to learn? Unfortunately, one group of exceedingly important qualities cannot be taught. Such factors as skill in communications, understanding, and judgment must be developed in practice.

This makes even more important the fundamental information which can be included in a description of the best available professional knowledge. Expert practitioners have developed a wide body of basic facts and principles which can be portrayed and then studied by those who want to increase their proficiency.

## THE INSTRUMENTS OF REAL ESTATE FINANCING

Before proceeding with other questions, it is important that all concerned with the problems of real estate financing obtain a general picture of some of the specifically legal problems and terms met with in this field.

As in all areas of real property law, the legal problems attached to real estate financing are extremely complex. They have a long tradition of development in both common and civil law. The legal complexities differ widely from state to state and alter appreciably with time. No borrower or lender can afford not to seek advice from lawyers when actual legal problems arise. On the other hand, it is difficult to handle real estate transactions or even seek the necessary advice without a basic understanding of the terms involved.

## The Major Instruments

The three most common methods of obtaining real estate financing over and above an individual's equity are the mortgage, the deed of trust, and the contract of sale, or land contract. (Other methods are discussed in Chapter 15.) While each serves the same basic purpose, there are significant differences in the legal concepts of these three instruments and also in the rights which the borrower and the lender have under each type of loan. In effect, the types are listed and discussed in descending order of rights of the borrower, who is also called the debtor-mortgagor-trustor-vendee, depending on the instrument. In contrast, moving from the land contract through the mortgage, the lender, also called the creditor-mortgagee-beneficiary-vendor, has a more difficult time and meets with greater formalities and costs in obtaining possession of the property which has been used as security for the loan.

Throughout this volume, the term "mortgage" describes the various methods by which money is loaned on real property. Included are all the various types of written contract which pledge real estate as a security for repayment of debts. The debts may be long or short. They may arise from real estate transactions or may reflect other purposes.

1. A mortgage is a contract which pledges a specific property as security for the repayment of a debt. Both a contract to repay a debt and a pledge of security must exist for a mortgage to exist. The two parts may, however, be in separate documents. The majority of states operate under the so-called lien theory. In these states, the underlying property is merely hypothecated, or pledged. A lien is created against the land in favor of the mortgagee. If the borrower (mortgagor) fails to pay, the lender can go to court to enforce his lien. In a minority of states, the mortgage is considered as an instrument which conveys the title of the property to the lender in order to secure the debt. The transfer of title is defeated, or becomes void, when the debt is repaid. Such actual transfers of title by a defeasible deed go back to the common-law theory of mortgages.

2. The trust deed conveys the title to the property to a third party (trustee). The trustee has a power of sale which he is to exercise if the trustor (debtor) fails to meet the conditions of the loan which the trust deed secures. The trustee applies the proceeds of the sale to pay the obligation held by the beneficiary (creditor). The trustee only takes such title as is necessary. When no default is in existence, the trustee's title lies dormant. The trustor has all the normal rights of ownership subject to the encumbrance of the debt and trust deed.

In some states mortgages may carry a power of sale. The effect of such powers is to enable lenders to have the property sold without a judicial procedure. The results are much like the results when there is a trust deed, but no third-party trustee exists.

Usually real estate credit takes the form of the mortgage or the deed of trust. It may, however, also be granted in the form of contracts of sale, or land contracts; leases, and bonds and debentures. There are also special techniques such as syndication, cooperatives, and condominiums, which are methods of obtaining real estate equity funds and which are closely related to other forms of financing.

3. The long-term, or installment, land contract differs considerably from the mortgage even though it serves the same general purpose. In a land contract, the selling owner, or vendor, agrees to convey title to the purchaser, or vendee, at some future time when the contractual payments have been met. The contract gives the purchaser equitable ownership. Normally this includes the right to use the property while he continues his payments. The vendee may sell or borrow on his interest in the property. He can compel that he be granted full title when he has met his side of the bargain, with only such encumbrances as are spelled out in the initial contract. The vendor also may sell or borrow on his interest in the property subject to the terms of the land contract.

## Requirements in Lending

Any interest in land can be borrowed against and pledged under a mortgage. A common example is borrowing against a long-term lease. The mortgage must be in writing. The recording statutes apply to mortgages which must contain the necessary legal descriptions and acknowledgments required by law. When recorded, the mortgage obtains a priority and a protection against future recordings. While priority is usually granted in order of recording, certain other liens may be given preference. This is usually true of tax liens or assessments. Depending upon the particular state and circumstances, mechanic's liens may also gain priority. The mortgage itself or later subordination agreements may spell out a change in the order of preference from the simple order of recording. Such arrangements are particularly important in land development agreements.

The obligation secured by a mortgage is usually evidenced by a promissory note or notes (bond). These notes may be negotiable instruments in and of themselves. Their owner has the right to sue to collect on them in the normal manner. The mortgage lien is simply an additional form of security. The critical factor is the debt. The mortgage has no standing without the debt. The mortgage may contain a description of the obligation, or, more commonly, the note may simply be referred to in sufficient detail to put other parties on notice of its existence.

The obligation may refer to money previously loaned, to future advances, as in construction lending, or to optional future advances (open-end mortgage). The priorities and right of other parties may differ depending on the type of advance. Commonly, purchase-money mortgages, which are extensions of credits as part of a purchase, are treated specially. They are given extra priorities, but in many states they cannot claim deficiency judgments.

Mortgages frequently spell out certain duties and rights. Acceleration clauses are common. These specify that upon default of certain conditions such as failure to meet amortization payments or failure to insure or to pay taxes, the entire debt becomes due and payable. Action may be taken to collect the whole sum rather than merely those parts otherwise due. Under assignment-of-rents clauses the lender can step in and collect rents to apply to the debt. This stops the borrower from collecting moneys and putting them to other uses. Similarly borrowers are required to maintain properties and to avoid waste or injury to property.

In the usual case, owners can sell properties which are mortgaged, while lenders can sell the mortgages to others. The sale or assignment of the debt to a third party can be recorded, which puts all on notice as to the new creditor. A borrower can sell his property subject to the mortgage debt. In such cases the new owner may or may not assume liability for the existing mortgages. He may assume the mortgage or buy subject to, but not assuming, the debt. In either case, the property remains as security for the debt.

When a new owner assumes the mortgage, he becomes the principal debtor. The seller, or original mortgagor, remains liable for any deficiency in addition to the new buyer unless there is a specific agreement by the lender to substitute the new owner in place of the original borrower.

## Remedies of Lender

When a debtor fails to make payments or defaults on his agreement in other ways, the lender has the right to attempt to satisfy his claim against the property. We loosely use the term "foreclosure" to apply to this procedure even though several alternative techniques may be involved.

Foreclosure is the sale of whatever right, title, and interest in the property the mortgagor had when the mortgage was executed. The mortgagee goes to court to claim his rights. Parties whose claims are superior to those of the mortgagee are not affected. The court determines the amount due. It orders a public foreclosure sale. This usually requires that cash bids be made except for the beneficiary, who may bid the unpaid balance due to him. The sums received by the court are used to pay off the unsatisfied liens according to their priority, with any balance (which rarely occurs) going to the original owner.

If the proceeds of the sale do not cover the outstanding debt, the court may enter a deficiency judgment for the difference. The uses of deficiency judgments have been heavily circumscribed in many states. Some have abolished them completely. In some a judgment must be based on fair market value rather than merely the amount bid in the sale.

In most states, the mortgagor has a right called the equity of redemption. This allows him to pay the debt plus certain penalties up to the time of the foreclosure sale even though the mortgage is in default. This right to redeem may be held by junior lienholders and others. The foreclosure is the act of cutting off this right. In some states an additional statutory redemption period runs following the foreclosure sale for up to a year or more. As a rule mortgagors cannot waive their rights to redeem. In many states the mortgagor may remain in possession after the foreclosure until the period for redemption has ended.

The cost of judicial procedure is likely to be high. The problems of gaining possession and of potential losses during the redemption period are great. These are among the reasons for the use of the trust deed or mortgage with a power of sale. Under this procedure, the trustee or mortgagee records a notice of default. From the time of the notice, a fixed reinstatement period usually exists. An announcement of a public sale is published. The sale then takes place with public bidding. The trustee or the mortgagee with power of sale passes title. In most cases the deed carries the right of possession. The effect of both the judicial process and the trustee sale is normally to eliminate most junior liens but not Federal tax liens.

To save the expense and costs of foreclosure or the public sale, the lender will sometimes seek to obtain a deed in lieu of foreclosure. Since this deed is valuable to the lender to save expenses, courts may scrutinize the transaction with considerable care to be certain that a bona fide sale took place. They want to avoid situations where lenders, because of their superior knowledge and financial strength, could take advantage of the debtor.

### The Land Contract

The land contract, or contract of sale, is another way for the seller to extend credit and yet attempt to avoid some of the difficulties and costs of foreclosure. Such contracts are particularly common where the buyer puts up only a small equity. They are used because the seller can regain his property in a much simpler manner. As a corollary they mean that the buyer has fewer rights.

The contract is made between the vendor (seller) and vendee

(buyer). It usually provides that the vendor will pass the legal title when the agreed-upon price has been met through installments, which may be accompanied by a fixed lump-sum payment. The seller retains title. He can sell his rights, including those for future payments, to a third party. In other cases he may simply assign his rights to the payments. He can mortgage whatever interest he has under the contract. Judgments can be entered as liens against his interests. The contract continues even if the vendor dies.

The purchaser, or vendee, receives equitable ownership and many rights pertaining to it. He can sell or borrow against his interest. While this is not necessary, many contracts give him the right of possession. His interests can be made subject to a judgment lien, and his rights like those of the vendor are likewise not terminated by death.

In many areas, sellers are unwilling to record the contract, since they would then be forced to clear the title if the sale did not go through. In some cases, however, recording is necessary, and the vendee frequently desires it for added protection. This is typically true when he is not in possession, since it is the act of possession that gives him much protection. When the purchaser meets his obligations, he is entitled to a title free of any circumstances except those he has agreed to in the contract.

If the buyer fails to meet his payments, the vendor can, in most states, take many actions. He can evict the vendee. He can sue for specific performance, foreclose, sue for damages, and declare a forfeiture of previous payments under the contract. Normally the cost and expense of gaining possession are less than under a mortgage or deed of trust.

Buyers normally use contracts of sale because they have no choice. They lack sufficient funds to obtain ownership with a mortgage. Their interest is harder to transfer and borrow against. Claims against the vendor may cause difficulties in obtaining a clear title. The final title may turn out to be defective or at least will require expensive court action. If the buyer defaults, the losses of prior payments may be considerably greater than under a mortgage.

The legal literature and the real estate literature report many major attempts to simplify and reduce the costs of mortgages and foreclosures. The charges to both borrowers and lenders vary widely from state to state. These costs enter into the price of real property. They are particularly burdensome when properties turn over frequently. No simple solutions exist because of the problem of balancing opposing interests. The fact that some states have succeeded in lowering costs, however, makes them more attractive for outside lenders. This gives other states a goal toward which to strive.

## SELECTED REFERENCES

Bowman, Arthur G.: *Real Estate Law in California,* Prentice-Hall, Inc., Englewood Cliffs, N.J., 1958.

Bryant, Willis R.: *Mortgage Lending,* 2d ed., McGraw-Hill Book Company, New York, 1962.

Jones, Oliver, and Leo Grebler: *The Secondary Mortgage Market,* University of California, Los Angeles, 1961.

Klaman, Saul B.: *The Postwar Residential Mortgage Market,* Princeton University Press, Princeton, N.J., 1961.

Kratovil, Robert: *Real Estate Law,* 3d ed., Prentice-Hall, Inc., Englewood Cliffs, N.J., 1958.

Pease, Robert H., and Homer V. Cherrington: *Mortgage Banking,* McGraw-Hill Book Company, New York, 1953.

# The Loan and Mortgage Markets_____2

Students of medicine study anatomy and physiology as necessary prerequisites to an understanding of complex medical situations. Similarly, if they are to become skillful practitioners of their art, mortgage financiers must have a basic comprehension of the underlying structure of their market and business.

Such knowledge must extend beyond the area of real estate financing to the broader over-all credit market, of which real property financing is just a part. Lenders and borrowers frequently find their actions circumscribed and dominated by forces entirely foreign to the mortgage field. Shortages of available funds, shifts in discounts, and altered terms often reflect outside pressures to which the mortgage officer must react. He must possess the ability to analyze the entire saving and investing picture, not only his own segment. When the man concerned with real estate financing becomes aware of how and why the over-all lending climate changes, he has taken a major step toward understanding his own needs.

Describing this necessary institutional and market knowledge is the task of this chapter and the next. In them we move from a view of the total credit market to the mortgage sector and to the types of firms operating in the real estate market. Chapters 4 and 5 analyze the government's impact on the market. They show how as a result of changes in government policy, plus demand and supply, impor-

tant movements occur in the availability of mortgage money and the
rates charged for loans.

## THE SUPPLY OF, AND DEMAND FOR, LOANABLE FUNDS

Real estate financing must compete for its funds with all other potential uses of credit. Before money is made available, lenders must
choose whether to expand or contract investments in government or
corporate bonds, notes and bills, stocks, commercial or consumer
loans, or other types of potential assets in relation to their purchases
or sales of mortgages.

The amount available to real estate will depend both upon the
total supply of credit and upon the amount left after competitive
uses have been met. The basic source of funds is actual savings in a
given period by businesses, individuals, or governments. In addition,
money may be made available by repayment of existing loans. Thus,
to examine the impact on mortgages of movements in over-all
credit conditions, we must analyze the underlying source—net savings—as well as the percentage of total credit channeled to financial markets, repayments of previous loans, and demand from other
users.

At times the amount of funds available for investment expands
rapidly—for instance, when families or businesses or the government saves more, when previous borrowers speed up their rate of
repayments, or when the Federal Reserve allows the banks to create
new deposits.

The demand for funds as well as the supply of funds may fluctuate. Businesses may begin to finance more of their own investments
directly. The government may run a surplus. Fewer houses may be
started. All these various conditions can occur simultaneously.

Such movements in the supply of, and demand for, loans are reflected in shifting interest rates and in expanded or curtailed availability of funds in some or all of the submarkets. The mortgage market seems to be a sphere where all these various currents converge
and cause major fluctuations.

Sharp alterations in the flow of available funds have been a common characteristic of the mortgage market. In one year, lenders'

meetings and professional journals may be primarily concerned with shortages of funds, making dire predictions that the economy in the future will not succeed in generating enough money for mortgages. A year or two later, similar media may be concerned mainly with the glut of money and the difficulty of placing it at an adequate return.

## Meaning of the Market

In speaking of the loan and mortgage markets, we mean the interrelated points where requests to borrow are negotiated, transactions occur, money is borrowed and lent, and interest rates and fees are determined. The significant fact is that even though such loans may and do occur in thousands of separate cities and institutions, each loan has some impact upon the others.

There is no single organized market for funds. There is no large exchange as there is for listed stocks, not even a small group of dealers as there is for government bonds. Instead, there are thousands of submarkets in cities and towns throughout the country where a variety of items such as mortgages, bonds, and notes are traded. The due dates for particular loans may vary from one day to 50 years.

Actually, each of these forms of classification—by type, term, or area—creates within the loanable-fund market as a whole a submarket which tends to be interconnected with most others. Funds flow from one to another. Borrowers and lenders are willing to substitute investments in one place for those available elsewhere. When a corporation in Boston expands and requires a loan, it may become harder to buy a house in Dallas. The Boston corporation may seek funds from an insurance company or a local or New York bank. The bank in turn must decide whether or not to make the loan and if so what other potential customers not to accept. Each lender or borrower makes adjustments as a result of experiencing a slightly altered situation with respect to supply or demand. It is the existence of these interrelationships that enables us to analyze credit markets in over-all terms, while recognizing that the form and magnitude of impact at each separate lending point will vary.

## Savings by Sectors

The basic source of funds for investment is the excess in the amounts received by various individuals, businesses, or governmental units over what they spend for current consumption. They may lend these moneys directly to others who want to borrow and spend more than their receipts, or they may place them with financial units which in turn can lend them to others.

Table 2-1 shows some savings figures for the country for the years 1945 to 1963. The personal savings figures, which are net for all households, are influenced both by greater desires to save and by wishes of other families to borrow. Business savings are the total amounts of funds available to all businesses. In most years, businesses as a whole invest more than they save and are therefore net borrowers. The amount they must borrow is, however, directly related to the amount of received funds which need not be paid out for expenses of current production.

Governments save when they run a surplus. Such funds, which are either deposited in financial institutions or used to pay off debts, are in either case available to the loan market. On the other hand, when governments as a whole run deficits they must borrow funds in the market. A negative figure indicates they did not add savings in that year but instead required funds.

Table 2-1 shows that since the war there has been a steady expansion of savings. In fact, total savings in the first half of the 1960s were more than double those of the last half of the 1940s. Most of the expansion, however, has been in business savings. Consumer saving slumped after the war and has just returned to the 1945 level. Government savings have fluctuated from plus to minus. The total level of saving tends to be unstable from year to year. Fluctuations of 15 to 20 per cent are quite common.

Clearly, the most unstable factor has been the government sector. Here, as is well recognized, the sharp movements of the Federal budget from surplus to deficit within a year create major fluctuations in the demand for, and supply of, funds. It must be recalled that the measured flow for any unit does not necessarily reflect a change in

TABLE 2-1    *Savings by Sectors, 1945–1963* (In billions of dollars)

| Year | Net personal savings | Gross business savings | Governments' surplus or deficit (−) | Total |
|------|------|------|------|------|
| 1945 | 28.7 | 15.6 | −39.7 | 4.6 |
| 1946 | 13.5 | 13.1 | 4.1 | 30.7 |
| 1947 | 4.7 | 18.9 | 13.3 | 36.9 |
| 1948 | 11.0 | 26.6 | 8.2 | 45.8 |
| 1949 | 8.5 | 27.6 | −3.1 | 33.0 |
| 1950 | 12.6 | 27.7 | 8.2 | 48.6 |
| 1951 | 17.7 | 31.5 | 6.1 | 55.3 |
| 1952 | 18.9 | 33.2 | −3.9 | 48.2 |
| 1953 | 19.8 | 34.3 | −7.1 | 47.0 |
| 1954 | 18.9 | 35.5 | −6.7 | 47.7 |
| 1955 | 17.5 | 42.1 | 2.9 | 62.5 |
| 1956 | 23.0 | 43.0 | 5.2 | 71.3 |
| 1957 | 23.6 | 45.6 | 1.0 | 70.2 |
| 1958 | 24.7 | 44.8 | −11.4 | 58.1 |
| 1959 | 23.6 | 51.3 | −1.5 | 73.9 |
| 1960 | 21.7 | 50.7 | 3.9 | 76.3 |
| 1961 | 27.6 | 50.8 | −4.7 | 73.7 |
| 1962 | 29.1 | 57.6 | −3.9 | 82.8 |
| 1963 | 29.4 | 60.6 | −1.7 | 88.3 |

SOURCE: *Economic Report of the President*, 1964, pp. 216–217.

the desire to save or run surpluses. The actual savings depend as much on changes in income levels as they do on desires.

Business savings consist of undistributed profits (or the difference between dividend payments and net profits) plus capital-consumption allowances. Year-to-year alterations in business savings depend primarily upon the level of profits, which are among the most volatile items in the economy. In contrast, depreciation allowances and dividends are relatively stable. Fluctuating profits above stable dividends combine in such a way that business savings experience repercussions of changes in profit rates to a magnified degree.

The factors determining consumer saving in the short run are familiar. Many households have semipermanent commitments to save through insurance and pension funds. Additional savings depend primarily upon the amount of income they receive and upon the rate at which they buy automobiles. Big auto sales mean low savings. Since 1950, net personal savings have varied between 6 and 8 per cent of disposable income. A change of 2 per cent in disposable income is equal to over $8 billion, or over 25 per cent of net mortgage investment.

### Sources of Funds

The savers have the ability to invest directly in goods, to buy credit-market instruments, or to save through a financial intermediary which, in turn, will loan out their funds. In fact, most household saving takes place by an accumulation of claims against financial institutions. This differs distinctly from the actions of the other groups in the economy, which do the bulk of their savings directly through the credit market. Excluding money (demand deposits and currency), almost all current savings going into, and funds held by, financial institutions belong to households.

Table 2-2 gives the basic sources of funds for the credit markets. It shows rather minor year-to-year shifts in the amounts made available to financial institutions, with the exception of commercial banks. But it shows very significant movements in flows in the "other" category, where flows depend upon the direct savings of households and businesses, in commercial banks, and to some extent in governments. The existence of these fluctuations, which result from monetary and fiscal policy plus income changes, is one of the major reasons why the money markets swing from easy to stringent and back.

It should be recognized that most of the funds shown under the various financial institutions, plus any changes in them, also reflect movements in household saving rates. This tendency of households

TABLE 2-2  *Sources of Financial Funds in the United States, 1953–1963* (In billions of dollars)

| Source | 1953 | 1954 | 1955 | 1956 | 1957 | 1958* | 1959 | 1960 | 1961 | 1962 | 1963 |
|---|---|---|---|---|---|---|---|---|---|---|---|
| Savings and loan associations | 3.7 | 4.2 | 5.7 | 4.9 | 4.9 | 6.2 | 8.3 | 7.1 | 9.3 | 10.2 | 12.9 |
| Life insurance companies | 4.9 | 5.0 | 5.2 | 5.1 | 4.9 | 5.1 | 5.2 | 5.4 | 5.6 | 6.4 | 6.6 |
| Commercial banks | 4.0 | 10.3 | 5.0 | 4.3 | 5.0 | 15.2 | 4.2 | 9.3 | 15.9 | 19.4 | 19.1 |
| Mutual savings banks | 1.8 | 2.0 | 2.0 | 2.0 | 1.9 | 2.5 | 1.4 | 1.5 | 2.1 | 3.1 | 3.5 |
| Other financial institutions | 3.7 | 3.5 | 3.8 | 3.9 | 4.6 | 5.3 | 6.6 | 5.9 | 6.2 | 6.6 | 6.3 |
| Government | 2.6 | 2.6 | 2.2 | 3.0 | 3.6 | 2.3 | 5.7 | 5.1 | 3.6 | 4.0 | 3.2 |
| Other | 8.1 | 6.6 | 24.5 | 7.2 | 9.1 | 6.1 | 27.5 | 4.9 | 8.2 | 13.5 | 14.7 |
| Total | 28.8 | 34.2 | 48.2 | 30.4 | 34.0 | 42.7 | 58.9 | 39.2 | 50.9 | 63.2 | 66.3 |

* Figures after 1958 are not strictly comparable with that and previous years.

SOURCE: *Investment Outlook*, Bankers Trust Company, New York.

27

to prefer saving through institutions rather than directly is a primary force behind the current organization of the mortgage market. In effect, our system of individual saving is based on trusting our money to banks, savings institutions, or insurance and pension funds, which then spend these sums so as to get the best mixtures of returns and risks.

Mortgage loans, which used to average about two-thirds of the amount of personal savings, in recent years have been as large as total personal savings. When the supply of savings is unstable or the demand from other uses fluctuates, the amount of money made available to the mortgage market may be squeezed. In other periods, it may rise so rapidly as to force lenders to increase greatly their solicitation of loan applications.

## Uses of Funds

Table 2-3 shows annual changes in the uses of funds. The mortgage market must compete in terms of yield, risk, and profitability with all other potential uses for funds. The interactions among all the various submarkets determine the actual flows as shown in the table. We see that mortgages were by far the main use for all investment and credit funds. In the last two years, the net investment in mortgages averaged higher than $27 billion annually—nearly 50 per cent of the total available funds. No other major instrument accounted for even a quarter as much of the market for funds as did mortgages.

The rate of lending on mortgages was among the most unstable in absolute, although not in percentage, terms. The other areas with major fluctuations included bank loans to business, closely related to rapid fluctuations in inventories; consumer credit, which varied with years of high and low auto sales; and the rapid changes in government financing, which, as already noted, reflected the oscillations between deficits and surpluses.

The critical fact is that the fluctuations in the supply of savings available through financial institutions and the shifting demand from other users have caused the amount of money available in the mortgage market to be violently squeezed in certain years. This has led

TABLE 2-3  *Uses of Financial Funds in the United States, 1953–1963* (In billions of dollars)

| Use | 1953 | 1954 | 1955 | 1956 | 1957 | 1958* | 1959 | 1960 | 1961 | 1962 | 1963 |
|---|---|---|---|---|---|---|---|---|---|---|---|
| Mortgages............... | 9.9 | 12.4 | 16.2 | 14.6 | 12.0 | 15.3 | 19.0 | 16.0 | 19.5 | 25.3 | 29.7 |
| U.S. government securities... | 4.2 | 3.2 | 1.6 | −6.1 | .... | 6.2 | 10.5 | −2.7 | 5.9 | 6.0 | 2.5 |
| State and local bonds........ | 3.5 | 4.2 | 3.5 | 3.3 | 4.8 | 5.7 | 5.0 | 4.0 | 5.3 | 5.7 | 6.8 |
| Corporate bonds............. | 4.8 | 3.8 | 4.2 | 4.7 | 7.1 | 5.9 | 4.1 | 5.0 | 5.1 | 5.0 | 5.6 |
| Corporate stocks............ | 1.9 | 1.8 | 1.9 | 2.5 | 2.7 | 2.1 | 2.4 | 1.8 | 2.9 | 0.6 | −0.3 |
| Foreign securities........... | −0.1 | 0.2 | .... | 0.5 | 0.7 | 1.4 | 0.7 | 0.6 | 0.8 | 1.0 | 1.1 |
| Consumer credit............. | 3.9 | 1.1 | 6.3 | 3.5 | 2.6 | 0.2 | 6.3 | 4.5 | 1.6 | 5.5 | 6.7 |
| Bank loans.................. | 0.8 | 1.1 | 7.5 | 4.6 | 1.7 | 1.8 | 6.9 | 3.5 | 4.0 | 7.6 | 8.3 |
| Other...................... | −0.1 | 6.4 | 7.0 | 2.8 | 2.4 | 4.1 | 4.0 | 6.5 | 5.8 | 6.5 | 5.9 |
| Total.................. | 28.8 | 34.2 | 48.2 | 30.4 | 34.0 | 42.7 | 58.9 | 39.2 | 50.9 | 63.2 | 66.3 |

* Figures after 1958 are not strictly comparable with that and previous years.
SOURCE: *Investment Outlook*, Bankers Trust Company, New York.

to jumps in interest rates, fees, and discounts.[1] It has caused sharp alterations in normal lending patterns and in the relationships among those in the market. These are the factors which make a knowledge of the general market so important to mortgage firms.

## Gross Flow of Funds

Tables 2-1 to 2-3 deal with net savings and with the net sources and uses of loanable funds. The volume of lending, however, far surpasses these amounts. In fact, net loans amount to less than half of all loans made. The market movements which we observe can be caused as much by reinvestments or lack of them as by net investment. While there is some pressure to reinvest funds back to their sources, this is far from a necessary procedure.

## The Insurance Flow of Funds

One of the few segments of the market for which we have an adequate picture of the total flows and total investments is in the insurance industry.

The first section of Table 2-4 reports gross income and expenses for the whole insurance industry in 1962. The difference between them is the money that was available for net investment. Thus the industry received over $19 billion in premium payments plus nearly $6 billion either from investment income or from miscellaneous sources, a total of $25 billion gross receipts. From this total income, companies made benefit payments and furnished moneys for dividends and cash surrenders and for operating expenses. Deducting the $18.5 billion required for these purposes, a difference of $6.475 billion was available for purchases of additional investment.

[1] When the market interest rate shifts, outstanding mortgages with interest rates below the market will be sold at discounts. Discounts are also used to adjust the market to small interest rate changes. A discount is simply the difference between the outstanding principal on a loan and the amount the loan sells for in the market. The way in which discounts or fees (payments above the principal) affect the actual yield on mortgages is discussed at length in the Appendix to Chapter 6.

TABLE 2-4   *Cash Flow of Life Insurance Companies, 1962* (In millions of dollars)

| *Gross inflow of funds* | | *Gross outflow of funds* | |
|---|---|---|---|
| **Income:** | | **Expenses:** | |
| Premium | | Payments....... $9,338 | |
|   receipts..... $19,373 | | Policy surren- | |
| Investment | |   ders or | |
|   income....... 5,044 | |   dividends..... 3,753 | |
| Other income... 605 | | Operating | |
|     Gross income........ $25,022 | |   expenses..... 5,456 | |
| | |     Total.............. $18,547 | |
| **Sales and repayments of assets:** | | **Purchases of assets:** | |
| Bonds......... $15,688 | | Bonds......... $18,487 | |
| Stocks......... 722 | | Stocks......... 766 | |
| Mortgages.... 4,779 | | Mortgages.... 7,478 | |
| Others......... 894 | | Others........ 1,827 | |
|     Total.............. 22,083 | |     Total.............. 28,558 | |
| **Total inflow of funds....** $47,105 | | **Total outflow of funds..** $47,105 | |
| Memo: net inflow and | | | |
|   net investment | | | |
| Bonds......... $2,799 | | | |
| Stocks.......... 44 | | | |
| Mortgages..... 2,699 | | | |
| Others.......... 933 | | | |
|     Total........ $6,475 | | | |

SOURCE: *Life Insurance Fact Book*, 1963, pp. 51, 52, 54, 69.

The second section of the table shows that gross investments far surpassed the net flow of funds. Investment officers of insurance companies purchased over $28.5 billion in assets in the course of the year. The largest inflow was from sales and repayments in the bond account. Much of this $15.6 billion turnover is accounted for by short-term governments, but other bonds also matured or were called during the year. The second largest gross inflow of funds came from the payment of amortization and principal on mortgages.

Money from these various repayments, amounting to over $22 billion, was available for new and different types of investments. While a large-scale shift in reinvestments by all companies would have caused major market reactions, sizable realignments of assets were possible. For any single firm, very large transfers among types of holdings could have been made without this result.

The final section of the table, showing how the firms as a whole did invest their net flow of income, indicates the net change in assets over and above the very large reinvestments. The table as a whole shows the source of funds for investment and the way in which they are distributed.

## THE MORTGAGE MARKET

Just as we have discussed movements in the over-all demand for, and supply of, loanable funds, so can we analyze alterations in the mortgage market. Here, however, we must be concerned with more than the simple flows. Since mortgages are the heart of our interest, we want to examine movements in this market in far more detail. This means that as an aid to future analysis we must classify our information in logical divisions.

### The Diversity of Mortgages

Unlike the other major instruments in the capital market, a mortgage tends to be a personal and highly differentiated claim. Differences among mortgages are caused by variations in the laws of each state, in the practices of each lender, in the types of borrowers, and in the property used as collateral.

Borrowers are a highly diverse group. They include individual consumers, investors and corporations entering the market to obtain funds needed primarily in businesses outside the real estate field, and investors and corporations needing money for their real estate transactions. Loans may be required for the development or construction of new property, for the purchase of existing buildings, or perhaps to remove equity accumulated in real estate in order to use it in an entirely different field.

Mortgages may be classified according to areas, borrowers, and type and use of the property. Thus mortgages are said to be on (1) one- to four-family residential structures, (2) other multifamily dwellings, (3) commercial properties, including stores and office buildings, (4) hotels and motels, (5) industrial plants, (6) farms, (7) special-purpose uses (churches, theaters, service stations, bowling alleys, etc.), and (8) unimproved land.

There may also be differentiation between government-insured or government-guaranteed and conventional types of mortgages.

## Legal Factors

Each state or supervisory authority establishes complex legal requirements specifying what the lenders under its supervision may hold in their mortgage portfolio. Frequently particular terms are set forth with respect to minimum equities or down payments (for example, loans may not be more than 90 per cent of value), the maximum period of amortization and its form (say 25 years of level payments), and the amount of interest that can be charged.

In addition, the area within which many institutions can lend is limited. Much savings and loan lending must be transacted within 100 miles of the firm's headquarters. Almost all institutions must meet special requirements as to the percentage of assets that can be invested in particular kinds of loans.

Legal influences are felt still more strongly through the differences in the real property laws of the 50 states. Foreclosure procedures, for example, vary dramatically. The period required for foreclosure may run from under a month to over two years. Costs incurred range from small sums to over $1,000. Clearly, all these legal factors cause every mortgage to differ from every other.

Other difficulties arise because of the need for construction supervision. Since the structure forms a major share of the security, the manner of construction and how plans are followed influence the worth of the final loan. A need for interim financing also exists. As in most industries, builders require loans for working capital. The fact that the amount lent is tied to construction progress means that lenders must walk a fine line, desiring to furnish sufficient capital but not wanting to pay out more than the builder has invested in his partially completed unit. Only astute judgment and continuous loan supervision during construction can assure the lender that he actually receives the security upon which he thought he loaned his money.

## Loans or Commitments

The analysis of the data in the mortgage market is complicated further by the fact that there may be a wide difference between conditions when the loan was agreed to and those prevailing when it was actually made. The data available on flow of funds and on rates of interest and other terms usually apply to the time that the money was paid out. There is frequently a long lag between the time of commitment and the actual loan. Buildings usually cannot be started without a guarantee that a loan will be made upon completion. A lender makes a commitment to lend money when and if the unit is finished and the potential borrower wants to take up the commitment. Such an arrangement ties up future funds. In cases of large structures, tracts, or shopping centers, the money will not be paid out for one to three or four years, during which time money markets may shift drastically. In addition, because so many propositions fall through before completion, the lender can never be certain that the money will actually be used. Borrowers may find more favorable terms in the interim and fail to exercise the option implicit in an advance commitment.

## Net Mortgage Lending

Table 2-3 shows that borrowers on mortgages are by far the largest demanders of funds in our credit market. Figure 2-1 charts the movements over time in mortgage lending, together with some related data. From section A of the figure, we note that while mortgage lending has grown rapidly, its path has been far from smooth. The net flows expanded from about $6 billion in 1945 to about $30 billion in 1963. However, the gains were marked by several sizable

FIGURE 2-1 *Mortgage-market Indicators*

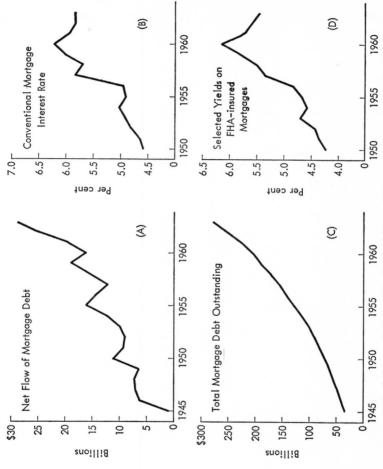

SOURCES: *Federal Reserve Bulletin*; Housing and Home Finance Agency, *Annual Report and Housing Statistics*.

fluctuations, with important dips in mortgaging activity taking place in 1949, 1951, 1956, and 1960.

Related movements occurred in mortgage interest rates, as demonstrated by sections B and D of Figure 2-1. A much higher level of rates prevailed at the end of the period than at the start. We also note very significant variations in shorter periods. While mortgage interest rates and yields move more sluggishly than other market rates, substantial changes have taken place. The shifts shown in the figure, when translated into quoted prices or values of existing loans, as is done daily in the bond market when interest rates move, would indicate alterations in the value or price of existing mortgages of 10 to 20 per cent.

The factors that cause these movements in net lending, in current yields, and in the value of existing loans are of critical importance to those engaged in real estate financing. It is rare for any part of the market to escape untouched when such movements occur. Shifts in the demand for, and supply of, mortgage funds cause rapid changes in the borrowing positions of borrowers and lenders and in their agreed-upon terms.

### Total Mortgage Lending

The net additions to mortgage loans form only one (and actually the smallest) measure of the mortgage business. Other important data are shown in section C of Figure 2-1 and in Table 2-5. The former shows that the total amount of loans outstanding has gone up steadily, with only minor hesitations. It is this volume of loans held that determines the total income of lenders and the amounts paid by borrowers. The relationship between the total volume of debt and net lending also shows that such income reacts only gradually to current fluctuations in the market.

More of the total debt turns over each year, however, than appears from the net lending data. The actual mortgages held reflect movements not in net loans but rather in the type of gross mortgage lending. It is clear also that from the point of view of those in the industry, it is the amount of gross business done in the year that determines many factors such as the size, organization, and problems of the lenders. We saw in Table 2-4 the sharp differences for insurance companies between gross and net mortgage lending. This difference is still greater for mortgage lenders as a whole.

While accurate figures exist neither on the amount of mortgage loans made in any period nor on the uses to which these funds

TABLE 2-5 *Mortgage Lending by Type of Lender, 1962* (In billions of dollars)

| Institutions | Gross mortgage lending | Repay- ments | Net increases | Total mortgages held, 1963 |
|---|---|---|---|---|
| Savings and loans....... | 20.8 | 10.7 | 10.1 | 84.7 |
| Commercial banks....... | 10.0 | 6.0 | 4.0 | 36.9 |
| Mutual savings banks.... | 6.2* | 3.0 | 3.2 | 34.3 |
| Insurance companies..... | 7.5* | 4.7 | 2.8 | 48.4 |
| Others............... | 11.0 | 6.5 | 4.5 | 58.9 |
| Total............... | 55.5 | 30.9 | 24.6 | 263.2 |

Gross loans: 55.5

| | | | |
|---|---|---|---|
| New construction.......... 26.5 | | Amortization............ 13.9 | |
| Purchases of existing | | Partial payment......... 1.7 | |
| buildings.............. 16.2 | | Payments in full........ 15.3 | |
| Refinancing.............. 12.8 | | Net increases.......... 24.6 | |

* A high percentage is recorded initially by mortgage companies.
SOURCES: *Federal Reserve Bulletin;* estimates of the author.

are put, some educated guesses are possible. While several groups of institutions report their total loans accurately, only the most general type of data exist concerning others and for individuals. Table 2-5 is based on informed guesses. According to these estimates, mortgage loans of over $55 billion were made in 1962. They resulted in net increases of about $25 billion in the amount owed on real estate.

Nearly half of the amounts lent went to finance the construction and purchasing of new properties. Construction loans per se showed a very rapid turnover. Made to finance the builders' needs, they were extinguished when the purchaser obtained a final mortgage. These loans reappear again as a significant factor increasing the amounts shown as paid in full. They inflate the annual difference between gross and net lending.

Large sums are also borrowed when ownership of existing buildings is transferred. Owner-occupied houses are sold on an average of every 8 to 10 years. Investment or income properties also turn over frequently. In these cases, either the existing loan is extinguished and a new one granted, or additional funds may be lent through second or third mortgages.

The amount of refinancing of existing loans surprises many observers. Increased equities or shifting market conditions enable property owners to borrow additional sums or change the terms of their loans through refinancing. Such refinancing accounts for a significant share of gross lending in every period.

In contrast, the bulk of money collected on mortgages in any year comes from the payments in full of construction loans or debts extinguished in the process of refinancing a credit or of obtaining a new loan for the sale of property. These repayments, however, do not add to the supply of mortgage money even though they are a most significant part of a firm's business. For the market as a whole, they give rise to offsetting accounting transactions. Funds for new uses are made available by the transaction which extinguishes the older loan. For firms and individuals, of course, such turnover of loans may be crucial in enabling a sale to be made or funds to be borrowed. Such transactions also form a most significant part of lenders' daily business.

During the life of a loan, money flows in from amortization and partial prepayments. Until the Depression, regular amortization was not as common as now. In the postwar period, the amounts of amortization rose steadily as outstanding loans increased. Such sums are important because they enable lenders to grant new loans. Prepayments and amortization also make it possible for institutions to shift their type of assets and liquidate some of their commitments in mortgages if they so desire.

## Mortgage Lending's Share of the Economy

Section C of Figure 2-1 reveals a huge and expanding volume of outstanding mortgage loans. The amount rose from under $35 billion at the start of 1945 to well over $280 billion less than 20 years later, an expansion of more than 700 per cent. How does this expansion compare with the growth in other parts of the economy and the money markets?

The value of outstanding mortgages increased more rapidly than the wealth of the country, whether measured relative to the current gross national product or relative to the value of real property. Figure 2-2 indicates that total mortgage debts in 1963 were over 47 per cent of the GNP, compared with less than 10 per cent in 1945. This percentage also exceeds the peak of slightly over 35 per cent reached in the boom of the 1920s.

There was about a 50 per cent increase in the number of dwellings from 1945 to 1963. The percentage of dwellings occupied by their owners went up from 50.8 to about 63 per cent. The two changes together meant more than 17 million additional owner-occupants. Of the approximately 35 million owner-occupied dwellings in 1963, nearly 50 per cent carried a mortgage.

Figure 2-2 also compares the $280 billion owed on mortgages in 1963 with the total debt structure of the country. We note that approximately 37.2 per cent of all private debt instruments are in the form of mortgages. The share of all debts was 25.5 per cent. Furthermore, these ratios result from a steady increase in the share of our credit and credit structure accounted for by mortgage lending. In 1945 the $34.7 billion mortgage total was 23.9 per cent of all private debts; in 1950 the $72.8 billion outstanding was 30.4 per cent of the private total; in 1963 the share was over 37.7 per cent.

We have already noted the major role played by mortgage lending in the functioning of financial institutions. That this role has been expanding is clear from the last section of Figure 2-2. Mortgages

FIGURE 2-2   *Mortgage Debt in the United States Economy*

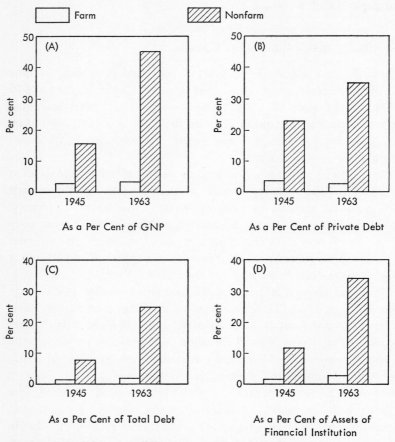

As a Per Cent of GNP

As a Per Cent of Private Debt

As a Per Cent of Total Debt

As a Per Cent of Assets of
Financial Institution

SOURCES: *Federal Reserve Bulletin; Survey of Current Business.*

as a share of the total assests of financial institutions rose from under 13 per cent to over 40 per cent by 1964.

## Other Measures

Figure 2-3 depicts the activities of the real estate financing industry in several other ways. It shows the tremendous diversity and broad impact of the industry as well as some of its major sub-

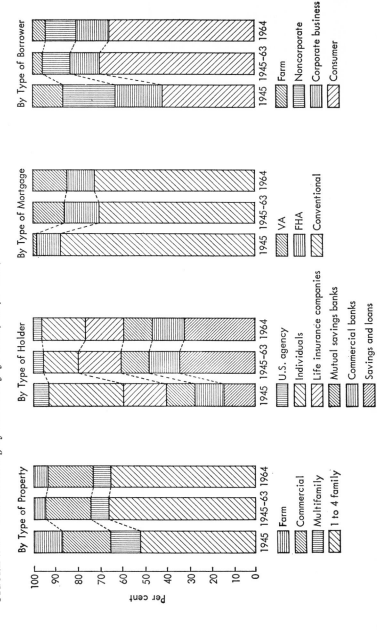

FIGURE 2-3    *The Anatomy of the Mortgage Debt, 1945–1964*

By Type of Property

Farm
Commercial
Multifamily
1 to 4 family

By Type of Holder

U.S. agency
Individuals
Life insurance companies
Mutual savings banks
Commercial banks
Savings and loans

By Type of Mortgage

VA
FHA
Conventional

By Type of Borrower

Farm
Noncorporate
Corporate business
Consumer

Per cent

SOURCES: Federal Reserve; Housing and Home Finance Agency.

41

divisions. The figure classifies loans by type of property holder, lender, mortgage, and borrower in 1945 and at the start of 1964. Furthermore, it shows the category of the loans made between 1945 and 1964.

Nearly 70 per cent of mortgage loans are secured by liens against one- to four-family units. Residential loans, which include those on one- to four-family and multifamily units, make up nearly 80 per cent of the total. Income properties have been a sharply fluctuating part of the lending picture. In the middle 1950s multifamily units took less than 10 per cent of the residential total; by 1964 they took more than a third.

Loans on farms constitute a steadily decreasing share of the total, even though there has been some increase in their absolute amounts. By 1964, they had fallen to about 6 per cent of all loans outstanding. Loans against commercial and industrial properties are by far the largest in individual size, but since their number is much smaller, they make up only about 15 per cent of amounts owed.

The impression we receive of various lending groups active in the mortgage market differs radically depending on whether we examine data on recordings, net increases in a year, or total holdings. Recordings show commercial banks, individuals, and miscellaneous mortgagors doing nearly half of all lending. In terms of holdings, on the other hand, as shown by Figure 2-3, savings and loans, life insurance companies, and mutual savings banks show more than 60 per cent of the total—a much larger share of outstanding loans than they originate. The increasing share of savings associations in the market and the decline of individuals also constitute a most significant phenomenon.

Several factors account for the differences between originations and holdings. Life insurance companies and savings banks buy many mortgages originated by mortgage companies or other firms; i.e., they are much more active as buyers than as sellers in the secondary market. They also tend to make loans which remain outstanding for longer periods.

These same factors account for the major difference between the percentage of recordings and holdings of conventional loans, as compared with those insured or guaranteed by the Federal Housing Administration and the Veterans Administration. A bulk of FHA and VA loans remain in existence for many years. On the other hand, because they include construction and other short-period mortgages, the average turnover on conventional loans is much faster.

The final classification on Figure 2-3 is by the borrower. Households owe about 70 per cent of mortgage debts. About 18 per cent of loans are made to corporations. Approximately 10 per cent of loans are to individuals who operate their properties as a business but do not incorporate. Still smaller amounts are used by farmers and nonprofit organizations, such as churches or colleges.

## SUMMARY

The volume of lending and the rates charged for loans are determined by millions of bargains struck in the loosely interconnected market for loanable funds. The mortgage market is a major segment of the wider market. Its terms and conditions are influenced both by its own special features and by the movements in the over-all market.

Funds to be loaned come from the savings of individuals, businesses, and the government as well as from the creation of deposits in commercial banks and the repayments of outstanding debts. All these sources vary in the amount they make available to the market in any year.

Demand for funds shifts in response to the needs of consumers, businesses, the government, and particularly the real estate market. As supply and demand alter, the charges and terms for new loans and the prices of existing loans also shift. The amount of funds loaned in each market also varies.

The mortgage market is the largest single part of the market for loanable funds. It is diverse, complex, and has many unique features. It has expanded rapidly in relation to most other major economic activities. Because of the size of the market and its many specialized parts, all attempts to explain and predict its movements require a broad background of knowledge and many specialized analytic concepts and tools.

## SELECTED REFERENCES

Bryant, Willis R.: *Mortgage Lending,* 2d ed., McGraw-Hill Book Company, New York, 1962, chaps. 1, and 2.

*Economic Report of the President* (annual).

Jones, Oliver, and Leo Grebler: *The Secondary Mortgage Market,* University of California, Los Angeles, 1961.

Klaman, Saul B.: *The Postwar Residential Mortgage Market,* Princeton University Press, Princeton, N.J., 1961, chaps. 1–5.

U.S. Senate, Subcommittee of the Committee on Banking and Currency: *Study of Mortgage Credit,* 86th Cong., 1st Sess., Government Printing Office, Washington, 1959.

Walter, James E.: *The Investment Process,* Harvard Business School, Boston, 1962.

# Lenders in the Mortgage Market_____3

On the lending side, the mortgage business is dominated by financial institutions. Table 3-1 shows that at the start of 1964 the main financial intermediaries held more than $215 billion in mortgages, or over 75 per cent of the total. These 22,000 or so firms keep nearly 35 per cent of their $600 billion in assets in the form of mortgages. This chapter gives an overview of the role of financial institutions in the mortgage market. Chapters 6 to 11 consider their problems, procedures, and effects in more detail.

The importance of mortgage financing to any particular institution depends upon that institution's position in the saving and lending structure as well as upon its own individual portfolio policy, which in turn is determined by law, by traditions, and by its management. However, the share of the total assets each group holds in mortgages does serve as an indicator both of the importance of mortgages to that particular industry and of the probability that any given firm within it will be active in the mortgage field. Thus lending on real property will be the core of the operations of almost any savings and loan association, mutual savings bank, or mortgage bank. On the other hand, while mortgage lending is important to insurance companies, commercial banks, and pension funds, there are firms in all these industries which pay little or no attention to opportunities in the mortgage field.

In dealing with the lending side of the market, we must also consider carefully the role of government, not primarily because the government is an important direct source of mortgage funds (which it is), but because it wields certain other vital influences.

TABLE 3-1    *Number and Assets of Major Types of Financial Intermediaries*

| | Commercial banks | Savings and loan associations | Mutual savings banks | Life insurance companies |
|---|---|---|---|---|
| **Number** | | | | |
| Financial institutions....... | 13,569 | 6,360 | 509 | 1,500 |
| Branches......... ........ | 13,498 | 2,300 | 624 | |
| Assets (in billions of dollars): | | | | |
| Total assets, 1959......... | 244.7 | 63.5 | 38.9 | 113.7 |
| Additions of assets, 1959–1964.............. | 67.2 | 43.8 | 10.9 | 27.1 |
| Total assets, January, 1964. | 311.9 | 107.3 | 49.8 | 140.8 |
| Total mortgages, 1959...... | 28.1 | 53.1 | 24.8 | 39.2 |
| Net increase of mortgages, 1959–1964.............. | 11.5 | 37.8 | 11.2 | 10.9 |
| Total mortgages, January, 1964.................. | 39.6 | 90.9 | 36.0 | 50.1 |

SOURCES: *Federal Reserve Bulletin; Life Insurance Fact Book; Savings and Loan Fact Book.*

These result from the government's role in the money market, its part as a supervisor of financial institutions, and the fact that it has been a major mortgage underwriter and promoter of a secondary mortgage market.

## A VIEW OF THE MORTGAGE MARKET

Even with 22,000 lenders, there may be periods when many potential borrowers are handicapped in obtaining funds because the structure of the mortgage market is so complex that lenders do not compete vigorously. Lenders are not evenly distributed geographically. All must meet specific legal requirements. Firms' skills and knowledge vary widely.

These geographical, legal, and institutional differences fragment the market into pieces like those of a jigsaw puzzle. A unified view is possible only through a careful piecing together of the parts and a recognition of their mutual influences and interdependences. Only through an overview of the completed picture can we examine the total United States mortgage market. Only by understanding the uniqueness of each part can the borrower and lender avail themselves of the full opportunities within the market.

### The Market's Unifying and Divisive Forces

The market is held together by the fact that all lenders make some funds available as long-term credits on real estate. Diversity arises from their methods of operation, their reasons for making mortgage loans, and their legal and informal organizational structures. What are some of the major factors differentiating their market performance?

Institutions vary in their primary reasons for existence; each group was organized to meet a separate credit or saving need. As a result, they have highly distinct policies as to the position of mortgage credit in their operations and as to whether or not they feel a continuing responsibility to particular classes of potential borrowers.

Another contrast is evident in the source and stability of their funds. Since mortgages are relatively frozen assets, lenders must relate their holdings to their possible cash requirements. Some lenders consider a large share of their deposits as temporary or subject to rapid withdrawal. Others expect that funds will remain with the institution over long periods.

Firms have many different approaches to lending. Some specialize in mortgages made only in their immediate vicinity; others operate over the entire nation. Some make and service their own loans; others purchase almost all mortgages through intermediaries. Some can handle small, individual properties; others find it easier to place their money in larger sums through tracts or expensive buildings.

Significant variety exists in the types of property upon which loans will be made, the terms or conditions of typical mortgages, and the prevailing interest rates charged.

Lending institutions range from banks and savings associations so small that they may make only one loan a week to mammoth financial institutions—institutions so large, whether banks, savings and loans, or insurance companies, that they process hundreds of loans weekly.

The market's fragmentation is due to the extreme diversity of the individual types of operation. To obtain a usable view of what is occurring at any time, as well as to learn where to look for money and what to expect, we need to understand how the various lenders operate and to see where they fit with respect to these main differentiating factors.

## A Local-market View

Some picture of this complexity can be gained by examining actual mortgage recordings in a few local markets. While the types of institutions making loans will vary among localities, the general picture will remain about the same.

In a fairly large California county (Santa Clara), nearly 40,000 mortgage loans totaling slightly over $800 million were recorded in 1962. Of these, about a third in number and a quarter in value were granted by individuals.

Among the financial institutions, savings and loan associations as a whole just nosed out commercial banks. Forty associations made 10,000 loans totaling nearly $250 million. The range in their lending was great. The 5 largest companies accounted for about half of the market, while 4 others made only 1 loan apiece. The 20 commercial banks making loans in this period recorded about

7,500 loans totaling $240 million. In this case the 2 largest banks accounted for over 60 per cent of the total issued by all the banks, while the top 5 banks did over 90 per cent of the volume.

The next largest group was formed by the mortgage companies. They acted as correspondents for insurance companies and mutual savings banks in the East. Thirty mortgage companies recorded about 6,600 loans worth $140 million. Among this group the 5 largest did half the business. Twenty insurance companies made loans directly in their own name, placing 1,225 loans for $40 million. In this category, the top 5 firms accounted for 80 per cent of the total.

In summary, in Santa Clara County in 1962 there were 110 financial institutions that made 25,593 loans for a total of $666 million, while 14,000 individuals loaned $150 million. The largest lender made 3,000 loans, or about 8 per cent of the total number, and about 10 per cent of the total value. The 10 largest lenders together made about one-third of the loans and accounted for about 40 per cent of the value.

This large county can be contrasted to a small one (Napa) in the same (San Francisco Bay) area, a county with a population of about 80,000. Here, there were 2,800 loans totaling $36 million. They were made by 20 institutional lenders (7 savings associations, 5 banks, and 8 mortgage companies) and 1,200 individuals. The institutions accounted for about two-thirds of the value and slightly more than half the number of loans.

The 5 largest lenders in this county included 2 savings associations, 2 banks, and 1 mortgage company. They made 40 per cent of all the loans, which made up about 80 per cent of the institutional mortgages. The largest single lender accounted for about 15 per cent of the total.

What conclusions can be drawn from these and similar data concerning the mortgage picture at the local level? We see a market divided among institutions and individuals. The number of institutions lending in any local area will depend upon the area's size but will range usually between 5 and 100. Again, in all but the smallest markets, there will probably be some competition from each of the main financial intermediaries plus mortgage companies.

Rarely will there be a single firm that dominates the entire market. Even the 10 largest firms will normally not account for more than half of total loans.

The situation becomes still more complex when differences in types of structure and conditions of loans are taken into account. These factors often cause the number of potential lenders for any property to drop drastically. A borrower looking for specific terms on a given structure may find only a single lender or, in other cases, no one. Whether this happens is determined by the number and types of lenders in the local market. To see what differences exist among submarkets, we must examine the conditions under which the various lenders exist and operate.

The following sections deal with the typical organization and operations of each of the main types of lenders. A system of classification based on type of institution is used because it takes into account differences in missions, legal frameworks and types of supervision. Still it cannot be used universally. There may be as much difference between a small and a large bank as between the small bank and a small savings association.

## SAVINGS AND LOAN ASSOCIATIONS

The largest source of funds to the mortgage market comes from the more than 6,000 savings and loan associations. They held over $90 billion in mortgages in 1964, or more than 40 per cent of the total owned by all financial institutions. Mortgages make up well over 80 per cent of their assets. Their only other principal holding is a liquidity reserve composed of cash and United States government bonds.

### Organization

Savings associations are primarily local, traditionally small-scale organizations, but they have grown steadily in size in the postwar period. Recently the total assets of the average (median) association were about $5 million. A typical association has several thousand savers and maintains a stock of between 500 and 1,000 mortgage loans outstanding at any given time.

The average firm contrasts sharply with the giant holding companies in the savings and loan field which own assets of over $1½ billion. More than half of the industry's volume is accounted for by less than 500 firms, each of which holds over $35 million in assets.

Savings associations are found in every state and in communities of all sizes. Their assets are distributed across the nation fairly evenly in accordance with population and wealth. Exceptions are some underrepresentation in the New England and Middle Atlantic States, the main home of mutual savings banks, and some overrepresentation in California, where the growth of savings associations and that of the state have reinforced each other.

## Operations

The unique organizational feature of savings and loan associations is that they exist primarily to make mortgage loans and to help finance homeownership. They specialize in individual home loans and are usually legally limited in the amount they can loan on other types of mortgages.

Most savings association loans are made directly from their own offices. They have been limited for the bulk of their business to lending within 100 miles of their headquarters. While most have sufficient outlets for their funds locally, this restriction has pinched a few.

Because of their local knowledge, they have been able to specialize in loans on existing houses. The proper valuation of these loans frequently depends on special local circumstances. Because they have neighborhood knowledge and can work out arrangements to fit the individual needs, they have been able to judge the market more carefully and lend to borrowers whom other types of lenders could not reach. They also have been permitted to lend a higher percentage of value than most other conventional lenders. This specialized market, fairly well protected from competition of other lenders, has enabled savings associations to charge somewhat higher interest rates on their loans than any of the other lending institutions.

As long as the demand for funds from their traditional borrowers is adequate, most associations are not willing to invest in government-underwritten mortgages with their lower returns and more time-consuming processing. Some larger associations, however, with a need for a mass market or for loans above average size, have vigorously entered into the tract and multi-unit markets, making loans on land, construction loans, and final permanent loans.

The degree to which associations have departed from their traditional pattern of local loans on existing homes has depended upon particular situations. In periods of easy money and insufficient high-interest loans, they have accepted government-underwritten and other special-type loans. They have participated in shared loans in other areas. In tighter periods they have been able to stick to their preferred market of direct conventional loans serviced by their own staff.

## LIFE INSURANCE COMPANIES

In recent years, life insurance companies have been the second largest mortgage lenders. Although their total assets are much smaller than those of commercial banks and recently their share of savings growth has fallen below that of savings associations, life insurance companies still hold the largest portion of the country's savings. Their holdings of mortgages rose from less than $7 billion at the end of World War II to over $50 billion in 1964. The share of mortgages in total assets climbed from under 15 to over 35 per cent. As this ratio indicates, a still higher proportion of current funds has been going into real estate loans. In the middle fifties, more than 60 per cent of new money received by life insurance companies flowed into the mortgage market.

### Organization

There are about 1,500 life insurance companies in the United States. They vary in size from small to multibillion dollar companies, with the largest companies holding the bulk of the assets. The 80-odd companies with over $1 billion of life insurance in force do most of the purchasing of mortgages.

Life insurance companies are domiciled in every state of the Union. The largest number have headquarters in Texas, Louisiana, and Arizona, but those with the largest assets are in the Northeast. Most companies perform their mortgage operations at their head offices. Some handle all transactions directly. Most use a system of mortgage correspondents spread throughout the country for originations and servicing. A few use their own branches. While most take mortgages anywhere in the country, insurance companies frequently are not represented in small areas.

Life insurance companies enter the mortgage market for the benefit of their policyholders, not of borrowers. Their investment funds are policyholders' reserves. Much life insurance is sold on a level-premium basis. Reserves are accumulated systematically during a policyholder's younger days, when risk of death is less, to build sufficient funds to pay the higher insurance costs expected in later years. These moneys, which require investment, are accumulating at a rate of over $6 billion a year.

Consistent with adequate safety, insurance companies want to achieve the highest possible yields on these policyholders' funds. Because of their huge size, these companies must be somewhat concerned with the total impact of their lending decisions, but such considerations are secondary compared with their primary duty to policyholders.

## Operations

Given their basic objectives, insurance companies attempt to adjust their lending among markets so as to achieve as high a yield as possible. They will lend on mortgages only when the expected net return is as high as, or higher than, that obtainable from other investments. Because mortgages have traditionally had a high yield, mortgage loans have been granted up to a point where companies felt constrained by questions of portfolio policies and general risks. In recent years, mortgage investment at about 35 per cent of total assets seems to have been thought a proper balance of these risks and yields.

In attempting to balance their yields among types of assets, the insurance companies as a whole have varied their net annual investment in mortgages by 30 or 40 per cent. Individual companies have found their ability to shift markets highly dependent on how they have organized their mortgage purchases. The larger companies have well-established organizations and correspondence relationships. Their steady flow of funds requires investment of large sums each year. They make long-run advance commitments and weigh heavily the organizational losses of sharp shifts in policy. Under these conditions, they have a limited flexibility at any given time.

Smaller companies, purchasing loans primarily through headquarters officers, may be in a more responsive position. They can and do vary sharply the percentage of their current flow going into mortgages. The larger lenders do have the possibility of changing their investments periodically through altering radically their rate of secondary-market purchases from mortgage bankers or the Federal National Mortgage Association (FNMA).

The type of loans purchased by insurance companies can be related to their mode of operations. They work from home offices and find it difficult and costly to control the risks in loans furnished by correspondents and brokers spread throughout the country. Excluding farms, about 25 per cent of their loans are on commercial and income properties, and over 40 per cent on government-insured or government-guaranteed loans. The remaining loans are primarily on high-priced, new or fairly recently built individual houses.

The insurance companies are the largest lenders on commercial and income properties. They are not restricted to local areas and have had more flexibility in this market than other lenders. Furthermore, since the individual loans on these properties are large, the company can spend the time, effort, and money needed to make certain that the loan is suitable.

Such controls are much more difficult on individual houses. In contrast to savings and loans that lend on older houses in their own localities, life insurance companies tend to restrict their conventional home loans to newer, more expensive units, with a decidedly lower percentage of the total value covered by the loan. They compete in this market by keeping their interest rate below that of other lenders. Still, by its nature this is a limited sphere.

These loans appeal primarily to cost-conscious borrowers who have sufficient funds to make fairly high down payments.

The problems of controlling moderate loans on individual houses over long distances account for the extensive use made by the insurance companies of FHA-VA guarantees and insurance. In this sphere, the Federal agencies' responsibility for underwriting can replace the company's need for more complete inspection of the unit and the borrower. The risk involved is far easier to calculate. Furthermore, government-guaranteed loans are most frequently offered by brokers in volume either as a result of large-scale building operations or because the correspondents are willing to accumulate and process batches of individual loans.

Because government-guaranteed loans are simpler to purchase and because bulk amounts are available, the lender can tailor his purchases more carefully to his needs. Insurance companies can move in and out of the FHA-VA market on the basis of relative yields with far greater ease than is true of the conventional-loan market.

## COMMERCIAL BANKS

Commercial banks are by far the largest financial intermediaries in both numbers and assets. Their assets in 1964 totaled over $310 billion. Their real estate loans, at $40 billion, were a modest 13 per cent of all assets, but they had risen considerably from only $4.7 billion in 1945. As a group the banks form the third largest market for mortgages.

The market impact of the banks far surpasses their relative share. They perform many supplemental functions in the process of making loans available to final lenders. Furthermore, their sharp year-to-year shifts in commitments to buy mortgages have caused magnified repercussions on yields, terms, and the demand from other lenders.

### Organization

There are nearly 14,000 commercial banks. They vary in size from several with assets of well over $10 billion to 1,250 with less than $1 million. Spread throughout the nation, they normally lend locally, but in many states, because of branch banking, the concept of local loans almost always encompasses entire metropolitan areas and may include whole states.

The importance of mortgage lending to individual banks varies tremendously. For example, the share of assets of the large money-market banks invested in real estate loans has been only about 3 per cent. On the other hand, many of the smaller country banks are usually loaned up to their maximum legal limit.

Their traditional view of themselves as purveyors mainly of short-term credit complicates the role of commercial banks in the mortgage market. By statute and tradition, they have sought assets more liquid than mortgages as investment outlets for their demand deposits. On the other hand, because mortgages have offered the advantage of higher yields for their time deposits, they have been particularly active in mortgage lending when such deposits were expanding. Recently, their mortgage holdings have averaged about 30 per cent of these savings-type deposits.

Banks have also served as originators and servicing agents for mortgages sold in the secondary market. Many banks have been concerned over their position as major local lenders. They have not wanted to turn regular customers away, and so felt obligated to make mortgage loans. But when their portfolios of mortgages expanded beyond a sum felt to be reasonable, they sold blocks of these loans. They then continued to service the mortgages for the new purchasers, thus both realizing profits and maintaining customer relations.

**Operations**

The legal lending requirements for banks, particularly nationally chartered banks, have been far stricter than those for most other lenders. While these regulations have gradually been liberalized, banks still tend to be more circumscribed in their conventional mortgage lending powers than other groups because of the fear of a lack of liquidity.

Banks play the most significant role in construction lending and in warehousing, or the advancing of interim credit for mortgage and real estate companies. Such loans most closely fit the banks' traditional role as providers of working capital. While many banks take no part in this market, others, including some of the largest, do a heavy volume of interim lending. Several New York money-market banks make participation loans with correspondent banks throughout the country. Without such participation, small local banks would frequently find that requested construction loans exceeded their legal maximum amount for individual loans.

In the long-term market, banks are a major force in the non-residential and FHA-VA sectors. Their participation in the conventional single-family market has varied widely. While heavily restricted, their terms for income properties have been more liberal than could be granted by savings associations. As a result, as much as 25 per cent of their portfolios is outside the residential field.

In the one- to four-family category, they have been primarily over-the-counter lenders to local customers, competitive in the markets both for existing houses and for new, larger units. Half or more of their loans have been on this conventional basis.

About a quarter of their total outstanding loans have been FHA-VA. At times, however, these have accounted for as much as 55 per cent of their volume. For banks, government-underwritten loans have the important advantage of not having to be counted as part of the mortgage total, which is limited by law.

Banks' new mortgage commitments have depended on available funds, which have varied with monetary policy and with their share of savings. Since both of these have been unstable, commercial banks' mortgage loans have fluctuated by as much as several hundred per cent on a year-to-year basis.

## MUTUAL SAVINGS BANKS

Mutual savings banks form a unique part of the savings industry. There are only a few more than 500 savings banks, concentrated heavily in the Northeast area, particularly in New York and Massachusetts. With less than about one-sixth of the assets of the commercial banks, they hold almost as many mortgages. Their holdings rose from slightly over $4 billion of real estate loans in 1945 to $36 billion by 1964. In addition to being the major lenders in their home states, they have in recent years played a significant part in establishing and maintaining a national mortgage market.

## Organization

As their name implies, these savings banks are mutual organizations, founded originally with a decided philanthropic purpose. A major aim was the promotion of thrift and savings among working men. As a means of achieving their goal, they have placed great stress on paying high interest rates on deposits. As a result, they have been eager to purchase mortgages as a method of gaining higher earnings.

Their portfolio policy lies between those of the commercial banks and savings associations. Their liquidity requirements also fall between the two but come closer to savings associations. In recent years, real estate loans have made up over 70 per cent of their assets. They have met their liquidity needs through cash and government securities plus some corporate bonds and stock. Their ratio of mortgages to all corporate-type investments has exceeded 5 to 1.

Although there are only about 8 mutual savings banks for every 100 savings and loans, mutual savings banks have been considerably larger. Recently their average size has been about six times as great. Comparatively, far fewer savings banks fall in the category of assets under $5 million. Until the 1950s, their total assets were also larger than those of the savings and loans. Because of their concentrated geographical area (they exist in only 17 states, and more than 70 per cent of their assets are in the top two) and for other reasons, their rate of expansion has been far slower. As a result, in 1964 their assets were less than half those of the savings associations.

## Operations

The mortgage operations of savings banks stem directly from their initial purpose and general philosophy. They feel some obligation to promote better housing and welfare in their own cities; but when they lend outside their own boundaries, they are primarily interested in competitive yields and safety.

In their home cities many perform a complete mortgage service. They operate an over-the-counter individual and tract mortgage service making conventional or insured loans on new and existing houses. They also make construction loans, do mortgage warehousing, sell stand-by commitments, and make loans on multifamily and nonresidential properties.

The percentage of savings banks operating in the national market has not been large, but those in it have been the banks with the highest assets making the largest share of mortgage loans. These banks have concentrated on purchases of large blocks in the secondary market from mortgage companies, commercial banks, and savings and loans. Their lending outside their own areas usually consists of government-underwritten mortgages.

Because their flow of funds has not been as even as that of other lenders and because they have been particularly conscious of competitive yields, savings banks have been in and out of the national market in a rather erratic manner. Mortgage brokers have had to develop special techniques of handling commitments in order to be able to deliver a volume of loans to savings banks in short periods.

About 10 per cent of the mutual savings banks' portfolios have been on nonresidential units, plus nearly a quarter on apartment houses. This reflects the fact that these banks are concentrated in the large Eastern cities, where apartment living has been both traditional and a significant part of the housing market. Over 50 per cent of total holdings have been loans on one- to four-family units underwritten by FHA or VA. Of course their national lending must be of this type, but they have also tended to use government underwriting in their own neighborhoods. A final 15 per cent of their portfolios consists of conventional loans on individual homes.

## MORTGAGE COMPANIES OR MORTGAGE BANKS

The expansion of mortgage companies, or mortgage banks, has been part of the growth of the correspondent system in real estate financing. As the names imply, these firms are almost totally concerned with the financing of real estate. While mortgage firms existed in the prewar period, the last 20 years have seen a tremendous growth in the industry, together with rapid changes in operations and functions.

Many specialized terms that have grown up around the operations of mortgage companies are defined in the Glossary. These include origination and servicing; interim loan, warehousing, and final, or take-out, loan; fee and discount; and commitment. Those previously unfamiliar with these concepts will find their definitions an aid to understanding the working of mortgage companies.

### Organization

Data are poor, but it is frequently estimated that about 1,000 mortgage companies exist. These firms participate in the market primarily as correspondents for other lenders, originating and servicing real estate loans but tending not to hold them in their own portfolio. While the average firm is small, 25 or more are so large that they service over $200 million of mortgages at any time, and at least one services well over $1 billion. As a whole, this group originates from 15 to 20 per cent of all new loans and probably services a still higher percentage of outstandings.

Most mortgage companies are local firms, although some have expanded onto a regional basis. In addition to the origination, selling, and servicing of loans, they frequently handle construction lending and related activities. They have been one of the main forces behind the rapid emergence of a more national market in the postwar period.

The traditional correspondent relationships grew out of the needs of insurance companies. They could and in some cases did set up their own loan offices. Working through their own offices, however, limited their loans to populous areas and also increased their fixed costs. In most cases, they preferred to handle their lending through local firms. Local correspondents would accept loan applications and process them for submission to insurance companies. The latter would then decide whether or not to make the loans. Depending on the market, fees might be paid by the prospective borrower or by the lender. If the servicing was to be done by the correspondent, additional fees were paid.

Gradually the system became more formal. To increase flexibility and to be certain of the availability of funds, mortgage companies obtained quarterly or semiannual advance commitments. These specified the number and type of loans the final lender would accept. Each tentative loan had to be submitted to the company for final approval. Loans might be closed either in the name of the insurance company or in that of the mortgage company and later transferred. The advance commitments specified the type and amount of loans, locations, size, etc. They also specified the fee that would be paid for origination and for servicing.

In addition to insurance firms, mortgage companies have become correspondents for other institutional lenders whose charters limit them to specific areas or for those, such as pension funds or college endowment funds, that would never find it worthwhile to build their own staffs. The mortgage companies perform all the functions necessary in originating the loans, packaging them as suitable investment instruments, and finally servicing them.

The mortgage companies are necessary for geographical diversification and also to fill a void caused by the lag between the start of construction and the final insurance or guarantee of a loan made to an individual borrower. A great deal of uncertainty exists during this period. The builder may not finish his construction. The final sale may be delayed. The approval by the insuring agency of the prospective borrower must be obtained. The necessary daily negotiations between lender and builder cannot be carried on by the distant or ultimate lender. At the same time, most local mortgage companies lack the cash for the ultimate loan and would not be able to get interim financing if local lenders were not certain that a final loan was available.

**Operations**

Under present techniques the mortgage company takes advance commitments from institutional lenders and in turn issues commitments to builders and construction lenders for a final take-out loan.

The mortgage banker may receive his commitments from several firms as a result of long-standing correspondent relationships. On the other hand, he may actively canvass many institutions seeking to buy commitments from them. A typical commitment might specify that the final lender agrees to buy a block of loans in a given period, from a specified area, and at a fixed price, providing the loans have been insured or guaranteed by the FHA or VA. Individual mortgages which do not measure up to the lender's credit or property specifications can be rejected.

Commitments may be purchased in various forms. Many are still of the traditional types based on the final lender's approval of individual tracts, suburbs, or properties. Other agreements may cover blocks, such as 500 FHA loans from the state of California to be delivered during the first quarter of 1965. Prices may be quoted on a net basis, for example, a return to the lender of 5.10 per cent net of service charges, and with an agreed-upon assumed life of, say, 12 years. Other forms of agreement might specify that the block will contain $5\frac{1}{4}$ per cent, 30-year mortgages to be delivered with an agreed discount of 2 per cent and an agreed servicing payment from the lender to the correspondent of $\frac{3}{8}$ or $\frac{1}{2}$ per cent per year on the outstanding balance.

The mortgage banker may agree to pay for the commitment, for example, 1 per cent at the time of purchase of the commitment, with the understanding that the fee will be returned if he delivers the mortgages as agreed but that the fee will be forfeited otherwise. Such commitment fees partially protect the lender against a mortgage company's failure to deliver loans when interest rates fall. Mortgage companies may, within the limit of their capital, take positions in the market. If they expect interest rate shifts, they may at one time hold more commitments than they have issued to builders and at another time issue more commitments to builders than they have bought from final lenders.

The mortgage company gradually accumulates loans under these commitments, and it also buys spot loans over its counters. These are mortgages on existing houses. They come in daily from real estate brokers on an individual basis. As the various loans are accumulated, they are warehoused with the local bank. The growing package of mortgages, some of which may be partially completed loans on construction, is turned into the bank as collateral behind the firm's notes.

When a sufficient block has been accumulated, they are delivered to an institutional lender. In most cases, the delivery will be against an outstanding commitment. In other cases, the mortgage company may accumulate the portfolio for its own account. It then has to offer them in the market at whatever current prices prevail.

For loans on shopping centers, apartments, or other large structures, the commitment is usually granted only after considerable bargaining and then with very specific terms which must be met.

In most cases, the servicing contract forms a major part of the transaction. It specifies the exact services which the mortgage company must furnish. It details the way in which funds must be treated, the type of reports that must be submitted, the action that the correspondent must take if loans become delinquent. The contract also specifies the fees which the correspondent may retain—usually some or all of the origination fee and $\frac{1}{4}$ or $\frac{1}{2}$ per cent of the interest payment based on the outstanding balance. Normally there are also subsidiary agreements as to management and sales procedures and fees if the property has to be foreclosed or title is taken in other ways.

Problems have arisen in cases where mortgage companies depend primarily on one or a few lenders. The advantage to lenders of having correspondents who represent only a few lenders is that they can entrust more of the decision process with respect to individual loans to the correspondent. Long-standing working relationships are valuable to each party. On the other hand, when the correspondent becomes too dependent on one or a few lenders, the latter no longer can consider the correspondent's operations as variable costs. The lender assumes a responsibility to see that the mortgage company can maintain an adequate volume of business.

The mortgage company has brought additional lenders into the mortgage market and particularly into local submarkets. Because they can be small, or need not have large accumulations of capital, and because they use funds primarily of lenders rather than the public, mortgage companies can be established with far greater ease than other types of financial institutions. Their highly pragmatic approach to the mortgage market has added a great deal of flexibility, as well as competition in local areas. They have faced difficult problems in the past—and may encounter new ones—because of the heavy dependence of most firms on handling government-insured or government-guaranteed loans.

## OTHER LENDERS

Mortgage companies are only one part of a large group of relatively little-known lenders which account for about a quarter of mortgage holdings and a larger share of initial recordings. Included in this category, in addition to mortgage companies, are certain Federal agencies discussed in the next chapter, other types of financial institutions, and individuals.

### Other Financial Institutions

Other financial institutions include many types with a large volume of assets. In 1964 their total resources amounted to over $130 billion. The largest holdings were those of pension funds. Also sizable are fire and casualty companies and credit unions. We also include in this group foundations, universities, and other trusts with similar investment problems.

There is a wide gap between the saving assets and mortgage investments of these groups. The fact that in 1964 less than 2 per cent of their assets took the form of real estate loans establishes them as a prime potential market for those trying to develop new sources of mortgage funds. Since they are primarily interested in high yields and have low liquidity needs compared to other financial agencies, most of these groups, at least in theory, could be a major force in the mortgage market. In fact, however, this market has been extremely hard to tap.

The difference between available funds and actual mortgage lending is usually attributed to the peculiarities of the mortgage market and the unfamiliarity with it of pension fund trustees. In recent years, several new organizations have been established in an attempt to remove the roadblocks to these investments. They are specialized intermediaries between pension funds and mortgage originators; they act as advisers for pension funds and perform functions equivalent to insurance companies' home-office mortgage staffs.

The gap between potential and actuality is so large in this area that even if it is closed only slightly, large amounts of new funds will be made available.

### Individuals

A large number of mortgages are recorded every year in the names of individuals. The average amount for these loans is small, and they are paid off fairly rapidly. The share of individuals in total holdings is about 10 per cent—far lower than their importance as measured by new recordings.

Mortgage loans made by individuals either tend to be purchase-money contracts, usually in the form of second, or junior, mortgages taken back when property is sold, or else they are consumer or family loans, providing funds needed for nonhousing purposes but with property utilized as an additional security.

Although our knowledge of individual loans is very spotty, it is quite clear that this is a chaotic and unorganized market. Volume and importance rise and fall contra-cyclically to the availability of funds from other lenders.

Lacking data, many observers until recently believed that the second-mortgage market was far larger during the 1920s than in recent years. Their beliefs stemmed from the fact that in the earlier period, conventional lenders required far higher down payments. Purchases were possible only with second or third loans. When high loan-to-value terms can be granted, junior mortgages would appear to be far less necessary.

Now observers are not as certain that this reasoning is correct. Although second mortgages have almost certainly become far less significant for *new* houses, even in this market tight-money periods show increased junior liens. On the other hand, in the market for *existing* houses, terms on available loans do not seem to have expanded to anywhere near the same degree as have those on new homes. Consequently, if they have wanted their properties to be competitive with new houses, sellers of existing houses have been forced to take back junior liens.

There has also been a growing market for junior liens in connection with income properties. In these cases, speculators have been willing to pay exceedingly high rates for second, third, or even higher mortgages. As Chapter 12 demonstrates, these loans have been thought worthwhile even at these high rates because they sharply increase the leverage and therefore the potential gain, although the risk and possible loss to the owner are also enhanced.

### Junior Mortgages

A typical case will illustrate how the junior-mortgage market thrives on discounts and high rates. An owner, finding that a prospective purchaser lacks $1,500 of the required down payment, decides that it is worth $500 to sell the property immediately instead of waiting for a future purchaser to show up with the necessary cash. He therefore agrees to accept a $1,500 second mortgage as part of the down payment instead of $1,500 cash. The mortgage calls for 6 per cent interest and is payable in level payments over 10 years with the proviso that it will become due immediately if the house is resold.

The seller may decide to hold the second mortgage for a time; or he can ask his broker to attempt to sell the loan. Most areas have either individuals or firms that specialize in such mortgages, or brokers may develop lists of people who will purchase occasional loans. Frequently such loans will be sold at 20 per cent, 30 per cent, or even 40 per cent discounts. In this case, assume the loan is sold for $1,000. By accepting and then selling the second mortgage, the seller in effect has cut his cash price by the $500 he felt was necessary.

The new owner has been able to buy a house before accumulating sufficient capital. As a result, he pays $500 more for the house than he would have had to if he had the required down payment.

His monthly payments for the first 10 years are $16.65 more than on the first mortgage alone. Consequently, the risks to himself, the first-mortgage lender, and the second-mortgage owner are higher.

The new second-mortgage owner has a high prospective yield. By the procedure shown in the Appendix to Chapter 6, his annual yield, if all payments are met on time, can be calculated as 16 per cent. This, however, will be a gross and not a net yield. Since the monthly payments are small, he will have considerable administrative costs or effort. In addition, his risk will be relatively great, at least during the early years of the loan. On the other hand, assuming no interest return, he will have his actual cash back at the end of five years.

The high theoretical returns attract investors to this market. Firms exist to handle the brokerage and even collections on these loans. In California, firms known as ten-percenters promised a 10 per cent interest to buyers of the loans, pocketing the difference to pay their costs and profits. To generate more business, these firms also arranged to buy blocks of loans from builders of new houses. The builders found they could more than compensate for the discount paid the second-mortgage lender because the lower down payment made possible by the existence of two mortgages enabled them to price their houses higher and sell them more rapidly.

Firms and individuals also do second-mortgage lending to families who need funds but have no other source of credit except the equity accumulated in their homes. In effect these second mortgages are a type of consumer financing. Their rates may or may not be competitive with other loan agencies. Frequently the yield, or rate to the lender, will be higher. However, because the loan extends over a longer period, the borrower may repay less per month than on a typical consumer loan.

## LENDERS AND THEIR LOANS

Figure 2-3 and Table 2-2 showed the effect of these various lenders on the gross and net flow of mortgage funds. We noted the large share of the various institutional lenders, led by the savings associations, followed by the insurance companies and commercial banks. We have also seen that because of their legal limitations, geographical concentration, and portfolio needs, the types of properties handled by the different lenders vary markedly.

While only second among the lenders, insurance companies do the largest volume of lending on commercial and income properties. Mutual savings banks are particularly significant in the apartment house field. Commercial banks are important in both these categories and are especially so in the markets for construction lending and mortgage warehousing.

The 1960 Census of Financing and recent studies of the Federal Home Loan Bank Board (FHLBB) make it clear that notable differences exist in types of loans made on one- to four-family units. The first and most obvious difference lies in whether or not the institutions' mortgages are government-underwritten. In 1960, among the financial institutions, about 70 per cent of the mortgages held by the mutual savings banks and life insurance companies on one-family, owner-occupied homes had some form of government underwriting. The percentage was about half for commercial banks and less than a quarter for savings and loan associations.

For conventional loans, other differences are also clear. Life insurance companies make the largest loans on the newest and most expensive houses. The average value of properties on which life insurance loans were made was nearly 50 per cent higher than that of properties on which savings and loan associations made loans, with mutual savings banks between. The life insurance houses were priced almost twice as high as those on which commercial banks lent money. Savings and loans lend on considerably older houses than other agencies. Except for individuals, they are the main lenders on pre-1930 houses. The ratio of loan to value also varies considerably. By 1964, for conventional loans, savings and loan associations were lending 75 per cent of the price of houses, compared to slightly under 70 per cent for insurance companies and mutual savings banks. Commercial banks lent only about 62 per cent of value. In length of loans, life insurance companies and savings banks gave the longest amortization periods—between 25 and 26 years for new houses and 20 to 25 for existing houses. Savings and loan average periods were about two to three years shorter, probably because savings and loans lend more on older units. The average contract term for commercial banks was under 15 years.

The differences in type of units lent on are also reflected in interest rates charged. Life insurance companies lending on prime properties have the lowest rates. The amounts charged by mutual savings banks, which are concentrated in the high-savings Eastern market, also tend to be low. The savings and loan associations lending on the older properties charge about ½ per cent more in the interest rate than do the insurance companies or savings banks.

These basic distinctions in type of loan and market availability are obviously important for most borrowers. Still more significant differences arise when some lenders leave their traditional market because of a shortage of funds. At such times, gaps open in the usual relationships, and some borrowers may have to pay unusually high premiums to attract lenders to a market they normally avoid. These differences among markets also cause yield gaps which cannot be accounted for on logical grounds.

## SUMMARY

The mortgage market is fragmented into submarkets by the lending habits, desires, and requirements of different types of financial institutions. Any local market is likely to have a fairly large number of potential lenders. If the market is of any size, no single firm or even a few are likely to dominate the total lending.

On the other hand, each institution in a local market will have a particular pattern of lending. The type of loan it will make, the amount of lending it does, and the rates it asks will depend upon the type of institution it is, its size, and market conditions. Savings and loans and savings banks are the largest lenders. They lend primarily on mortgages. Yet among them, some offer one type of loan while others may specialize in a different class. Insurance companies and commercial banks, because they have wider opportunities, are more likely to pick and choose and even to leave the mortgage market completely if they do not find competitive yields.

Knowledge of how each type of lender is likely to react to a given loan as well as to movements in the over-all market for loanable funds is significant for both borrowers seeking funds and for other lenders who must determine their own competitive patterns.

## SELECTED REFERENCES

American Bankers Association: *The Commercial Banking Industry,* Prentice-Hall, Inc., Englewood Cliffs, N.J., 1962.

Colean, Miles L.: *Mortgage Companies,* Prentice-Hall, Inc., Englewood Cliffs, N.J., 1962.

Kendall, Leon T.: *The Savings and Loan Business,* Prentice-Hall, Inc., Englewood Cliffs, N.J., 1962.

Klaman, Saul B.: *The Postwar Residential Mortgage Market,* Princeton University Press, Princeton, N.J., 1961.

Life Insurance Association: *Life Insurance Companies as Financial Institutions,* Prentice-Hall, Inc., Englewood Cliffs, N.J., 1962.

National Association of Mutual Savings Banks: *Mutual Savings Banking,* Prentice-Hall, Inc., Englewood Cliffs, N.J., 1962.

# The Government and the Mortgage Market___4

Attempting to operate in the mortgage market without a full recognition and understanding of the part played in it by local, state, and Federal government agencies is like attempting to build a bridge without knowledge of the basic laws of physics. It can be done, but it will not be efficient, and it may be extremely dangerous. Whether that influence is obvious or not, the government has a widespread influence on our credit structure. The borrower and lender must remain constantly alert and ready to react to changes in government policies.

Throughout our economic history, striking alterations in our financial institutions have come about because of new developments in both the political and business spheres. Financial institutions ultimately owe their existence to the constitutional prerogative given the Federal government of establishing and controlling our monetary system and to the Federal and state governments' power to charter.

Monetary chronicles contain details of the agonizing national decisions which have been required to determine what type of financial institutions should exist, and how their ability to lend and to create deposits or near deposits should be regulated. These relationships are still in the process of steady evolution.

Governmental influences are transmitted to the mortgage market and to real estate financing decisions in five primary ways:

1. Through their legal and supervisory functions, the governments, both state and Federal, determine the ground rules of mortgage lending.
2. Monetary and debt-management policies dominate available funds and interest rates. At times, selective credit controls have also directly affected mortgage credit.
3. The Federal government has facilitated the movements of additional funds in significant amounts to the mortgage market primarily through two special agencies, the Federal Home Loan Bank System and the Federal National Mortgage Association.
4. Through the Federal Housing Administration and the loan guarantee service of the Veterans Administration, the Federal government insures or guarantees mortgage loans.
5. Tax regulations and rates exert a major influence on most real estate financing decisions.

The first three channels of impact are discussed in this chapter. The FHA and VA programs are taken up in the next. Tax factors are considered in the many separate spheres where they play a significant role. In each case stress is placed on the chain of causation through which the government action moves to its final effects upon real estate financing. Even though they are frequently not obvious because the areas of influence are widespread, government actions tend to create major problems, solutions for which are constantly sought by borrowers and lenders.

## SUPERVISION AND INSURANCE

As supervisors of financial institutions, governments exert a pervasive influence on the lending process. After the early disastrous history of laissez-faire approaches to the chartering of financial institutions, our country gradually evolved a dual Federal and state system of banking based upon governmental charters and supervision. The equally disastrous effect of the 1930s on the liquidity and solvency of the savings and loan companies led to a similar system for that industry. The country determined that fiduciary institutions which gathered in the savings of millions of individuals must meet certain basic minimal criteria in their operations.

Banks, savings and loans, and insurance companies are all required to observe specific standards with respect to the loans they make. Legal restrictions define the type and conditions of mortgages they can write. In almost all cases, the manner in which they obey these regulations is subject to examination.

Controls and regulations have not, however, all been negative. The Federal Reserve System was established in an attempt to give banking institutions more flexibility by making available a source of additional reserves. Other types of financial institutions can obtain advances and the use of secondary funds through the Federal Home Loan Bank System.

As a result of the Great Depression and particularly, it might be noted, because of the collapse of the mortgage lending system, two major institutions to insure depositors were established. The Federal Deposit Insurance Corporation and the Federal Savings and Loan Insurance Corporation perform examination and supervisory functions in order to make certain that in their role of insurer they are not assuming too large or unwise risks.

The government's interest in financial institutions extends far beyond the potential insolvency of individual firms. By law and custom, it has a deep concern with the value and amount of money in existence. To influence the value of money and the price level, the Federal government constantly alters its monetary and public debt policies. Monetary policy includes the Federal government's steps to control the amount of currency and the level of deposits in the banking system. Public debt policy includes decisions as to what type, maturity, and amounts of public debt to offer in any period in order to influence financial markets.

All changes in these policies strongly affect the availability of real estate financing and the amounts that will be charged for any particular loan.

## THE MARKET FOR MONEY

The over-all manner in which the amounts of money and credit shift is not hard to follow. A brief overview of the market is useful before examining its specific details. Congress and the President have entrusted to the Federal Reserve System the duty and authority of attempting to control the economy's supply of money and credit. The Federal Reserve is to regulate the amount of money so as to aid in achieving full employment with stable prices. When business conditions are poor and unemployment exists, the Federal Reserve attempts to expand the amount of money and credit. If it believes that inflation threatens, it acts to curtail them.

## Reserves and the Amount of Money

The basis of all our monetary controls is the requirement that commercial banks maintain a certain per cent of reserves behind each dollar of deposits. The Federal Reserve influences credit by expanding or contracting these reserves. For Federal Reserve member banks, reserves include vault cash and deposits with the Federal Reserve Bank. If the reserve requirement is $16\frac{2}{3}$ per cent, then each bank must have $1 in reserves for each $6 in demand deposits on its books. If it obtains an additional $1 in reserves, it has the right to purchase investments or issue loans up to a total of $5 in addition. The new deposits of $5 issued to make the loans plus the initial $1 in reserves deposited with the bank will once again restore the legal ratio of deposits to reserves.[1] The banks are not required to use their new $1 in reserves to increase investments or loans, but it is profitable to do so because they can earn interest on the additional loans or investments. Therefore, they usually do expand fairly rapidly.

When the amount of reserves drops, the banking system as a whole must change its level of deposits and its holdings of loans and investments. When banks as a whole lose $1 in reserves, they must sell $5 in loans in order to contract their deposits by the required amount. This is the point of impact of the monetary authorities. The Federal Reserve has three basic weapons by which it can alter either the reserves or the level of potential deposits or loans based upon them. These are (1) open-market operations (2)

[1] For a complete description of how our system works, see Board of Governors of the Federal Reserve System, *The Federal Reserve System: Purposes and Functions*, Washington.

changes in discounts, and (3) changes in the reserve ratio. All are discussed in more detail shortly.

There are other influences which tend to shift reserves on a seasonal or special basis; but they tend to be small, and it is the policy of the Federal Reserve to offset and neutralize them.

If the reserves in the system remain constant, some banks may lose and others may gain reserves. Except for minor differences in reserve requirements among banks, this shifting would have no overall effect. The assets and deposits based on the total reserves are traded around among the banks so that each bank can retain its proper ratio, even as some gain and others lose deposits.

When the Federal Reserve increases reserves, banks can create money or deposits, which are equivalent in our modern economy. The new deposits lead to an expansion of credit. The demand for loans and investments rises. Unless an unexpected expansion occurs in the demand for credit, interest rates fall.

Through their expanded lending, the commercial banks make it easier to qualify for loans, and they pay more for investments. Market prices of notes and bonds rise. The shifting prices and rates and the greater availability of money affect other lenders. Their funds expand in turn. Recipients of new money make deposits in other financial institutions, or they pay off previously existing debts. The banks' bidding increases the value of all loan portfolios. Other institutions may sell some assets and gain funds for direct mortgage lending.

Since all of the main lenders in the mortgage market now have more funds, they lend on more liberal terms and at lower interest rates. Activity increases. Potential borrowers find themselves in a preferred position. They receive a hearty welcome at all lending institutions, and are offered easier terms.

When the Federal Reserve wants to contract credit, the whole process is reversed. It reduces reserves. Commercial banks sell loans. Buyers can be found only at lower prices or higher interest rates. The commercial banks move out of the mortgage market. Other lenders have less money to loan. They slam the door in the face of prospective borrowers whom they would have welcomed only a short while before. Real estate men, land developers, promoters of income property find they cannot get financing on the same reasonable terms that had previously prevailed.

## Open-market Operations

The Federal Reserve authorities excercise their primary control over member bank reserves through buying and selling government bills, notes, and bonds in the open market. At frequent intervals the System's open-market committee meets to determine whether the amount of credit requires loosening or tightening or should stay as it is. If the decision is for change, the committee instructs the manager of the System's security account to alter the System's holding of securities in order to move credit in the desired direction.

When the System decides to tighten credit, bills or bonds are sold in the government bond market. The impact on interest rates is immediate. The market takes additional bonds only if their price is marked down or, conversely, if their interest rate is raised.

Because of our fractional reserve system, this immediate market reaction is only the first of several. The buyer pays the Federal Reserve with a check drawn on his commercial bank. When this check is presented, the member bank's reserve balances at the Federal Reserve are debited for the amount of the bond. The open-market sale, therefore, has the effect of simultaneously cutting the Federal Reserve's assets of bonds and its liabilities to commercial banks. Since these liabilities, or deposits of the commercial banks, serve as their reserves, the amount of reserves now available falls as a result of the open-market operation.

The commercial bank that loses reserves must now curtail its loans or sell investments. For each $1 lost, it must contract its deposits by the $5 necessary to bring its reserve-deposit ratio back to the legal requirement. To sell its bonds, the bank in turn must mark down their price sufficiently to attract individuals who will buy and hold them. They pay the bank from their deposits, so it in turn reduces its assets and liabilities together.

The fact that the Federal Reserve can sell or buy assets at its own discretion and that its payments or receipts are made in the form of its own deposits gives it its primary power over the money market. When it decreases reserves, the commercial banks, because of our fractional reserve system, must decrease their holdings and their related deposits by a magnified amount.

### Discount Operations

Member banks can temporarily adjust their reserves and give themselves time to make the necessary changes in their assets through discount operations. By borrowing from the Federal Reserve, they can gain deposits to adjust their individual reserve positions. Under established procedures, they can borrow on their notes with required collateral, or rediscount, at a fixed cost called the discount note.

This discount rate is the charge the member banks must pay to the Federal Reserve on their borrowings. The Federal Reserve publicly establishes and announces changes in the discount rate. An increase in the rate raises the member banks' cost and lowers the desirability of borrowing. It also indicates a changed view of the money market by the Federal Reserve. Such signals of an increased tightening of monetary policy have an immediate impact on all lenders' and borrowers' expectations with respect to future interest rates.

Discounting is normally considered a temporary measure to gain time in the adjustment of reserves. Loans can be run off (i.e., funds from maturing bonds or notes are not reinvested in similar securities) more slowly or securities liquidated in an orderly manner. However, if banks attempt to borrow to increase their reserves and assets in contradistinction to Federal Reserve policy, they may be subject to more direct pressure.

Since banks pay off their discounts by adjusting their assets, the volume of discounting by member banks (or the opposite, the amount of free reserves they hold which could be used as a base for expanded credit) is a primary indicator of the degree of tightness or ease in the banking system.

Figure 4-1, for example, shows the close relationship between the amount of member bank borrowings, or discounts, and the short-term interest rate. It is clear that when banks have to borrow in any sizable amount from the Federal Reserve, the yields on treasury bills

FIGURE 4-1    *Money-market Indicators*

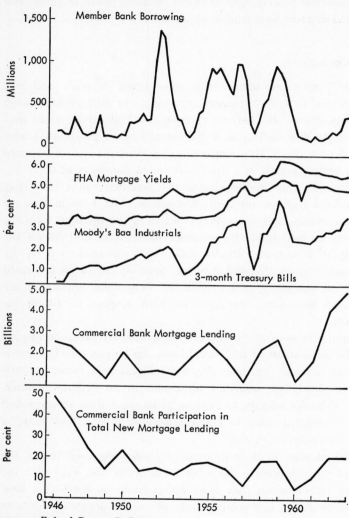

rise sharply above previous levels. These movements in short-term rates are in turn transmitted to the long-run rates on bonds and mortgages. Because they have longer maturities during which they may experience many fluctuations of short-run rates, however, the latter show less amplitude in the amount of their movements than do treasury bills.

### Changes in Reserve Requirements

The Federal Reserve has a third control, one so powerful that it is loath to use it. Congress has granted the Board of Governors of the Federal Reserve the right to alter within established legal maximums and minimums the amount of reserves the banks must maintain for each dollar of deposits. These limits for 1964 required Reserve city banks to hold between 10 and 22 per cent of reserves against demand deposits, while lower limits existed for country banks and for time deposits.

An example of this control's effect can be cited. The Board once changed required reserves from 18 to 20 per cent. The power of such a move is obvious. The increase of 2 points on a basis of 18 meant that, except for some additional reserves made available on a temporary basis, the banks had to decrease their deposits by more than 10 per cent. When this power has been used, it has been a sharp shock to our entire monetary system.

Between 1951 and 1964, no increases occurred in reserve requirements. However, in about a dozen instances, reserve requirements were reduced. These reductions served partly to increase the level of bank earnings and partly to ease the money markets in periods when the Federal Reserve felt more credit would benefit the economy.

## COMMERCIAL BANKS' REACTIONS TO CHANGED RESERVES

Commercial banks must adjust their portfolios and lending operations when they lose reserves, and they may expand when they gain funds. The manner and rate at which adjustments occur depend on individual managements. Although the initial impact may be met through discount operations, this is only a temporary expedient. If the losses are not unusual or peculiar and are expected to last, each bank that has lost reserves and the system as a whole will have to shift their investment policies.

### Nonmortgage Loans and Investments

Banks hold large amounts of short-term governments as liquidity, or secondary, reserves. Most initial adjustments to meet shifting reserves are handled through this account. Banks sell their short-term governments or let them run off. Notes or certificates are offered at increasingly higher yields. They are bought by individuals, corporations, or other financial institutions that find it worthwhile to hold these securities instead of bank deposits. They pay for their new assets with their existing deposits. The banks lose the assets, and their deposits fall as the checks they receive in payment are debited to the purchasers' accounts. The sharp movements in yields on treasury bills which occur when reserves are shifted were noted in Figure 4-1.

As the rates of return on short-term governments rise, banks must make other decisions. Have short-term rates risen far enough to make it worthwhile to refuse new loans or sell other investments instead of liquidating more of the short-term items? The banks must examine their business loans, consumer loans, security accounts, and mortgage loans in turn. The particular impact in each market depends on the banks' general portfolio policy plus the manner in which they react to the shifting market interest rates. In addition to more than 20 per cent of assets in United States governments, banks hold, roughly, 20 per cent of their assets in loans to commerce and industry; 10 per cent in other types of business loans, primarily to farmers, brokers, and financial institutions; and between 10 and 15 per cent in each of the three categories of loans to individuals and consumers, state and local and other securities, and mortgages.

After governments, the largest possible area of adjustment is found in the banks' portfolios of business loans. The making of commercial loans is the banks' most traditional function. Under tight-money conditions, these loans may also be the most profitable. As a result, banks primarily attempt to adjust this part of their portfolio through shifting rates rather than volumes. In the past decade, the prime lending rate for banks changed on an average of just over once a year. While normal rises or falls from one year to the next have been ½ per cent, some year-to-year changes of 1 per cent have occurred. The rates on short-term business loans average ¼ to ½ per cent above the prime rate and vary when it does.

Changing reserves seem to have less effect on consumer credit than on that for business. In consumer loans, the change in money rates alters profitability only slightly. A great deal of the money collected on them goes to cover overhead, clerical, and other fixed expenses. In addition, because banks have spent money to build up a consumer-loan business and working relationships with appliance, auto, and other dealers, they hesitate to tighten this credit drastically. If they turn away business, they lose large contributions to profits plus important future customers. As a result, tight money has little direct effect on the volume of consumer loans.

Banks tend to make more adjustments in their holdings of non-federal securities. When money is easy, they make large investments in tax-exempt bonds. They gradually increase the average period to maturity of their portfolios. When money tightens, they let the short end run off. They tend not to sell bonds, but the expansion of this segment of their assets slows down.

### Mortgage Loans

Thus far we have seen that the impact of decreased reserves causes banks to make major adjustments through their short-term governments, to raise commercial money rates and tighten access somewhat, to change consumer lending but slightly, and to change their rate of investment in other securities. Figure 4-1 shows that the mortgage market constitutes a major area of adjustment.

In tight-money periods of the past, banks have made few if any commitments of additional funds to the mortgage market, and particularly not to the residential section. There were some reinvestment of pay-offs and some loans against prior commitments, but on the whole, mortgage lending was one of the main areas that felt pressure when the banks adjusted their portfolios. In the tight-money periods of 1957 and 1959–1960, banks cut their new mortgage lending by more than 20 per cent. Banks' share of total mortgage lending also moved sharply, as shown in Figure 4-1. Even though banks make up only about 15 per cent of the total mortgage market, they have accounted for up to 70 per cent of the net changes in the market.

The banks' pressure on the mortgage market stems from two basic sources. One is the traditional uneasiness of the banks in making long-term loans. They consider themselves primarily commercial lenders. Mortgage lending falls outside many banks' usual mode of operation. Second, interest rates on mortgages tend to lag behind the market. This means that on a yield basis, a bank may be better off slowing down on its mortgage lending.

## THE REACTION OF OTHER FINANCIAL INSTITUTIONS

The rapid response of banks in the mortgage market is a major reason why Federal Reserve policy is so significant for mortgage financing. When reserves contract, banks have to adjust their lending. The immediate impact is on their liquid reserves of short-term governments, but they desire to return to previous liquidity ratios, and must therefore diminish their holdings of other assets. This pressure, plus the shifting yield differentials, rapidly leads to diminished willingness to make mortgage loan commitments.

As one would expect in a closely interrelated system of financial institutions, any major movement in one sector causes strong reactions in the others. As soon as the Federal Reserve alters bank reserves, other financial institutions feel pressure. One method of transmission is through the flow of funds. Movements in bank deposits influence savings in other institutions. Pressure is also imparted through the interest rate structure. The banks' adjustment of rates in their market spreads throughout the credit structure.

### Flow of Funds

The most immediate impact on other institutions is through their savings flow. When money becomes tight, a small decrease occurs in the rate of personal savings, and a large decrease in the share of savings that goes to financial intermediaries. This decrease occurs because banks have to raise security prices to induce savers to hold securities directly instead of through deposits. While most of the purchases are paid for by bank deposits, some are financed by withdrawals or fewer deposits in all other savings institutions.

In 1953, in 1957, and in 1959, the rate of savings in financial institutions fell. Each of these periods witnessed pressure on bank reserves and sharp increases in the rate of returns available on short-term securities.

The rising market yields also influence institutions' cash flows in another manner. As rates rise, the amounts of repayments fall on bonds, mortgages, and other loans. Such advance payments and refunding are in normal circumstances a significant part of institutions' gross flows. With rates increasing, borrowers avoid repayments as much as possible. New loans are more expensive and harder to get. Outstanding commitments based on previous levels of repayment may make still stronger the need to readjust current lending. In contrast, when rates fall, borrowers are eager to refinance at the lower rates.

### Interest Rates

Because all lenders share overlapping areas of competition in money markets, rate changes transmit themselves from one to another. With free reserves, commercial banks force the prices of securities up, and interest rates down. These changes move throughout the credit market as each lender adjusts his portfolio policy to close gaps in the interest structure.

When the Federal Reserve tightens reserve positions, the opposite occurs. Banks have to sell securities. Interest rates rise. Individuals and lenders alike adjust their holdings. Adjustment may be made difficult because shifting rates cause the value of portfolios to move also. If rates rise sharply, large-scale capital losses result.

The speed with which changes in reserve positions affect interest rates depends upon expectations and upon lenders' existing commitments. Most lenders may have committed a high percentage of their available funds for the next three to six months. These commitments will be honored at their original interest rates. As a result, yields on new loans will lag behind true market rates.

The speed with which markets react also depends upon the estimates of individuals and firms as to how rapidly the Federal Reserve will tighten credit and as to how long they expect tightened conditions to last. Clearly, if a lender thinks interest rates will rise for the next six months, he is better off selling as many securities and holding as many short-term assets as possible. The faster he acts, the less he will lose when rates finally rise.

This expectation of higher rates also results in refusals to lend or make new commitments. Lenders recognize that loans made after the market has adjusted will bring higher yields. Securities purchased before rates rise may have to be sold at a loss. The interaction between the unwillingness to lend and the desire to get out of securities can cause the money market to react very sharply. If lenders are certain that the Federal Reserve is determined to tighten money, rates may shoot far up before an appreciable reduction in reserves occurs. As reserves fall, they will simply underpin the higher rates that have already resulted from changed expectations.

### The Mortgage Market

The rate of lending on mortgages fluctuates sharply depending on the general ease or tightness of the money market. When the availability of credit changes, one should expect all markets to be affected. Less money and less savings mean fewer possible loans. However, the mortgage market is hit harder than the average. Rates on mortgages adjust more slowly than rates on other credit instruments. During the adjustment process, institutions that can avoid making mortgage loans are better off. Also, lenders can shift their portfolio policy more easily in periods of money-market movements. A lender who believes he has put too much money in mortgages can utilize a period of tightness to shift his lending ratios. In periods of ease, the development of mortgage loans may be simpler than for other types.

Life insurance companies, like commercial banks, appear to adjust their commitments on mortgage loans rather rapidly. In each period of market tightness, the insurance companies have shifted their emphasis away from the mortgage market. Their movements have been sharp. Other lenders have been forced to curtail mortgage expansions because the rate of increase in their inflow of funds has slowed.

The mortgage market, as we know, is extremely complex. Some lenders are unsophisticated. Some lenders fail to recognize that they have the ability to delay new commitments when money rates are shifting. Apparent market rates are confusing because current lending takes place partly at new rates and partly against old commitments. Furthermore, rates may hold steady until fairly sizable gaps of $\frac{1}{4}$ or $\frac{1}{2}$ per cent open up. All these factors cause mortgage interest rates to shift rather slowly compared to other markets.

This sluggish rate of change in mortgages contrasts sharply with the bond market, where interest rates may adjust by $\frac{1}{4}$ per cent in a week or less. Institutions that follow the money markets closely note the gaps among the markets and transfer their new lending accordingly.

Many observers believe that the impacts of money-market movements are increased by the existence of maximum ceilings on interest rates for loans made under the FHA-VA programs. While up to a point a system of discounts and premiums introduces greater flexibility into the market by allowing more exact adjustments, after discounts become large some lenders may completely avoid the market for psychological reasons. Mutual savings banks and insurance companies make much greater shifts in their commitments and loans on insured mortgages than on other types, and particularly so in comparison with bonds.

How much movement into and out of mortgages is due to a desire of institutions to shift their portfolios anyway is unknown. Many observers believe that unsophisticated lending officers tend to avoid the mortgage market, particularly less common types of mortgage loans, if they can do so. If their flow of funds diminishes or bonds become more readily available, they immediately withdraw from part of the mortgage market. On the other hand, with easier money, falling rates, and pressures to maintain earnings, they seek mortgages more aggressively.

These pressures result in wider fluctuations in the amount of mortgage money than in the amount of money for other loans. Under fluctuating credit conditions, mortgage interest rates do not move as rapidly as others, but larger movements do occur in the general availability of money and particularly in the conditions of lending. Borrowers who have less than optimum security or who want specialized types of financing are hit particularly hard when credit tightens. In contrast, in periods of ease the number of poor loans accepted rises faster than it should.

## SELECTIVE CREDIT POLICIES

Although the chief pressure of the government on the money market has traditionally been exerted through commercial bank reserves, other policies are or could be used. Because they deal more directly with specific segments of the market for credit than with the over-all supply of money, these policies have been given the title "selective controls." The title is something of a misnomer, since shifts in the total supply of reserves have selective impacts, particularly on mortgages, and selective controls may have significant influences on the total amount of credit.

### Debt Management

The United States Treasury sells large sums of money-market instruments—bills, certificates, notes, and bonds—every year. The amounts of yearly issues, most of which are refunding, exceed $100 billion. The action of the Treasury to adjust the proportions of issues of different lengths in order to affect the structure of interest rates is called debt management.

The theory of debt management is simple. Given the portfolio needs of lenders, a basic demand exists at any time for instruments of various length. If the supply of instruments in any sector of the range is shifted, the sectors where supply now exceeds demand will experience interest rises, and vice versa. As an example, assume there is a normal demand for $2 billion in new issues of United States bonds with a maturity of over 20 years. If the Treasury issued $5 billion in any year, the additional amounts could only be sold at higher interest rates required to attract purchasers whose normal preference was for bonds with shorter maturities, mortgages, or other loans.

A shift in relative interest rates may have some favorable effects in the credit market. An obvious example is the so-called operation twist. The Treasury believed that short-term interest rates in this country were not high enough to attract investment from abroad so that gold was being lost to enable short-term funds to be held overseas. It therefore increased its offerings of short-term bills and certificates. The excess supply of these instruments raised short-term rates relative to the longer maturities.

In contrast, when the Treasury felt that the amount of borrowing in the long-term market on mortgages and other instruments was too large, it stepped up its issues of long-period bonds to maintain or force long-term market rates higher.

While they agree that debt management has some role to play in credit controls, many observers feel that except in sharply defined cases it should not be great. The problems of related alterations in the proportions of the debt are difficult. The Treasury has to pay higher rates than would otherwise be the case. Such higher rates have important budgetary implications. As a result, the reasonableness of using debt management in contrast to other controls is not theoretically clear. Except in critical periods in the money market, it is difficult to obtain agreement as to what policy is proper. The fact that such policies are used, however, means that each person concerned with analyzing the credit market must understand how they work. He must also be prepared to forecast interest rate movements that follow shifts in debt-management policy.

### Direct Controls

There are other selective controls which may apply directly to the mortgage market. Two basic types have been used in the past, and others might be adopted in the future.

The most significant controls are those over required down payments and amortization periods. The number of families that can purchase houses or make new loans is directly related to the amount of down payment and monthly payments required. Each doubling of the down payment, say from 5 to 10 per cent, may remove nearly half the potential borrowers from the market. Similarly if a $15,000 house requires monthly payments of $120 instead of $90, the number of potential buyers will be greatly curtailed.

The emergency developing around the Korean War, caused Congress to vote powers over down payments and amortization to the lending authorities. The Federal Reserve established requirements for conventional loans through Regulation X, and the VA and FHA made related changes in their own regulations. It was hoped that decreasing the number eligible for loans would reduce the demand for houses and therefore for construction labor and materials.

While they were potentially important, the actual impact of these regulations was less than expected. A vast number of commitments were made just prior to the imposition of the regulations in the period during which their general terms were being discussed with interested builder and lender groups. By the time these commitments were used up, the need for the regulations had largely passed. The economic impact of the fighting was less than expected, and inflationary excesses following an initial scare period did not develop.

In the same period, a program of voluntary credit restraint was established under the aegis of the Federal Reserve. Local and regional committees were established which issued guidance and directions on a voluntary basis. These committees circulated statements about the need for cooperation in limiting inflationary loans. They attempted to establish general guidelines on what appeared to be inflationary under particular circumstances. They also issued information on what was happening in the lending field.

As a result of this program, it is probable that mortgage loans, particularly on shopping centers, large apartment houses, and existing properties, were at a somewhat lower level than they would otherwise have been. Fewer loans in turn moderated price rises and the demand for men and materials.

The controls of the Korean War followed both the much stricter direct controls of World War II and a basically unsatisfactory attempt to aid veterans in the period immediately after the war. They indicate possible efforts which may be followed in any future period when the country is worried about sharp inflationary pressures either in the economy as a whole or centered more specifically in the housing or construction spheres.

## THE FEDERAL HOME LOAN BANK SYSTEM

The Federal Home Loan Bank System was established in 1932 as a credit reserve system for thrift and home financing institutions. The System includes the Federal Home Loan Bank Board and twelve regional Federal Home Loan Banks. The National Housing Act added the Federal Savings and Loan Insurance Corporation, which is also administered by the Federal Home Loan Bank Board. There are approximately 4,800 members of the System, almost all of which are savings and loan associations. Insurance companies and mutual savings banks are also eligible, but not many have joined.

The FHLB Board, in addition to administering the System, has regulatory functions over Federal associations and over the insurance fund and insured member associations. It has a major money-market function as a secondary source of funds for member institutions. It serves as a source of extra liquidity to meet unusual withdrawal demands, to provide seasonal requirements, and to make possible an additional source of long-term home financing money.

The availability of short-term loans is important when a local crisis creates a sudden need for funds for a member institution. Since mortgages are hard to liquidate and most assets are in mortgages, the availability of another source of money means that an institution has time to accumulate cash through its normal flow of funds and through additional sales. Short-term loans for seasonal purposes increase the amount of mortgages the members can hold. If they had to hold cash to meet a normal seasonal withdrawal pattern, they could make fewer loans. Under the present system, associations can plan to meet these seasonal needs through borrowing.

Advances can also be made on a long-term basis of up to 10 years. They increase the money available to the whole mortgage market and particularly to localities where the need for money outruns local savings. In a typical year half or more of the members associations have been borrowers from the FHL Banks. The amount of advances has been growing steadily. In 1963, $5.6 billion was lent, while the maximum outstanding at one time was $4.8 billion.

An examination of the advances shows that they tend to grow faster when the mortgage market is active and rates are rising. On the other hand, in slack periods, members tend to repay a higher percentage of the advances.

Short-term loans to members can be based on the notes of the individual borrowing institution. Long-term advances require specific collateral, usually in the form of a pledge of particular first-mortgage loans held by the member. The amount of borrowing is limited in rather complex ways. In effect, the ability to get funds from the banks depends on the institution's own capital, the amount of its withdrawable accounts, and the amount of stock it holds in its regional Federal Home Loan Bank.

The funds made available to the Federal Home Loan Banks come from three sources. Member associations are required to purchase capital stock. Until 1962 members had to own stock equal to 2 per cent of their aggregate mortgage loans, but this requirement was then modified, so that the rate of growth in stock has slowed. As of the start of 1964, the stock outstanding totaled $1.5 billion, a sum equivalent to 31 per cent of the funds loaned out at that time.

As their second source of funds, the Federal Home Loan Banks accept deposits from their members, on which they pay a small interest rate which varies among regions. In almost all cases, the rate is below that paid by the member associations to their depositors. These deposits are primarily liquidity reserves. They increase when members' new deposits outrun their ability to find mortgages. As a result, the deposits move cyclically, rising when the mortgage market is weak and declining in high-interest-rate periods when the demand for mortgage funds and the returns on government issues are high. At the start of 1964, deposits were about $1.2 billion.

The final and most important source of funds arises from the ability of the FHL Banks to issue consolidated obligations of bonds, notes, or certificates in the general money market. These instruments are secured by the capital of the banks, the notes of their members, and the underlying mortgages. In effect, this technique makes it possible for the System to attract money into mortgages that could not or would not buy mortgages directly. A bank or insurance company will buy these notes in competition with other bonds even if its own mortgage portfolio is filled. As a result, the total money available to the mortgage market is greater than it would otherwise be.

This ability to attract additional funds is an important accomplishment of the System. It also acts to widen the geographical distribution of mortgage funds. Most borrowing by the FHL Banks is done in areas with ample money supplies, while their advances to members tend to go to areas of shortages.

The improved liquidity for emergencies and the ability to meet seasonal fluctuations are also significant plus factors. Member associations can put more money into mortgages than would otherwise be possible. The pooling of the liquidity reserves of all members results in decreased costs and more strength for each individual institution. It should be noted that the System enables the members to borrow on, or discount, their mortgages. It does not furnish a secondary market where they can buy and sell mortgages if they so desire.

## THE FEDERAL NATIONAL MORTGAGE ASSOCIATION

The Federal National Mortgage Association, more commonly known as the FNMA or "Fanny May," has existed since 1938. Congress furnished its charter and voted it its original capital and surplus from funds of the Reconstruction Finance Corporation. It was intended as an example for private lenders of how a secondary mortgage market for FHA loans could operate. It failed, however, in its task of encouraging private secondary-market operations. Through most of its history, it has served primarily as a method whereby the government guaranteed a market for certain FHA-VA loans which the private market considered marginal.

There have been numerous reorganizations of the FNMA. We

examine the organization resulting from the Act of 1954, which gave the FNMA three separate functions: (1) a secondary-mortgage-market operation, (2) assistance to special mortgages, and (3) liquidation of previous mortgage purchases. It was hoped that under the rechartering, eventually both the capital and the money used in the organization could be obtained from the private capital market, as is the case for the Federal Home Loan Banks. Each function was to be handled separately.

## The Secondary-market Operation

The first objective of Fanny May was to provide supplementary assistance to the secondary market for home mortgages. It was to provide additional liquidity for FHA-VA loans and thus improve their distribution. It also would aid the commitment process and offer repurchase agreements. Finally it would increase the total flow of money to the mortgage market by attracting new funds through its notes in a manner completely analogous to the FHLB System.

The capital for the private secondary-market operation is subscribed by those who wish to sell mortgages to the Association. With this capital and its mortgage holdings, the FNMA can sell debentures in the private market. These may equal ten times its capital and surplus. The debentures are not guaranteed by the government.

With money provided by the capital and debentures, Fanny May makes a market in insured and guaranteed mortgages. The types of loans it buys have been limited in their size, amounts, and dates. The Association also stands ready to sell any loans from its portfolio to private lenders.

The FNMA announces prices at which it will buy or sell. The prices vary with the location of the property, amount of equity, and face interest rate. It trades groups of loans through negotiations and insists that the loans meet certain standards. Mortgage firms which sell loans usually retain their servicing. The FNMA also issues stand-by commitments and agrees to take certain mortgages under repurchase agreements. Sellers get an option to repurchase the loans they sell at fixed prices in fixed periods.

While the Association attempts to set its prices inside the market range, it is usually slightly above or below. Consequently, in any period most transactions have tended to be on one side. Most of its purchases have been from mortgage companies, which use it to gain flexibility and to obtain an additional market in periods of tight money. The adjustments made by other financial intermediaries through Fanny May have not been great.

In periods of tight money, Fanny May has been almost entirely a buyer. When other mortgages have been less readily available, it has been able to sell. Part of its difficulties arise from criticism by builders and Congress that it tightens credit when it sells loans. Those in favor of easier credit can rarely agree that there is a proper time to tighten it. Since any increase of the supply of mortgages by FNMA sales has that effect, they always prefer Fanny May to be buying rather than selling.

The stand-by commitments and repurchase agreements have increased the market's flexibility. They have enabled mortgage companies to offer commitments to builders even when they were hard to obtain in the private market. The mortgage companies use the FNMA as an emergency backstop. They can issue commitments farther into the future knowing that if the market settles down, private sources of funds will come forward and they will not have to use their Fanny May commitments.

### Special Programs

In addition to the secondary-market operation, which in theory may become privately financed, the FNMA has other functions more in the direct tradition of governmental services. Under the special assistance program, the FNMA buys special mortgages at above the market rate. These mortgages are for programs such as FHA-insured loans to redevelopment and renewal housing and housing for the aged.

In these categories, Congress has determined that as a matter of public policy the FHA should insure loans with more than traditional risks or with mortgage yields below the current market. Since lenders are unwilling to make loans under the established terms, the FHA's authorization to insure them would have no effect unless the government furnished a market. Thus it is the task of Fanny May to see that loans uneconomic for the private market will be purchased.

Congress and the executive establish the prices and amounts of possible loans in these special assistance programs. Since many of these programs call for very specialized types of development that are outside the traditional skills of the building industry, building under them has lagged far behind congressional authorizations. The process of getting the programs approved by the interested agencies, built, and finally rented takes a great deal of complicated maneuvering. Most builders have been willing to leave the expense of pathbreaking in these fields to a few specialists. These assistance programs are growing slowly but steadily.

For another type of program in this area, builders and mortgage companies evidenced a rapid acceptance, which may be a portent for the future. In 1958 when the level of new housing starts was falling rapidly, Congress authorized the FNMA to purchase special mortgages for small single-family homes. The terms were favorable enough to give a form of subsidy to the builders and owners of these projects. The commitments under this program were taken up with great speed. The results seemed to show that under particular circumstances, Congress through Fanny May could give a short-period impetus to the level of building and the amount of national output.

The FNMA was given another group of special functions in order to liquidate the portfolio of mortgages held when the program was established in its present form on November 1, 1954. These prior loans carried low interest rates and were hard to sell in the open market. They have fallen drastically in amount, however, because of amortizations, repayments, and special trades for United States bonds carrying higher interest rates.

The special assistance programs of Fanny May are financed by Treasury capital. For peculiar administrative reasons, the way in which Fanny May obtains its money, either from the Treasury or private markets, makes a significant difference in the government's fiscal budget. Fanny May financing has consequently become a political football, kicked from side to side in order to show budget results which in fact have virtually no relation to economic reality. All recent administrations have attempted to show a better record in budget deficits at critical periods by altering Fanny May's financing. Frequently the improved look has been obtained only at an actual increased cost to the government.

Many serious unresolved problems exist in the relationship of the FHA-FNMA programs to the private market. The FHA and the FNMA make it possible for the government to play a significant role in the housing market. However, few have been willing to face up to the various implications of the programs. The techniques depend upon a mixed use of private markets and governmental intervention. The net results appear to have many advantages in contrast to purely private or purely public mortgage markets. However, the programs might work still better if interested persons recognized more completely how and why the present mixture has developed, what its operations actually do, and what implications they have for the future.

## SUMMARY

The government has played a very important role in the mortgage market. Its influence has been exercised directly and indirectly, with the indirect influence being more significant.

When the Federal Reserve acts to tighten credit, banks must readjust their loans and holdings of securities. Banks' mortgage lending tends to be a major sector in which they make adjustments. At the same time, banks' sales of other assets and their losses in deposits cause reactions in other financial institutions. Savers may want to buy securities directly rather than hold them through financial intermediaries. The market interest rates on notes and bonds rise. Lenders may want to buy them rather than make as many new commitments on mortgages, whose rates tend to lag behind other markets.

The government may use other selective credit controls, either in the money market in general or specifically on mortgages. Mortgage-market controls were used during the Korean War period. They caused rather violent movements in loans and probably curtailed the total lending on mortgages.

Through the establishment of the Federal Home Loan Bank System and the Federal National Mortgage Association, the government has facilitated a flow of funds into mortgages which might not otherwise be available. These organizations issue notes and bonds based on their capital and mortgage holdings. As a result, investors who want shorter-term, more liquid assets are able to add money to the mortgage market. These organizations also have other significant influences that facilitate the functioning of the mortgage market.

## SELECTED REFERENCES

American Bankers Association: *The Commercial Banking Industry,* Prentice-Hall, Inc., Englewood Cliffs, N.J., 1962.

Board of Governors of the Federal Reserve System: *The Federal Reserve System: Purposes and Functions,* Washington.

Jones, Oliver, and Leo Grebler: *The Secondary Mortgage Market,* University of California, Los Angeles, 1961.

Kendall, Leon T.: *The Savings and Loan Business,* Prentice-Hall, Inc., Englewood Cliffs, N.J., 1962.

Samuelson, Paul A.: *Economics,* 5th ed., McGraw-Hill Book Company, New York, 1961, chaps. 16, 17.

Walter, James E.: *The Investment Process,* Harvard Business School, Boston, 1962.

# The Mortgage Programs of the
# Federal Housing and Veterans
# Administrations_____5

The mortgage insurance and guarantee programs of the Federal government have been among the most significant dynamic forces in the postwar mortgage market. To recognize the extent of their impact and to evaluate future possibilities and probabilities of change, we must fully understand how these programs work and how they influence mortgage financing.

The mortgage insurance program of the Federal Housing Administration and the guarantee program of the Veterans Administration broke new paths in several directions. A complete revolution occurred in our concepts of reasonable terms for new loans with respect to down payments and amortization periods as well. Mortgage instruments that could be traded nationally developed. Institutions previously in the mortgage market only occasionally made more extensive portfolio commitments.

Better procedures for underwriting mortgages developed. Fixed standards and risk rating were introduced. Mortgage banking experienced a rapid growth. Local and regional lenders faced greater competition, but they also had increased opportunities to buy mortgages on a national scale. More houses were built and sold, and they were of different types than they otherwise might have been. The structure of our cities today has been altered by these programs.

Government intervention in the mortgage markets has been so popular that other related programs are constantly being proposed. The FHA has been utilized as a vehicle to aid in getting more and different housing built through the special assistance programs. These programs use contingent rather than outright subsidies. Their costs to the government depend upon their efficiency and upon future market developments rather than upon immediate subsidies, as in the previously enacted public housing programs.

The growth of the FHA-VA programs may also have introduced some additional instability into mortgage lending. Their existence has increased the impact of governmental monetary policies. While the question of whether more unstable conditions are a direct or indirect effect of the programs is debatable, the growth of a national market dependent upon institutions each strongly affected by government policies would probably increase fluctuations no matter how operated. Many, believe, furthermore, that the programs have been regulated and administered in such a manner as to have added instability.

Table 5-1 shows various measures of the relative importance of the FHA-VA programs in the residential mortgage market. They appear least significant with respect to nonfarm mortgage recordings. Here the government programs reached a maximum of 36 per cent in 1955. By 1964 they were running only a little over 20 per cent. However, these figures understate their significance, since the figures for the governmental programs are based on the actual FHA-VA reports while a great deal of duplication exists in the series for conventional recordings.

A better measure of importance may be the data showing the total mortgage loans outstanding. The government-underwritten loans were nearly 45 per cent of the total in 1955. By 1964, they had dropped to not much over 35 per cent. The difference between the FHA-VA recordings and outstandings stems from the fact that conventional loans have both duplication and a shorter life because they include construction lending and that for short-period financing.

TABLE 5-1 *Comparison of Conventional and Government-insured and Government-guaranteed Residential Mortgage Lending* (In billions of dollars)

| Year | Nonfarm recordings of $20,000 or less | | | | | Mortgage debt outstanding, one- to four-family properties | | |
|---|---|---|---|---|---|---|---|---|
| | Con-ven-tional | VA | | FHA | | VA | FHA | Con-ven-tional |
| | | Pro-posed | Exist-ing | Pro-posed | Exist-ing | | | |
| 1950 | 10.6 | 1.9 | 1.2 | 1.6 | 0.9 | 10.3 | 8.6 | 26.3 |
| 1951 | 10.9 | 2.7 | 0.9 | 1.2 | 0.7 | 13.2 | 9.7 | 28.8 |
| 1952 | 13.4 | 1.8 | 0.9 | 1.0 | 1.0 | 14.6 | 10.8 | 33.1 |
| 1953 | 14.4 | 2.0 | 1.0 | 1.3 | 1.0 | 16.1 | 12.0 | 38.0 |
| 1954 | 16.8 | 2.7 | 1.6 | 1.0 | 0.9 | 19.3 | 12.8 | 43.6 |
| 1955 | 18.2 | 4.6 | 2.6 | 1.3 | 1.8 | 24.6 | 14.3 | 49.3 |
| 1956 | 18.6 | 3.9 | 1.9 | 1.1 | 1.5 | 28.4 | 15.5 | 55.1 |
| 1957 | 18.2 | 2.9 | 0.9 | 0.9 | 1.4 | 30.7 | 16.5 | 60.4 |
| 1958 | 21.0 | 1.3 | 0.5 | 1.7 | 2.9 | 30.4 | 19.7 | 67.6 |
| 1959 | 23.4 | 2.1 | 0.7 | 2.6 | 3.5 | 30.0 | 23.8 | 77.0 |
| 1960 | 22.7 | 1.6 | 0.4 | 2.2 | 2.4 | 29.7 | 26.7 | 84.8 |
| 1961 | 24.6 | 1.2 | 0.7 | 1.8 | 3.0 | 29.6 | 29.5 | 93.9 |
| 1962 | 26.2 | 1.4 | 1.3 | 1.8 | 3.4 | 29.7 | 32.3 | 106.4 |
| 1963 | 28.0 | 1.3 | 1.7 | 1.7 | 3.9 | 30.0 | 34.2 | 117.5 |

SOURCE: *Federal Reserve Bulletin.*

The share of government programs in the new-house market is hard to estimate because of problems in the underlying statistics. It appears, however, that in 1950 and 1954, the government programs accounted for nearly half of all starts and more than half of those new dwellings that carried mortgages. By 1964, the government programs' share of housing starts was under 20 per cent. The erosion of this share was fairly steady after 1955, with only a minor reversal due to the FNMA special assistance programs of 1958–1959.


## OPERATIONS OF THE FHA PROGRAM

The Federal Housing Administration insurance programs started in the depth of the Great Depression. The chaotic conditions of the mortgage market and the almost complete cessation of residential construction demanded some type of action. Almost all the groups concerned with housing, such as real estate groups, builders, labor, material suppliers, and financial institutions, advocated the adoption of some new approach to the mortgage market in order to stabilize it and make possible an expansion of building. Their desires were realized when Congress passed the National Housing Act in June, 1934, establishing the Federal Housing Administration.


### Purposes and Functions

The initial act entrusted to the FHA three major goals which still remain part of its functioning. However, the importance of these different objectives has varied greatly in the ensuing periods. Some who at certain times supported the Act because they believed in one of these purposes became disaffected when other goals played a more prominent part in total operations.

Initially the FHA's most important aim was to reduce the risks of the mortgage market in order to make savings institutions lend more willingly on real estate. This increased lending would foster a step-up in building, more employment, and an increase in the gross national product. The failure of the housing industry to re-establish itself was recognized as a major drag on the entire economy. From its start, the FHA was concerned with influencing the level of housing production.

The means of reducing risks and attracting more money into the mortgage market were twofold. The mutual mortgage insurance plan pooled risks of the individual lenders, giving each the benefit of the law of large numbers, which observes that regularity of certain types of behavior becomes more predictable as a larger universe becomes involved. Still more significant, the ultimate risks of loss were transferred from the individual lenders to the government. Risks were also reduced by bringing more knowledge and scientific methods into the procedures of mortgage underwriting. The fore-closure experience of the early 1930s demonstrated that the tradi-tional mortgage lending techniques were not suitable for their tasks. It was hoped that the FHA could bring about major improvements in mortgage lending practices.

The second purpose of the FHA, stated in the preamble of the Act creating it, is "to encourage improvements in housing standards and conditions." Changing ideas of how to improve housing condi-tions have led to major alterations in FHA policy over time.

From the start, the FHA took more interest in the construction and location of houses it insured than has been typical of con-ventional lenders. The FHA has established minimum property re-quirements which, if not met, mean a building is completely in-eligible for a loan. In contrast, private lenders normally lower the amount which will be loaned on substandard units. Similarly, the FHA has established maximum interest rates.

The desire to improve housing conditions has also led to the use of the program to promote the construction of houses which Congress felt would otherwise not have been built. Under major defense and war housing programs, the government assumed risks and additional costs of building for nonstable areas and for areas which had previously lacked standard housing and financing condi-tions. The concept of special aid expanded to include loans to margi-nal groups or others needing special assistance who would not qualify under usual lending standards. Periodically Congress has changed the terms, conditions, and interest rates of mortgages which the FHA could insure. The objective has been to improve the hous-ing conditions of particular groups when Congress believed special aids were necessary.

The third purpose of the FHA was to establish a national mortgage market. It was hoped that a private secondary-market mechanism could be promoted along lines similar to those now being followed by the FNMA. That did not occur. On the other hand, many incidental acts of the FHA did lead to an expanded secondary market. The existence of insurance led to a removal of state restrictions on terms and areas of lending for mortgages which carried the FHA approval. The uncertainty of lenders operating in distant markets was reduced. Instruments with the FHA imprint became negotiable throughout the nation.

### Eligible Loans

The FHA insures against losses on money advanced by the lender. The FHA lends no money of its own. Thus, before the FHA becomes involved, a borrower must find an approved lender that is willing to put up the money on a mortgage which the FHA will insure.

To be insured, loans must be held or made by an FHA-approved mortgagee. Commercial banks, mutual savings banks, Federal savings and loan associations, and life insurance companies are, by the nature of their regulation by other authorities, eligible for approval upon application. Other lenders, such as mortgage banks, pension funds, or specialized financial institutions, may be approved as mortgagees. They must meet particular FHA requirements with respect to their capital and their ability to originate and service insured loans in accordance with normal practices of prudent lending institutions.

An approved mortgagee has the right to apply for insurance of mortgages which meet certain minimum FHA requirements. The property underlying the mortgage must be eligible according to FHA standards. It must be in the United States or its possessions. The property must be held in fee simple or in accordance with limited types of leaseholds. Certain restrictions, such as those which attempt to discriminate by race or color, must be absent. The FHA-insured mortgage must be the only one on the property when it is recorded. Each specific FHA title has certain minimum property requirements as to type of construction, design, condition, land development, neighborhood, and similar factors.

Loans are insured only for eligible borrowers who meet specific credit standards. Except in particular circumstances, they cannot be above sixty-two years in age. The required mortgage payments and other housing expenses must fall within prescribed ratios to the borrower's current and prospective income.

The mortgage terms also must meet FHA requirements. The interest rate may not exceed the maximum established by the Commissioner. Loans are limited in absolute amount and in the ratio of amount to the selling price of the house. Monthly amortization sufficient to extinguish the loan over a given period must be established. Escrow funds must be set up and credited monthly with funds for future payments of taxes and insurance.

### The FHA Insurance

Approved lenders make applications for FHA commitments to insure particular loans which are to be closed under specific conditions. The conditions include forms to be used, the title regulations, and FHA approval of the eligibility of the property and borrower. Conditional commitments are granted for a specific property and prospective terms but with an unknown mortgagor. Firm commitments are issued upon approval of the eligible borrower.

With a firm commitment, the mortgagee can advance the money and close the loan. If all the terms of the commitment are met, the FHA issues an insurance contract. The contract specifies the fees to be paid and lists the conditions and manner in which the lender will be reimbursed for losses.

The FHA charges a commitment fee, other initial processing charges, and an insurance premium of $\frac{1}{2}$ per cent per year on the unpaid balance. Different types of loans are insured under various FHA titles, each of which may have a separate insurance fund. The largest funds are created under section 203 of the National Housing Act. This section establishes mutual mortgage funds. If the amounts received in a fund exceed the estimated requirements for payments against insurance contracts written under the fund, a refund of some of the previously collected premiums will be made to the mortgagor when his mortgage and the insurance are extinguished by his final payment.

When a borrower defaults on his loan, the insurance contract becomes effective. Lenders must inform the insuring office within 60 days after default and periodically thereafter. Within a year of default, the lender must acquire title by some means, or he must institute foreclosure procedures.

To secure the insurance benefits, the mortgagee must be able to deliver title to the FHA within 30 days after acquisition with the property free of waste (loss of value due to undermaintenance). Upon delivery of title, the insured lender receives from the mortgage insurance fund negotiable debentures whose interest and principal are guaranteed by the United States government. While the due date of the debentures varies somewhat among the FHA titles, they normally run for 20 years from the date foreclosure was instituted. They carry interest rates set periodically by the Commissioner with the approval of the Treasury. Rates depend upon the going interest rate for government bonds. The debentures can be used to make payments due the mutual mortgage insurance fund. The fact that they can be turned into cash through the normal ½ per cent insurance premium payments reduces the risk of capital loss due to shifting interest rates.

Insurance claims are divided. Debentures are issued immediately for the entire unpaid principal balance of the mortgage plus amounts for such things as taxes, assessments, insurance, part of foreclosure costs and those necessary for protecting, preserving or operating the property.

In addition the mortgagee receives a contingent-claim certificate to cover the difference between the debentures he receives and his total necessary expenses. The contingent claims cover the remaining foreclosure costs, unpaid interest, and repairs necessary to restore the property to proper condition. The amount received on this claim will depend on the housing market and the cost of sale. When a property is sold, the Federal Housing Commissioner calculates his total costs including debentures. If the net receipts exceed all these costs, the difference is used to pay as much as possible of the certificate of claim.

The system of debentures enables the FHA to spread losses over future periods and to hold properties for longer periods. It also means future income may offset periodic sharp losses. Since the lender must stand at least part of the losses, the system of certificates of claim forces him to use diligence in order to avoid unpaid interest or deterioration of the property.

This system may also decrease the FHA's work load. To avoid debentures and certificates, lenders may dispose of properties themselves rather than invoke the insurance. In strong housing markets, numerous defaults are handled directly by the lenders. The debenture-claim system, however, does lessen the usefulness of the insurance. Some observers believe that the psychological cost of the uncertainty which it introduces may far exceed any sums it saves through greater lender diligence.

### Terms For Title 2 Loans

A lengthy description of the terms required for FHA or VA guarantees is not worthwhile because every Congress makes alterations. It is useful, however, to see how criteria have developed historically and how drastically concepts of a relatively safe mortgage have altered.

In the area of minimum requirements for property or borrowers, developments have been steady but minor. There have been periodic complaints of standards set too high, but controversy has been relatively subdued. The major changes have occurred in maximum interest rates, amortization periods, and minimum down payments. The terms of section 203, which provide for the insurance of home mortgages and which have accounted for over 60 per cent of normal mortgage volume, have had the greatest impact on both the total FHA program and conventional lenders.

When the FHA was established in 1934, mortgages eligible for insurance required down payments of at least 20 per cent. The longest period of amortization was 20 years. No insured loan could be over $16,000. The maximum interest rate was $5\frac{1}{2}$ per cent plus an insurance premium of $\frac{1}{2}$ per cent of the original balance. This meant a total average payment of about $6\frac{1}{2}$ per cent. Since then, each of these terms has been altered many times.

The maximum interest rate has fluctuated. The insurance fee was reduced to $\frac{1}{2}$ per cent of the outstanding balance. At one point, a minimum rate of 4¼ per cent plus the insurance premium was reached, or a total charge of 4¾ per cent. The maximum allowed in any postwar period was 5¾ per cent plus the insurance, or a total of 6¼ per cent. This amount was just below the initial maximum. The highest authorized rate was about a third above the lowest.

Although interest rates have fluctuated, down payments, or their converse, the maximum percentage of loan to value, have decreased steadily except during the Korean crisis. In marked contrast to the original required 20 per cent down payment for any house, by 1961 a house costing $15,000 or less could be bought with only 3 per cent down. The 1965 regulations authorized insurance of loans for 97 per cent of the first $15,000 of the FHA-estimated value, plus 90 per cent of the next $5,000 plus 75 per cent of the remaining amount, with a maximum loan of $30,000. Under these regulations, typical down payments would be $300 for a $10,000 house; $450 for a $15,000 house; $1,000 for a $20,000 house; $2,250 for a $25,000 house, and $3,500 for a $30,000 house.

In each period a maximum mortgage was specified. This maximum has risen from $16,000 to $30,000. Higher-priced houses can carry an FHA mortgage, but the entire difference between the selling price and the maximum FHA mortgage must be paid by the buyer as a down payment.

Throughout most of the FHA's history, a major differential existed between the minimum down payment required on existing units and that required on those properties with plans approved prior to construction and whose construction was inspected by the FHA or VA. The law has in theory now removed this differential. In fact, existing units will probably have higher required down payments, since the FHA valuation is more likely to fall below the selling price. The difference between the FHA value and the selling price must be added to his down payment by the buyer as part of his cash requirement.

The amortization period has also increased steadily. Starting at a maximum of 20 years, it grew to 25, to 30, and finally to 35 years for property inspected during construction. For existing units, the maximum amortization period is 30 years or less, depending on the expected life of the property.

The impact of these changed terms can best be judged by seeing how they influenced the down payments and monthly payments required initially and in 1964. These data are shown in Table 5-2. Required payments for each price house are shown at three different interest rates, even though it must be recognized that a single rate prevailed in each period.

Most obvious is the vast difference in down-payment requirements. The 1934 regulations required down payments three to six times higher than more recent ones, depending upon the price of the house.

The changed amortization lengths mean a potentially sharp difference in monthly payments. The bottom line of the table shows the amount of payment per $1,000 of loan required at the given interest rates and with amortization periods of 20 years for 1934, and 35 years in 1964.

We note that at $4\frac{3}{4}$ per cent interest, the lengthening of the amortization period reduces the required monthly payment per $1,000 of loan from $6.44 to $4.89—a total of $1.55, or 24 per cent. At $6\frac{1}{4}$ per cent interest, the reduction is $1.39, or 19 per cent. The higher the interest rate, the less dramatic is the impact of lengthening the amortization period. It is also true that the longer the amortization period, the less is the effect of increasing the period by a similar additional number of years. This occurs because the interest share of any payment becomes more significant as the amortization period becomes longer.

Table 5-2 also shows that at the total $5\frac{3}{4}$ per cent rates prevailing in 1964, the borrower must pay $5.54 per $1,000 of loan, 24 per cent less than the $7.26 required in 1934. It is also true, however, that most of this lower payment per $1,000 borrowed simply enables a person to carry the additional loan made possible by the lower down payment requirement. Thus a borrower who bought a $15,000 house with maximum loans would actually have to pay $80.53 per month in 1964, compared to $87.15 per month in 1934. At identical interest rates of $5\frac{3}{4}$ per cent, a difference of only $3.25 would separate the two. For a person who bought a $25,000 house with minimum down payment, actual monthly payments in 1964 would have been less than in 1964, even with the higher interest rates and shorter amortization period at the earlier time.

TABLE 5-2  *Comparison of Mortgage Patterns and Required Monthly Payments under Various FHA Terms*

| Value of house | Down payment | | Monthly payment on basis of annual interest including FHA insurance rates* | | | | | | | |
|---|---|---|---|---|---|---|---|---|---|---|
| | | | 4¾% | | 5¾% | | 6¼% | | | |
| | 1934 | 1964 | 1934 | 1964 | 1934 | 1964 | 1934 | 1964 | | |
| $15,000 | $ 3,000 | $ 450 | $ 77.24 | $ 71.13 | $ 83.78 | $ 80.53 | $ 87.15 | $ 85.42 | | |
| 20,000 | 4,000 | 1,000 | 102.99 | 92.88 | 111.72 | 105.17 | 116.20 | 111.54 | | |
| 25,000 | 9,000 | 2,200 | 102.99 | 111.46 | 111.72 | 126.20 | 116.20 | 133.85 | | |
| 30,000 | 14,000 | 3,500 | 102.99 | 129.55 | 111.72 | 146.68 | 116.20 | 155.58 | | |
| Monthly payment per $1,000 loan...... | | | 6.44 | 4.89 | 6.98 | 5.54 | 7.26 | 5.87 | | |

* The 1934 figures are for 20-year amortization; the 1964 figures are for 35-year amortization.

## Special Assistance Titles

The sharp differences in required payments shown in Table 5-2 underlie the logic of the various special assistance programs of the FHA. Congress has decreed that more liberal terms and lower interest rates should be made available to special groups whose housing conditions it believes require public aid. These special programs are established under individual titles such as sections 203(h) and (i), 213, 221, 222, 223, 809, 810, etc. These titles aid disaster areas, servicemen, defense workers, the aged, low-income groups, urban renewal areas, and similar cases.

The general technique is similar. Congress determines that to help a particular group afford housing, special terms or interest rates are necessary. Again, as demonstrated by the table, the better the terms and the lower the interest rates, the less is the required monthly payment or rent. The less the payment, the more easily can a group at a given income level afford a particular level of housing. The easier terms may include a zero or only a $200 down payment, a 40-year amortization period, or below-market interest rates. As an example, one program pays only the current yield on all marketable United States Treasury obligations, or between 3 and $3\frac{3}{4}$ per cent interest. The FHA also waives the mortgage insurance premiums.

As noted in the previous chapter, since these loans are not at competitive rates, they depend upon commitments and purchases by the FNMA. Mortgage companies agree to make the loans, but only because of FNMA participation. The line between this type of operation and a direct-lending program by the government is very thin.

Since these terms increase the FHA's risk, Congress authorizes a special title and a special insurance fund for each program. In effect, Congress agrees to pay for any losses for these titles from future appropriations if necessary. The amount of losses will depend on how well the programs are managed and how closely the established terms approach economic rents. Many programs may be self-supporting. Others may require outside funds. The point to recognize is that Congress, with much popular support but also over a great deal of political opposition, has determined that such special programs are a proper use of the FHA organization and insuring function.

## THE VA MORTGAGE LOAN GUARANTEE PROGRAM

The GI Home Loan Guarantee program of the Veterans Administration was not thought of initially as a housing-market program. In 1944, Congress passed the Serviceman's Readjustment Act, frequently called the GI Bill of Rights. As indicated by its title, Congress was concerned primarily with aiding the veteran to shift from a war footing back to a normal way of life. The program included education, job, and housing provisions.

As an aid to readjustment, Congress wanted to aid the veteran in purchasing a better-quality house or one with more reasonable terms than might otherwise be available. The technique devised was to guarantee lenders against some or all of the losses that might arise as a result of the additional risks assumed when the GI was granted better terms than those prevailing in the market. The original guarantee scheme applied to many types of loans, including those on businesses, farms, and for alterations and repairs. The bulk of the guarantees, however, have been made on the veterans' own residential properties.

Because the Act was to aid servicemen's readjustment, a time limit was initially placed on its operations. This time limit has been extended periodically. Since each extension requires congressional action, a possibility always exists that the program may end.

In its first 20 years, the program guaranteed over 6 million loans. While the VA program theoretically has been concerned with the individual veteran, in fact it has been far more significant as a housing-market instrument. The program and its changes have been shaped more by builders and lending institutions than by veterans' groups. As it developed, the program served almost the identical purposes of the FHA with, however, slight differences in procedures and clientele.

The VA guarantee established an additional type of negotiable instrument for the national market. The lowered risks to lenders which resulted and the improved secondary market have paralleled

FHA results. The VA has similarly been concerned with the terms of lending, borrowers' eligibility, and property standards. The similarities to the FHA program are so great that it is proper to analyze the results of the two programs jointly. In a vast number of cases, houses have had tentative commitments from both the VA and FHA. The form of the final loan depended primarily on the eligibility of the purchaser.

While terms, conditions, and eligibility have differed only slightly most of the time, greater differences have occurred in particular periods. Each program has seen its use rise or fall depending upon the particular market circumstances. Except for the years 1954 to 1956, the FHA handled the largest share of inspections for new-house construction under the government programs. On the other hand, with the exception of 1949, the number of loans made under the VA program exceeded the FHA for each year from 1946 through 1957. The FHA program became the largest again in 1958 and has since been two to three times as large.

## Eligibility and Terms

The VA program consists primarily of a system of guarantees. There has also been a small direct-loan program primarily for semi-rural areas or others where financing under the guarantee program was difficult to obtain. In the years 1950 through 1963, 235,000 direct loans were made.

Initially the guarantee was for $2,000. The figure was later raised to $4,000 and eventually to either $7,500 or 60 per cent of the amount of the loan, whichever is less. The VA covers all the loss up to the amount of the guarantee. However, the amount of the guarantee declines pro rata with payments on the loan. For example, if the original loan was $10,000, the guarantee would be $6,000. The VA would cover the total loss up to $6,000, but the lender would be responsible for any beyond that amount. When the lender had received $5,000 in payments and the loan was reduced to $5,000, the guarantee would still cover 60 per cent but would be only for $3,000. The VA would pay up to this amount, and the lender would be responsible for the remaining $2,000.

This type of program, as opposed to that of the FHA, has a twofold effect. The lender increases his risk somewhat as the size of the loan increases, since the maximum $7,500 guarantee does not expand. Thus the chances of there being a loss of over $7,500 on a $13,000 house are much less than the chances of a loss above this amount on a $50,000 house. Second, as the amount of the unpaid balance decreases, the VA's potential payment may become so small a part of the total that the lender may be better off handling all foreclosure and disposal procedures himself rather than entrusting them to the VA.

Under the loan guarantee program, the VA does not furnish any money. As with FHA loans, the veteran must find a lender who will make the funds available. The lender then applies for a loan guarantee. Lenders are divided into supervised and nonsupervised. Supervised lenders include banks, savings and loans, insurance companies, and other mortgagees subject to examination and supervision by an agency of the United States government or a state. These lenders can create VA loans that will be automatically guaranteed without prior approval of the VA. In effect they have a firm commitment that all eligible loans will be guaranteed. Many supervised lenders prefer, however, to ask the VA for specific prior approval of each loan to make certain that it is eligible. Nonsupervised lenders must get prior approval for each specific loan.

The terms for eligible loans depend upon congressional rulings and regulations issued by the VA Administrator. Many of the requirements parallel those of the FHA, but there are some significant differences. The VA specifies that a loan is eligible for guarantee only if the purchase price paid by the veteran does not exceed the reasonable value of the property as determined by the Administrator. In contrast, the FHA restricts the amount of the loan but, providing the difference is in cash, the purchaser may pay as much above the FHA value as he desires. The VA requirement sets up a cut-off point that rules out many loans completely. The object is to protect the unwary veteran.

Borrower requirements parallel those of the FHA also, but with the obvious difference that the buyer must be a veteran eligible for the VA loan guarantee benefits. Specific eligibility is determined by the VA in accordance with acts of Congress. The loan-to-income ratios required by the VA tend not to be as strict as those of the FHA. Limits are established by the individual lender, who is charged with being prudent in determining that the burden on the veteran borrower will not be too great.

A maximum interest rate is set in any period. It has tended to be at or below that of the FHA and has moved less frequently. It was 4 per cent for the initial period and rose in steps to $5\frac{1}{4}$ per cent. Since no insurance fee is required, at equivalent interest rates the veteran pays less on a guaranteed than on an FHA-insured loan. The losses on the guarantees and the administrative costs of the program are absorbed by the government as one form of veterans' benefit.

There is no minimum-down-payment requirement. While the amount of guarantee is limited, the lender can lend as much as he sees fit and with as little or as much down payment as he feels is necessary. In one period, so-called no-no-down-payment loans were made. At that time, even closing costs could be included in the amount of the loan. In most periods, however, the VA has required that the borrower furnish money for the closing costs. During the Korean period, one of the direct mortgage controls suggested and used was to require specific-percentage down payments. The number of loans guaranteed without down payments has exceeded 60 per cent in several years.

A maximum period of amortization is authorized. As with the FHA, it has gradually increased, rising from 20 to 30 years.

The increased ease of eligibility reflects the favorable experience of low-down-payment, long-maturity loans. During the entire program, claims have been relatively low, ranging from only $\frac{1}{10}$ to $\frac{3}{10}$ per cent of all loans outstanding in any period. This good risk experience, however, occurred primarily during a period of rising prices for houses. With prices always going up, borrowers or lenders could sell the house at a price high enough so that no claim was necessary against the guarantee.

In periods of stable prices, such loan experience has been poorer. With no down payments, the owner has no equity to cover the selling costs of a house such as agent fees and title transfers. If

depreciation is greater than amortization, he may have a negative
equity. In all such cases, the percentage of foreclosures and claims
is likely to be much higher than where an equity has been built
up through rising prices.

### The Guarantee

Since it has no continuing insurance premiums to collect, the
VA does not establish continuing accounts with lenders as does
the FHA. Once it has issued a guarantee, it retains no continuing
relation to the loan. It steps in only in case of default. The lender
services the account. If a default occurs, he must notify the VA.
Since the guarantee is a form of veteran benefit, the VA has rather
liberal default requirements in order to aid the veteran. The lender
can use extra time in attempting to cure the default. He can also
modify or extend the terms if this will help the veteran. With the
prior approval of the VA, a voluntary deed may be accepted by
the lender, and the guarantee will remain in effect.

When all efforts to cure the default have failed, the lender may
file his claim for the full amount of the guarantee. All expenses
of the lender, including interest and other expenditures, are included,
providing they do not exceed the amount of the VA guarantee.

Upon receiving a claim for payment, the VA has 30 days in
which to take either of two options. It may require the lender to
transfer the loan and security to the VA. In this case it pays all
the outstanding indebtedness owed the lender as of the date of transfer. If the VA prefers, it may take the second option and tell the
lender to foreclose. It can specify the minimum amount which will
be credited to the debt as a result of the security. This means the
lender in foreclosures knows what amount the VA will pay against
the guarantee and what portion the VA expects to come from liquidation of the security. If the market price is below the upset price, the
VA will take over the security.

The VA guarantee has been thought to be worth slightly more
than the FHA insurance. The claim procedure is simpler. No debentures are involved. The VA guarantee covers all costs and expenses
incurred up to the time of claim, in contrast to the FHA settlement

of only part of those included in the certificate of claim. The sphere in which the guarantee is weaker is on expensive houses or in cases of complete disaster, where the amount of the guarantee does not cover the entire difference between the indebtedness and the liquidating value of the property assigned as security.

The VA guarantee can only be granted for loans to specific individual veterans. However, if the veteran sells the house subject to the existing mortgage, the guarantee continues even if the new owner is a nonveteran. An important point frequently neglected is that the VA holds the veteran for whom the guarantee was initially issued responsible if any loss occurs to the VA. The VA has the right to make a claim against the veteran if at any time it has to make good on its guarantee to the lender. Claims of this type have been made against veterans who many years previously sold their houses subject to mortgages. In theory the VA has the right to offset such a claim against any benefits that the veteran can claim in the future from the government.

## EVALUATION

The government's intervention in the mortgage market stems partly from its necessary functions of organizing and regulating the monetary and public debt systems. In addition, however, specific programs have been enacted and operated which aim at increasing the flow of funds into mortgages, increasing the rate of homeownership, perhaps adjusting the rate of construction, and certainly improving housing standards by making it possible for each family to live in a more expensive house. It must be recognized that the enactment and carrying out of these programs does not necessarily mean that they have achieved their goals, particularly since some of the goals may be conflicting.

### The Availability of Mortgage Funds

There is general agreement that the government programs have succeeded in attracting additional funds to the mortgage market. Important lenders such as insurance companies, pension funds, and commercial and savings banks have found it possible to lend more freely and to operate on a wider geographical basis. The programs of the FNMA and the FHLB System have, by the issuance of debentures, made money available on mortgages which otherwise would have had to remain in the market for short-term funds.

These successful developments have occurred because government insurance and guarantees have made the mortgage a more standard commodity and have removed legal restrictions in the national market. The conventional mortgage has caused problems in classifying borrowers and properties with sufficient accuracy for lenders at a distance to evaluate their risk properly. The FHA-VA programs ensure that a borrower has met certain minimum standards. Furthermore, the maximum loss of the lender, even if the borrower defaults, is fixed. Table 11-1 shows the significant role played by the government-aided loans in the additions to the portfolios of most national lenders.

Insurance companies that had been lending on a national scale were able to expand in the moderate-priced market. The costs of their lending in smaller units were reduced. Mutual savings banks located in areas of surplus funds in the East could lend at wider distances. Other financial institutions, likewise limited either by legal requirements or by their small scale, have also been enabled to increase their mortgage loans. The percentage of their loans held in mortgages continues small, however, so that this remains a fruitful market for the future.

The increased money has almost certainly kept down rates, particularly in the rapidly expanding areas of growth where local savings could not have sufficed. The government programs also, without doubt, aided the specific programs they were planned to assist.

## Stability and Instability in Construction

Whether the government's intervention has improved the stability of the real estate markets is less certain. First it may be noted that there is not unanimous agreement that stability of construction is a proper goal. Most observers certainly believe it to be. They feel that a housing and construction industry that turns out a stable amount of production instead of fluctuating widely up and down is more efficient and makes an important contribution to the stability of the entire economy. Houses are cheaper and better. The level of national income is higher.

The few who disagree point out that in many periods the economy's demands run ahead of its ability to produce. This leads to inflation and perhaps to later shortages of demand. These analysts welcome the fact that tight money cuts back on construction. They wonder how inflation could be stopped if no area had to curtail production. They claim to be pleased that construction is flexible and that its resources can be transferred elsewhere more easily than in most industries. They do not answer the question of what the cost of this instability may be in terms of construction costs and standards, nor do they consider whether the economy might not be better off if the construction sector needed to worry only about its own stability and not that of the economy as a whole.

Why should the expansion of the governmental programs have increased construction instability? It does appear that mortgage lending varies more than other types of credit. When the country passes from a period of monetary ease to one of restraint, or vice versa, movements in the mortgage market are further magnified. The change in the amounts and costs of funds has a decided impact on levels of construction and their prices. Builders and borrowers may not be as eager or find it possible to build or buy at the new levels of credit prices.

Much of this instability is directly due to the nature of the money markets. Their interrelationships and their institutional structures are such as to concentrate much of any pressure in the mortgage markets. The simple fact that government programs have expanded the market and brought in new institutions has probably increased this instability. This is particularly true because the new institutions can move in and out of the mortgage market relatively easily. Life insurance companies and the banks have large and well-operated security departments. If mortgages fail to be competitive, they cut their commitments.

Many people believe that instability has been increased by the maintenance of fixed maximum interest rates on FHA-VA loans, especially since changes in their rates tend to lag behind those of the market. Although it is now recognized that discounting is a natural market phenomenon, they still feel that the system of discounting leads to instability.

The reason behind the practice of discounting is easy to understand. When interest rates shift, lenders have their choice of many loans. For mortgage companies, builders, or owners to get money, they must offer mortgages competitive in price with other loans. They agree to accept a certain number of dollars per hundred (called points) below the face value of the mortgage. The amount they pay through taking less than the face value of the loan is the discount.

Discounting is a standard practice in the bond market, where most bonds are quoted on a yield basis rather than in terms of prices or face values. The price necessary to give a particular yield depends on the length of the maturity and the promised interest. Prices necessary to equal the quoted yields are found in a bond table. The same is now true of mortgages. In mortgages, however, the price depends on the rate of amortization and on particular assumptions as to whether the note will be paid off before it is completely amortized.

Who pays for the discount depends on the competitive situation of the housing and lending markets in any area. The idea behind ceilings on interest rates was that home purchasers tended to be in the market so rarely that they could be fleeced by sharp operators among the builders or lenders. The fact that rates offered rarely fell below the maximum and that when they did, premiums were frequently paid to the agents rather than to the borrower confirmed many people in their beliefs.

Some people make a strong argument in favor of shifting rates and against the use of discounts on the claim that discounts are probably paid for by the borrower anyway. That need not be the case, however. Whether or not borrowers pay for the discounts depends on the appraising practices of the FHA and VA. Where they include the discounts as builders' costs, they are passed on. Where they do not, the builder frequently absorbs them through lowering his profit margin. He is better off paying the discount and accepting lower profits than shutting down construction. The same may be true of an individual owner. He may pay the discount. thus in effect accepting a lower price, or fail to sell his house.

The system of discounting is supported as logical by those whc think it gives a more flexible pricing system. Pointing out that its flexibility accounts for its use in the bond market, they say that it may increase the willingness of lenders to enter the mortgage market, since it decreases their risk. When the discount rate is 3 points on an FHA loan, the lender puts out only $97 for each $100 of the mortgage. The insurance covers the $100 listed on the mortgage note. If the borrower defaults and the FHA makes good its insurance, the lender, depending on the value of debentures and his certificate of claim, may make an immediate profit. In any case, he will be better off than if he had paid 100 per cent for the mortgage.

On the other hand, some point out that this lowered lender risk may means higher costs elsewhere. They hold that in calculating the discount and risks, lenders are likely to err on the conservative side. As a result they will charge more than the true risk involved. There is also considerable agreement that when discounts get to 6 points or more, lenders may hesitate to make loans because they fear a blackening of their public image.

Lenders explain that it is difficult to convince the public that discounting is simply another form of adjusting rates. When a veteran has to pay 8 points, the image of the harsh, hardhearted lender appears. While no one objects to a bank buying a corporate or even a government bond at 92, the same may not always be true for an individual's mortgage.

This fear is particularly strong because initially there were popular and congressional attacks on the legal and moral aspects of discounting. The FHA and VA made various regulations attempting to control it. The memory of the past may still continue to make institutions hesitant when the amount of the discount becomes too great.

It appears quite certain, however, that those who believe that prompter movement of the maximum interest rates on FHA-VA loans would solve the problems of instability in the mortgage market are not correct. Because both the money markets and the construction markets are unstable by nature, discounting is only one minor aspect of the entire question.

## Housing Standards and Living Conditions

One of the chief arguments for the government programs has been that they have raised housing standards and improved living conditions. While the truth of this argument seems clear on the surface, the facts become slightly murky when they are probed.

The FHA-VA programs have certainly had very favorable influences on the terms, conditions, and techniques of mortgage lending. The consideration given by the FHA to evaluations of the property and borrowers has led to improved techniques throughout the mortgage industry. The spread of the fixed-monthly-payment plan, with money included for interest, amortization, taxes, and insurance, has also been salutary. It has made it far simpler for the borrower to budget his housing expenses.

Still more significant has been the spread of low-down-payment mortgages, or those with a high loan-to-value ratio; this has tremendously increased the number of potential purchasers of homes. The low down payment has been able to work because of longer amortization periods. A man with a given income can afford a higher loan because of the smaller required monthly payments for each dollar borrowed.

The spread of low down payments and longer amortizations has led to a rapid expansion of homeownership. The percentage of owner-occupied homes was 44 in 1940 and about 63 in 1963. It is probable that this expansion improved housing conditions because in most cases the single-family owner-occupied home is more efficient in terms of cost and living standards. On the other hand, some wastes probably occurred because the programs discriminated too much in favor of the new as opposed to existing houses and in favor of the suburb over the central city. Because of the nature of the programs, these discriminations are difficult to stop. However, as they have become more obvious, the FHA has attempted to improve its procedures so as to aid all sections of the market more equitably.

Another area of improvement has been in the special assistance programs. It has been possible to plan and build dwelling units for many groups and areas of the country that would have been completely excluded from the conventional market. Important national policies such as defense, military housing, and urban renewal have been carried out through a combination of private and public initiative; otherwise they would probably have been entirely public programs.

### Costs of Housing and Borrowing

The major area in which the results are most difficult to analyze is that of the government programs' impact on costs. The costs which must be considered are those for borrowed money, the government's insurance and guarantees, and the amount it takes to live in a house.

Because more money is available for mortgages, interest costs should be less. That will be true, however, only if the increase in money has been greater than the increase in the demand for it. The rising ability to pay for mortgages and live in better houses may have meant that more money was demanded than was made available by the new governmental techniques.

The spread between government-insured mortgages and new public bond issues has varied, but on the whole it has been large. If the government insurance or guarantee makes the mortgage fairly equivalent to a bond, how large should the spread between the two be? Since 1950, the spread has varied between 75 and 200 basis points. Most of the time it has been in the vicinity of 125 to 150 points, or $1\frac{1}{4}$ to $1\frac{1}{2}$ per cent interest. Perhaps $\frac{1}{2}$ to $\frac{3}{4}$ per cent difference is accounted for by servicing costs and other handling charges. Why have mortgage rates not fallen by the additional difference?

While the programs have not brought in enough competition to bring rates down to the bond rate, they have cut the costs of conventional mortgage rates with which they are in competition. The owner of a new, moderate-priced house has almost certainly paid less for borrowed money than he would have had to otherwise.

The cost to the government is uncertain also. Thus far all the various FHA insurance funds have been more or less self-supporting.

While in certain cases very conservative estimates show that individual funds have greater contingent liabilities than they have assets, the final results are not at all clear. Final costs will be determined by the future economy and housing market. With severe depression conditions and a sadly disorganized housing market, the government might have to meet some costs for the various programs from the Treasury.

It is not obvious, however, that an actual monetary subsidy from the government will be necessary. Risks assumed by the government may become so small that their costs become slight. Risks which would be impossible for a private firm to assume and which would require tremendous insurance premiums may be minimal under a government underwriting program. If that is the case, it is a tremendous advantage for the present system.

The evaluation of the programs' effects on the cost of buying a house is the most difficult of all. (For additional considerations, see Chapter 13.) Easier terms enable a buyer to carry a large loan. Does he actually get more house for his additional money, or does he get the same house at a higher price? If the house price rises by nearly the increased amount he can borrow, then he is simply living in the same house but building his equity more slowly and paying for it over a longer period.

What actually happens depends on demand and supply conditions in the housing market. When mortgage terms are reduced, a buyer can borrow more and bid more for a house. That was part of the theory of the GI Bill. Because he had better terms, a veteran could readjust more easily by bidding a house away from a nonveteran. However, if he were bidding only against other veterans, all might end up by paying more.

If the supply of houses were fixed, it is fairly clear that the only gainers from the government programs would be the former owners. However, there is not a fixed supply, since new houses are constantly built. If, as a result of the government programs, construction efficiency is improved and houses are built more cheaply than otherwise, all gain. On the other hand, if the instability of the programs and sudden large expansions of demand lead to inefficiency and higher costs, many of the programs' advantages may be dissipated.

Keen observers may be found on both sides of this argument. Their split makes clear the fact that cheaper and better terms need not lead to fewer sacrifices for housing or better living conditions but rather may lead primarily to higher costs. The new programs must be administered with their true goals of lowered final costs in mind. Policy makers should not be misled by more loans on better terms if the result is to be simply higher payments for equivalent housing.

## SUMMARY

The FHA and VA programs primarily guarantee or insure loans made by private lenders. Direct loans are a minor part of the government programs, although the purchase of special assistance loans by the FNMA from mortgage companies comes close to being a direct-lending operation.

The purpose of both programs is to increase the amount of mortgage loans that will be made on properties with risks that lenders would otherwise consider too great to accept. The risks may arise because of lower down payments, longer amortization periods, or because they are in the national market away from the home offices of the lenders. Lenders look to the insurance or guarantee as another, and actually most important, source from which the loans will be repaid if necessary.

Both programs have established minimum standards and basic procedures that all loans must meet before being accepted for insurance and guarantee. These standards attempt to minimize the risk that the government takes in carrying out its policies and to assure the government that the risks which are assumed are related to its goals.

The experience of the programs has led to a steady improvement in terms for down payments and amortization (but not for interest rates) of mortgage contracts. The more favorable terms have spread from the government-aided to the conventional market. At several times in the past, the government programs have nearly dominated the mass housing markets. However, as the terms available on conventional loans have improved and as small apartments have increased in importance, the share of new loans with insurance or guarantees has fallen.

The programs have had a major impact in broadening the national mortgage market. They have made it possible for the new lenders to enter the mortgage field and for others to spread out on a national basis. The fact that the added lenders are probably more sensitive to changes in the over-all money market may have increased instability in mortgage lending.

There is lack of agreement as to how effective the programs have been in reducing the costs of housing. It is recognized that previously ineligible families have been brought into the homeownership market. Significant changes have occurred in land development, construction, and lending practices. The evidence as to what has happened to costs and prices as a result of these changes is mixed.

## SELECTED REFERENCES

Break, G. F.: *The Economic Impact of Federal Loan Insurance,* National Planning Association, Washington, 1961.

Colean, M. L.: *The Impact of Government on Real Estate Finance in the United States,* National Bureau of Economic Research, Inc., New York, 1948.

Fisher, E. M., and R. M. Fisher: *Urban Real Estate,* Holt, Rinehart and Winston, Inc., New York, 1954.

Fisher, E. M., and C. Rapkin: *The Mutual Mortgage Insurance Fund,* Columbia University Press, New York, 1956.

Jones, Oliver, and Leo Grebler: *The Secondary Mortgage Market,* University of California, Los Angeles, 1961.

Saulnier, R. J., et. al.: *Federal Lending and Loan Insurance,* Princeton University Press, Princeton, N.J., 1958.

U.S. Housing and Home Finance Agency: *Annual Report.*

# The Lending Decision_____6

The supply of funds to the mortgage market depends upon the decision to lend of thousands of individual lenders and their willingness to make funds available to borrowers at particular interest rates and terms. The wisdom with which these decisions are made is extremely important for borrowers, and the economy as a whole. This chapter and the five which follow examine in detail the criteria which should govern lending decisions, as well as examples of good lending procedures. The Appendix to this chapter explains in detail the mathematics of financing real estate. It shows both by table and formulas how to calculate yields, necessary payments, and remaining balances.

At all times, the mortgage lender must be ready to make two not completely unrelated decisions: (1) Should it increase or decrease its loans on mortgages in proportion to its cash holdings or other investments? (2) If it decides to lend on mortgages, which loans should it grant and which should it reject?

Safety and liquidity are usually ranked first among the factors influencing a firm's willingness to lend. As fiduciary institutions entrusted with funds by thousands of individuals, lenders are required by both law and tradition to give utmost priority among all operating criteria to the safe return of these funds. Therefore, a decision to buy more mortgages or to buy any individual mortgage must

125

be weighed in the light of the lender's ability to repay deposited funds.

The second factor to be considered is the relative profitability of a given mortgage in comparison with other potential investments. Mortgages bear a certain interest rate and may yield additional sums through fees or discounts allowed from their face value. On the other hand, they engender operating costs, carry risks of loss, and may create a tax liability. When these factors are weighed together, a net yield can be calculated. Does this potential yield make it worthwhile to make the loan on real property or would a bond or equity investment be preferable? Perhaps the decision may be to hold cash or liquid assets, on the assumption that a more profitable mortgage may be offered in the future.

These various considerations may result in a go-slow decision for mortgages as a whole; or they may result simply in an increase in individual selectivity, which will have the same effect. More stringent conditions will be likely if the firm is close to its legal or traditional limit for mortgage lending.

## RISKS

A risk is the degree of probability of loss of expected income or capital from a mortgage loan. If the losses in income and capital due to accepting poor risks are sufficiently large or concentrated, the total safety of the institution may be endangered. While the penalties of assuming too many poor risks are all too obvious, avoiding them altogether is impossible. At best, firms can attempt to make the most judicious selection among risks so as to minimize the threat of loss of safety, while maximizing the net yield which will remain after paying for the probable losses.

The three basic types of events in the mortgage market which lead to losses are: (1) random movements causing losses on a small percentage of loans which meet all standard normal criteria, (2) the failure to use proper care in the underwriting or selection of loans, so that substandard mortgages enter the portfolio, and (3) changing economic conditions which create losses among all the loans affected by them.

## Mortgages and Risks

Mortgages appear to carry more risks, or possibilities of loss, than many other types of investment. The history of mortgages shows that because they are long-term loans made under very diverse conditions, a somewhat higher percentage are likely to run into difficulties than is true of bonds or even of commercial or consumer loans.

This factor of risk, once recognized, should not be unduly feared. Because of it, the net return on mortgages, after adequate reserves have been established and all losses and costs have been paid, appears to be higher than that on most other parts of the investment portfolio.

This paradoxical fact stems from the basic conservatism and ignorance of many financial officers who, recognizing the inherent risks in mortgages, distrust them and develop an irrational bias against such loans. The mortgage market tends to overcompensate for its risks. Lenders who see the dangers and take proper precautions find that the high-risk premiums paid on mortgages much more than cover the actual losses involved.

The skilled mortgage officer does not attempt to avoid all risks but rather calculates their true costs. He then measures the costs against the risk premium which the mortgage carries so as to arrive at an estimate of the true yield. He establishes proper reserves and other institutional protections. Such analysis calls on the highest skill of the mortgage man. When this task is properly performed, he can demonstrate to other officers in his institution how much should be lent on mortgages and how reaching such limits will increase profits and decrease risks.

## Risks of Random Individual Losses

Every financial transaction carries some risk of loss. A great deal of such risk is a purely random element in the borrowing of money for the purpose of purchasing real property. Insofar as this hazard is purely random, it could be insured against on an actuarial basis if sufficient knowledge were available. In fact, both the FHA and mortgage guarantee companies do attempt to insure such risks. If they could properly separate these random risks from others, it would be no more difficult—and might even be easier—to establish the necessary actuarial reserves against mortgage losses than it is to establish them against losses from fire, auto accidents, or health costs.

Conceptually, it is not difficult to distinguish the types of losses from each other. Consider any portfolio of mortgages with properly made loans. The borrowers have assumed contracts which they can meet. A reasonable expectation exists that they will desire to fulfill their loan commitments. The lending process was error-free, and the economy continues at an even keel. Even with all these conditions met, some delinquencies, foreclosures, and losses will occur. These losses will result simply from the random occurrence of normal events which, while not predictable for any single loan, can be predicted for an entire class.

What are some of these events to which every group of loans will be exposed but against which it cannot be protected by better lending practices?

Most important are various family difficulties or catastrophes. Every time a divorce, death, serious illness, or separation occurs, payments on the mortgage are likely to be endangered. Losses will result from delayed payments; in especially serious cases, the family may have to move out of its home. Whether a forced sale causes a loss depends on how soon the difficulty occurs after the mortgage has been granted and on the state of the market.

Similarly, in any period a responsible worker or businessman may suddenly experience a sharp drop in income or even a loss of his job. Such an occurrence may sharply curtail his ability to meet loan payments, with a consequent loss to the lender.

Finally, the value of individual properties may fluctuate randomly as a result of shifts in neighborhoods, changes in tastes, or even physical disasters not fully protected against. Any of these may lead to a cessation in payments and foreclosures with losses.

In all these cases, losses could have been avoided only by halting all normal lending. While they cannot be forecast, with a sufficiently large and diversified mortgage portfolio such losses can be estimated and covered by reserves established for that purpose. Experience shows that these reserves need not be large.

## Losses from Improper Risk Analysis

The second cause of losses is improper risk analysis. The concept of random losses applies only when the original loan has been properly made. Every loan, in addition to a random factor, contains certain potentialities of misfortune which vary with the circumstances of the borrower, the property offered as security, and the terms of the loan. The purpose of mortgage risk analysis is to ensure that loans are properly classified so that the amount of risk being engendered by these variables will be recognized. Furthermore, the potential losses related to each class of loans must also be estimated.

The ability of particular lenders to accept high-risk loans will depend on the size of their portfolio and their liquidity requirements. The vital consideration is that the job of risk analysis be done properly. Careless or ill-advised lending will increase potential losses.

## Losses from Changed Economic Conditions

The final—and historically the most important—type of risk is that related to major economic movements. Such movements, affecting the entire national income, alter the ability to pay for buildings, the prices that particular types of property realize in the market, the costs or charges applicable to real estate, and the interest rate.

The most obvious danger is that another major economic depression, like that of 1929 to 1932, will occur. That depression caused enormous losses in most mortgage portfolios. It wiped out large numbers of lending institutions. As the level of income fell, individuals found it harder and harder to meet their mortgage payments. Because the market for foreclosed property was so poor and because houses deteriorated more rapidly in lenders' hands than in those of the erstwhile owners, lenders frequently found that it did not pay to foreclose.

A related possibility is that the real estate market as a whole or particular parts of it may go through a major depression separate and distinct from one in the over-all economy. Specific depressions and losses are particularly likely to occur in individual submarkets, such as those for hotels, apartment houses, and office buildings or in individual cities or suburbs. Submarkets can meet with disasters because of overbuilding or collapses of local demand.

The probability of a major economic downturn or of submarkets going bad cannot be exactly calculated. In the past, lenders and others have made major errors of both pessimism and optimism. To be on the safe side, these potential risks of shifting economic conditions should be estimated as some function of the worst experience of the past. Significant miscalculations may result from a policy of attempting to measure these risks entirely on the basis of recent experience. It should also be clear that large national lenders have important advantages in absorbing losses in submarkets. To them such losses appear comparable to random individual risks. If the per cent of loans of a lender in any submarket is small, it will not hurt badly if the submarket deteriorates. On the other hand, an institution that, because of laws or poor management, has, concentrated loans in a single area assumes much heavier risks.

Losses from movements in the interest rate, in taxes, or in expenses of foreclosures can also occur with economic change. While costly in terms of net yields, these losses are less likely to lead to disaster.

## Types of Risks

Closely related to the basic types of events which cause risks are three separate types of risk. Some occurrences are more likely to lead to one type of risk than to another. In planning its lending strategy, a firm must consider each of these types. Action to protect against one may at times increase the likelihood of one of the others.

1. The first type of risk is the risk that losses will be suffered on any individual loan. Many observers feel that this is the most prevalent type of risk. We have noted that some losses occur because individual borrowers will not or cannot meet their commitments on time. In fact, they may fall so far behind that foreclosure becomes necessary.

When the individual or firm fails to pay, the property is the next source of security. If it has been properly evaluated, it may reduce the loss to zero. On the other hand, if the physical aspects were not properly evaluated, if income fell, or if the neighborhood or community declined, it may not suffice to cover the outstanding loan.

2. Threats to the safety or solvency of the entire institution are a second type of risk called the portfolio risk. This risk is frequently confused with that just described. For the institution to be threatened, however, there must be more than simply random losses. No one worries too much about occasional losses in individual cases; they are the normal risks of any business. What causes tremendous concern is the threat to the safety of the institution which would result if whole classes of loans were subject to a large simultaneous run of losses or foreclosures. The portfolio risk is based on the possibility that groups of loans will go bad together, in contrast to the first type of risk in which individual failures to pay occur more or less randomly and can be absorbed by reserves.

Various forces cause portfolio risks over and above the simple summation of the risks of losses on individual loans. The possibility is always present that a national economic catastrophe such as that of the 1930s will destroy both the ability of large numbers of borrowers to pay and the desire of others to purchase. Another threat is the danger to a portfolio of local loans that a major local industry may close down. Finally, individual institutions may overload themselves with loans based on a single builder, a new subdivision, or a special type of tract house. In case of a sudden loss of value, the safety of the entire institution may be jeopardized.

Losses from portfolio risks may be increased by the fact that if a class of loans goes bad and many foreclosures occur simultaneously, the resulting losses must be liquidated or handled outside of normal channels. The history of the thirties shows that, barring major errors, with adequate time the security gained from the property is sufficient to repay most of the outstanding debt. This ability to sell the property if the borrower fails to meet his contract is one of the popular features of mortgage lending. On the other hand, if many loans go bad at the same time, sales of property do not offer the lender the same opportunity to collect. When its portfolio is cluttered with slow payments, foreclosures, and other problems, it may have to sacrifice properties rather than give the market a chance to absorb them at nondistress prices. As a result, additional losses are suffered in liquidation that would not have occurred if the same loans could have been handled through routine procedures.

Such handling of losses threatens the institution's solvency. If capital reserves are wiped out, distress liquidation may require the whole organization to be closed. When major portions of the portfolio go bad, risks to the organization's existence rise astronomically.

Portfolio risks and their threat to safety give mortgages a poor name. Lenders remember a history of large portfolios going bad but fail to recognize that these risks can be calculated and protected against. Instead they go to either of two extremes. Some lenders, noting that present yields more than compensate for the individual risks and neglecting portfolio risks, overestimate the true net yield of mortgages; others, remembering past dangers to safety from a bunching of bad loans, fail to take advantage of the profitability of diversified individual mortgages. What is needed is a policy between the extremes which takes account of each threat and protects adequately but not excessively against it.

3. A third type of risk in mortgages is their potential lack of liquidity. Mortgages are long-term loans. The lender normally cannot require repayment at his own convenience. The liquidity risk is the possibility that extra costs may be engendered if part of the mortgage portfolio must be sold to obtain a larger than normal supply of funds.

Most lending institutions can experience a sudden demand for funds. If this occurs, the entire portfolio must be examined to see where cash can be raised at the most reasonable rates. If the mortgage portfolio cannot free sufficient funds to meet the institution's needs except at an excessive cost, a further risk is added. In determining its investment policy, the institution must either protect against this risk directly or recognize that the face amount of mortgage yields must be reduced by the potential losses which would result from the need to liquidate part of the mortgage portfolio in order to obtain cash.

## Type of Costs

We have defined a risk as the probability that the stated rate of return on a loan or a portfolio will not be received. Risk is measured by the amount of reserve required as a charge against gross income to offset probable losses from failures by borrowers to pay loans as agreed.

With risk defined as equal to a loss reserve against a whole class or portfolio of loans, it becomes clear that risks must be measured on some type of statistical or actuarial basis. Not all loans will turn out identically. Most mortgages will earn their contract interest rate, but for others the gross yield will be reduced in large or small amounts. The risk reserve applies to an entire class of loans in such a manner as just to offset expected losses.

We do not have mortality or loss tables for mortgages. Because losses are due to a variety of causes, most of which cannot be measured exactly, risk reserves must be based on statistics and judgment. The causes for loss may be personal, institutional, or economic.

The costs for which possible losses must be estimated include (1) the various costs of collecting delinquent payments up to and including foreclosures, (2) costs of liquidating properties that have to be taken over in place of original loans, (3) the cost of selling mortgages if cash is required, and (4) the losses in interest or principal due to increases in market interest rates above the terms contained in the mortgage.

The first costs arise from the additional administration required to collect on loans which cannot be handled normally. Servicing costs rise if a family runs into difficulties and fails to meet regular payments. Loans may have to be renegotiated with forgiveness of interest, extension of the payment period, or similar changes in the contract.

More serious costs arise if the property must be taken over when payments cease. Losses from this source will equal the difference between the amount of net return received on liquidation of the property and the outstanding loan. This difference will depend on how much was loaned originally and how much has been paid off; on changes in the value of the property due to movements either in the market or in prices in general; and on such factors as the costs of foreclosure, maintenance and administration, and selling the property.

Other losses are possible if the lender must sell an outstanding mortgage in the secondary market. It is frequently not recognized that the lender should be concerned with the timing of loan repayments and the problems which may arise in reinvesting these funds.

Consider, for example, an alternative decision to lend on a bond or mortgage. A risk charge against the higher face yield on the mortgage should be based on the possibilities that it will be less easy to sell in case of need and that its value will alter as the going interest rates fluctuate, with the amount depending on its terms.

The market for mortgages is far more local and segmented than that for most bonds. Therefore, a forced liquidation of mortgages will cost more. Furthermore, liquidation costs will vary among mortgages.

Bond-market experience and fluctuating discounts on FHA-VA loans prove that the value or selling price of a mortgage will depend upon how the face interest rate on the loan compares with the existing market rate for loans of similar length. If a 5 per cent mortgage is sold when the going rate has risen to 6 per cent, it will be possible to sell it only at a decided discount from its face value. The amount of the discount will be determined by the length it has to run and the expected repayments in each future period.

## LESSONS FROM PAST LENDING EXPERIENCE

It is necessary to make a proper estimate of losses which current loans will suffer in order to measure the risks to the institution from its mortgage lending. Such a measure is also necessary to determine what charges should logically be made against current income in order to estimate properly the anticipated net yields, or returns. A careful analysis of the forces bringing about losses and an attempt to forecast them for the future are essential. History must be the main basis for such predictions.

The most valuable facts for forecasting are found in the individual lender's own portfolio data, which can tell the specific forces that have caused past losses. These data can underline present weaknesses that foretell future danger. An institution's analysis of its own history can show recent portfolio trends and the areas of particular pressure. Such an examination can also measure past underwriting errors so that they may be protected against in the future.

To its own individual data, however, the firm must add the experience of the whole mortgage market. Its own records are not a sufficient basis for a prediction because they may cover only a special market, a certain period in time, or too limited a range of loans with respect to types of property and terms as well. A firm's experience may have included no major depression; yet it must consider this and other possibilities in the light of total mortgage lending history.

Analyzing past losses in mortgages can only be done in a fragmentary manner and with considerable hazard. Data are scarce and in far from ideal forms. Still, a good many studies of lending and foreclosure experience have recently been completed which add immeasurably to our knowledge.[1] Each study has some unique features that make it difficult to generalize to other cases. Recent data are primarily concentrated on FHA and VA experience; the earlier studies dealt primarily with the experience of the Great Depression. Some facts on conventional loans are at present becoming available. One way to use these special studies is to consider them as extreme cases, recognizing that current experience with conventional loans should approach but not exceed the indicated losses.

FHA and VA data may be taken as illustrative of trends of the conventional market. While the amount of movement of government-insured loans with their low down payments may exceed that of conventionals, all do tend to move in the same directions. Danger signals in one sector may well be applied to all.

### Numbers of Losses

Periodically the FHA and the VA publish the number of loans that they have insured or guaranteed which lenders report as in default. Defaults are defined as loans with three or more missed monthly

[1] Interested readers should consult the following publications: U.S. Housing and Home Finance Agency, *Mortgage Foreclosures in Six Metropolitan Areas,* Washington, 1964. U.S. Federal Housing Administration, *FHA Experience with Mortgage Foreclosures and Property Acquisitions,* Government Printing Office, Washington, 1963. U.S. Veterans Administration, *Report of Loan Service and Claims Study,* Washington, 1962. J. E. Morton, *Urban Mortgage Lending,* Princeton University Press, Princeton, N.J., 1956. John Lintner, *Mutual Savings Banks,* Harvard Business School, Boston, 1948. E. M. Fisher and C. Rapkin, *The Mutual Mortgage Insurance Fund,* Columbia University Press, New York, 1954.

FIGURE 6-1   (A) Delinquencies of Conventional Mortgages Serviced by Mortgage Bankers   (B) FHA and VA Mortgage Default Rates (As per cent of outstanding mortgages)

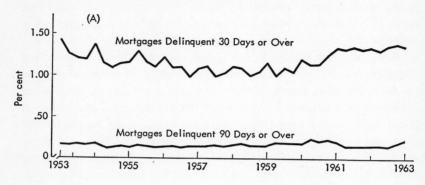

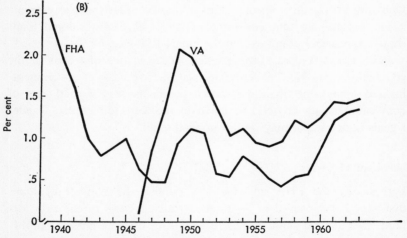

SOURCES: Mortgage Bankers Association Delinquency Survey; Housing and Home Finance Agency, *Annual Report* and *Housing Statistics*.

payments. Figure 6-1 shows that the per cent of defaults has fluctuated primarily with changes in income and unemployment. The number also increased rapidly after 1957.

The number of loans in default rose more sharply than the percentages because the total loans under each program continued to expand. By 1963, the percentage of FHA loans in default was about 1.25 per cent, while for VA loans the ratio was 1.50 per cent. No equivalent data exist for all conventional loans. However, the Mortgage Bankers Association, in its reports of loans delinquent at the end of each quarter, shows conventional and FHA delinquencies as about equal until 1960. For the next three years, the conventional rate was only about half that of the insured loans.

These figures are not an indication of the number of loans causing trouble at any time. There are other loans which may require extra servicing because they are delinquent, but for too short a time to be included in the report. Many delinquencies are cured during the course of the quarter, while the data show only units in default at the end. The number of loans in default at sometime during the year in the early 1960s ran from 3 to 5 per cent. No similar data exist for the prewar period, but judging from the number of actual foreclosures, the delinquency rate must have been much higher.

Figure 6-2 shows the major movements in total foreclosures following the Great Depression when in 1933 foreclosures rose to 250,000. The demoralization of the market was so complete that many believe that without moratorium laws and the active intervention of the Home Owners Loan Corporation, which took mortgages in danger of foreclosure off the hands of lending institutions, the actual number of foreclosures might have been three or four times as great in 1934 and 1935.

The number of foreclosures decreased sharply in the postwar boom market. It then rose steadily and at a fairly rapid rate following 1957. By the end of 1964 foreclosures had passed 100,000 to move back once again above the 1939 level. But the number of outstanding mortgages should be related to the actual number of foreclosures. While no exact data are available, it is probable that between 3 and 4 per cent of mortgages were foreclosed in the year 1933, close to 1 per cent in 1939, and less than ½ per cent in 1963.

The figure also shows the experience of FHA foreclosures and the number of VA claims paid. Again a sharp increase is noted. For the FHA, 2,500 foreclosures, or less than 0.20 per cent of the outstanding mortgages, occurred in 1950. The level remained this low through 1954. Subsequently, foreclosures rose steadily, until by 1963 they were about 1.0 per cent of those outstanding. Similarly, the number of VA claims paid was very low in the middle 1950s and then rose steadily to a higher per cent of outstandings in 1963. The FHLBB shows that in 1963, savings and loan associations

FIGURE 6-2 (*A*) *Total Nonfarm Foreclosures* (*B*) *FHA Foreclosure and VA Claims Payment Rates* (As per cent of outstanding mortgages)

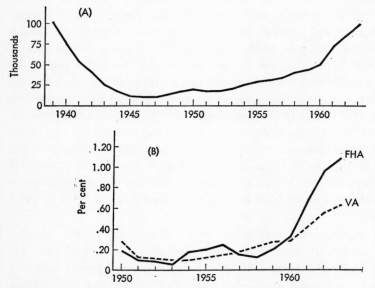

SOURCE: Housing and Home Finance Agency, *Housing Statistics.*

foreclosed on 0.42 per cent of the conventional mortgages in their portfolios.

These recent foreclosures rates may be compared with the experience of the Great Depression. Estimates based on spotty data indicate that between 15 and 20 per cent of all loans made during the years 1927 to 1930 were foreclosed. The percentage varied by type of lender and property, but it was high for all.

## Amounts of Losses on Foreclosures

The rate of foreclosures is only one measure of the risks involved in mortgage lending. Even more significant is the total amount lost on each foreclosure. Three major factors influence the amount forfeited on a particular property.

1. After foreclosure, depending on the state's foreclosure and redemption laws, title may pass to an outside buyer or to the lender. If the lender holds the title, it can then sell the property, taking as much time as it believes advantageous given its estimate of future markets. For example, the FHA retains ownership of foreclosed properties on an average of two to three years, but individual properties may be retained as long as 10 years.

The capital loss is the difference between the amount of the loan balance at the time of foreclosure and the actual selling price when the property is disposed of. The size of the outstanding loan balance will depend on the loan-to-value ratio when the loan was made, on the amount of amortization between the loan period and date of foreclosure, and on accrued but unpaid interest and other expenses. The market will determine the selling price of the foreclosed structure. The price received will differ from the value estimated when the loan was made depending on the amount of true depreciation, changes in house prices in general, fluctuations in the local market, and any errors in the initial appraisal.

Some indication of possible capital losses may be gained from past FHA experience for single-family homes. For 11,125 properties sold between 1936 and 1960, capital losses averaged only about $550 per property, or about 7 per cent of the amount of the average outstanding loan at the time of foreclosure. On the other hand, for the houses sold in the first half of 1961 the average loss was $1,225, or 12.5 per cent of the loan. For the year ending June 30, 1962, it was $1,575 or 15.8 per cent of the value of the loan.

Clearly, market movements have been the most important determinants of capital losses. With generally rising prices, market values rose sufficiently so that losses were held to a minimum. On the other hand, when house prices stabilized, considerable losses occurred on the marginal units which went into foreclosure.

2. Another type of cost from foreclosure is that of holding the property between the date of acquisition and the date of sale. Such costs include taxes and insurance, additions and improvements, maintenance and operations, and most importantly, the income lost on the money tied up in the property because no interest is being received on the foreclosed loan. Rents or other income received from the property will offset some of the expenses.

The interest rate the lender assumes for the money tied up in the foreclosed property will be an important share of these costs. The FHA does not show these costs; but allowing for conceptual differences, the FHA experience seems to indicate that net holding costs average about 10 per cent a year. This means that as a result of these costs, the lender's investment in a house held two years will be about 120 per cent of the loan value at the time of foreclosure.

3. The final charges are the expenses of foreclosure and of selling the property. Such costs vary tremendously from state to state, and must be estimated by each lender from his own local knowledge. In this category, the FHA experienced expenses of between 5 and 6 per cent of loan value. Its data do not, however, include all foreclosures expenses.

All three types of costs must be totaled to obtain the average loss to the firm on each foreclosure. On the basis of FHA experience, for a favorable period such as 1936 to 1960, the total losses including forgone interest would run between 25 and 30 per cent of the amount of loans foreclosed. Based on experience such as that of 1961 and 1962, losses would be expected to total between 30 and 40 per cent of the loan value at the time of foreclosure. The FHA accounts in this period show a loss of 18 per cent. Actual FHA interest rates were lower than those an individual firm would have to allow on its own investments.

The FHA has drawn up tables of estimated possible losses under extremely unfavorable conditions, assuming the very negative expectation, that a major depression will prevail for the next five years. Expected losses vary with the original loan-to-value ratio and the time expected to elapse between the original loan and foreclosure. In the case of mortgages made at 85 per cent of value, the tables indicate that for foreclosures made during the loan's first eight years, the average loss may be assumed to be about 26 per cent of the outstanding balance. After eight years, the expected loss falls rapidly to under 5 per cent.

Other lenders calculate similar expected losses under related assumptions. The amounts depend upon (1) their actual loan-to-value ratio, (2) the expectations of a depression in their own house markets, (3) the depression's length, and (4) the opportunity-cost interest rate they apply to investments in foreclosed property. For most lenders, the expected losses through foreclosure would be some what above those expected by the FHA and might equal 30 to 40 per cent of the loan balance at the time the borrower stopped making payments.

Some check of this assumption may be made against the Depression experience. Recent data on average losses on conventional loans, however, are not suitable for such estimates. From the end of the war until 1960, actual losses were exceedingly small. With rising prices in the housing market, most properties that had to be taken over were sold at close to their loan values. While losses increased after 1960, no major studies of their size are available.

Estimates do exist in the National Bureau studies of loss rates for the entire period from 1920 to 1947 and for loans originated during the years 1920 to 1929. Such losses vary considerably by type of lender and obviously to an even greater degree among individual institutions. They do not include lost interest. These studies show losses varying from 9 to 21 per cent of the amount of loans foreclosed. Because the studies include the period through World War II, the average loss shown is slightly lower than in the Depression years alone.

## ESTIMATING FUTURE LOSSES FROM FORECLOSURES

This past over-all experience plus a firm's own recent history can be used in estimating the losses which are likely to be sustained from any batch of new loans. Mortgage lenders do not as commonly set up specific reserves against losses as do other types of lenders.

Tax and regulatory authorities allow or require general reserves, but they are usually not based on the specific risks involved in a given set of loans.

The reason that regulations do not require more specific reserves, like those against insurance risks or those of the FHA, would seem to be the lack of actuarial experience for mortgage losses. With enough experience, estimates could be made of the risks of random losses. Expected losses due to economic changes, however, would still require a forecast of the economy over the life of the loan. Losses from poor lending practices are also hard to estimate, since they could be avoided by improving procedures and supervision and would not require the establishment of reserves.

Difficult as it is, estimates of future losses must be made or the firm can never decide whether a prospective loan will be profitable. Clearly it makes no sense simply to assume that the promised interest rate will be the true yield. Losses are too common. This is especially true when deciding on potential loans of different types and of unlike payments, since losses do vary from one type of loan to the next. Unless differences in expected losses are estimated, the firm that assumes all loans to have equal risks is likely to suffer from adverse selection and end up with the least profitable portfolio.

The possible losses on each type of property or loan vary widely around the average. A useful technique, however, is to determine the average and then estimate the variations from it of particular loans. As noted, the most accurate assumptions will flow from the firm's own experience, but they will always have to be tempered by knowledge of previous figures for the entire real estate market.

The calculations require a combination of anticipated foreclosure rates with the expected losses on each foreclosure. Estimates of additional servicing costs from delinquencies which are cured before foreclosure should be handled separately. Various assumptions can be made as to probable future economic conditions. The type of losses to be expected under each set of conditions can be calculated and compared. The firm can then decide which level of losses it considers most likely for the period during which the loan under consideration will be outstanding.

For these calculations, it is convenient to pick a fixed period for the expected average life of the new loans. Many firms use eight years, which is close to present averages. To indicate possible variations in economic experience and their effect on returns, they may use results of the 1950s, when both prices and incomes were rising; the experience of 1960 to 1963, when housing prices were more stable but incomes rose steadily; and the conventional-loan outcomes for the Depression.

TABLE 6-1  *Estimated Loss Ratios and Required Reserves for 90 Per Cent Loans on One-family Houses* (Percentages)

| State of economy | (1) Annual fore-closure rate | (2) Proba-bility of fore-closure over lifetime of 8 years | (3) Average loss on each fore-closed loan | (4) Proba-bility of loss on each new loan | (5) Re-quired annual appro-pria-tion to loss reserve |
|---|---|---|---|---|---|
| Rising prices and incomes (1950s)....... | 0.2 | 1.6 | 20 | 0.32 | 0.04 |
| Stable prices, rising incomes (1960-1963)... | 1.0 | 8.0 | 25 | 2.0 | 0.25 |
| Depression............ | 3.0 | 24.0 | 35 | 8.4 | 1.05 |

Table 6-1 shows the caluculations for required risk reserves under the various assumptions. A primary requirement is for a prediction of average foreclosures which can be expected against loans on single-family homes now in the process of being made. An experience similar to that of the FHA in the 1950s would indicate foreclosures of about 0.2 per cent per year; the years 1960 to 1963 show a probable level of 1.0 per cent per year, finally, assumptions based on the Depression experience yield a potential rate of 3.0 per cent per year.

When each of these annual rates is multiplied by 8, the number of years of average expected life, it appears that only 1.6 per cent of loans being made currently would be foreclosed under the favorable conditions. More recent trends would indicate that on the average 8.0 per cent of any new group of loans in this category could be expected to experience foreclosure in their lifetime, while under assumptions of a severe depression starting in the next year or two, the rate of foreclosures expected against new loans might reach 24.0 per cent.

For each of these three conditions, there are separate expected losses on the foreclosed properties. Again many factors cause variations around the anticipated mean. However, the previous and following analyses lead to an assumption of a 20 per cent loss rate for each foreclosure under favorable circumstances, 25 per cent under more recent experience, and 35 per cent in case of a major depression.

Multiplying these expected losses per foreclosed property by the rate of foreclosure (column 2 times column 3 equals column 4) indicates that 0.32 per cent of the amount to be loaned would be lost through foreclosure under most favorable conditions, 2.0 per cent would be lost under recent experience, and 8.40 per cent would have to be charged off in case of a major depression. These percentages are the charges required against anticipated interest income from new loans to exactly compensate the firm for capital losses which are anticipated from future foreclosures on average, well-made one family-house loans.

The assumption that each loan will be outstanding for eight years means (neglecting the complications of discounting) that under the favorable conditions only 0.04 per cent would be required annually as a reserve or charge against gross interest on new loans.

Necessary annual charge

$$= \frac{\text{expected foreclosure loss from group of loans}}{\text{number of years of interest to be received}} = \frac{0.32}{8} = 0.04$$

Future foreclosure losses would be charged against this reserve. It would be reduced to zero when the loans had all been paid off. This nearly negligible amount approximates the experience of many lenders in the 1950s.

THE LENDING DECISION 145

On the other hand, more recent experience indicates an expected loss charge of $2.0/8 = 0.25$ per cent annually against new loans. (The FHA annually puts aside about this 0.25 per cent in its insurance funds; the other half of its fees goes for administrative expenses.) Finally, the amount of reserves needed from current interest to handle losses from a severe depression would approximate 1.05 per cent per year.

**Actual Past Losses**

These assumptions as to possible risks can be compared with Lintner's and the National Bureau's estimates of actual losses (excluding lost interest) on loans made in the 1920s. Lintner shows that if Massachusetts savings banks had made the charges necessary to anticipate their losses against single-family loans made during the period from 1918 through 1931, they would have had to appropriate 0.42 per cent per year of loans outstanding to a specific loss reserve. For all types of mortgage loans made during this period, the rate would have been about 0.85 per cent per year.[2] Similarly, Morton shows that the necessary charges for future losses experienced on home loans made in the period from 1925 to 1929 by life insurance companies were 0.86 per cent per year and that for commercial banks the charges were 0.67 per cent.[3] Losses on loans made during the Depression were somewhat higher. The loss rate on income property mortgages issued at the peak of the boom was nearly twice as high as the loss rate on homes.

Analyzing data similar to these, Grebler and Brigham judge that under early conditions of the 1960s appropriations to loss reserves of 0.25 to 0.40 per cent per year would be proper for California savings and loans associations.[4] They assume average market conditions without sharply rising or falling prices. Such an estimate of possible losses from home loans appears reasonable as a starting point when a firm attempts to project its probable mortgage yields

[2] Lintner, *Mutual Savings Bank*, p. 339.
[3] Morton, *Urban Mortgage Lending*, pp. 114–115.
[4] L. Grebler and E. F. Brigham, *Savings and Mortgage Markets in California*, California Savings and Loan League, 1963, p. 209.

compared to those from other investments. These average expected losses against home loans form a base which must be adjusted according to type of property, conditions of the loan, and state of the economy.

## SUMMARY

Critical in each lending decision is the proper evaluation of risks. Lenders daily are offered potential investments with promised interest payments of 3 to 30 per cent. A logical choice among these offers can be made only after the lender determines how much of the promised yield is likely to disappear through additional costs. He must also determine what effect accepting certain risks may have on the over-all safety of his institution.

Some risks arise from factors influencing the individual loan directly. They may be increased or decreased depending upon the care and wisdom which a lender exercises in processing and controlling the risk factors in each loan. Some of the individual risks, however, cannot be avoided. They can only be estimated and prepared for by a proper use of reserves.

Expected losses for a normal batch of loans will depend on what happens to the economy both nationally and locally. If prosperity and rising prices prevail during the first five years after loans are made, their average losses will be negligible. On the other hand, if a severe depression hits, probably 8 per cent or more of the amount lent will be lost.

## SELECTED REFERENCES

Fisher, E. M., and C. Rapkin: *The Mutual Mortgage Insurance Fund,* Columbia University Press, New York, 1954.

Grebler, L., and E. F. Brigham: *Savings and Mortgage Markets in California,* California Savings and Loan League, 1963.

Lintner, J.: *Mutual Savings Banks,* Harvard Business School, Boston, 1948.

Martin, P.: *Real Estate Principles and Practices,* The Macmillan Company, New York, 1959.

Morton, J. E.: *Urban Mortgage Lending,* Princeton University Press, Princeton, N.J., 1956.

U.S. Federal Housing Administration: *FHA Experience with Mortgage Foreclosures and Property Acquisitions,* Government Printing Office, Washington, 1963.

U.S. Housing and Home Finance Agency: *Mortgage Foreclosures in Six Metropolitan Areas,* Washington, 1964.

U.S. Veterans Administration: *Reports of Loan Service and Claims Study,* Washington, 1962.

## APPENDIX TO CHAPTER 6

### The Mathematics of Financing Real Estate

The problems of calculating yields and costs for borrowers and lenders on real estate are closely connected. They primarily are concerned with the accurate estimation of expected income streams. Both are complicated by the fact that since today's investments or loans can earn compound-interest payments, money to be received next year is not worth as much as money received today.

The general methods used in the mathematics of real estate finance calculate the expected payments or income that will be received in the future as a result of a loan or investment. This stream must then be divided into repayments of the initial principal and earnings on the outstanding principal. In loans, the repayments are called amortization and the earnings are called interest or net yield on the loan balance. In investments, the measurement of the loss in principal is called depreciation and the earnings are called yield or return on equity. In the actual calculations of the value of an investment, an estimate is made of the present worth of the stream of income, which includes repayments for any losses in value due to depreciation. Depreciation is not considered as an expense to be subtracted separately from the income stream. To do so would be to count it twice. It would not lead to the real value.

### The Present Value of Future Receipts

We are all familiar with the idea that if a sum of money can be invested so as to yield a return, it will grow to a larger sum in the future. Thus, if we have $1 today and a borrower will pay us back the $1 plus 6 per cent interest at the end of a year, we will have $1.06 at that time. Similarly, if the $1.06 can be reinvested at the same rate, it will be worth $1.1236 at the end of the second year ($1.06 × 1.06 = $1.1236).

This concept is expressed by the familiar compound-interest formula of

$$A = P(1 + i)^n$$

where $A$ = the amount to which $P$ will grow at compound interest
$P$ = the principal invested
$i$ = the interest rate, or yield for one interest-earning period
$n$ = the number of interest-earning periods

Thus our $1, invested to earn 6 per cent annually, will be worth $1.7908 at the end of 10 years [$1.7908 = 1(1 + 0.06)^{10}$]. The amount to which $1 will grow or the amount to be multiplied by the principal can be looked up in any compound-interest table, usually under the title "the amount of 1 at compound interest." (See Tables 6-2 and 6-3.)

Because of this fact that money now in hand can earn interest, we will not pay as much for $1 to be received next year as $1 today. Thus, if we were offered $1 next year and we knew we could invest our current $1 at 6 per cent interest, we would today pay only $0.9434 for next year's payment. Similarly, for $1 payable in two years we would pay only $0.89, and for $1 payable in 10 years, we would pay only $0.5584. A United States savings bond which will pay $100 in less than 10 years can be bought in any bank for $75.00.

The value of a future payment is estimated by following the rule that a promise to pay $1 at the end of $n$ years is worth today an amount which invested at compound interest would grow in value in the given number of years to the promised $1 or

$$0.9434 = \frac{1}{1.06} \qquad 0.8900 = \frac{1}{(1.06)^2} \qquad 0.5584 = \frac{1}{(1.06)^{10}}$$

This says we can get the present value of a future payment by dividing it by the number to which $1 will grow in the given time at compound interest. In more general terms, the formula for finding the present value of a future amount to be received is

$$P = \frac{A}{(1 + i)^n}$$

The value of each $1 to be received in any future year can be looked up in financial tables under the title "the present value or worth of 1" or, as in Table 6-2, "the present value of the reversion of 1."

### The Present Value of a Stream of Receipts

What if we were promised the right to receive $1 each year for the next 10 years? How much would that promise be worth? Let us assume again that we could earn 6 per cent compounded annually through investing in an equally risky venture. We note from above that the present value of the first year's payment is $0.9434, of the second year's payment is $0.8900, and of the tenth year's payment is $0.5584. We can find the present value of all of these payments by adding together the worth of what we will receive in year 1, plus year 2, plus year 3, etc., to and including year 10. The present value of a promise to pay $1 for each of the next 10 years when discounted at 6 per cent is $7.36. This is found by looking in a compound-interest table to the column headed "the present value of an annuity of 1 per period" or by solving the formula

$$a_{\overline{n}|i} = \frac{1 - (1 + i)^{-n}}{i}$$

where $a_{\overline{n}|i}$ is the present discounted value of an annuity which pays 1 in each of $n$ periods discounted back to the present at a rate of interest of $i$ (Table 6-3). An annuity is simply a series of income payments each a year further removed.

### Payments Needed to Amortize a Loan

When we make an amortized mortgage loan, we lend a certain sum of money and receive in return a promise of certain monthly or annual payments for a given number of periods. In effect, we are purchasing with our loan or principal an agreed-upon annuity or future stream of receipts. We could solve to find what interest we would earn through this bargain. We will solve for such a yield in the next section.

More commonly, we determined what rate we want to charge for the use of our money. We call this the interest rate, which

TABLE 6-2 *Monthly Compound-interest Table at 6 Per Cent per Annum (Effective rate = ½ per cent; i = 0.005)*

| | (1) | (2) | (3) | (4) | (5) | (6) | |
|---|---|---|---|---|---|---|---|
| Time | Amount of 1 at compound interest $s = (1+i)^n$ | Accumulation of 1 per period $s_{\overline{n}} = \dfrac{s-1}{i}$ | Sinking-fund factor $\dfrac{1}{s_{\overline{n}}} = \dfrac{1}{s-1}$ | Present value reversion of 1 $v^n = \dfrac{1}{s}$ | Present value ordinary annuity 1 per period $a_{\overline{n}} = \dfrac{s-1}{si}$ | Installment to amortize 1 $\dfrac{1}{a_{\overline{n}}} = \dfrac{si}{s-1}$ | n months |
| **Months** | | | | | | | |
| 1 | 1.005000 | 1.000000 | 1.000000 | 0.995025 | 0.995025 | 1.005000 | 1 |
| 2 | 1.010025 | 2.005000 | 0.498753 | 0.990075 | 1.985099 | 0.503753 | 2 |
| 3 | 1.015075 | 3.015025 | 0.331672 | 0.985149 | 2.970248 | 0.336672 | 3 |
| 4 | 1.020151 | 4.030100 | 0.248133 | 0.980248 | 3.950496 | 0.253133 | 4 |
| 5 | 1.025251 | 5.050251 | 0.198010 | 0.975371 | 4.925866 | 0.203010 | 5 |
| 6 | 1.030378 | 6.075502 | 0.164595 | 0.970518 | 5.896384 | 0.169595 | 6 |
| 7 | 1.035529 | 7.105879 | 0.140729 | 0.965690 | 6.862074 | 0.145729 | 7 |
| 8 | 1.040707 | 8.141409 | 0.122829 | 0.960885 | 7.822959 | 0.127829 | 8 |
| 9 | 1.045911 | 9.182116 | 0.108907 | 0.956105 | 8.779064 | 0.113907 | 9 |
| 10 | 1.051140 | 10.228026 | 0.097771 | 0.951348 | 9.730412 | 0.102771 | 10 |
| 11 | 1.056396 | 11.279167 | 0.088659 | 0.946615 | 10.677027 | 0.093659 | 11 |

150

| Years | | | | | | | Months |
|---|---|---|---|---|---|---|---|
| 1 | 1.061678 | 12.335562 | 0.081066 | 0.941905 | 11.618932 | 0.086066 | 12 |
| 2 | 1.127160 | 25.431955 | 0.039321 | 0.887186 | 22.562866 | 0.044321 | 24 |
| 3 | 1.196681 | 39.336105 | 0.025422 | 0.835645 | 32.871016 | 0.030422 | 36 |
| 4 | 1.270489 | 54.097832 | 0.018485 | 0.787098 | 42.580318 | 0.023485 | 48 |
| 5 | 1.348850 | 69.770031 | 0.014333 | 0.741372 | 51.725561 | 0.019333 | 60 |
| 6 | 1.432044 | 86.408856 | 0.011573 | 0.698302 | 60.339514 | 0.016573 | 72 |
| 7 | 1.520370 | 104.073927 | 0.009609 | 0.657735 | 68.453042 | 0.014609 | 84 |
| 8 | 1.614143 | 122.828542 | 0.008141 | 0.619524 | 76.095218 | 0.013141 | 96 |
| 9 | 1.713699 | 142.739900 | 0.007006 | 0.583533 | 83.293424 | 0.012006 | 108 |
| 10 | 1.819397 | 163.879347 | 0.006102 | 0.549633 | 90.073453 | 0.011102 | 120 |
| 11 | 1.931613 | 186.322629 | 0.005367 | 0.517702 | 96.459599 | 0.010367 | 132 |
| 12 | 2.050751 | 210.150163 | 0.004759 | 0.487626 | 102.474743 | 0.009759 | 144 |
| 13 | 2.177237 | 235.447328 | 0.004247 | 0.459298 | 108.140440 | 0.009247 | 156 |
| 14 | 2.311524 | 262.304766 | 0.003812 | 0.432615 | 113.476990 | 0.008812 | 168 |
| 15 | 2.454094 | 290.818713 | 0.003439 | 0.407482 | 118.503514 | 0.008439 | 180 |
| 16 | 2.605457 | 321.091337 | 0.003114 | 0.383810 | 123.238025 | 0.008114 | 192 |
| 17 | 2.766156 | 353.231110 | 0.002831 | 0.361513 | 127.697486 | 0.007831 | 204 |
| 18 | 2.936766 | 387.353195 | 0.002582 | 0.340511 | 131.897876 | 0.007582 | 216 |
| 19 | 3.117899 | 423.579854 | 0.002361 | 0.320729 | 135.854246 | 0.007361 | 228 |
| 20 | 3.310204 | 462.040895 | 0.002164 | 0.302096 | 139.580771 | 0.007164 | 240 |

TABLE 6-2  (Continued)

| Time | (1) Amount of 1 at compound interest $s = (1+i)^n$ | (2) Accumulation of 1 per period $s_{\overline{n}|} = \dfrac{s-1}{i}$ | (3) Sinking-fund factor $\dfrac{1}{s_{\overline{n}|}} = \dfrac{1}{s-1}$ | (4) Present value reversion of 1 $v^n = \dfrac{1}{s}$ | (5) Present value ordinary annuity 1 per period $a_{\overline{n}|} = \dfrac{s-1}{si}$ | (6) Installment to amortize 1 $\dfrac{1}{a_{\overline{n}|}} = \dfrac{si}{s-1}$ | $n$ months |
|---|---|---|---|---|---|---|---|
| **Years** | | | | | | | |
| 21 | 3.514371 | 502.874129 | 0.001989 | 0.284546 | 143.090806 | 0.006989 | 252 |
| 22 | 3.731129 | 546.225867 | 0.001831 | 0.268015 | 146.396926 | 0.006831 | 264 |
| 23 | 3.961257 | 592.251446 | 0.001688 | 0.252445 | 149.510979 | 0.006688 | 276 |
| 24 | 4.205579 | 641.115782 | 0.001560 | 0.237779 | 152.444121 | 0.006560 | 288 |
| 25 | 4.464970 | 692.993963 | 0.001443 | 0.223966 | 155.206864 | 0.006443 | 300 |
| 26 | 4.740359 | 748.071876 | 0.001337 | 0.210954 | 157.809106 | 0.006337 | 312 |
| 27 | 5.032734 | 806.546875 | 0.001240 | 0.198699 | 160.260171 | 0.006240 | 324 |
| 28 | 5.343142 | 868.628484 | 0.001151 | 0.187156 | 162.568843 | 0.006151 | 336 |
| 29 | 5.672696 | 934.539150 | 0.001070 | 0.176283 | 164.743393 | 0.006070 | 348 |
| 30 | 6.022575 | 1004.515043 | 0.000996 | 0.166042 | 166.791614 | 0.005996 | 360 |
| 31 | 6.394034 | 1078.806895 | 0.000927 | 0.156396 | 168.720844 | 0.005927 | 372 |
| 32 | 6.788405 | 1157.680906 | 0.000864 | 0.147310 | 170.537996 | 0.005864 | 384 |

| | | | | | | | |
|---|---|---|---|---|---|---|---|
| 33 | 7.207098 | 1241.419694 | 0.000806 | 0.138752 | 172.249581 | 0.005806 | 396 |
| 34 | 7.651617 | 1330.323306 | 0.000752 | 0.130691 | 173.861732 | 0.005752 | 408 |
| 35 | 8.123551 | 1424.710299 | 0.000702 | 0.123099 | 175.380226 | 0.005702 | 420 |
| 36 | 8.624594 | 1524.918875 | 0.000656 | 0.115947 | 176.810503 | 0.005656 | 432 |
| 37 | 9.156540 | 1631.308097 | 0.000613 | 0.109212 | 178.157689 | 0.005613 | 444 |
| 38 | 9.721296 | 1744.259174 | 0.000573 | 0.102867 | 179.426611 | 0.005573 | 456 |
| 39 | 10.320884 | 1864.176825 | 0.000536 | 0.096891 | 180.621815 | 0.005536 | 468 |
| 40 | 10.957454 | 1991.490735 | 0.000502 | 0.091262 | 181.747584 | 0.005502 | 480 |
| 41 | 11.633285 | 2126.657088 | 0.000470 | 0.085960 | 182.807952 | 0.005470 | 492 |
| 42 | 12.350801 | 2270.160207 | 0.000440 | 0.080966 | 183.806718 | 0.005440 | 504 |
| 43 | 13.112571 | 2422.514283 | 0.000413 | 0.076263 | 184.747461 | 0.005413 | 516 |
| 44 | 13.921326 | 2584.265226 | 0.000387 | 0.071832 | 185.633552 | 0.005387 | 528 |
| 45 | 14.779963 | 2755.992612 | 0.000363 | 0.067659 | 186.468166 | 0.005363 | 540 |
| 46 | 15.691559 | 2938.311769 | 0.000340 | 0.063729 | 187.254293 | 0.005340 | 552 |
| 47 | 16.659380 | 3131.875972 | 0.000319 | 0.060026 | 187.994750 | 0.005319 | 564 |
| 48 | 17.686894 | 3337.378791 | 0.000300 | 0.056539 | 188.692191 | 0.005300 | 576 |
| 49 | 18.777783 | 3555.556574 | 0.000281 | 0.053254 | 189.349115 | 0.005281 | 588 |
| 50 | 19.935955 | 3787.191086 | 0.000264 | 0.050161 | 189.967874 | 0.005264 | 600 |

SOURCE: Reprinted by permission, from *Ellwood's Tables for Real Estate Appraising and Financing*, Ridgewood, N.J., 1959.

TABLE 6-3   *Annual Compound-interest Table at 6 Per Cent (Effective rate = 6 per cent; $i = 0.06$)*

| Years | (1) Amount of 1 at compound interest $s = (1+i)^n$ | (2) Accumulation of 1 per period $s_{\overline{n}|} = \frac{s-1}{i}$ | (3) Sinking-fund factor $\frac{1}{s_{\overline{n}|}} = \frac{i}{s-1}$ | (4) Present value reversion of 1 $v^n = \frac{1}{s}$ | (5) Present value ordinary annuity 1 per period $a_{\overline{n}|} = \frac{s-1}{si}$ | (6) Installment to amortize 1 $\frac{1}{a_{\overline{n}|}} = \frac{si}{s-1}$ | n years |
|---|---|---|---|---|---|---|---|
| 1 | 1.060000 | 1.000000 | 1.000000 | 0.943396 | 0.943396 | 1.060000 | 1 |
| 2 | 1.123600 | 2.060000 | 0.485437 | 0.889996 | 1.833393 | 0.545437 | 2 |
| 3 | 1.191016 | 3.183600 | 0.314110 | 0.839619 | 2.673012 | 0.374110 | 3 |
| 4 | 1.262477 | 4.374616 | 0.228591 | 0.792094 | 3.465106 | 0.288591 | 4 |
| 5 | 1.338226 | 5.637093 | 0.177396 | 0.747258 | 4.212364 | 0.237396 | 5 |
| 6 | 1.418519 | 6.975319 | 0.143363 | 0.704961 | 4.917324 | 0.203363 | 6 |
| 7 | 1.503630 | 8.393838 | 0.119135 | 0.665057 | 5.582381 | 0.179135 | 7 |
| 8 | 1.593848 | 9.897468 | 0.101036 | 0.627412 | 6.209794 | 0.161036 | 8 |
| 9 | 1.689479 | 11.491316 | 0.087022 | 0.591898 | 6.801692 | 0.147022 | 9 |
| 10 | 1.790848 | 13.180795 | 0.075868 | 0.558395 | 7.360087 | 0.135868 | 10 |
| 11 | 1.898299 | 14.971643 | 0.066793 | 0.526788 | 7.886875 | 0.126793 | 11 |
| 12 | 2.012196 | 16.869941 | 0.059277 | 0.496969 | 8.383844 | 0.119277 | 12 |
| 13 | 2.132928 | 18.882138 | 0.052960 | 0.468839 | 8.852683 | 0.112960 | 13 |

154

| | | | | | | |
|---|---|---|---|---|---|---|
| 14 | 2.260904 | 21.015066 | 0.047585 | 0.442301 | 9.294984 | 0.107585 |
| 15 | 2.396558 | 23.275970 | 0.042963 | 0.417265 | 9.712249 | 0.102963 |
| 16 | 2.540352 | 25.672528 | 0.038952 | 0.393646 | 10.105895 | 0.098952 |
| 17 | 2.692773 | 28.212880 | 0.035445 | 0.371364 | 10.477260 | 0.095445 |
| 18 | 2.854339 | 30.905653 | 0.032357 | 0.350344 | 10.827603 | 0.092357 |
| 19 | 3.025600 | 33.759992 | 0.029621 | 0.330513 | 11.158116 | 0.089621 |
| 20 | 3.207135 | 36.785591 | 0.027185 | 0.311805 | 11.469921 | 0.087185 |
| 21 | 3.399564 | 39.992727 | 0.025005 | 0.294155 | 11.764077 | 0.085005 |
| 22 | 3.603537 | 43.392290 | 0.023046 | 0.277505 | 12.041582 | 0.083046 |
| 23 | 3.819750 | 46.995828 | 0.021278 | 0.261797 | 12.303379 | 0.081278 |
| 24 | 4.048935 | 50.815577 | 0.019679 | 0.246979 | 12.550358 | 0.079679 |
| 25 | 4.291871 | 54.864512 | 0.018227 | 0.232999 | 12.783356 | 0.078227 |
| 26 | 4.549383 | 59.156383 | 0.016904 | 0.219810 | 13.003166 | 0.076904 |
| 27 | 4.822346 | 63.705766 | 0.015697 | 0.207368 | 13.210534 | 0.075697 |
| 28 | 5.111687 | 68.528112 | 0.014593 | 0.195630 | 13.406164 | 0.074593 |
| 29 | 5.418388 | 73.639798 | 0.013580 | 0.184557 | 13.590721 | 0.073580 |
| 30 | 5.743491 | 79.058186 | 0.012649 | 0.174110 | 13.764831 | 0.072649 |
| 31 | 6.088101 | 84.801677 | 0.011792 | 0.164255 | 13.929086 | 0.071792 |
| 32 | 6.453387 | 90.889778 | 0.011002 | 0.154957 | 14.084043 | 0.071002 |
| 33 | 6.840590 | 97.343165 | 0.010273 | 0.146186 | 14.230230 | 0.070273 |
| 34 | 7.251025 | 104.183755 | 0.009598 | 0.137912 | 14.368141 | 0.069598 |
| 35 | 7.686087 | 111.434780 | 0.008974 | 0.130105 | 14.498246 | 0.068974 |

TABLE 6-3  *(Continued)*

| Years | (1) Amount of 1 at compound interest $s = (1+i)^n$ | (2) Accumulation of 1 per period $s_{\overline{n}|} = \dfrac{s-1}{i}$ | (3) Sinking-fund factor $\dfrac{1}{s_{\overline{n}|}} = \dfrac{i}{s-1}$ | (4) Present value reversion of 1 $v^n = \dfrac{1}{s}$ | (5) Present value ordinary annuity 1 per period $a_{\overline{n}|} = \dfrac{s-1}{si}$ | (6) Installment to amortize 1 $\dfrac{1}{a_{\overline{n}|}} = \dfrac{si}{s-1}$ | n years |
|---|---|---|---|---|---|---|---|
| 36 | 8.147252 | 119.120867 | 0.008395 | 0.122741 | 14.620987 | 0.068395 | 36 |
| 37 | 8.636087 | 127.268119 | 0.007857 | 0.115793 | 14.736780 | 0.067857 | 37 |
| 38 | 9.154252 | 135.904206 | 0.007358 | 0.109239 | 14.846019 | 0.067358 | 38 |
| 39 | 9.703507 | 145.058458 | 0.006894 | 0.103056 | 14.949075 | 0.066894 | 39 |
| 40 | 10.285718 | 154.761966 | 0.006462 | 0.097222 | 15.046297 | 0.066462 | 40 |
| 41 | 10.902861 | 165.047684 | 0.006059 | 0.091719 | 15.138016 | 0.066059 | 41 |
| 42 | 11.557033 | 175.950545 | 0.005683 | 0.086527 | 15.224543 | 0.065683 | 42 |
| 43 | 12.250455 | 187.507577 | 0.005333 | 0.081630 | 15.306173 | 0.065333 | 43 |
| 44 | 12.985482 | 199.758032 | 0.005006 | 0.077009 | 15.383182 | 0.065006 | 44 |
| 45 | 13.764611 | 212.743514 | 0.004700 | 0.072650 | 15.455832 | 0.064700 | 45 |
| 46 | 14.590487 | 226.508125 | 0.004415 | 0.068538 | 15.524370 | 0.064415 | 46 |
| 47 | 15.465917 | 241.098612 | 0.004148 | 0.064658 | 15.589028 | 0.064148 | 47 |
| 48 | 16.393872 | 256.564529 | 0.003898 | 0.060998 | 15.650027 | 0.063898 | 48 |

| | | | | | | | |
|---|---|---|---|---|---|---|---|
| 49 | 17.377504 | 272.958401 | 0.003664 | 0.057546 | 15.707572 | 0.063664 | 49 |
| 50 | 18.420154 | 290.335905 | 0.003444 | 0.054288 | 15.761861 | 0.063444 | 40 |
| 51 | 19.525364 | 308.756059 | 0.003239 | 0.051215 | 15.813076 | 0.063239 | 51 |
| 52 | 20.696885 | 328.281422 | 0.003046 | 0.048316 | 15.861393 | 0.063046 | 52 |
| 53 | 21.938698 | 348.978308 | 0.002866 | 0.045582 | 15.906974 | 0.062866 | 53 |
| 54 | 23.255020 | 370.917006 | 0.002696 | 0.043001 | 15.949976 | 0.062696 | 54 |
| 55 | 24.650322 | 394.172027 | 0.002537 | 0.040567 | 15.990543 | 0.062537 | 55 |
| 56 | 26.129341 | 418.822348 | 0.002388 | 0.038271 | 16.028814 | 0.062388 | 56 |
| 57 | 27.697101 | 444.951689 | 0.002247 | 0.036105 | 16.064919 | 0.062247 | 57 |
| 58 | 29.358927 | 472.648790 | 0.002116 | 0.034061 | 16.098980 | 0.062116 | 58 |
| 59 | 31.120463 | 502.007718 | 0.001992 | 0.032133 | 16.131113 | 0.061992 | 59 |
| 60 | 32.987691 | 533.128181 | 0.001876 | 0.030314 | 16.161428 | 0.061876 | 60 |

SOURCE: Reprinted by permission, from *Ellwood's Tables for Real Estate Appraising and Financing*, Ridgewood, N.J., 1959.

is the percentage of a sum of money charged for its use. We usually state that the interest charge or rate is a given per cent per year of the principal.

When we have agreed upon the principal to be loaned and the interest rate, we may next agree as to the length of period over which the loan is to be repaid, i.e., over which the principal is to be amortized, or reduced to zero. This involves finding the size of the payments which will exactly accomplish our desires. Under another type of arrangement, we may agree as to the amount to be paid in each period. In this case, we will have to solve to find the necessary number of periods over which payments will have to be made to reduce the principal to zero at the given interest rate. In a third, mixed case, we may fix both the size and the number of periodic payments. Under such agreements we have to solve to find how large a payment on principal must be made at the end. Such a larger principal payment at the end is called a balloon payment.

In all these examples, it was assumed that the payment each period would be the same, i.e., a constant amount. These are called level constant payments. Another type of agreement calls for a constant level of payments on principal rather than in total. Interest is paid only on the remaining, or unamortized, principal. Since the outstanding principal is less each period, the interest payments decrease. As a result, even though principal payments are level, total payments of interest and principal decrease each period.

If a loan is to be amortized with level payments, the size of each payment must be greater than the interest owed. Some of the payment covers interest and some principal. Since at the end of each payment the amount owed has been reduced, the interest payable next time, which is figured on the outstanding balance, is also lower. As a result, in the next period, the amount of the constant payment going to repay principal is greater and the amount for interest is less. This is obvious from Table 6-4. It shows the amount going to interest and principal in each payment on a $1,000 loan at 6 per cent for 20 years with level monthly payments. The table also shows the amount still owed at the end of each period.

The table shows that such a loan contract would require a monthly payment of $7.17. In the first payment the division would be $5.00 to interest and $2.17 to principal. In the last payment, of $7.17, the amounts would have shifted to $0.06 and $7.11.

TABLE 6-4  *Monthly-payment Direct-reduction 20-year Loan Amortization Schedule at 6 Per Cent* (Monthly payment per $1,000 = $7.17; exact figure = $7.164311)

| Time | | Payment on— | | Balance of loan | Time | | Payment on— | | Balance of loan |
|---|---|---|---|---|---|---|---|---|---|
| Years | Months | Interest | Principal | | Years | Months | Interest | Principal | |
| 0 | 1 | $5.00 | $2.17 | $997.83 | 3 | 1 | $4.57 | $2.60 | $912.04 |
| 0 | 2 | 4.99 | 2.18 | 995.65 | 3 | 2 | 4.56 | 2.61 | 909.43 |
| 0 | 3 | 4.98 | 2.19 | 993.46 | 3 | 3 | 4.55 | 2.62 | 906.81 |
| 0 | 4 | 4.97 | 2.20 | 991.26 | 3 | 4 | 4.53 | 2.64 | 904.17 |
| 0 | 5 | 4.96 | 2.21 | 989.05 | 3 | 5 | 4.52 | 2.65 | 901.52 |
| 0 | 6 | 4.95 | 2.22 | 986.83 | 3 | 6 | 4.51 | 2.66 | 898.86 |
| 0 | 7 | 4.93 | 2.24 | 984.59 | 3 | 7 | 4.49 | 2.68 | 896.18 |
| 0 | 8 | 4.92 | 2.25 | 982.34 | 3 | 8 | 4.48 | 2.69 | 893.49 |
| 0 | 9 | 4.91 | 2.26 | 980.08 | 3 | 9 | 4.47 | 2.70 | 890.79 |
| 0 | 10 | 4.90 | 2.27 | 977.81 | 3 | 10 | 4.45 | 2.72 | 888.07 |
| 0 | 11 | 4.89 | 2.28 | 975.53 | 3 | 11 | 4.44 | 2.73 | 885.34 |
| 1 | 0 | 4.88 | 2.29 | 973.24 | 4 | 0 | 4.43 | 2.74 | 882.60 |
| 1 | 1 | 4.87 | 2.30 | 970.94 | 4 | 1 | 4.41 | 2.76 | 879.84 |
| 1 | 2 | 4.85 | 2.32 | 968.62 | 4 | 2 | 4.40 | 2.77 | 877.07 |
| 1 | 3 | 4.84 | 2.33 | 966.29 | 4 | 3 | 4.39 | 2.78 | 874.29 |
| 1 | 4 | 4.83 | 2.34 | 963.95 | 4 | 4 | 4.37 | 2.80 | 871.49 |
| 1 | 5 | 4.82 | 2.35 | 961.60 | 4 | 5 | 4.36 | 2.81 | 868.68 |
| 1 | 6 | 4.81 | 2.36 | 959.24 | 4 | 6 | 4.34 | 2.83 | 865.85 |
| 1 | 7 | 4.80 | 2.37 | 956.87 | 4 | 7 | 4.33 | 2.84 | 863.01 |
| 1 | 8 | 4.78 | 2.39 | 954.48 | 4 | 8 | 4.32 | 2.85 | 860.16 |
| 1 | 9 | 4.77 | 2.40 | 952.08 | 4 | 9 | 4.30 | 2.87 | 857.29 |
| 1 | 10 | 4.76 | 2.41 | 949.67 | 4 | 10 | 4.29 | 2.88 | 854.41 |
| 1 | 11 | 4.75 | 2.42 | 947.25 | 4 | 11 | 4.27 | 2.90 | 851.51 |
| 2 | 0 | 4.74 | 2.43 | 944.82 | 5 | 0 | 4.26 | 2.91 | 848.60 |
| 2 | 1 | 4.72 | 2.45 | 942.37 | 5 | 1 | 4.24 | 2.93 | 845.67 |
| 2 | 2 | 4.71 | 2.46 | 939.91 | 5 | 2 | 4.23 | 2.94 | 842.73 |
| 2 | 3 | 4.70 | 2.47 | 937.44 | 5 | 3 | 4.21 | 2.96 | 839.77 |
| 2 | 4 | 4.69 | 2.48 | 934.96 | 5 | 4 | 4.20 | 2.97 | 836.80 |
| 2 | 5 | 4.67 | 2.50 | 932.46 | 5 | 5 | 4.18 | 2.99 | 833.81 |
| 2 | 6 | 4.66 | 2.51 | 929.95 | 5 | 6 | 4.17 | 3.00 | 830.81 |
| 2 | 7 | 4.65 | 2.52 | 929.43 | 5 | 7 | 4.15 | 3.02 | 827.79 |
| 2 | 8 | 4.64 | 2.53 | 924.90 | 5 | 8 | 4.14 | 3.03 | 824.76 |
| 2 | 9 | 4.62 | 2.55 | 922.35 | 5 | 9 | 4.12 | 3.05 | 821.71 |
| 2 | 10 | 4.61 | 2.56 | 919.79 | 5 | 10 | 4.11 | 3.06 | 818.65 |
| 2 | 11 | 4.60 | 2.57 | 917.22 | 5 | 11 | 4.09 | 3.08 | 815.57 |
| 3 | 0 | 4.59 | 2.58 | 914.64 | 6 | 0 | 4.08 | 3.09 | 812.48 |

TABLE 6-4 *(Continued)*

| Years | Months | Interest | Principal | Balance of loan | Years | Months | Interest | Principal | Balance of loan |
|---|---|---|---|---|---|---|---|---|---|
| 6 | 1 | $4.06 | $3.11 | $809.37 | 9 | 1 | $3.45 | $3.72 | $686.51 |
| 6 | 2 | 4.05 | 3.12 | 806.25 | 9 | 2 | 3.43 | 3.74 | 682.77 |
| 6 | 3 | 4.03 | 3.14 | 803.11 | 9 | 3 | 3.41 | 3.76 | 679.01 |
| 6 | 4 | 4.02 | 3.15 | 799.96 | 9 | 4 | 3.40 | 3.77 | 675.24 |
| 6 | 5 | 4.00 | 3.17 | 796.79 | 9 | 5 | 3.38 | 3.79 | 671.45 |
| 6 | 6 | 3.98 | 3.19 | 793.60 | 9 | 6 | 3.36 | 3.81 | 667.64 |
| 6 | 7 | 3.97 | 3.20 | 790.40 | 9 | 7 | 3.34 | 3.83 | 663.81 |
| 6 | 8 | 3.95 | 3.22 | 787.18 | 9 | 8 | 3.32 | 3.85 | 659.96 |
| 6 | 9 | 3.94 | 3.23 | 783.95 | 9 | 9 | 3.30 | 3.87 | 656.09 |
| 6 | 10 | 3.92 | 3.25 | 780.70 | 9 | 10 | 3.28 | 3.89 | 652.20 |
| 6 | 11 | 3.90 | 3.27 | 777.43 | 9 | 11 | 3.26 | 3.91 | 648.29 |
| 7 | 0 | 3.89 | 3.28 | 774.15 | 10 | 0 | 3.24 | 3.93 | 644.36 |
| 7 | 1 | 3.87 | 3.30 | 770.85 | 10 | 1 | 3.22 | 3.95 | 640.41 |
| 7 | 2 | 3.85 | 3.32 | 767.53 | 10 | 2 | 3.20 | 3.97 | 636.44 |
| 7 | 3 | 3.84 | 3.33 | 764.20 | 10 | 3 | 3.18 | 3.99 | 632.45 |
| 7 | 4 | 3.82 | 3.35 | 760.85 | 10 | 4 | 3.16 | 4.01 | 628.44 |
| 7 | 5 | 3.80 | 3.37 | 757.48 | 10 | 5 | 3.14 | 4.03 | 624.41 |
| 7 | 6 | 3.79 | 3.38 | 754.10 | 10 | 6 | 3.12 | 4.05 | 620.36 |
| 7 | 7 | 3.77 | 3.40 | 750.70 | 10 | 7 | 3.10 | 4.07 | 616.29 |
| 7 | 8 | 3.75 | 3.42 | 747.28 | 10 | 8 | 3.08 | 4.09 | 612.20 |
| 7 | 9 | 3.74 | 3.43 | 743.85 | 10 | 9 | 3.06 | 4.11 | 608.09 |
| 7 | 10 | 3.72 | 3.45 | 740.40 | 10 | 10 | 3.04 | 4.13 | 603.96 |
| 7 | 11 | 3.70 | 3.47 | 736.93 | 10 | 11 | 3.02 | 4.15 | 599.81 |
| 8 | 0 | 3.68 | 3.49 | 733.44 | 11 | 0 | 3.00 | 4.17 | 595.64 |
| 8 | 1 | 3.67 | 3.50 | 729.94 | 11 | 1 | 2.98 | 4.19 | 591.45 |
| 8 | 2 | 3.65 | 3.52 | 726.42 | 11 | 2 | 2.96 | 4.21 | 587.24 |
| 8 | 3 | 3.63 | 3.54 | 722.88 | 11 | 3 | 2.94 | 4.23 | 583.01 |
| 8 | 4 | 3.61 | 3.56 | 719.32 | 11 | 4 | 2.92 | 4.25 | 578.76 |
| 8 | 5 | 3.60 | 3.57 | 715.75 | 11 | 5 | 2.89 | 4.28 | 574.48 |
| 8 | 6 | 3.58 | 3.59 | 712.16 | 11 | 6 | 2.87 | 4.30 | 570.18 |
| 8 | 7 | 3.56 | 3.61 | 708.55 | 11 | 7 | 2.85 | 4.32 | 565.86 |
| 8 | 8 | 3.54 | 3.63 | 704.92 | 11 | 8 | 2.83 | 4.34 | 561.52 |
| 8 | 9 | 3.52 | 3.65 | 701.27 | 11 | 9 | 2.81 | 4.36 | 557.16 |
| 8 | 10 | 3.51 | 3.66 | 697.61 | 11 | 10 | 2.79 | 4.38 | 552.78 |
| 8 | 11 | 3.49 | 3.68 | 693.93 | 11 | 11 | 2.76 | 4.41 | 548.37 |
| 9 | 0 | 3.47 | 3.70 | 690.23 | 12 | 0 | 2.74 | 4.43 | 543.94 |

TABLE 6-4   (*Continued*)

| Time | | Payment on— | | Bal- ance of loan | Time | | Payment on— | | Bal- ance of loan |
|---|---|---|---|---|---|---|---|---|---|
| Years | Months | Inter- est | Princi- pal | | Years | Months | Inter- est | Princi- pal | |
| 12 | 1 | $2.72 | $4.45 | $539.49 | 15 | 1 | $1.84 | $5.33 | $363.56 |
| 12 | 2 | 2.70 | 4.47 | 535.02 | 15 | 2 | 1.82 | 5.35 | 358.21 |
| 12 | 3 | 2.68 | 4.49 | 530.53 | 15 | 3 | 1.79 | 5.38 | 352.83 |
| 12 | 4 | 2.65 | 4.52 | 526.01 | 15 | 4 | 1.76 | 5.41 | 347.42 |
| 12 | 5 | 2.63 | 4.54 | 521.47 | 15 | 5 | 1.74 | 5.43 | 341.99 |
| 12 | 6 | 2.61 | 4.56 | 516.91 | 15 | 6 | 1.71 | 5.46 | 336.53 |
| 12 | 7 | 2.58 | 4.59 | 512.32 | 15 | 7 | 1.68 | 5.49 | 331.04 |
| 12 | 8 | 2.56 | 4.61 | 507.71 | 15 | 8 | 1.66 | 5.51 | 325.53 |
| 12 | 9 | 2.54 | 4.63 | 503.08 | 15 | 9 | 1.63 | 5.54 | 319.99 |
| 12 | 10 | 2.52 | 4.65 | 498.43 | 15 | 10 | 1.60 | 5.57 | 314.42 |
| 12 | 11 | 2.49 | 4.68 | 493.75 | 15 | 11 | 1.57 | 5.60 | 308.82 |
| 13 | 0 | 2.47 | 4.70 | 489.05 | 16 | 0 | 1.54 | 5.63 | 303.19 |
| 13 | 1 | 2.45 | 4.72 | 484.33 | 16 | 1 | 1.52 | 5.65 | 297.54 |
| 13 | 2 | 2.42 | 4.75 | 479.58 | 16 | 2 | 1.49 | 5.68 | 291.86 |
| 13 | 3 | 2.40 | 4.77 | 474.81 | 16 | 3 | 1.46 | 5.71 | 286.15 |
| 13 | 4 | 2.37 | 4.80 | 470.01 | 16 | 4 | 1.43 | 5.74 | 280.41 |
| 13 | 5 | 2.35 | 4.82 | 465.19 | 16 | 5 | 1.40 | 5.77 | 274.64 |
| 13 | 6 | 2.33 | 4.84 | 460.35 | 16 | 6 | 1.37 | 5.80 | 268.84 |
| 13 | 7 | 2.30 | 4.87 | 455.48 | 16 | 7 | 1.34 | 5.83 | 283.01 |
| 13 | 8 | 2.28 | 4.89 | 450.59 | 16 | 8 | 1.32 | 5.85 | 257.16 |
| 13 | 9 | 2.25 | 4.92 | 445.67 | 16 | 9 | 1.29 | 5.88 | 251.28 |
| 13 | 10 | 2.23 | 4.94 | 440.73 | 16 | 10 | 1.26 | 5.91 | 245.37 |
| 13 | 11 | 2.20 | 4.97 | 435.76 | 16 | 11 | 1.23 | 5.94 | 239.43 |
| 14 | 0 | 2.18 | 4.99 | 430.77 | 17 | 0 | 1.20 | 5.97 | 233.46 |
| 14 | 1 | 2.15 | 5.02 | 425.75 | 17 | 1 | 1.17 | 6.00 | 227.46 |
| 14 | 2 | 2.13 | 5.04 | 420.71 | 17 | 2 | 1.14 | 6.03 | 221.43 |
| 14 | 3 | 2.10 | 5.07 | 415.64 | 17 | 3 | 1.11 | 6.06 | 215.37 |
| 14 | 4 | 2.08 | 5.09 | 410.55 | 17 | 4 | 1.08 | 6.09 | 209.28 |
| 14 | 5 | 2.05 | 5.12 | 405.43 | 17 | 5 | 1.05 | 6.12 | 203.16 |
| 14 | 6 | 2.03 | 5.14 | 400.29 | 17 | 6 | 1.02 | 6.15 | 197.01 |
| 14 | 7 | 2.00 | 5.17 | 395.12 | 17 | 7 | 0.99 | 6.18 | 190.83 |
| 14 | 8 | 1.98 | 5.19 | 389.93 | 17 | 8 | 0.95 | 6.22 | 184.61 |
| 14 | 9 | 1.95 | 5.22 | 384.71 | 17 | 9 | 0.92 | 6.25 | 178.36 |
| 14 | 10 | 1.92 | 5.25 | 379.46 | 17 | 10 | 0.89 | 6.28 | 172.08 |
| 14 | 11 | 1.90 | 5.27 | 374.19 | 17 | 11 | 0.86 | 6.31 | 165.77 |
| 15 | 0 | 1.87 | 5.30 | 368.89 | 18 | 0 | 0.83 | 6.34 | 159.43 |

TABLE 6-4    (*Continued*)

| Time | | Payment on— | | Bal-ance of loan | Time | | Payment on— | | Bal-ance of loan |
|---|---|---|---|---|---|---|---|---|---|
| Years | Months | Inter-est | Princi-pal | | Years | Months | Inter-est | Princi-pal | |
| 18 | 1 | $0.80 | $6.37 | $153.06 | 19 | 1 | $0.40 | $6.77 | $74.05 |
| 18 | 2 | 0.77 | 6.40 | 146.66 | 19 | 2 | 0.37 | 6.80 | 67.25 |
| 18 | 3 | 0.73 | 6.44 | 140.22 | 19 | 3 | 0.34 | 6.83 | 60.42 |
| 18 | 4 | 0.70 | 6.47 | 133.75 | 19 | 4 | 0.30 | 6.87 | 53.55 |
| 18 | 5 | 0.67 | 6.50 | 127.25 | 19 | 5 | 0.27 | 6.90 | 46.65 |
| 18 | 6 | 0.64 | 6.53 | 120.72 | 19 | 6 | 0.23 | 6.94 | 39.71 |
| 18 | 7 | 0.60 | 6.57 | 114.15 | 19 | 7 | 0.20 | 6.97 | 32.74 |
| 18 | 8 | 0.57 | 6.60 | 107.55 | 19 | 8 | 0.16 | 7.01 | 25.73 |
| 18 | 9 | 0.54 | 6.63 | 100.92 | 19 | 9 | 0.13 | 7.04 | 18.69 |
| 18 | 10 | 0.50 | 6.67 | 94.25 | 19 | 10 | 0.09 | 7.08 | 11.61 |
| 18 | 11 | 0.47 | 6.70 | 87.55 | 19 | 11 | 0.06 | 7.11 | 4.50 |
| 19 | 0 | 0.44 | 6.73 | 80.82 | 20 | 0 | 0.02* | 4.50* | 0.00 |

SOURCE: Financial Publishing Co., Boston.
*Final payment = $4.52

## Mathematics of Amortization with Level Payments

The mathematics of the amortization table are interesting. Understanding them may help in recognizing the formulas underlying the table. We can ask the present value of a promise to pay $7.17 for each of the next 240 months, or 20 years, discounted at 6 per cent interest. Clearly, the value must be $1,000, since we have just determined that this is the amount that would be paid or lent on such a contract. This can be checked in Table 6-2 where we find that 139.580771 is the present value of an annuity of 1 per period at the end of 20 years. Multiplying this by $7.17 will give us $1,000 (with errors in rounding), or $7.17 \times 139.580771 = \$1,000$

$$\text{Monthly payment} \times a_{\overline{n}|} = \text{principal}$$

We could as easily solve for the monthly payment if we knew the principal. Thus

$$\text{Monthly payment} = \frac{\text{principal}}{a_{\overline{n}|}} = \text{principal} \times \frac{1}{a_{\overline{n}|}}$$

or the required level monthly payment to amortize a given loan at a fixed interest in a certain period can be found by multiplying the principal by the reciprocal of the present value of an annuity of 1 per period. Such reciprocals $(1/a_{\overline{n}|})$ are commonly contained in financial tables under the title "installment to amortize 1."

We can also ask how much principal has been repaid at any time. We saw that this can be found directly from Table 6-4. How is the table derived? On the level-payment loan, the first payment contains an initial payment to principal. In the next period a similar payment is made plus an additional principal payment equal to the interest saved on the first payment. In the third period the original payment plus the interest on both previous payments is returned on principal. In effect, the amount of principal paid in each period is simply the first payment times the amount it grows to at compound interest. Such a sum can be found in the column labeled "the amount of 1 at compound interest" in Table 6-2.

If we want to approximate the amount that will have been paid on principal at the end of any period, all we need to do is add up the previous principal payments. This can be found calculated in tables of the form of Table 6-4. If we do not have such tables available, we can approximate through the more common interest tables. Thus we find the compound-interest payments accumulated under the title "accumulation of 1 per period." Taking the initial payment of $2.17 on principal and looking up the accumulation of 1 at the end of 10 years, we have $2.17 \times 163.879347 = \$356$; the payments on the $1,000 loan would be $356 in its first half. The principal outstanding would be about $644. The values we get from such calculations are only roughly right because they contain errors of rounding, while the printed tables have been worked out with more exactness.

This same type of formula will allow us to estimate how long it will take to pay off a loan if we agree on the amount of the monthly payments rather than on the length of the period of amortization. Thus we could agree to lend $10,000 at 6 per cent interest and to accept $75 per month in payment. When would the loan be paid off? The simplest way would be to use a table. Level payments of $75 per month on $10,000 are the equivalent of a 9 per cent annual payment ($75 \times 12 = 900$). We find from Table 6-5 that at this rate a loan charging 6 per cent interest will be

TABLE 6-5    *Mortgage Constant-payment Plans: Amounts Paid in Given Periods*

| Total constant rate, % | Interest rate, % | Per cent paid off in— | | | | Full term | |
|---|---|---|---|---|---|---|---|
| | | 5 years | 10 years | 15 years | 20 years | Years | Months |
| $5\frac{1}{2}$ | $4\frac{1}{4}$ | 7.0 | 15.5 | 26.2 | 39.3 | 35 | 0 |
| | $4\frac{1}{2}$ | 5.6 | 12.6 | 21.4 | 32.3 | 38 | 0 |
| 6 | $4\frac{1}{4}$ | 9.7 | 21.8 | 36.6 | 55.0 | 29 | 1 |
| | $4\frac{1}{2}$ | 8.4 | 18.9 | 32.1 | 48.5 | 30 | 11 |
| | $4\frac{3}{4}$ | 7.0 | 16.0 | 27.3 | 41.6 | 33 | 2 |
| | 5 | 5.7 | 12.9 | 22.3 | 34.3 | 35 | 11 |
| $6\frac{1}{2}$ | $4\frac{1}{4}$ | 12.5 | 28.0 | 47.1 | 70.7 | 25 | 1 |
| | $4\frac{1}{2}$ | 11.2 | 25.2 | 42.7 | 64.7 | 26 | 3 |
| | $4\frac{3}{4}$ | 9.9 | 22.3 | 38.2 | 58.2 | 27 | 9 |
| | 5 | 8.5 | 19.4 | 33.4 | 51.4 | 29 | 5 |
| | $5\frac{1}{4}$ | 7.1 | 16.4 | 28.4 | 44.1 | 31 | 6 |
| | $5\frac{1}{2}$ | 5.7 | 13.3 | 23.2 | 36.3 | 34 | 2 |
| 7 | $4\frac{1}{4}$ | 15.3 | 34.2 | 57.6 | 86.5 | 22 | 1 |
| | $4\frac{1}{2}$ | 14.0 | 31.5 | 53.4 | 80.9 | 23 | 0 |
| | $4\frac{3}{4}$ | 12.7 | 28.7 | 49.1 | 74.9 | 24 | 0 |
| | 5 | 11.3 | 25.9 | 44.5 | 68.5 | 25 | 2 |
| | $5\frac{1}{4}$ | 10.0 | 23.0 | 39.8 | 61.7 | 26 | 6 |
| | $5\frac{1}{2}$ | 8.6 | 19.9 | 34.8 | 54.5 | 28 | 1 |
| | $5\frac{3}{4}$ | 7.2 | 16.8 | 29.7 | 46.7 | 30 | 1 |
| | 6 | 5.8 | 13.7 | 24.2 | 38.5 | 32 | 7 |
| $7\frac{1}{4}$ | $4\frac{1}{4}$ | 16.7 | 37.3 | 62.8 | 94.3 | 20 | 10 |
| | $4\frac{1}{2}$ | 15.4 | 34.6 | 58.8 | 88.9 | 21 | 7 |
| | $4\frac{3}{4}$ | 14.1 | 31.9 | 54.5 | 83.2 | 22 | 6 |
| | 5 | 12.8 | 29.1 | 50.1 | 77.1 | 23 | 6 |
| | $5\frac{1}{4}$ | 11.4 | 26.2 | 45.5 | 70.5 | 24 | 8 |

TABLE 6-5 *(Continued)*

| *Total constant rate, %* | *Interest rate, %* | *Per cent paid off in—* | | | | *Full term* | |
|---|---|---|---|---|---|---|---|
| | | *5 years* | *10 years* | *15 years* | *20 years* | *Years* | *Months* |
| | 5½ | 10.0 | 23.3 | 40.7 | 63.5 | 25 | 11 |
| 7¼ | 5¾ | 8.7 | 20.2 | 35.6 | 56.1 | 27 | 6 |
| | 6 | 7.3 | 17.1 | 30.3 | 48.1 | 29 | 5 |
| | 4¼ | 18.1 | 40.4 | 68.0 | | 19 | 9 |
| | 4½ | 16.8 | 37.8 | 64.1 | 97.0 | 20 | 5 |
| | 4¾ | 15.5 | 35.1 | 60.0 | 91.5 | 21 | 2 |
| | 5 | 14.2 | 32.4 | 55.7 | 85.6 | 22 | 1 |
| 7½ | 5¼ | 12.8 | 29.5 | 51.2 | 79.3 | 23 | 0 |
| | 5½ | 11.5 | 26.6 | 46.5 | 72.6 | 24 | 2 |
| | 5¾ | 10.1 | 23.6 | 41.5 | 65.4 | 25 | 5 |
| | 6 | 8.7 | 20.5 | 36.4 | 57.8 | 26 | 11 |
| | 6½ | 5.9 | 14.0 | 25.3 | 40.9 | 31 | 1 |
| | 4¼ | 19.5 | 43.5 | 73.3 | | 18 | 9 |
| | 4½ | 18.2 | 40.9 | 69.4 | | 19 | 5 |
| | 4¾ | 16.9 | 38.3 | 65.4 | 99.8 | 20 | 1 |
| | 5 | 15.6 | 35.6 | 61.3 | 94.2 | 20 | 10 |
| 7¾ | 5¼ | 14.3 | 32.8 | 56.9 | 88.1 | 21 | 8 |
| | 5½ | 12.9 | 29.9 | 52.3 | 81.7 | 22 | 7 |
| | 5¾ | 11.6 | 26.9 | 47.5 | 74.8 | 23 | 8 |
| | 6 | 10.2 | 23.9 | 42.4 | 67.4 | 24 | 11 |
| | 6½ | 7.4 | 17.5 | 31.6 | 51.1 | 28 | 2 |
| | 4¼ | 20.9 | 46.6 | 78.5 | | 17 | 11 |
| | 4½ | 19.6 | 44.1 | 74.8 | | 18 | 5 |
| 8 | 4¾ | 18.3 | 41.5 | 70.9 | | 19 | 1 |
| | 5 | 17.0 | 38.8 | 66.8 | | 19 | 8 |
| | 5¼ | 15.7 | 36.1 | 62.5 | 97.0 | 20 | 5 |

TABLE 6-5 (*Continued*)

| Total constant rate, % | Interest rate, % | Per cent paid off in— | | | | Full term | |
|---|---|---|---|---|---|---|---|
| | | 5 years | 10 years | 15 years | 20 years | Years | Months |
| 8 | 5½ | 14.4 | 33.2 | 58.1 | 90.8 | 21 | 3 |
| | 5¾ | 13.0 | 30.3 | 53.4 | 84.1 | 22 | 2 |
| | 6 | 11.6 | 27.3 | 48.5 | 77.0 | 23 | 2 |
| | 6½ | 8.8 | 21.1 | 37.9 | 61.3 | 25 | 10 |
| | 7 | 6.0 | 14.4 | 26.4 | 43.4 | 29 | 10 |
| 8¼ | 4¼ | 22.2 | 49.7 | 83.7 | | 17 | 1 |
| | 4½ | 21.0 | 47.2 | 80.1 | | 17 | 7 |
| | 4¾ | 19.7 | 44.7 | 76.4 | | 18 | 2 |
| | 5 | 18.4 | 42.1 | 72.4 | | 18 | 9 |
| | 5¼ | 17.1 | 39.3 | 68.2 | | 19 | 4 |
| | 5½ | 15.8 | 36.6 | 63.9 | 99.8 | 20 | 1 |
| | 5¾ | 14.4 | 33.7 | 59.3 | 93.5 | 20 | 10 |
| | 6 | 13.1 | 30.7 | 54.5 | 86.6 | 21 | 9 |
| | 6½ | 10.3 | 24.6 | 44.3 | 71.5 | 24 | 0 |
| | 7 | 7.5 | 18.0 | 35.0 | 54.3 | 27 | 1 |
| 8½ | 4¼ | 23.6 | 52.8 | 89.0 | | 16 | 5 |
| | 4½ | 22.4 | 50.4 | 85.5 | | 16 | 10 |
| | 4¾ | 21.1 | 47.9 | 81.8 | | 17 | 4 |
| | 5 | 19.8 | 45.3 | 78.0 | | 17 | 10 |
| | 5¼ | 18.5 | 42.6 | 73.9 | | 18 | 5 |
| | 5½ | 17.2 | 39.9 | 69.7 | | 19 | 0 |
| | 5¾ | 15.9 | 37.1 | 65.2 | | 19 | 9 |
| | 6 | 14.5 | 34.1 | 60.6 | 96.3 | 20 | 6 |
| | 6½ | 11.9 | 28.1 | 50.6 | 81.7 | 22 | 4 |
| | 7 | 8.9 | 21.6 | 39.6 | 65.1 | 24 | 11 |
| | 7½ | 6.0 | 14.8 | 27.6 | 46.1 | 28 | 8 |

TABLE 6-5 *(Continued)*

| *Total con- stant rate, %* | *Inter- est rate, %* | *Per cent paid off in—* | | | | *Full term* | |
|---|---|---|---|---|---|---|---|
| | | *5 years* | *10 years* | *15 years* | *20 years* | *Years* | *Months* |
| | $4\frac{1}{4}$ | 25.0 | 56.0 | 94.2 | | 15 | 9 |
| | $4\frac{1}{2}$ | 23.8 | 53.5 | 90.8 | | 16 | 1 |
| | $4\frac{3}{4}$ | 22.5 | 51.1 | 87.3 | | 16 | 7 |
| | 5 | 21.3 | 48.5 | 83.5 | | 17 | 0 |
| $8\frac{3}{4}$ | $5\frac{1}{4}$ | 20.0 | 45.9 | 79.6 | | 17 | 6 |
| | $5\frac{1}{2}$ | 18.7 | 43.2 | 75.5 | | 18 | 1 |
| | $5\frac{3}{4}$ | 17.3 | 40.4 | 71.2 | | 18 | 8 |
| | 6 | 16.0 | 37.6 | 66.6 | | 19 | 5 |
| | $6\frac{1}{2}$ | 13.3 | 31.6 | 56.9 | 92.0 | 21 | 0 |
| | 7 | 10.4 | 25.2 | 46.2 | 76.0 | 23 | 1 |
| | $4\frac{1}{4}$ | 26.4 | 59.1 | 99.4 | | 15 | 1 |
| | $4\frac{1}{2}$ | 25.2 | 56.7 | 96.2 | | 15 | 6 |
| | $4\frac{3}{4}$ | 23.9 | 54.3 | 92.7 | | 15 | 10 |
| | 5 | 22.7 | 51.8 | 89.1 | | 16 | 4 |
| | $5\frac{1}{4}$ | 21.4 | 49.2 | 85.3 | | 16 | 9 |
| 9 | $5\frac{1}{2}$ | 20.1 | 46.5 | 81.3 | | 17 | 3 |
| | $5\frac{3}{4}$ | 18.8 | 43.8 | 77.1 | | 17 | 10 |
| | 6 | 17.4 | 41.0 | 72.7 | | 18 | 5 |
| | $6\frac{1}{2}$ | 14.7 | 35.1 | 63.2 | | 19 | 10 |
| | 7 | 11.9 | 28.8 | 52.8 | 86.8 | 21 | 7 |
| | $7\frac{1}{2}$ | 9.1 | 22.2 | 41.4 | 69.2 | 24 | 0 |
| | 8 | 6.1 | 15.2 | 28.8 | 49.1 | 27 | 7 |
| | $4\frac{1}{4}$ | 29.2 | 65.3 | | | 14 | 0 |
| | $4\frac{1}{2}$ | 28.0 | 63.0 | | | 14 | 4 |
| $9\frac{1}{2}$ | $4\frac{3}{4}$ | 26.7 | 60.7 | | | 14 | 8 |
| | 5 | 25.5 | 58.2 | | | 15 | 0 |
| | $5\frac{1}{4}$ | 24.2 | 55.7 | 96.7 | | 15 | 5 |

TABLE 6-5 *(Continued)*

| *Total constant rate, %* | *Interest rate, %* | *Per cent paid off in— 5 years* | *10 years* | *15 years* | *20 years* | *Full term Years* | *Months* |
|---|---|---|---|---|---|---|---|
| | 5½ | 23.0 | 53.2 | 92.9 | | 15 | 10 |
| | 6 | 21.7 | 50.5 | 89.0 | | 16 | 3 |
| | 5¾ | 20.3 | 47.8 | 84.8 | | 16 | 9 |
| 9½ | 6½ | 17.7 | 42.1 | 75.9 | | 17 | 10 |
| | 7 | 14.9 | 36.1 | 66.0 | | 19 | 2 |
| | 7½ | 12.1 | 29.7 | 55.2 | 92.3 | 20 | 11 |
| | 8 | 9.2 | 22.9 | 43.3 | 73.6 | 23 | 2 |
| | 4¼ | 32.0 | 71.5 | | | 13 | 1 |
| | 4½ | 30.8 | 69.3 | | | 13 | 4 |
| | 4¾ | 29.6 | 67.0 | | | 13 | 8 |
| | 5 | 28.3 | 64.7 | | | 13 | 11 |
| | 5¼ | 27.1 | 62.3 | | | 14 | 3 |
| | 5½ | 25.8 | 59.8 | | | 14 | 7 |
| 10 | 5¾ | 24.6 | 57.3 | | | 15 | 0 |
| | 6 | 23.3 | 54.6 | 96.9 | | 15 | 4 |
| | 6½ | 20.6 | 49.1 | 88.5 | | 16 | 3 |
| | 7 | 17.9 | 43.3 | 79.2 | | 17 | 4 |
| | 7½ | 15.1 | 37.1 | 69.0 | | 18 | 7 |
| | 8 | 12.2 | 30.5 | 57.7 | 98.2 | 20 | 3 |
| | 4¼ | 34.8 | 77.7 | | | 12 | 3 |
| | 4½ | 33.6 | 75.6 | | | 12 | 6 |
| | 4¾ | 32.4 | 73.4 | | | 12 | 9 |
| | 5 | 31.2 | 71.2 | | | 13 | 0 |
| 10½ | 5¼ | 29.9 | 68.9 | | | 13 | 3 |
| | 5½ | 28.7 | 66.5 | | | 13 | 7 |
| | 5¾ | 27.4 | 64.0 | | | 13 | 10 |
| | 6 | 26.2 | 61.5 | | | 14 | 2 |
| | 6½ | 23.6 | 56.1 | | | 14 | 11 |

TABLE 6-5   (*Continued*)

| Total con- stant rate, % | Inter- est rate, % | Per cent paid off in— | | | | Full term | |
|---|---|---|---|---|---|---|---|
| | | 5 years | 10 years | 15 years | 20 years | Years | Months |
| | 7 | 20.9 | 50.5 | 92.4 | | 15 | 9 |
| | 7½ | 18.1 | 44.5 | 82.8 | | 16 | 11 |
| | 8 | 15.3 | 38.1 | 72.1 | | 18 | 0 |
| | 4¼ | 37.5 | 83.9 | | | 11 | 7 |
| | 4½ | 36.4 | 81.9 | | | 11 | 9 |
| | 4¾ | 35.2 | 79.8 | | | 12 | 0 |
| | 5 | 34.0 | 77.6 | | | 12 | 2 |
| | 5¼ | 32.8 | 75.4 | | | 12 | 5 |
| | 5½ | 31.6 | 73.1 | | | 12 | 8 |
| 11 | 5¾ | 30.3 | 70.7 | | | 12 | 11 |
| | 6 | 29.1 | 68.3 | | | 13 | 3 |
| | 6½ | 26.5 | 63.2 | | | 13 | 10 |
| | 7 | 23.9 | 57.7 | | | 14 | 6 |
| | 7½ | 21.2 | 51.9 | 96.6 | | 15 | 4 |
| | 8 | 18.4 | 45.7 | 86.5 | | 16 | 4 |
| | 4¼ | 40.3 | 90.1 | | | 10 | 11 |
| | 4½ | 39.2 | 88.2 | | | 11 | 1 |
| | 4¾ | 38.0 | 86.2 | | | 11 | 3 |
| | 5 | 36.8 | 84.1 | | | 11 | 6 |
| | 5¼ | 35.6 | 82.0 | | | 11 | 8 |
| 11½ | 5½ | 34.4 | 79.8 | | | 11 | 11 |
| | 5¾ | 33.2 | 77.5 | | | 12 | 1 |
| | 6 | 32.0 | 75.1 | | | 12 | 4 |
| | 6½ | 29.4 | 70.2 | | | 12 | 11 |
| | 7 | 26.8 | 64.9 | | | 13 | 6 |
| | 7½ | 24.2 | 59.3 | | | 14 | 2 |
| | 8 | 21.4 | 53.4 | | | 15 | 0 |

SOURCE: Financial Publishing Co., Boston.

paid off in 18 years and 5 months. We note it will be slightly more than 40 per cent paid off in 10 years.

If we lacked such a table but had the usual compound-interest table, we could approximate the period required in the following way. The first payment of $75 would include $50 in interest and $25 on principal. When would this $25 payment on principal plus all additional payments which grow at the rate of compound interest accumulate to $10,000? This would take as long as it would take for $1 to accumulate to $400, since $10,000/25 = 400$. Looking down the column headed "accumulation of 1 per period" in Table 6-2, we see that an initial payment of $1.00 plus additional payments growing by compound interest in each period will accumulate to $400 in between 18 and 19 years. The two systems give approximately the same answer, as they should.

### Real versus Nominal Interest Rates

Mortgages carry agreed-upon interest rates. Thus the previously discussed mortgages carried rates of 6 per cent, and the monthly payments and amortization were calculated on this basis. These are the nominal or face interest rates. If we want to find the real interest rate—the yield, or net return to the lender—we will have to make two types of adjustment.

As indicated earlier, the more common one consists of correcting for expenses such as operating costs and risks of loss. The second and less understood adjustment consists of correcting for fees or discounts which may cause the actual amount of money loaned to differ from the amount of principal stated in the debt document. We now want to discuss how to estimate the yield under such conditions.

Yield is the percentage return per year to the lender on the actual funds he has paid out. The actual price paid for mortgages differs from their face value either because the market rate of interest has altered or in order to give the originator or seller of the mortgage a source of income. Let us consider again the 20-year $1,000 mortgage, at 6 per cent. When interest rates tighten, the original lender or owner of such a mortgage might find that in order to sell it, he would have to accept a lower price. He might discount the mortgage. In lending, each per cent of discount is normally spoken of as a point. Thus the seller might discount the mortgage by 3 per cent, or pay 3 points. The new buyer would pay only $970 for a mortgage which required the borrower to pay back $1,000 at 6 per cent interest over 20 years. This contract, as we saw, would call for 240 monthly payments of $7.17 each. The new buyer is interested in calculating his real yield. He will find that his yield depends upon whether the mortgage is outstanding for the full time or, as happens frequently, is refinanced or paid off in a lump sum at an earlier date.

Again we find that convenient tables have been printed for our purpose. Thus if we look at Table 6-6, we can see immediately that a 6 per cent mortgage with 20 years to maturity bought at a price of 97 has an annual yield of 6.38 per cent. Similarly we see that if this mortgage is paid off at the end of 10 years, the actual yield will have been still higher, 6.47 per cent. The table shows yield calculations for mortgages bought at either discounts or premium.

The idea behind the changing yield should be clear. The interest collected is figured on $1,000. The actual amount loaned was only $970. This means a somewhat higher real interest rate. In addition, though, the actual amount repaid on principal is also more than was lent. This $30 difference is an added interest payment which goes to increase the yield by still more. The yield on the loan repaid at an earlier date is still higher because this $30 is averaged over a shorter period. More of it is added to the return in each period, since it is all repaid in a shorter time.

What is the logic behind these tables? What the buyer has done is to pay $970 for an annuity which promises to pay him $7.17 for the next 20 years. We know that the present value of such a contract discounted at 6 per cent is $1,000. Clearly the contract in this case must be discounted at a higher rate to give the lower present value. We must solve the equation

$$a_{\overline{n}|i} = \frac{\text{principal}}{\text{monthly payment}} = \frac{970}{7.17} = 135.380$$

Looking in a set of compound-interest tables, we find that for 240 months the present value of an annuity of 1 per period is 136.8123 with discounting at 6.25 per cent, and it is 134.1250 at 6.50 per cent. The 135.3800 falls between, so interpolation is necessary to get the approximate yield.

TABLE 6-6    *Annual Mortgage Yields at 6 Per Cent Mortgage Rate for 20 Years*

| Price | 2 years | 5 years | 8 years | 10 years | 12 years | 15 years | 18 years | To maturity |
|---|---|---|---|---|---|---|---|---|
| 80 | 18.32 | 11.65 | 10.07 | 9.59 | 9.29 | 9.05 | 8.95 | 8.93 |
| 80½ | 17.97 | 11.49 | 9.96 | 9.48 | 9.20 | 8.96 | 8.86 | 8.85 |
| 81 | 17.62 | 11.33 | 9.84 | 9.38 | 9.10 | 8.87 | 8.78 | 8.76 |
| 81½ | 17.28 | 11.18 | 9.72 | 9.28 | 9.01 | 8.79 | 8.69 | 8.68 |
| 82 | 16.94 | 11.02 | 9.61 | 9.18 | 8.91 | 8.70 | 8.61 | 8.59 |
| 82½ | 16.60 | 10.86 | 9.50 | 9.08 | 8.82 | 8.61 | 8.52 | 8.51 |
| 83 | 16.26 | 10.71 | 9.38 | 8.98 | 8.73 | 8.53 | 8.44 | 8.43 |
| 83½ | 15.93 | 10.55 | 9.27 | 8.88 | 8.64 | 8.44 | 8.36 | 8.34 |
| 84 | 15.60 | 10.40 | 9.16 | 8.78 | 8.55 | 8.36 | 8.28 | 8.26 |
| 84½ | 15.27 | 10.25 | 9.05 | 8.68 | 8.46 | 8.27 | 8.20 | 8.18 |
| 85 | 14.94 | 10.10 | 8.94 | 8.59 | 8.37 | 8.19 | 8.12 | 8.10 |
| 85½ | 14.62 | 9.95 | 8.83 | 8.49 | 8.28 | 8.11 | 8.04 | 8.02 |
| 86 | 14.29 | 9.80 | 8.73 | 8.40 | 8.19 | 8.03 | 7.96 | 7.95 |
| 86½ | 13.97 | 9.65 | 8.62 | 8.30 | 8.11 | 7.95 | 7.88 | 7.87 |
| 87 | 13.65 | 9.50 | 8.51 | 8.21 | 8.02 | 7.87 | 7.80 | 7.79 |
| 87½ | 13.34 | 9.36 | 8.41 | 8.11 | 7.94 | 7.79 | 7.73 | 7.71 |
| 88 | 13.02 | 9.21 | 8.30 | 8.02 | 7.85 | 7.71 | 7.65 | 7.64 |
| 88½ | 12.71 | 9.07 | 8.20 | 7.93 | 7.77 | 7.63 | 7.57 | 7.56 |
| 89 | 12.40 | 8.93 | 8.10 | 7.84 | 7.68 | 7.55 | 7.50 | 7.49 |
| 89½ | 12.09 | 8.78 | 7.99 | 7.75 | 7.60 | 7.48 | 7.43 | 7.42 |
| 90 | 11.78 | 8.64 | 7.89 | 7.66 | 7.52 | 7.40 | 7.35 | 7.34 |
| 90½ | 11.47 | 8.50 | 7.79 | 7.57 | 7.44 | 7.33 | 7.28 | 7.27 |
| 91 | 11.17 | 8.36 | 7.69 | 7.48 | 7.36 | 7.25 | 7.21 | 7.20 |
| 91½ | 10.87 | 8.22 | 7.59 | 7.40 | 7.28 | 7.18 | 7.14 | 7.13 |
| 92 | 10.57 | 8.09 | 7.49 | 7.31 | 7.20 | 7.10 | 7.06 | 7.06 |
| 92½ | 10.27 | 7.95 | 7.40 | 7.22 | 7.12 | 7.03 | 6.99 | 6.99 |
| 93 | 9.97 | 7.81 | 7.30 | 7.14 | 7.04 | 6.96 | 6.92 | 6.92 |
| 93½ | 9.68 | 7.68 | 7.20 | 7.05 | 6.96 | 6.89 | 6.85 | 6.85 |

TABLE 6-6   (*Continued*)

| Price | *Prepaid in—* | | | | | | | To maturity |
|---|---|---|---|---|---|---|---|---|
| | 2 years | 5 years | 8 years | 10 years | 12 years | 15 years | 18 years | |
| 94 | 9.39 | 7.55 | 7.11 | 6.97 | 6.89 | 6.82 | 6.79 | 6.78 |
| 94½ | 9.10 | 7.41 | 7.01 | 6.88 | 6.81 | 6.74 | 6.72 | 6.71 |
| 95 | 8.81 | 7.28 | 6.92 | 6.80 | 6.73 | 6.67 | 6.65 | 6.65 |
| 95½ | 8.52 | 7.15 | 6.82 | 6.72 | 6.66 | 6.60 | 6.58 | 6.58 |
| 96 | 8.23 | 7.02 | 6.73 | 6.64 | 6.58 | 6.54 | 6.52 | 6.51 |
| 96½ | 7.95 | 6.89 | 6.63 | 6.56 | 6.51 | 6.47 | 6.45 | 6.45 |
| 97 | 7.66 | 6.76 | 6.54 | 6.47 | 6.43 | 6.40 | 6.38 | 6.38 |
| 97½ | 7.38 | 6.63 | 6.45 | 6.39 | 6.36 | 6.33 | 6.32 | 6.32 |
| 98 | 7.10 | 6.50 | 6.36 | 6.31 | 6.29 | 6.26 | 6.25 | 6.25 |
| 98½ | 6.83 | 6.38 | 6.27 | 6.23 | 6.21 | 6.20 | 6.19 | 6.19 |
| 99 | 6.55 | 6.25 | 6.18 | 6.16 | 6.14 | 6.13 | 6.13 | 6.13 |
| 99½ | 6.27 | 6.12 | 6.09 | 6.08 | 6.07 | 6.07 | 6.06 | 6.06 |
| 100 | 6.00 | 6.00 | 6.00 | 6.00 | 6.00 | 6.00 | 6.00 | 6.00 |
| 100½ | 5.73 | 5.88 | 5.91 | 5.92 | 5.93 | 5.94 | 5.94 | 5.94 |
| 101 | 5.46 | 5.75 | 5.82 | 5.85 | 5.86 | 5.87 | 5.88 | 5.88 |
| 101½ | 5.19 | 5.63 | 5.74 | 5.77 | 5.79 | 5.81 | 5.81 | 5.82 |
| 102 | 4.92 | 5.51 | 5.65 | 5.69 | 5.72 | 5.74 | 5.75 | 5.76 |
| 102½ | 4.65 | 5.39 | 5.56 | 5.62 | 5.65 | 5.68 | 5.69 | 5.70 |
| 103 | 4.39 | 5.27 | 5.48 | 5.54 | 5.58 | 5.62 | 5.63 | 5.64 |
| 103½ | 4.13 | 5.15 | 5.39 | 5.47 | 5.52 | 5.56 | 5.57 | 5.58 |
| 104 | 3.86 | 5.03 | 5.31 | 5.40 | 5.45 | 5.49 | 5.51 | 5.52 |
| 104½ | 3.60 | 4.91 | 5.22 | 5.32 | 5.38 | 5.43 | 5.46 | 5.46 |
| 105 | 3.34 | 4.79 | 5.14 | 5.25 | 5.32 | 5.37 | 5.40 | 5.40 |
| 105½ | 3.09 | 4.67 | 5.06 | 5.18 | 5.25 | 5.31 | 5.34 | 5.34 |
| 106 | 2.83 | 4.56 | 4.97 | 5.10 | 5.18 | 5.25 | 5.28 | 5.29 |
| 106½ | 2.57 | 4.44 | 4.89 | 5.03 | 5.12 | 5.19 | 5.22 | 5.23 |
| 107 | 2.32 | 4.33 | 4.81 | 4.96 | 5.05 | 5.13 | 5.17 | 5.17 |

SOURCE: Financial Publishing Co., Boston.

We must solve

| Yield | Present value factor |
|-------|---------------------|
| 6.25 | 136.8123 |
| X | 135.3800 |
| 6.50 | 134.1250 |

$$X = 6.25 + 0.25 \frac{136.8123 - 135.3800}{136.8123 - 134.1250} = 6.383$$

Thus the 3-point discount raises the actual yield by about 38.3 percentage points.

One way of seeing why the yield changes is to look at the following formula, which approximates the true yield.

$$Y = \frac{i\frac{B}{2} + \frac{B - C}{n}}{\frac{C}{2}} \times 100$$

where $Y$ = yield

$B$ = balance of unpaid principal on loan

$C$ = cost or payment to buy loan

$i$ = face or nominal interest rate on loan

$n$ = number of years loan has to maturity

The logic of this formula is not hard to see. The term $i(B/2)$ gives an approximation of annual income from interest, since the principal $B$ divided by 2 shows the average amount of the loan outstanding against which interest is calculated. The term $(B - C)/n$ shows the average annual amount received from the extra principal received, since $B - C$ is this extra amount, or discount. The term $C/2$ shows the average amount the investor will have invested at any time.

For the previous example we find

$$Y = \frac{0.06\frac{1,000}{2} + \frac{1,000 - 970}{20}}{970/2} \times 100$$

$$Y = \frac{30 + 1.5}{485} \times 100 = \frac{3,150}{485} = 6.49$$

What happens when the loan is paid off at the end of 10 years? The same general type of calculation takes place, but it is more complex. The problem is to find the interest rate which will equate $970 to 120 monthly payments of $7.17 plus a lump-sum payment of $644, which is the amount which will remain unpaid at that time on the original loan of $1,000. In other words, there is some interest rate or yield (actually 6.47 per cent) which will discount back the monthly-payment series and the final reversion to give a present value of $970, the amount which the new buyer pays for the loan.

There is no simple formula to solve this latter problem analytically. It can be done either by a trial-and-error method or by a computer program. It seems complex because we must find equal yields to discount both the monthly payments and the final reversion. Since the data we get in our normal tables do not enable us to do this, we must look directly into a table such as Table 6-6 that has been properly calculated or use a trial-and-error method as explained in the next section.

### Estimating the Yield on Property

When we become concerned with the yield on property, we find a mathematical problem identical to that of loans. We frequently are given a development cost or a selling price for a property, an expected stream of income, and a final value or sales price or reversion at the end of a given period. From these data we want to calculate the yield. The mathematical problem is the same as that for a discounted loan. We seek the interest or yield rate that will make the discounted value of the future payments including the final lump sum equal to today's price. Again the yield must be found directly in a yield table or by a trial-and-error technique from a corresponding mortgage or bond table.

To find the yield, the owner must forecast all future revenues and expenses up to the time he plans either to sell the property or to transfer it to another use. He must also forecast the selling price or the value of the property at the end of this income stream. He then can find the yield (rate) which will discount these two figures—the income stream and the reversion—to equal exactly the actual value or selling price of the property today.

The problem is to find a given yield rate which, when used to discount the future income stream and the final worth or reversion, will make their sum exactly equal to today's cost or investment. The formula is

$$I = R \frac{1 - (1 + y)^{-n}}{y} + \frac{I_n}{(1 + y)^n}$$

where $I$ = present cost
$R$ = estimated annual net income
$y$ = yield
$n$ = number of years for income
$I_n$ = value of property at end of period

The problem is complicated because no table carries the combined yield rate. Instead we must estimate the expected yield, use it on a trial basis to get the present value of the reversion, subtract this from the investment, and then use the rate on the income stream to see how far its discounted value differs from the remaining investment.

Assume that we have a property which costs $1,000,000 which has an annual net income of $86,000 that can be collected for 25 years and which during that period will depreciate so that its sales price at the end of it will be $400,000. (For example, think of a property with a 25-year net-net lease.) Substituting in the equation we find

$$1,000,000 = 86,000 \frac{1 - (1 + y)^{-25}}{y} + \frac{400,000}{(1 + y)^{25}}$$

$$\frac{1 - (1 + y)^{-25}}{y} = \frac{1,000,000 - \dfrac{400,000}{(1 + y)^{25}}}{86,000}$$

Try 8.00 per cent for $y$. We must look in a table similar to Table 6-2 showing the present value of a reversion of 1 after 25 years for different interest rates.

$$\frac{400,000}{(1 + y)^{25}} = 400,000 \times 0.146 = 58,400$$

$$\frac{1 - (1 + y)^{-25}}{y} = \frac{1,000,000 - (400,000 \times 0.146)}{86,000}$$

$$= \frac{941,600}{86,000} = 10.9488$$

Looking up the present value of an annuity of 1 at 8 per cent for 25 years, we find that our discount rate or yield is too high. A simple inspection of such as annuity table makes it clear that the yield will be between 7.7 and 7.75 per cent. The exact amount can be found easily on a computer or approximately by trial and error of rates between these limits.

### Other Estimates of Yields

Because the problems of this joint discounting are difficult, most investors actually use a short cut to figure the yield. They make either of two assumptions: (1) that the income stream will continue forever—in which case no problems of a reversion exist—or (2) that the income stream will continue for a given number of years and at the end of that time the property will be worthless. Again no problem of a reversion will arise.

Examples of the first type of calculation are found in Chapters 14 and 15. They are discussed there at length. The net income (free and clear income) is calculated before depreciation, financing charges, and income taxes. The net yield is found directly from the capitalization formula for a perpetual annuity.

$$y = \frac{R}{I}$$

where $y$ = annual yield

$R$ = annual net income

$I$ = total investment, developed cost, or cost to purchase

Thus a property which costs $1,000,000 and has $86,000 annual income is said to yield 8.6 per cent.

$$y = \frac{86,000}{1,000,000} = 8.6 \text{ per cent}$$

In many cases the owner wishes to calculate the yield on his equity rather than on the total investment. In this case $R'$ will be net income after financing charges, while $I'$ will be the equity rather than total investment.

The problem which arises in these cases is that the income is assumed to remain constant forever. The owner must decide how likely this assumption is and must determine whether the yield is high enough to cover the risks that this assumption is incorrect. As a safety factor, therefore, some owners take the opposite point of view and assume that the stream of income will disappear completely at the end of a fixed period. The owner may assume that income will continue at the present rate for 25 years and then drop to zero. To draw again on our previous example of a property with a 25-year net-net lease, assume that the property will be worthless when the lease ends. This problem is again one of valuing an annuity for a given number of years. We saw that the formula for the present value of an annuity of 1 per period is

$$a_{\overline{n}|i} = \frac{1 - (1 + i)^{-n}}{i}$$

If our $1,000,000 property were assumed to pay its income for 25 years, we would solve the equation

$$1,000,000 = 86,000 \frac{1 - (1 + i)^{-25}}{i}$$

$$\frac{1 - (1 + i)^{-25}}{i} = \frac{1,000,000}{86,000} = 11.628$$

Looking in a "present value of an annuity" table at 25 years, we find we must solve the following problem by interpolation:

$$a_{\overline{25}|0.065} = 11.991$$
$$a_{\overline{25}|X} = 11.628$$
$$a_{\overline{25}|0.070} = 11.469$$

$$X = 6.50 + 0.50 \frac{11.991 - 11.628}{11.991 - 11.469} = 6.848$$

It is clear that to assume that no income or reversion will be available at the end of 25 years cuts the estimated yield considerably. It is far less than the estimated yield based on a perpetual return. One method is overly conservative, and one is not conservative enough. The true yield falls between these two extremes.

In any of these cases it is possible, by complicating the arithmetic, to take into account possible future declines in income. Thus, assume a lease for only 10 years, and a new lease that could be negotiated only for $50,000 for years 11 through 25. In this case, we would simply work with the present values of two separate streams, one for the first part of the period and the second for the later part.

## Capitalization

The problem of estimating the yield on a property with a known price and an estimated future income stream is closely related to the typical appraisal problem of determining the investment value of the property. The appraiser is asked to estimate the value of a property by projecting its future income stream, its value or reversion at the time the income stream stops, and the proper capitalization rate, or

$$V = R\frac{1 - (1 + i)^{-n}}{i} + \frac{V_{-n}}{(1 + i)^n}$$

In this case, the appraiser must estimate the net return $R$. He must estimate the length of time over which such an average return can be expected. He estimates the value that the property will have at the end of the period $V_{-n}$. He next estimates the proper capitalization rate or rates $i$. Having decided upon the various numbers, he can solve for the present investment value by using the tables for the present discounted value of the future annuity (income stream) and the present value of a future lump-sum payment (reversion).

The skill of appraising and the literature on this subject are concerned primarily with how to estimate future returns and how to determine the proper capitalization rates. When these have been determined, however, the actual mathematical problem is simple. Thus if the estimated amounts were a net return of $86,000 for 25 years, a value of the property of $400,000 at the end of that period, and a capitalization rate of 7.50 per cent, the required equation would be

$$V = 86,000\frac{1 - (1 + 0.075)^{-25}}{0.075} + \frac{400,000}{(1 + 0.075)^{25}}$$

Looking up the present value of an annuity for 25 years, discounted at 7.50 per cent interest, we find 11.1469. Under the present value of 1 at the end of 25 years and discounted at 7.50 per cent, we find 0.163979.

The value therefore is

$$V = 86,000(11.1469) + 400,000(0.163979) = 1,024,225$$

## Depreciation

The factor which has been omnipresent in all the previous discussions but has not appeared explicitly is depreciation. The concept of depreciation is simple. It is the loss in value of the property due to the passage of time. In the real estate field, property is said to lose value because of physical deterioration and functional or economic obsolescence. Property can also appreciate in value because of changes in the price level or because of economic improvement in the conditions surrounding the building. In the previous formulas, depreciation was not shown directly. Its effect was measured through estimating any changes in future net receipts and through estimating the difference between the present value of a property and its value after a fixed number of years.

Depreciation is a complex problem both because it is hard to estimate and because, for tax and accounting purposes, certain rather arbitrary charges for depreciation are allowed against income. If an investor assumes that these charges are arbitrary, he will want to correct for them in his value or yield estimates. The form in which depreciation deductions are taken will also affect his estimated yields. These problems are discussed in Chapter 14.

Mathematically there are three main methods of calculating depreciation accepted for most tax purposes by the Bureau of Internal Revenue. Other methods may be used, however, if they can be proved more logical or correct.

The base against which depreciation can be figured is often important. As a general rule, land cannot be depreciated. In addition, depreciation may be figured on the difference between the cost and salvage value. In the following discussion, we assume that the property will depreciate to zero.

### Straight-line Method

This technique assumes a constant decline in the value of a property. For example, assume a property will become worthless after 40 years. Its depreciation rate $D$ then would be $100/40 = 2\frac{1}{2}$ per cent per year. To find the expected depreciated value of a property at the end of any period we have

$$V_{-n} = I - (D \times I \times n)$$

where $I$ = original value

$V_{-n}$ = depreciated value

$D$ = depreciation rate

$n$ = number of years

or, for a \$1,000,000 property and a 20-year period at $2\frac{1}{2}$ per cent depreciation,

$$V_{-n} = 1,000,000 - (20 \times 0.025 \times 1,000,000) = 500,000$$

## Declining-balance Method

In this technique, a property is assumed to decline in value each year by a fixed percentage of its value (original cost less depreciation) at the beginning of the year. Its value at the end of any period is

$$V_{-n} = I(1 - D)^n$$

or, in the previous case,

$$V_{-n} = 1,000,000(1 - 0.025)^{20} = 602,600$$

To see what is happening, note that the values at the ends of years 1, 2, and 3 are

$$
\begin{aligned}
&\qquad\qquad\qquad\qquad\qquad\qquad\qquad\quad \textit{Depreciation}\\
&\qquad\qquad\qquad\qquad\qquad\qquad\qquad\qquad\; \textit{in year}\\
&V_{-1} = 1,000,000(1 - 0.025)^1 = 975,000 \qquad 25,000\\
&V_{-2} = 1,000,000(1 - 0.025)^2 = 950,625 \qquad 24,375
\end{aligned}
$$

(which is the same as $V_{-2} = 975,000(1 - 0.025)^1 = 950,625$)

$$V_{-3} = 1,000,000(1 - 0.025)^3 = 926,859 \qquad 23,766$$

The declining balance is primarily used because the Bureau of Internal Revenue for accelerated-depreciation purposes allows the rate of depreciation $D$ used in calculations for income tax purposes to be $1\frac{1}{2}$ or 2 times the straight-line rate. Thus, instead of $1 - 0.025$ in the above calculation, for tax purposes we might use $1 - 0.050$ or $1 - 0.0375$. This means that in early stages the amount of authorized depreciation will be greater than under the straight-line method. This is demonstrated in Table 6-7, which shows the relationship among the different methods of depreciation for a property assumed to have a 40-year life.

## "Sum of the Years' Digits" Method

Under this procedure the firm is allowed to charge off a percentage based upon the length of time the building has been depreciated compared to its total life. For example, for the property with a

TABLE 6-7 *Comparative Depreciation Rates for Properties with Assumed 40-year Life*

| Year | Straight line | | 200% declining balance | | 150% declining balance | | Sum of digits | |
|---|---|---|---|---|---|---|---|---|
| | Annual % | Cumulative % | Annual % | Cumulative % | Annual % | Cumulative % | Annual % | Cumulative % |
| 1 | 2.50 | 2.50 | 5.00 | 5.00 | 3.75 | 3.75 | 4.88 | 4.88 |
| 2 | 2.50 | 5.00 | 4.75 | 9.75 | 3.61 | 7.36 | 4.75 | 9.63 |
| 3 | 2.50 | 7.50 | 4.51 | 14.26 | 3.47 | 10.83 | 4.64 | 14.27 |
| 4 | 2.50 | 10.00 | 4.29 | 18.55 | 3.34 | 14.17 | 4.51 | 18.78 |
| 5 | 2.50 | 12.50 | 4.07 | 22.62 | 3.22 | 17.49 | 4.39 | 23.17 |
| 6 | 2.50 | 15.00 | 3.87 | 26.49 | 3.10 | 20.59 | 4.27 | 27.44 |
| 7 | 2.50 | 17.50 | 3.68 | 30.17 | 2.98 | 23.57 | 4.14 | 31.58 |
| 8 | 2.50 | 20.00 | 3.49 | 33.66 | 2.87 | 26.44 | 4.03 | 35.61 |
| 9 | 2.50 | 22.50 | 3.32 | 36.98 | 2.76 | 29.20 | 3.90 | 39.51 |
| 10 | 2.50 | 25.00 | 3.15 | 40.13 | 2.66 | 31.86 | 3.78 | 43.29 |
| 11 | 2.50 | 27.50 | 2.99 | 43.12 | 2.56 | 34.42 | 3.66 | 46.95 |
| 12 | 2.50 | 30.00 | 2.84 | 45.96 | 2.46 | 36.88 | 3.54 | 50.49 |
| 13 | 2.50 | 32.50 | 2.71 | 48.67 | 2.37 | 39.25 | 3.41 | 53.90 |
| 14 | 2.50 | 35.00 | 2.56 | 51.23 | 2.28 | 41.53 | 3.29 | 57.19 |
| 15 | 2.50 | 37.50 | 2.44 | 53.67 | 2.20 | 43.63 | 3.18 | 60.37 |
| 16 | 2.50 | 40.00 | 2.32 | 55.99 | 2.11 | 45.74 | 3.04 | 63.41 |
| 17 | 2.50 | 42.50 | 2.20 | 58.19 | 2.03 | 47.77 | 2.93 | 66.34 |
| 18 | 2.50 | 45.00 | 2.09 | 60.28 | 1.96 | 49.73 | 2.81 | 69.15 |
| 19 | 2.50 | 47.50 | 1.99 | 62.27 | 1.88 | 51.61 | 2.68 | 71.83 |
| 20 | 2.50 | 50.00 | 1.88 | 64.15 | 1.81 | 53.42 | 2.56 | 74.39 |
| 21 | 2.50 | 52.50 | 1.79 | 65.94 | 1.75 | 55.17 | 2.44 | 76.83 |
| 22 | 2.50 | 55.00 | 1.71 | 67.65 | 1.68 | 56.85 | 2.32 | 79.15 |
| 23 | 2.50 | 57.50 | 1.62 | 69.27 | 1.62 | 58.47 | 2.19 | 81.34 |
| 24 | 2.50 | 60.00 | 1.53 | 70.80 | 1.56 | 60.03 | 2.07 | 83.41 |
| 25 | 2.50 | 62.50 | 1.46 | 72.26 | 1.50 | 61.53 | 1.94 | 85.37 |

TABLE 6-7 (Continued)

| Year | Straight line | | 200% declining balance | | 150% declining balance | | Sum of digits | |
|---|---|---|---|---|---|---|---|---|
| | Annual % | Cumulative % | Annual % | Cumulative % | Annual % | Cumulative % | Annual % | Cumulative % |
| 26 | 2.50 | 65.00 | 1.39 | 73.65 | 1.44 | 62.97 | 1.82 | 87.19 |
| 27 | 2.50 | 67.50 | 1.32 | 74.97 | 1.39 | 64.36 | 1.71 | 88.90 |
| 28 | 2.50 | 70.00 | 1.25 | 76.22 | 1.34 | 65.70 | 1.59 | 90.49 |
| 29 | 2.50 | 72.50 | 1.19 | 77.41 | 1.29 | 66.99 | 1.46 | 91.95 |
| 30 | 2.50 | 75.00 | 1.13 | 78.54 | 1.24 | 68.23 | 1.34 | 93.29 |
| 31 | 2.50 | 77.50 | 1.07 | 79.61 | 1.19 | 69.42 | 1.22 | 94.51 |
| 32 | 2.50 | 80.00 | 1.02 | 80.63 | 1.15 | 70.57 | 1.10 | 95.61 |
| 33 | 2.50 | 82.50 | 0.97 | 81.60 | 1.10 | 71.67 | 0.98 | 96.58 |
| 34 | 2.50 | 85.00 | 0.92 | 85.52 | 1.06 | 72.73 | 0.86 | 97.44 |
| 35 | 2.50 | 87.50 | 0.87 | 83.39 | 1.02 | 73.75 | 0.73 | 98.17 |
| 36 | 2.50 | 90.00 | 0.83 | 84.22 | 0.98 | 74.73 | 0.61 | 98.78 |
| 37 | 2.50 | 92.50 | 0.79 | 85.01 | 0.95 | 75.68 | 0.49 | 99.27 |
| 38 | 2.50 | 95.00 | 0.75 | 85.76 | 0.91 | 76.59 | 0.36 | 99.63 |
| 39 | 2.50 | 97.50 | 0.71 | 86.47 | 0.88 | 77.47 | 0.25 | 99.88 |
| 40 | 2.50 | 100.00 | 0.68 | 87.15 | 0.85 | 78.32 | 0.12 | 100.00 |

40-year expected life, the denominator of the depreciation rate is always the sum of the digits from 1 to 40; i.e.,

$$1 + 2 + 3 + \cdots + 39 + 40 = \frac{n(n+1)}{2} = \frac{40 \times 41}{2} = 820$$

The numerator the first year would be 40, the second 39, down to 1 in the fortieth year; i.e., $D = 40/820, 39/820, \ldots, 1/820$. This system would give a $D$ of 4.88 in the first year, a $D$ of 4.75 in the second year, and a lower one each year thereafter. (See Table 6-7.)

The important point in discussions of depreciation is usually not the technique of calculating the particular rates, because this is a mechanical process. The problem is to project a logical rate that can be expected to occur. This expected rate can then be compared with the authorized tax rate.

This same general problem exists in all computations of yield or even of loan repayments. The mathematics are relatively simple. If one wants, he can find tables which solve nearly all computational problems. However, one must not confuse the answers found in the table with what may happen in the real world. Actual results will depend more on the accuracy of the forecasts of the income stream than on extra digits or greater or lesser approximations in the mathematical processes.

# Causes of Individual Risks and
# Their Control_____7

In every program of risk management, first attention must be paid to the analysis of individual loans. The basic causes of the types of delinquencies and foreclosures likely to strike any loan must be understood. In addition to knowing what dangers exist, every firm needs a sound processing procedure to ensure that each loan application is carefully analyzed and that its risks are evaluated in accordance with these procedures. Only then can the decision be made as to whether a prospective loan qualifies and is worth making.

Table 6-1 showed estimates of losses for an average well-made loan on a single-family house under three separate economic conditions. Many loans, however, will not meet the standards of the average. Their own particular features may increase or decrease their risks and probability of loss.

Previous studies of mortgage experiences list 10 to 15 separate factors in any given loan which will cause its risks to deviate from the average. An examination of these factors and their impact upon the probability of losses is vital to potential lenders or borrowers. An understanding of real estate financing requires that participants in a loan recognize what probable losses they are engendering when some features are included rather than others.

Lending officers require a basic check list of risk factors in order to determine the desirability and potential profitability of any loan. Figure 7-1 presents such a list. It can serve as an introduction to the influences creating differential losses. The list is not complete because much work still remains to be done in establishing mortgage

FIGURE 7-1   *Factors Affecting Risks*

A. Loan characteristics
   1. The time at which the loan is made
   2. Mortgage terms
      a. Amortization provisions
      b. Loan-to-value ratio
      c. The existence of junior liens
   3. Interest rate
   4. Type of loan
B. Borrower's characteristics
   1. Ownership and occupancy
   2. Income
      a. Income-expense ratio
      b. Occupation
      c. Credit rating
   3. Family difficulties
   4. Transfers of title
C. Property characteristics
   1. Type
   2. Price
   3. Design
   4. Age
   5. Location

evaluation systems. Each mortgage officer must add his own experience to this framework.

## LOAN CHARACTERISTICS

Existing studies of mortgage experience show why each of the factors listed in Figure 7-1 appear to alter the risks of any loan. An examination of the results of these studies forms a background against which borrowers and lenders may measure the risks of future loans.

## Time and Age

Risks incurred in individual loans are much greater in some years than in others, partially because a loan's success in its first five years is heavily influenced by the state of the economy. When incomes and housing prices are rising, only the poorest of loans will not succeed. On the other hand, even mild recessions or periods of stable building costs lead to foreclosures of loans that otherwise would be bailed out by a voluntary transfer of the property.

Over and above the danger of market changes, new loans have a higher risk than older ones. The younger a loan, the more likely it is that the property or borrower will have hidden defects that will show up with time. Furthermore, the newer the loan, the less the reduction in principal. The borrower has a smaller equity and less interest in maintaining payments. Most loans experience the largest losses in their second or third year.

At certain periods, lenders tend to be carried away with enthusiasm. They overvalue the security of the property, overestimate the income it and its owner will receive, and underestimate normal risks. Such contagious optimism, which stands out clearly throughout lending history, results in greater than normal losses.

Because the period and the age of a loan have such a strong effect, lending officers should always work with a specific forecast clearly in mind of the next several years' property market. Trends of the recent past cannot simply be projected for the future. Current experience must be tempered by a recognition of the likelihood that overbuilding will occur. Furthermore, because young loans are so much more dangerous, the reserves held behind an unseasoned portfolio must be much higher than those against mortgages five years of age or older.

## Mortgage Terms

Mortgage terms significantly influence risk because they determine the purchaser's equity and the relationship between the loan and the property value. The lender wants borrowers with sufficient equity either to make it worth their while to continue to meet the payments or to permit the property to be sold for more than the outstanding loan. If equity is negative or close to zero, the borrower may not go to the trouble and expense of trying to sell the property. The owners may also milk the property, making minimal or no payments while gathering income or occupying the unit.

The lender's risk may rise because of the borrower's low original down payment, because of physical depreciation or obsolescence, or because a fall in the price level causes the property's value to decline faster than the rate of amortization of the loan.

Previous studies show that foreclosures and losses do rise as down payments fall. They also demonstrate that the lender is not protected purely by his own loan-to-value ratio. A low down payment resulting from a junior mortgage increases considerably the risk of loss to the holder of a first mortgage, even though the value of his loan is far below the initial selling price.

There is evidence of greater losses due to longer amortization periods, but probably a threshold exists before which length makes little difference. It may be that any length of 20 years or less has little influence on risk. Loans encounter their greatest danger in their first few years. During this period, no type of amortization arrangement may give adequate protection to basically poor loans. But if a loan survives the first danger period, its risks will be reduced the faster the owner's equity rises.

### Interest Rates

The contract interest rate carried by a mortgage affects its risk in two ways.

First, it might be thought that at higher interest rates, borrowers would have more trouble meeting payments, and therefore risks would be higher. While this is true if rates are very high, it appears not to be so in the range of normal rates. Probably lenders adjust the amount loaned the borrowers so that even with higher interest payments are not too high. In fact, foreclosures seem to become higher as the interest rate becomes lower. This higher foreclosure rate probably reflects, for reasons made obvious in the following pages, the fact that lenders are less willing to grant extensions and other aids when there is a considerable gap between the contract interest rate and rates current in the market.

A second risk related to interest rates is that the market value of the mortgage will fall if current interest rates exceed the contract rate. This risk arises from the familiar fact that no lender will pay par for a loan carrying a contract rate below that prevailing in the market. Thus a loan made at 4¾ per cent which the lender cannot renegotiate will, depending on its length, sell at 90 or less if the current market interest rate goes to 5¾ per cent.

Such changes in the market values of mortgages are reflected in the constantly shifting discounts on older FHA or VA mortgages. Thus in 1957, VA and FHA 4½ per cent mortgages sold as low as 87 in the market.

Since borrowers normally have rights to repay loans (although frequently with a penalty) but lenders cannot change the terms, the lower the contract interest rate, the greater the risk to the lender.

**Type of Loan**

Many real property loans are a far cry from the traditional amortized regular-payment mortgages on completed buildings. Lenders make loans for the development of raw land. They furnish construction money. Some engage in warehousing of portfolios for other lenders. Junior liens are still exceedingly common even though usually avoided by financial intermediaries. Some properties are sold on contracts of sale.

In each of these cases, potential dangers rise rapidly. Although risks may be somewhat controlled by proper lending techniques and safeguards, they are likely to be high. The promised payments and face yields tend to be high also. The mortgage officer must carefully judge this relationship between risk and return in order to make logical decisions.

## CHARACTERISTICS OF BORROWERS

Mortgage experience based upon the characteristics of the borrower differ sharply depending on whether the conditions considered are those at the time of the loan or at foreclosure. Many defaults occur because of family problems. Except for those which may be guarded against by better underwriting at the time the loan is made, they must be thought of as random risks. Allowances must be made for them, but they cannot be avoided.

## Ownership and Occupancy

Significant differences exist between risks on owner-occupied properties and those held for income purposes. The likelihood of a loss on an owner-occupied unit is tied more closely to the borrower than to the property.

With an owner-occupier, personal income and assets play a significant role in determining losses. As long as they are adequate, the property is not likely to be tested as to market value. Normally, a stable person who is a good credit risk and meets with no misfortune will not stop payments on his own home even if the value of his equity becomes negative for short periods. When he runs into temporary difficulties, payments may continue if he has assets to draw upon.

This situation holds for income properties only when the debt service on a property is a minor share of the borrower's total income. For example, with plants, stores, and similar units where a fiscally sound corporation is on the note or the lease, debts will continue to be paid even if the particular location does not live up to expectations. Consequently, much risk evaluation of income properties such as shopping centers and office buildings has been primarily based on the financial statement of the lessor rather than on an adequate income analysis of the property. Lenders have tried to assure repayment by insisting that good names be on sufficient leases to carry the financing.

On the other hand, properties such as apartment houses, small shopping centers, and individual stores are normally not in a position where leases can carry the loan. They are frequently owned by real estate corporations whose only asset is the property under loan. Each property must stand on its own feet. If the income does not meet the financial costs, foreclosure or voluntary transfer of the property to the lender is inevitable.

Clearly the risks involved in loans on this latter type of property are considerably greater than in the former cases.

### Income of Borrower

The income of the owner-occupier is the most important single factor determining whether or not foreclosure takes place. About 40 per cent or more of foreclosures occur because the owner's income has fallen. Some differences can be predicted at the time the loan is made. Risks are higher for lower-income families, for those who assume a higher than normal ratio of housing expense to income, and for those who have jobs or businesses less stable than the average.

The record indicates that some sharp falls in income must be considered as random or normal risks. Every family has some likelihood of experiencing an income drop. On the other hand, certain occupations, such as self-employed businessmen and manual workers, have above normal instability. Since unemployment and business losses are the two largest causes of foreclosures, in these cases the risks of loss must be greater.

Some families are poor credit risks for other reasons which can be ascertained through careful investigation. A family may make a habit of overextending itself. Even if a family has not overextended itself in the past, the risk will be increased if the mortgage loan raises its required payments too high. The ratio of expense to income is important. It becomes even more significant when future expenses are poorly forecast. Rising taxes, high maintenance on older houses, and unexpected repairs on new units all raise the expense-income ratio and frequently bring about higher foreclosure rates.

### Change in Borrowers' Characteristics

Next to income, the most significant causes of losses are other changes in the personal situation of borrowers. Marital difficulty is most common. Since average risks vary with age and number of years married, some predictions are possible in this sphere. On the whole, however, divorce, as well as death and illness, which also lead to losses, should probably be considered as a random risk.

Housing mobility is another factor leading to losses. A man may be transferred, or he may sell his house with its existing loan because of a desire for new quarters. Both situations cause the risk of loss to rise. Some judgment as to stability of job or location when the loan is under consideration will help to reduce losses.

## PROPERTY CHARACTERISTICS

Types of property and related characteristics are the final major factors influencing risks in loans. Again, differences in losses are very high. As reported by Morton, Lintner, and the FHA, losses on some types of property run six or eight times as high as losses on others.

### Type

We have already noted that form of ownership, which is closely related to type of property, is a factor that causes differential risks. In addition, fluctuations in the market for certain properties tend to be much greater than for others. Overbuilding, undue optimism, and lack of careful controls are all far more common in connection with income properties than with individual homes.

As an example, for the years 1950 to 1960 the FHA foreclosure or default termination rate for apartment houses ran more than ten times as high as that for single-family homes. Some of this poor experience was due to special programs; but differences of such magnitude were not unexpected.

With losses on single-family houses measured as 1, Lintner showed losses on stores and office buildings of 2.25, on apartment houses of 3.25, and on garages of 5.50. Morton, using the various National Bureau studies, shows that for the years 1920 to 1947 losses on all other properties than one to four-family homes were about 50 to 100 per cent higher than losses on these homes.

These data indicate that the lending officer probably ought to multiply whatever risk factor he applies to single-family houses by 2 or 3 in calculating expected yields on income properties. The specific amount will, of course, vary greatly with ownership, location, and similar characteristics.

**Price and Design**

Risks related to the price of a house or other property are not well defined. They rise rapidly if an error occurs in appraising the true value. Market price, if not based on an efficient, knowledgeable, well-operating market, may diverge sharply from the true market value. If such gaps are not caught in the appraisal process, the loan may be based on an inflated price, and the dangers of loss are multiplied.

The evidence does not make clear whether houses found at the bottom or at the top of the real price range are more risky securities. It is possible that the conditions which apply in a depression may be reversed under normal circumstances.

In a depression, the ease of selling houses and their percentage decrease in value seem negatively correlated with their price. The higher the initial selling price, the greater the relative fall in the value of a house, and vice versa. All markets lose in value, but high-priced units are hurt relatively more. Expensive houses lose most of their potential market as families move down in income. On the other hand, because in a depression a higher percentage of families are at lower incomes, the market for inexpensive houses may improve relatively. The middle market remains unchanged in size, as losses of families to the lower-income groups are made up by those moving down from above.

In normal times with expanding incomes, in contrast, the lowest-priced houses seem to carry the greatest dangers. Low prices and poor quality often go hand in hand. If incomes or tastes rise, cheap houses of inferior quality are harder to sell.

Losses are more probable also if the design is substandard. By design is meant the physical characteristics, livability, visual appeal, continuing usefulness for the particular functions of a property, and ease of maintenance. Properties that fail to compete with buildings erected later often experience defaults on their loans. Good design determines whether or not values can be maintained.

The quality of construction is significant. Buildings that have been skimped on with respect to structural features can compete only when they are new and in tight markets. In competitive situations, their values fall. Physical characteristics also determine future operating and maintenance costs. Rising operating costs have been a serious cause of foreclosures, as homeowners find that they have insufficient income to meet the new expenses or that the net yield of income properties is eaten into by maintenance and repairs.

## Age and Location

There is little evidence that risks vary with age of property. There is, however, an indication that mortgages on new homes in tracts are riskier than individual mortgages, whether on new or older units. This is partly because new areas tend to be unstable, with a fairly high initial turnover. Any errors that have crept into the design or construction will make it hard to resell those units which can be expected to reappear fairly rapidly on the market.

It is also highly probable that the processing of individual borrowers in a tract will be less rigorous than in the case of individual loans. The prospective borrower has the strong support of the builder in qualifying for a loan. This support may take the form of advice on how to qualify, pressure on the lending officer, or outright chicanery. Whichever applies, mass sales and processing of loans increase the lender's danger.

Location may refer either to the geographical area—the city, suburb, metropolitan area, state, or similar unit—or to the particular site within the general area.

The geographical area is important because as the economy develops, some areas are passed by. They may decline sharply while others grow at a rate far above average. Loans in expanding areas will be more secure. Losses in a declining area may be heavy. In addition to growth, differences in taxes and foreclosure procedures and costs may have a significant impact on risks.

Some evidence of relative geographical risks can be gained from VA and FHA experience. The VA showed for 1961 several field stations with no claims. In contrast, the rate in San Antonio was 0.9 per cent of loans outstanding, and in Wichita it was over 2.7 per cent. The variance was so large that the cities at the third quartile had claim rates more than three times as high as those at the first.

The FHA experience by states indicates similar important geographical differences. For 1935 to 1961, the foreclosure rate of all home loans insured ranged from 0.04 per cent for Hawaii and 0.18 for Montana to 5.79 for South Carolina and 5.89 for Alaska. On December 31, 1961, the default percentage ranged from 0.20 for Hawaii and 0.33 for South Dakota to 2.97 for Vermont and 3.10 for Florida.

These very marked differences obviously reflect varying growth rates and basic foreclosure conditions. However, they are also an important indication of errors in market judgment on the part of both developers and lenders. Florida was an extremely rapid-growth area that was overlent and overbuilt at the end of 1961.

Specific location of individual sites introduces probably the most important single risk for loans on commercial or income properties. The amount available to meet the mortgage payment depends completely on how the building's market develops.

For residential property, long lists exist of specific location factors that significantly influence consumer's decisions. These include the general attractiveness of the site, location with respect to public services, transportation, general tax rates, school systems, and status in general. As these factors vary, the amount of risk shifts.

## LENDING PROCEDURES AND PROCESSING OF LOANS

Recognition of the problem areas in individual loans is only the start of a program to control risks. In order to make use of this knowledge, each firm must work out sound lending criteria and a careful control of the entire loan process. Firms find many advantages in establishing well-planned standard operating procedures. Managements need sufficient information to determine whether a loan should be made. The decision must be based on the legality of the proposed loan, knowledge of its inherent risks, and its expected net yield.

Formal procedures ensure the inclusion of all necessary information. They establish individual responsibilty. The reasons a particular loan was granted can be found in a single place. Weak loans that have not lived up to expectations may be reevaluated to see why they went wrong and what lessons might be learned for the future.

What are the ingredients in a well-operating standard procedure? First comes a set of standard forms used throughout the organization. They include forms for loan applications, for interviews, for appraisal reports, for credit reporting, for the final risk evaluation, for the loan recommendation, and for the loan approval.

The forms are accompanied by either verbal or written instructions to make certain that all are dealt with properly. Depending on the size of the organization, step-by-step processing will occur under either formal or informal procedures. Finally the procedures include the bases to be used for the lending decision and a technique for future reevaluations.

While many lenders have utilized primarily informal procedures in the past, such techniques are rapidly going out of use. Because of their many advantages, formal written procedures are taking their place. In the first place, they ensure that no important steps are left out of the lending process. Second, fixed routines tend to limit personal variations and ensure more complete agreement with the over-all organizational goals. While many loans may still be exceptions to general policies, formal procedures make more certain that logic and sure reasoning will be applied in the granting of the variances; they are less likely to result from mere whims. Finally the recording of the facts and reasoning behind the loans makes possible the process of reevaluation. In attempting to find what went wrong in the initial analysis of a poor loan, it is very frustrating to encounter only a simple notation of "granted" in the file.

Not as common as standard procedures but spreading rapidly are written risk-rating systems. Such systems tend to follow the basic technique worked out by the FHA. These methods go beyond the mere determination of whether or not a loan should be made. They assign each mortgage a numerical rating and measure the relative risk which it appears to contain. By assigning specific values to individual parts of the mortgage evaluation process, it becomes feasible to modify and strengthen the pattern at its weakest points. It becomes possible to negotiate with the prospective borrower in order to bring particular conditions up to a necessary minimum.

Where the loan is being made for nonmonetary reasons such as customer or public relations, a listing of possible risks shows what if anything is being sacrificed for this purpose.

Finally the rating systems allow a specific estimate of the potential risks, the reserves necessary to cover them, and the anticipated net yield from the mortgage. The assignment of numbers improves the judgment necessary both for determining whether to make a loan and for the management of the total portfolio.

However handled, the lending procedure must weigh the factors which influence the loan's risk, including the characteristics of the borrower, of the loan, and of the property itself.

The borrower's characteristics and the mortgage pattern influence the likelihood of prompt payments. Will the borrower want to meet his obligations, and will he be able to do so? The answers depend on the borrower's credit responsibility, on his future income and expenses, and on his other assets. These must be related to the amount of the loan and its repayment requirements.

The real estate offered as security becomes important only when the borrower fails to pay. Then the question arises whether the price of the property will suffice to discharge the outstanding obligation of the borrower to the mortgagee.

## THE LOAN APPLICATION

The loan application and the borrower's interview supplement each other. They serve (1) to welcome the prospective borrower, (2) to aid him in making his financial decisions, (3) to obtain a preliminary offer to borrow subject to further negotiations, (4) to obtain part of the information necessary for evaluating the loan and servicing it if granted, (5) to inform prospective borrowers of lending and servicing procedures, and (6) to screen out unlikely applicants in order to save unnecessary efforts.

Figure 7-2 is a typical application form for a loan on a residential property. A form for income property would ask for the same basic type of information but would differ considerably in detail.

The application starts with a statement of the amount of loan requested and the proposed terms of repayment. The application

FIGURE 7-2   *Loan Application Form*

## APPLICATION FOR RESIDENTIAL LOAN

Application is hereby made for a loan described below as to amount and terms, to be amortized by the payment of equal ☐ monthly; ☐ quarterly; ☐ semi-annual installments for principal and interest.

| Total Amount of Loan | Rate of Interest | Number of Years | Payment for Principal and Interest | Estimated Payment for Taxes and Hazard Insurance Premiums | Total Payment |
|---|---|---|---|---|---|
| $ | % | | $ | $ | $ |

Prepayment Privilege:

The mortgage (will) (will not) provide for escrow payments for taxes and insurance
Source of Equity
Details of secondary financing:
Purpose of loan:
The loan will be secured by a first mortgage or deed of trust upon real property located at:

(Street Address)          (City)          (P. O. Zone)   (County)          (State)
Legal Description:

Property Description:

Lot Size:

| | Cost | Date | Mtge. | Present Balance | Name of Holder | Interest | Payments |
|---|---|---|---|---|---|---|---|
| Land | $ | | 1st | $ | | % | $ |
| Building | $ | | 2nd | $ | | % | $ |
| Total | $ | | Estimated Annual Taxes: | | Applicant (will) (will not) occupy property. | | |

Improvements made since Purchase:

Special Judgments or Assessments:

Applicant                              Age      Spouse                                      Age
Ages of dependents
Applicant's Address
Applicant's Phone Numbers:  Home                          Business

| SOURCE OF ANNUAL INCOME | | PERSONAL INFORMATION |
|---|---|---|
| Base salary | $ | Occupation or Type of Business |
| Overtime wages | $ | |
| Bonus and commissions | $ | Employer |
| Dividends and interest income | $ | Address |
| Real Estate Income (Net) | $ | Position held                No. of years |
| Wife's income | $ | Partner or officer in any other venture or other employment |
| Other income—itemize | $ | |
| | | Previous Employer |
| | | Address |
| TOTAL | $ | Position held                No. of years |
| CONTINGENT LIABILITIES | | WIFE'S EMPLOYMENT |
| As Endorser or Co-maker on Notes | $ | Employer |
| Alimony payments (Annual) | $ | Address |
| Are you defendant in any legal action? | | |
| Have you ever taken bankruptcy? | | Position held                No. of years |

I (We) agree to pay all expenses incident to appraisal, credit investigation, photographs, title work, closing fees, attorney fees, survey, and any other necessary closing expense.

In the event I (We) do not close this loan, I (We) will pay _____ a fee of _____

I (We) agree to furnish through _____ agent, fire insurance with extended coverage for at least $_____

I hereby certify that the information contained in this application is true and complete to the best of my knowledge and belief.

Signed_____

Date_____          Signed_____

FIGURE 7-2 *(Continued)*

| ASSETS | | | | LIABILITIES | |
|---|---|---|---|---|---|
| Cash (Show Bank) | $ | | | Notes payable: (Show Payee) | |
| | | | | To | $ |
| Earnest Money Deposited | | | | To | |
| Investments: Bonds and Stocks —see schedule | | | | To | |
| Investment in own Business | | | | Installment Accounts Payable Automobile: Monthly ($ ) | |
| Accounts and Notes Receivable | | | | Other: Monthly ($ ) | |
| Real Estate owned—see schedule | | | | Other Accounts Payable | |
| Auto: Year Make | | | | Mortgages payable on Real Estate—see schedule | |
| Personal property and Furniture | | | | Unpaid Real Estate Taxes | |
| Life Insurance ($ ) Cash Surrender Value | | | | Unpaid Income Taxes | |
| | | | | Chattel Mortgages | |
| Other Assets—itemize | | | | Loans on Life Insurance Policies (Include Premium Advances) | |
| | | | | Other debts—itemize | |
| | | | | Total Liabilities | |
| | | | | Net Worth | |
| Total Assets | $ | | | Total Liabilities and Net Worth | $ |

## COMPLETE THE FOLLOWING SCHEDULES IN DETAIL

### SCHEDULE OF BONDS AND STOCKS

| AMOUNT OR NO. SHARES | DESCRIPTION *(Extend Valuation in Proper Column)* → | MARKETABLE ACTUAL MARKET VALUE | NON-MARKETABLE (UNLISTED SECURITIES) |
|---|---|---|---|
| | | | |
| | | | |
| | | | |
| | | | |

### SCHEDULE OF REAL ESTATE

| DESCRIPTION AND LOCATION | ACTUAL MARKET VALUE | MORTGAGE AMOUNT | MATURITY DATE |
|---|---|---|---|
| | | | |
| | | | |

*Indicates sold and awaiting closing

### SCHEDULE OF NOTES PAYABLE

*Specify any assets pledged as collateral, indicating the liabilities which they secure:*

| TO WHOM PAYABLE | DATE | AMOUNT | DUE | INTEREST | ASSETS PLEDGED AS SECURITY |
|---|---|---|---|---|---|
| | | | | | |
| | | | | | |

### SCHEDULE OF INSTALLMENT ACCOUNTS

| PROPERTY PURCHASED | AMOUNT OWED | MONTHLY PAYMENT |
|---|---|---|
| | | |
| | | |

### ADDITIONAL COMMENTS

Form No. 202A Mortgage Bankers Association of America, 111 West Washington Street, Chicago 2, Illinois is a preliminary offer of a contract by the prospective borrower. As in many real estate transactions, it may be accepted, rejected, or met by a counter-offer from the lender. Final terms may require substantial negotiations.

The second section of the application contains information on the real property which will form the security for the loan. First comes a legal description of the land. For a house the description is fairly compact, being concerned mainly with location, price, size, year built, and structural characteristics.

For an income property far more facts must be demanded. Because their importance is greater, locational factors need expansion. The description of the improvements must also be in greater detail. Financial and operating statements are needed so that the ability of the property to earn the required payments can be calculated. Other important facts may be attached, such as a list of leases showing terms and tenants.

As an example of how extensive the required information may be, the following list of exhibits was attached to a recent application for a mortgage to be insured by the FHA on a proposed apartment house. The total presentation was 55 pages in length.

### List of Exhibits

1. Aerial view of site.
2. Aerial view of site with improvements superimposed thereon.
3. Picture of model with outline of Phase I and project description.
4. Phase I plot plan and list of proposed improvements.
5. Designation of three phases and prorated land price.
6. Legal description of Phase I.
7. Outline of conveyancing transactions with chart.
8. Land disposition agreement.
9. Financial statements.
10. Construction contract and cost estimates.
11. Request for determination of prevailing wages.
12. Utilities expense, letter from engineering consultants.
13. Elevator maintenance expense.
14. Refuse-removal expense.

15. Operating payroll and table-of-organization chart.
16. Decorating and repair maintenance expense.
17. Detail of annual insurance expense.
18. Replacement-reserve computation.
19. Rental schedule.
20. Income from commercial shops.
21. Laundry-concession income.
22. Computation of estimated real property taxes.
23. Statistical data sheet.
24. Landscape budget.
25. Art costs with competition announcement.
26. Consultants, fees, permits, testing and inspection costs.
27. Insurance during construction.
28. Builder's general overhead.
29. Architect fees.
30. Legal and organization costs.
31. Area map listing schools and churches.
32. City zoning map.

The final section of the application contains information about the borrower. Included are statements concerning family status, employment, previous employment, and assets and liabilities. For an income property, the form requests information about both the corporation making the application—balance sheets, etc.—and its principal owners. Applications must be signed and the credit and other information contained therein certified as true.

The completed application form containing the basic information needed by the lender will be checked and supplemented by credit and appraisal reports. However, it is important because it contains the applicant's personal statements as to what loan he wants and his certification as to his own credit worthiness and the condition of the physical security.

**The Loan Interview**

Interviews may occur before or after receipt of the loan application. Many people shop for loans from several sources. They must be treated courteously. Frequently, however, no formal application follows. In other cases, the preliminary interview makes it clear that the applicant will not qualify for a loan. Such clients should be discouraged as soon as possible from making a formal application.

The interview is extremely important in the lending process. Its nature will depend on the size of the firm and its type of operations. Usually loan officers with the responsibility of analyzing the loan and recommending on it also handle the interviews. They may specialize by type of loan or deal with all sorts. The larger the amount or complexity of the loan, the higher in the organization's structure will the interview and final negotiations take place. As the complexity of the loan application and its attachments increases (for example, when a loan on a new shopping center is being proposed, rather than a single-house loan on an existing structure), so does the necessary skill and training of the interviewer.

The interviewer is a salesperson, a public relations man, and a lending analyst. He must obtain from the client information many people consider confidential without causing him to feel insulted or hurt. The interview serves as a screening device to avoid unnecessary paper work. Acceptance of applications for loans sure to be refused causes wasted effort and ill will. On the other hand, the unsatisfactory prospective borrower must be turned away without losing his respect or friendship.

The interviewer can serve as a valuable source of education for the borrower. In explaining the logic behind the information required on the application, he can aid the prospective borrower in making a proper decision as to what financial obligations to incur. Frequently families fall in love with a house and attempt to borrow far more than they can repay. The interviewer must explain why everyone will be better off if this is not done.

The interviewer can also ease future servicing of the loan. He can explain the firm's procedures. He can stress the need for promptness while pointing out that the borrower should take the initiative and seek out the lender if any problems develop. If the borrower knows what he is expected to do and why, future relations will be more cordial.

All these other duties, however, merely supplement the

interviewer's main function of obtaining as much information as he possibly can in order to judge the prospective borrower's credit worthiness. The loan officer must gather from the applicant all the specific details necessary for a proper evaluation. Part of this information is furnished on the application form. However, the information which the interviewer gathers from informal discussion and the give-and-take of questions and answers may be still more significant.

Loan repayments depend partly on the borrower's desires, partly on the likelihood of his income's continuing, and partly on family relations. Since judgment of these factors tends to be subjective, evaluation of the same data by different interviewers may vary greatly. The skilled loan officer has the best judgment in these spheres.

The interviewer must also be a negotiator. He must recognize during the discussion what prospective terms are likely to be unsatisfactory and where changes might be made to minimize future risk. In the interview process, he can probe to find whether the borrower is willing to make changes in critical items and can do so. It is frequently much easier to negotiate differences before they are put down in black and white.

When the conference is finished, the loan application and the interviewer's notes should contain the information necessary for the further processing of the loan. Unsatisfactory requests should have been withdrawn. At the end of the interview, the loan officer should be able to indicate whether a loan will probably be granted, but he must also be careful to point out that he does not have the final responsibility. Additional information will be obtained from the credit and appraisal reports. The loan committee will base its decision partly on the interview and partly on added facts but also on the firm's portfolio position.

## SUMMARY

This chapter considered some of the major factors which cause mortgages to go bad. Loans differ in their own characteristics, in those of the borrowers, and in the underlying security. The degree to which these individual features vary from the norm may increase the potential risk of any loan five- to tenfold. Particularly important in causing differential losses are the timing of the loan, the type of property, and its location.

Knowledge of potential dangers may not be useful unless lenders adopt specific procedures to make certain that their lending process gathers and uses the necessary information about individual applications. The loan application and interview and their processing form the key to a successful information system. When properly used, these forms save lenders time and effort and give them the necessary data to use in their risk evaluations.

## SELECTED REFERENCES

Bryant, Willis R.: *Mortgage Lending,* 2d ed., McGraw-Hill Book Company, New York, 1962.

Fisher, E. M., and C. Rapkin: *The Mutual Mortgage Insurance Fund,* Columbia University Press, New York, 1954.

Lintner, J.: *Mutual Savings Banks,* Harvard Business School, Boston, 1948.

McMichael, S. L., and P. T. O'Keefe: *How to Finance Real Estate,* 2d ed., Prentice-Hall, Inc., Englewood Cliffs, N.J., 1953.

Morton, J. E.: *Urban Mortgage Lending,* Princeton University Press, Princeton, N.J., 1956.

U.S. Federal Housing Administration: *FHA Experience with Mortgage Foreclosures and Property Acquisition,* Government Printing Office, Washington, 1963.

U.S. Housing and Home Finance Agency: *Mortgage Foreclosures in Six Metropolitan Areas,* Washington, 1964.

U.S. Veterans Administration: *Reports of Loan Service and Claims Study,* Washington, 1964.

# Evaluating the Individual Risk_____8

It is not sufficient for a firm to know the basic causes of bad loans and to have established procedures for obtaining necessary information on each application. There must be a specific analysis of each potential loan to evaluate its good and bad features. The characteristics of the borrower and the property must be checked against the known factors which affect risks. There must be an over-all estimate of the entire loan. Will the promised gross yield be earned? Is it high enough to offset the potential risks, so that a satisfactory net yield will result?

The measurement of the individual risk is also significant for the borrower. He frequently welcomes advice from the lender who may, from his broader experience, recognize that certain features of the loan may cause all parties to the proposal to run undue risks.

## BORROWER CHARACTERISTICS

The analysis of borrowers' characteristics attempts to estimate and control the possibility that the mortgagor will fail to fulfill his loan contract. The lender aims to choose borrowers who have the ability and the desire to protect their ownership. The evaluation must consider both intangible and tangible factors. Is the borrower a man of character? How does he view his responsibility as a signer of a note? Other influences will include his motivation, his family life, health, and future prospects, in addition to such specific factors as his income, assets, and liabilities.

The weight given these various factors can be determined either informally, through a credit-analysis check sheet, or more precisely through a rating system such as that of the FHA, shown in Figure 8-1. In any case, the analysis must show that the borrower's income and net assets are adequate to meet the contemplated loan, that

FIGURE 8-1  *FHA Mortgagor Rating Grid*

| Mortgagor features | Reject | 1 | 2 | 3 | 4 | 5 | Rating |
|---|---|---|---|---|---|---|---|
| Credit characteristics of mortgagor | | | 4 | 8 | 12 | 16 | 20 |
| Motivating interest in ownership of the property | | | 2 | 4 | 6 | 8 | 10 |
| Importance of monetary interest to mortgagor | | | 4 | 8 | 12 | 16 | 20 |
| Adequacy of available assets for transaction | | | 2 | 4 | 6 | 8 | 10 |
| Stability of effective income | | | 4 | 8 | 12 | 16 | 20 |
| Adequacy of effective income for total obligations | | | 4 | 8 | 12 | 16 | 20 |

SOURCE: Federal Housing Administration, *Underwriting Manual.*

his prospects are favorable, and that his motivation and character indicate he will continue to meet his obligations.

The facts on the loan application regarding income, employment, and balance sheet are basic sources of data. They are checked by the judgment of the interviewer and by the character and financial facts shown on a credit report. Each supplements the other. The skilled interviewer verifies the application and elicits additional consequential facts.

Credit reports, usually obtained from organized credit agencies, record the amount of credit previously obtained by borrowers and the promptness of payment. They also reveal significant factors such as reputation, mobility, assets, and any litigation, unpaid claims, or bankruptcy.

### The Rating Grid

The diverse pieces of credit information are gathered into one place and weighed by means of the rating grid. Figure 8-1 shows a grid issued by the FHA. Similar grids have been developed by the American Institute of Banking and by individual lenders. Such grids ensure greater uniformity throughout the organization. They supplement but do not replace the skill and judgment needed in interviewing and analysis.

The idea of the grid is simple. The analyst judges each credit feature separately and forms an opinion concerning the item's quality, deficiencies, and risks. If any single characteristic is not acceptable, the loan will be rejected.

Experience shows, furthermore, that defaults are likely to arise from a combination of comparatively weak elements. The larger the number of vulnerable features, the more likely a default. Even if no single factor is obviously bad but the factors combined indicate that the mortgagee's ability or willingness to pay is suspect, the loan should be denied. For example, if the total rating is less than 50 in the grid in Figure 8-1, the mortgage should be disapproved. This means the borrower must have average ratings between columns 2 and 3. Weakness in several areas will cause a rejection.

### Credit Characteristics of Mortgagor

The first factors rated are basic attitudes of the borrower such as honesty, integrity, and judgment. If any are unsuitable, the probability of default is high.

The borrower's past-payment record is assumed to measure his character and attitude toward debts. If credit reports show a long record of delinquencies or slow pays, the chances are high that the mortgage loan will be treated in a similar fashion.

Studies of defaulted loans have shown that divorce and broken homes are a significant cause of foreclosures. Risks of divorce are high for newlyweds who are very young. The mortgagor with an established family is a better risk than the single person. Finally the analyst should consider the borrower's past history in financial management. Serious past errors in judgment, whether in business or in contracting personal debts, raise questions of ability, whereas a successful record of personal saving with growing assets evidences the probability of continued success. This is true even if the assets are drawn down for the house purchase and therefore are not available for offsetting risks in and of themselves

### Motivation and Adequacy of Available Assets

The next three items on the grid measure different types of motivation. A borrower is assumed to be more highly motivated to continue payments if a loan is on his permanent home bought willingly in a normal market. Those buying for future sale, to save rent in a tight market, or for part-time use show a greater tendency to default.

The owner's equity is also important. Those desiring a loan for refinancing purposes in order to remove part of their accumulated equity in a property are looked upon with more suspicion than are new buyers. In addition, the higher the owner's equity, the greater his motivation to meet his mortgage payments. Conversely, low down payments and junior liens lead more rapidly to foreclosures. The FHA insists that the purchaser of a house must have sufficient assets over and above the loan to handle all required payments to close the transaction. If the buyer must borrow additional sums by a note or second mortgage, the FHA rejects the proposed loan.

### Stability of Effective Income

The fifth criterion concerns length of present employment, type of job, and sources of secondary income. The longer a man has been employed in a stable industry, the greater are the chances that his income will continue. For men with a history of job mobility, frequent unemployment, or seasonal or unskilled work, there is increased danger of future income losses.

Secondary income, if derived from a wife's or children's employment or from moonlighting, is also likely to be unstable. Wives become pregnant. Second jobs held for long periods become tiresome. Children marry and move away. If the mortgage payment requires the additional income from any such source, trouble is likely to result. Secondary income is, however, a valid source for clearing up other outstanding obligations, such as auto or furniture installment payments. With such money available, the danger of defaulting on these short-run debts is much less.

### Adequacy of Income

The FHA has collected a large amount of data showing the general relationships between income and housing expense for most families. Such relationships differ widely among local areas depending on custom, land prices, heat, water bills, etc., While for any lender the income-expense ratio must be based on local experience, Figure 8-2 shows what these data look like on an over-all basis and depicts a typical pattern.

The figure and all local studies illustrate a common phenomenon that has been known for 100 years as Schwabe's law. It has been proved valid over and over again. As incomes rise, the amount spent on housing increases, but the per cent of income used for housing falls. This law, which has no legal or moral implications, has been found valid by empirical lending experience.

The widths of the bands reflect the variations in ratios among individual families. The amounts spent differ because of tastes and local costs. People with incomes of $500 a month spend anywhere from $80 to $125 a month on housing. Ten per cent of households spend even more. The FHA suggests that those whose ratios are similar to the top curve be checked in the first column on the grid and that those near the bottom be given the full 20 points of column 5. Thus a high ratio is a signal of weakness, even though it may not require rejection.

For those whose ratios are above the curve, a special check is necessary. People with high incomes have a greater ability to rise above the norms and allocate more to housing if they so desire.

FIGURE 8-2  *Prospective Housing Expense Related to Income*

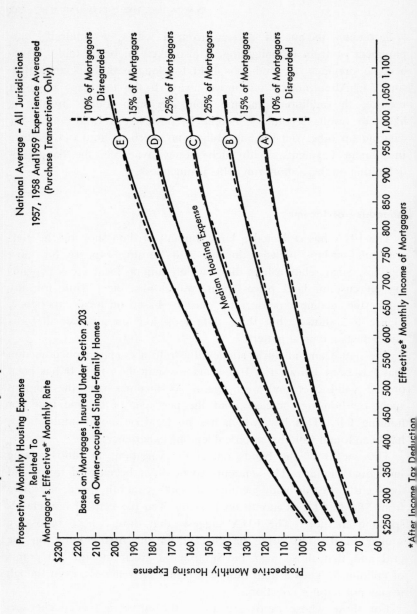

The fact that most high-income families show lower ratios is a question of taste, not necessity. Moreover, peoples' spending on housing is a good measure of their future ability to meet payments. The critical fact is that when the ratios get too high, families can no longer meet their loan payments by cutting other items from the budget. The sacrifice in terms of other goods may not be considered worthwhile, and they will give up the house.

Families may also fail to meet mortgage payments if their total fixed obligations are too high. Other payment requirements need to be considered. High installment payments, costs of college education, or medical fees endanger the mortgage.

## THE PROPERTY AND ITS APPRAISAL

For several reasons the real property underlying the mortgage loan constitutes a basic source of its security. In the first place, if the value of the property exceeds the loan balance, the borrower will want to retain ownership. Even when he cannot maintain payments, he will take the responsibility of selling the property or transferring ownership. The lender will be saved much turmoil and extra expense. Second, if payments are not made, the property's value will determine what can be obtained when it is sold after foreclosure. If the property is worth enough, the lender will suffer no loss.

Appraisal is the process of estimating the current value of the property. This estimate is the start of a calculation through which the lender can predict his risk. He can ascertain the current relationship of the proposed loan to the property's value and the owner's equity. Such an appraisal is important legally. Almost all fiduciary institutions are restricted by law and regulation to loans of no more than a certain per cent of value. If the appraisal is perfunctory or inaccurate, the lender may violate the law.

The risk of future loss depends not only on the current relationship of the debt to the property's value but also on future relationships. The lender must be concerned with the gap between the outstanding loan and the property's value during the entire period that the loan is outstanding. This gap will widen or narrow from its initial amount depending upon whether or not the rate of amortization exceeds the rate of depreciation. The lender must therefore use the appraisal as a basis for estimating the future pattern of depreciation. He must compare the projected amount and timing of losses in value through depreciation with the amortization schedule and the owner's initial equity in order to estimate the minimum equity the owner will hold at any future date.

Because the appraisal process is so central to lending activities, the art of appraising has expanded rapidly in recent years. Several professional societies, journals, and numerous books exist in the field. The literature is large and replete with many arguments concerning meaning of value, purpose of the appraisal, and similar problems. It must be recognized that many of these arguments apply primarily to unusual cases or are essays attempting to improve the knowledge and skills of the individual appraiser.

The sometimes wide discrepancies still existing among individual appraisals of a single property are often a source of concern. These differences arise partly because the act of appraising remains, as must an art, as a skill and partly because appraisers do not agree on what value they are attempting to estimate. Many appraisers feel that when hired by the seller they should arrive at a different estimate of value than when hired by the lender. Many others believe that such ideas of diverse values are wrong. They hold that a single value exists and should be estimated. Each user of this estimate can then adjust it for his own purposes. Since neither point of view is accepted completely, lenders find divergent estimates for the same property. They must be aware of what the appraisal is based on and what information it is attempting to convey in determining their own decision for lending purposes.

The process of appraisal is one of finding, estimating, and collating the particular variables and their influences on the value of a specific property. The FHA lists the following factors which must be analyzed and determined as part of the entire process of valuation analysis:

1. Quality and stability of locations environing a property.
2. Characteristics of the site.
3. Structural, functional, and aesthetic qualities of the building improvements.

4. Rights and utility included in the property.
5. Cost at which equivalent properties may be assembled.
6. Prices at which equivalent properties may be sold and bought.
7. Extent and amount of prospective benefits the property is capable of producing.
8. Price at which ownership of the property is warranted.

The form for such an analysis is shown in Figure 8-3, a typical appraisal form for a single-family house. The report contains an identification of the property, an analysis of its neighborhood, a description of its improvements, and an estimate of its value together with an enumeration of how the estimate was obtained. Appraisal reports for income properties tend to be far more detailed with respect to the market. Of necessity they also show an extensive analysis of the income and expense situation of the property.

**The Location**

Where a property is located plays a significant role in determining its value. Location may refer to the city or town, the neighborhood, or the specific site. Each of these influences the lender's valuation and willingness to grant a mortgage.

Institutions that lend primarily in their own areas are not too concerned with the impact of local growth. On the other hand, national lenders, like those that choose between mortgages and other assets, give careful thought to a city's growth and general stability. Loans on properties in a town dependent on a single industry are inherently more risky. In recent periods, some localities have developed thousands of bad loans due to the shutting down of an airplane plant or other major employer.

Locality analysis attempts to make clear the area's economic base. What types of jobs are available? What industries exist? Which have been growing, which declining? The rating of an area's economy takes into account factors such as population growth or decline, the type and distribution of employment, predictions of future employment, and average income levels. Risks rise with a concentration of employment in single industries, in a combination

FIGURE 8-3 *Property Appraisal Form*

## RESIDENTIAL APPRAISAL REPORT FOR CONVENTIONAL LOANS

Name of applicant

Address of security

                 (street and no.)             (city)             (state)

Legal description

### NEIGHBORHOOD

| Value range $ | to $ | Trend | | Built-up | % |
|---|---|---|---|---|---|
| Typical occupations | | Predominant nationality | | | |
| Quality of maintenance | | Home ownership | % | Vacancy | % |

Adverse physical or social influences or special amenities

### SITE

| Dimensions | x | Grade (slope) | In city limits? |
|---|---|---|---|

Zoning        Police and fire protection

Street improvements (specify type): Roadway      Curb

Sidewalk      Storm sewer      Street lights      Alleys

Utilities: Electricity      Gas      Public water      Sewerage system

Distance to (in blocks or miles): Major business district

Neighborhood shopping      Public transportation

Elementary schools      High schools      Churches

Adverse conditions or special amenities

### IMPROVEMENTS

| Date of erection | | If under construction, percentage completed | % |
|---|---|---|---|
| Construction: Foundation | | Exterior walls | Roofing |
| Gutters | | Other exterior features | |
| Interior: Walls | | Decoration | Floors |
| Windows | | Trim and cabinet work | |
| Number of: Rooms | Bedrooms | Bathrooms | Tile baths |
| Heating: Type and capacity of system | | Fuel | |
| Central air-conditioning | | Ceiling insulation | |
| Wall insulation | | Weatherstripping | |
| Storm sashes or thermopane | | Fireplace | Attic fan |
| Built-in features: Dishwasher | Disposer | Stove | Other |
| Number of porches: Open | Screened | Enclosed | |
| Basement: Full? | Wall construction | Concrete floor? | |
| Any leaks or dampness? | Finish work (describe if any) | | |
| Garage or carport: Type (attached, detached, or built-in) | | No. of cars | |
| Utilities | Construction | Floor | Roof |
| Site improvements: Driveway | Landscaping | Outbuildings | |
| Other (walks, concrete patios, fences, barbecue pits, etc.) | | | |
| Architectural type of home | | No. of units | |
| Conformity with neighborhood | Sales appeal | Desirability of room arrangement | |
| Adequacy of closets, cabinets, and storage | | Modernness of kitchen and bathrooms | |
| Quality of workmanship | Condition of structure | Future economic life | |

What repairs, painting, or termite treatment are required to make property readily salable (if none, so state)? Estimate approximate cost

## FIGURE 8-3   *(Continued)*

Locate lot and show
distance from corners

Sketch of Building Outline
(including exterior dimensions)

N

STREET:
PAVED?

W                E

STREET:
PAVED?

STREET:
PAVED?

STREET:
PAVED?

S

### VALUATION

**REPRODUCTION COST:**

| | | | | | |
|---|---|---|---|---|---|
| Lot | x | @ $ | per | ft. | $ |

Reproduction cost new of
House _____ ft. @ $ _____ per _____ ft. $ _____

Garage _____ ft. @ $ _____ per _____ ft. $ _____

Porch _____ ft. @ $ _____ per _____ ft. $ _____

Other _____ ft. @ $ _____ per _____ ft. $ _____

Extras (if over $500, please detail) _____ $ _____

Cost of improvements _____ $ _____

Total reproduction cost new _____ $ _____

**LESS DEPRECIATION:**

Physical deterioration _____ % _____ $ _____

Functional obsolescence _____ % _____ $ _____

Economic depreciation _____ % _____ $ _____

Total depreciation _____ $ _____

MARKET VALUE AS OF _____ , 19 ____ is ____ $ _____

Estimate of fair monthly rental $ _____

### Additional Comments

I have personally inspected the interior and exterior of the property described above for the purpose of estimating the Market
Value to enable the lender to underwrite the conventional loan applied for on this security. I warrant that the statements made
by me are, to the best of my knowledge and belief, true and correct. I have no interest in the property, nor in the loan applied
for, at present or contemplated.

(Signed) _____

(Appraiser)

Form No. 203 Mortgage Bankers Association of America, 111 West Washington Street, Chicago 2, Illinois of cyclically more volatile industries, or in areas of decline or slow growth.

Within cities, areas also have shifting value patterns. Neighborhoods rise and fall, sometimes to rise again. The likelihood of unsatisfactory change depends upon the design and planning of an area, the type of structure within it, its public image, community facilities and transportation, and the costs of utilities and taxes. All these must be judged in comparison with what is or may become available in competing locations.

For income properties, location becomes the paramount factor. A unit in a declining market will have falling income and will lack ability to meet mortgage payments. In this sphere, the type of locational analysis depends upon the particular kind of property involved. Retail locations compete with each other and with new shopping centers. Office buildings change in desirability and status. Warehouses are influenced by transportation patterns. In each of these cases, the appraiser must select a method of analysis related to the specific problems. The lending officer must check the appraiser's reasoning, holding in mind the history of overoptimism which has occasionally besmirched the past record of appraisals of income property.

Natural physical features, design, and zoning or protective covenants are the chief factors which influence the physical attractiveness of neighborhoods. The higher value of view sites, waterscapes, wooded areas, or similar features is familiar. The opposite impact of flood dangers, airport noises, or slide areas is as obvious. The design of streets, landscaping, and the placement of houses can enhance or detract from the natural values. Neighborhoods of dreary monotony suffer. Inharmonious land uses, such as factories or garages, are a danger. So are large numbers of houses whose design is becoming obsolete. Since loan risks depend upon the development of land uses, zoning and other controls over land use are important.

Values rise when more people want to live in an area. The quality of schools and the area's reputation are critical variables for families. Civic buildings of other types are important for these and other groups. Transportation increasingly means freeways and parking, but other forms still have an impact. The further a house is from transportation, stores, and other facilities, the more time and money must be spent on driving.

Recent studies show high rates of movement, delinquencies, and foreclosures due to unexpected increases in costs of insurance, utilities, and taxes. Many newly created suburban communities find themselves in an intolerable situation because of extreme demands on limited school facilities. Taxes skyrocket; double sessions occur; good teachers leave. Families move out to better districts or have to sell when they find their required tax escrows rising. The wise lender recognizes these dangers. His neighborhood analysis carefully estimates any unusual demands on public facilities.

## The Specific Property

In addition to location, the appraisal identifies the specific property and judges its general attributes and suitability for the purpose for which it is proposed. Even a sound estimate of current value cannot decrease the risk which will arise from a lack of suitability. A property with an old, obsolescent house may have a higher value if the land underlying it is worth most of the price or if there is a restricted market. The loan may be dangerous, however, if the livability of the house does not bring in enough income to cover the necessary loan payments.

The appraisal normally includes an exact description of the physical improvements and the rights included in the property. Only through a complete physical inspection can the required repairs and alterations be determined. Only by an examination of the site and title can other claims against the property be known. Restrictions, easements, and encroachments restrict the normal rights in a property and reduce its value.

The valuation process attempts to assemble all the elements affecting the present and future utility of the property and to judge the amount people are and will be willing to pay for this utility. Estimates of value are based upon three basic types of information. Depending upon the existing data, the appraiser may primarily use one of three approaches—the market data, or comparison approach, the replacement-cost approach, or the income-capitalization approach. He will usually place most reliance upon the particular approach which has the best available data for his needs. If he has adequate comparisons, most of his estimates will be based upon market information. He will use the other approaches to check his conclusions and in certain cases to get outside limits.

1. The market data, or comparison, method bases its estimate of value on recent actual purchase prices and on the current offers and asking prices for comparable properties. The problem of finding recent equivalent prices may be great. Adjustments frequently have to be made to allow for time variations and for the inclusion or exclusion of specific factors such as size, style, and location.

A series of actual prices is a quite firm base for value even though it is no guarantee of the future. However, in either highly exhilarated or depressed markets, the going price may differ from value. Allowances must also be made for special influences on the buyer and seller, such as motivation, market knowledge, and skills. Not every sale meets the value criteria of knowledgeable buyers and sellers entering freely into contracts with no duress.

2. The replacement-cost approach is particularly suitable for new buildings. It operates on the theory that no buyer should pay more than the current cost of a substitute property. Actual replacement costs of a new structure are calculated. Numerous methods exist of calculating such costs, ranging from a detailed analysis of the specific proposed construction to procedures based on much looser techniques, such as average costs per square or cubic foot. To the replacement cost must be added the market value of the site and other costs engendered in the construction and property transfer process.

For existing buildings, the replacement cost must be reduced by an estimate of accrued depreciation. The usefulness of this approach is sharply reduced by the need to subtract depreciation, which creates greater inaccuracies the older the building. Much depreciation is caused by obsolescence rather than by physical wear. The measurement of the actual value lost as a result of time is almost impossible except through some use of the market data process. No technique except actual comparisons can measure what has really happened.

Other problems are caused by under- or overimprovement of the property, by which is meant that improper amounts have been put into the structure in relation to its basic use. As an example, gold-plated bathtubs may be expensive and have a high replacement cost yet have little value to the average home purchaser. Even a complete and itemized bill for construction of a new unit may give too high a value if it contains features for which the average buyer will not bid.

3. The income-capitalization approach is primarily used for income properties. It starts with a computation of probable net earnings calculated from predictions of income and operating expenses. A capitalization rate is selected on the basis of the type of property and its location. The forecast net earnings stream is then capitalized into an estimate of present value based upon the selected rate. (See the Appendix to Chapter 6.) Even slight errors in the capitalization rate will cause large differences in the value estimate.

The appraiser bases his final estimate upon his judgment and the data developed through the three approaches. The separate approaches give his estimate outside limits. The final result, however, is not a summary or averaging of the three. Depending upon the type of property and market conditions, the appraiser will have far more confidence in one set of data than in the others.

The accuracy of the final estimate will also depend on the type of property. Certain types of appraisals are performed so frequently that plenty of data are available. They become almost routine. Others may be so rare and require so many different assumptions that even highly skilled men seeking the same value estimate will find themselves far apart.

## THE FINAL RISK RATING

The analysis of the loan application and its related interview, credit report, and appraisal finally lead to a decision to grant the loan, to negotiate changed terms, or to suggest that the applicant try elsewhere. The analysis also serves to classify the loan with respect to its estimated risk and yield.

The analysis of the loan application may show an unsatisfactory pattern that could be modified. Frequently such modification takes the form of a lesser amount to be loaned, a more rapid amortization, or occasionally a higher interest rate. Some lenders follow a policy of quoting interest rates which differ depending on the borrower's equity and speed of amortization. Such a policy which charges more for higher risks follows logically from a recognition of the existence of differential perils.

In other cases, negotiations take place with respect to the design of the structure or its proposed use. There may be insistence on

FIGURE 8-4 *Rating of Mortgage Pattern* (Rental-income properties)

| *Features* | *Weight* | *Rating* |
|---|---|---|
| Rating of mortgage terms                       Total | 58 | |
| Ratio of loan to value ____% | 25 | |
| Ratio of term of mortgage to remaining economic life ____% | 6 | |
| Ratio of debt service to net income ____% | 27 | |
| Rating of economic background | 6 | |
| Rating of net income expectancy | 20 | |
| Rating of mortgagor | 16 | |
| Rating of mortgage pattern | | |

more AA leases or insistence that part of the construction be delayed until a first section has experienced a market test. Such negotiated changes may lower the risk sufficiently to make the loan worthwhile.

In his final risk evaluation, the lender may follow either of two paths. He may include all risk features, no matter what type of property or loan, in a single evaluation. More probably, he will rate risks within a given category of loans and then determine, on the basis of collateral information, what the cut-off point for risks should be in each category.

Thus some assign ratings to classes of property, to years, and to types of loans, in addition to factors such as those indicated in Figure 8-4. This procedure allows all to be added into a single total. More common, however, is the rating of each mortgage in a category, such as new apartments or shopping centers or houses. Then, according to the relative risks among these categories, the lender decides what risks to accept in each category. The effort to place all on a single scale is difficult.

Figure 8-4 is based on the risk-rating system used by the FHA for income properties. This procedure gives effect to four different factors affecting risks—the terms of the mortgage, the area's economic background, the property's net income expectancy, and the mortgagor. Each of these items includes many elements. Thus value, remaining economic life, and estimate of net income depend upon a complete appraisal. That the other factors also include many elements can be seen from the following outline:

### Rating of Mortgage Terms

Ratio of loan to value
Ratio of term of mortgage to remaining economic life
Ratio of debt service to net income

### Rating of Economic Background

Type of economic base
Employment trends
Diversification of industry
Cyclical fluctuations
Scope of market and marketability

### Rating of Net Income Expectancy

Location
    Protection against inharmonious land uses
    Physical and social attractiveness
    Adequacy of civic, social, and commercial centers
    Adequacy of transportation
    Sufficiency of utilities and service
    Level of taxes and special assessments
    Relative marketability

Property
  Visual appearance
  Livability
  Natural light and ventilation
  Structural quality
  Resistance to elements and use
  Suitability of mechanical equipment
  Adjustment for nonconformity
Rentability of units
  Expense ratio
  Stability of effective gross income
  Variability of expenses

### Rating of Mortgagor

Credit characteristics of mortgagor
Motivating interest in ownership of property
Importance of monetary interest
Adequacy of available assets for transaction
Stability of effective income
Adequacy of effective income for total obligations

In each category the number of points awarded varies with the degree of risk involved. For example, a mortgage with a maximum loan compared to value will be awarded only 3 out of a possible 25 points in the first line of Figure 8-4. On the other hand, a loan that is only 60 per cent or less of the value will be given the full 25. Similarly Figure 8-1 showed a grid rating for the mortgagor. A barely eligible mortgagor with a rating of 50 on that grid would get 1 point in the rating-of-mortgagor category in Figure 8-4. On the other hand, a highly responsible mortgagor with a grid rating of 80 or more would be awarded the full 16 points in this category.

The total of points bestowed out of the possible 100 determines the over-all mortgage risk. The lender changes the cut-off point below which he will not lend depending on the state of the money market, the type of loan, or the gross income expected from the loan. The grid of Figure 8-4 gives him a specific estimate of the risk. He can attempt to lower the risk by negotiations to improve one or more of the factors in the pattern.

Although the use of these concepts is expanding rapidly, rating systems as complex as this are somewhat unusual for conventional lenders. The reasons for their spreading use, however, are obvious. Whether or not he does so formally, every lender must consider the elements on the grid when he makes a loan. Many loans based only on the subjective judgment of the lending officer as approved by the loan committee are later found wanting. Judgment may place too much weight on a single factor, such as the mortgagor or the property, and critical areas increasing the risk may have been completely overlooked.

## SUMMARY

All agree that judgment must remain the cornerstone of loan approvals. However, standard procedures improve judgment, make the considered factors uniform throughout a firm, and enable the degree of risk and potential yield to be quantified. For these reasons, some form of check list for analysis improves the lending process.

The basic factors considered in analyzing the individual loan are the borrower's characteristics as reported in the loan application, interview, and credit report. These must, however, be carefully related to the terms of the loan.

The data necessary to judge the property and its usefulness as a security are developed through the appraisal. It provides an estimate of the present value and becomes a basis for a projection of the future value of the property. Again, these factors must be related to the amount of the loan and its other terms.

The various features of the loan, borrower, and property and their relationships determine the potential risk of the loan. The lender uses this knowledge to calculate whether the proposed loan carries the promise of a sufficiently adequate yield. He uses the information to accept the loan, to negotiate modifications in the proposal, or to reject it.

## SELECTED REFERENCES

American Institute of Real Estate Appraisers: *The Appraisal of Real Estate*, 3d ed., Chicago, 1960.

Babcock, F. M.: *The Valuation of Real Estate,* McGraw-Hill Book Company, New York, 1932.

Bryant, Willis R.: *Mortgage Lending,* 2d ed., McGraw-Hill Book Company, New York, 1962.

Kahn, S. A., et al.: *Real Estate Appraisal and Investment,* The Ronald Press Company, New York, 1963.

Ratcliff, R. U.: *A Restatement of Appraisal Theory,* Bureau of Business Research, University of Wisconsin, Madison, Wis., 1963.

Ring, A. A.: *The Valuation of Real Estate,* Prentice-Hall, Inc., Englewood Cliffs, N.J., 1963.

U.S. Federal Housing Administration: *Underwriting Manual,* Government Printing Office, Washington, 1959.

Wendt, P. F.: *Real Estate Appraisal,* Holt, Rinehart and Winston, Inc., New York, 1956.

# Management of Portfolio Risks————————9

Preoccupation with individual loans will not solve all a lender's problems of risk management. The total composition of a firm's portfolio may lead to additional dangers. If many loans go bad simultaneously, the institution's solvency will be endangered. If the lender needs a substantial amount of cash that can only be obtained at high costs, the firm will face a crisis of liquidity. If interest rates shift suddenly, the firm may have sizable capital gains or losses.

In addition to lowering losses on individual loans, risk management has a second major goal—to obtain an over-all portfolio composition that will minimize the dangers of insolvency and illiquidity. This attention to the over-all composition of loans as distinct from their individual analysis is spoken of as the management of portfolio risks.

Preventative policies include careful regard for diversification, the planning of cash flows and liquidity, and the establishment and maintenance of sufficient reserves. The failure or near collapse of institutions almost always appears to result from unsuccessful efforts in one of these spheres.

## DIVERSIFICATION

Lack of diversification produces a major threat to a firm's safety. Under normal circumstances, when loans deteriorate as a result of random individual mishaps, the total number of loans in the portfolio determines the amount of risk. As in many insurance problems, the larger the number of loans, the smaller the total risk. The chances that an unusually high percentage will go bad in any period decrease with the size of the portfolio.

The law of large numbers leading to decreased risks applies, however, only if no correlation exists among the loans which could cause many of them to go bad simultaneously. In contrast, if loans are of a similar type, portfolio risk is greater because all may react in a uniformly unsatisfactory manner to the same outside forces. If a city is hit by an earthquake, closing of a military base, or a large excess of apartment houses, many loans may simultaneously be affected adversely.

Diversification of loans attempts to avoid such correlation, or covariance. There may be diversification with respect to time of lending, areas, neighborhoods or regions, types of properties and individuals, or any of a number of other possible bases of classification.

## Time of Lending

Risk analysis shows that it is dangerous for a portfolio to contain too many loans issued at the same period. Loans processed together in time are governed by the same underwriting and appraisal views and principles. A tendency usually prevails of depending too much on recent experiences. A class of loans that has been profitable may be pushed to the limit. When incomes are rising and jobs plentiful, predictions of future income may be too high. Clustering in time may increase the danger from an economic downturn because, under normal amortization procedures, a large body of young loans will not have had much of their principal repaid.

The risk manager must clearly recognize that high correlations in time sharply increase the amount of portfolio risk. A group of loans with a normal age distribution will be far safer than a collec-tion of new loans made under fairly uniform economic and underwriting conditions.

## Area of Lending

Regulations commonly require institutions to limit their mortgage loans to local areas, often defined as within 50 or 100 miles of their home office. Because lenders have the most knowledge of local conditions, it is assumed that they can make safer loans in their own neighborhood than elsewhere.

Although better knowledge may lower individual underwriting risks, area limitations may decrease total safety by curtailing diversification. Experience proves that the smaller the area, the greater the risks that its entire property market will go bad. The pressures on whole regions such as West Virginia, the coal areas of Pennsylvania, and other special-purpose locations are common knowledge. Still more common are towns which have experienced a boom and then a sharp drop due to the closing of a military base or major defense plant. Even in Los Angeles, one of the fastest-growing parts of the country, a small area found itself with several thousand unsold houses when the defense picture changed. In such situations, a large percentage of the properties in a town lose value simultaneously. Any institution with a high proportion of its portfolio concentrated in loans on a few locations within an area obviously faces greatly increased risks.

## Types of Property and Individuals

Lenders frequently find that for a period certain types of loans may be far more profitable than others. A savings association which financed John Smith when he was a small contractor may keep his account as he grows bigger and more and more successful. It may feel extremely lucky to have such an outstanding, profitable account. In many such situations, however, the association suddenly finds that the borrower has gone bankrupt and that its losses may run to several million dollars.

Similarly, in times of rapidly rising land prices, shortages of rental units, or expanding tourist traffic, special loans on raw land, apartments, or motels may yield excellent results. Suddenly prices level off, the boom ends, or overbuilding becomes obvious. Firms heavily concentrated in what they thought were fine loans take heavy losses.

While regulations unfortunately create concentration within areas, they usually attempt to limit concentration in other types of risk. They require diversification by type of loan and individual. Such compulsory diversification may look better on paper than it is in fact. It may not meet the problem of covariances of risks on loans all made at the same time. Correlations can exist among many seemingly different types of loans if all rest on the same basic premises. It is such covariances that must be avoided through proper risk management. The lending officer must do more than comply with the letter of regulations. He must recognize their intent and logic and make certain that true diversification is protecting the firm against many loans going bad at the same time. He must avoid the excess losses created by having to liquidate a large number of loans in a short period.

## PLANNING FOR LIQUIDITY

Liquidity has been defined as the ability to obtain cash when needed without incurring high costs or other risks. It also is frequently defined in very specific terms in the regulations affecting particular institutions as cash, treasury bills, or other short-term assets certain ratios of which to total resources may be fixed by law. The need for liquidity arises because most financial institutions, either contractually or by custom, agree to make available to their depositors funds entrusted to them on demand or upon short notice.

Even when, as with savings accounts, delays could be required, institutions are loath to demand such notices. Failure to pay on demand would shake major premises on which recent saving expansions have been based. The average family looks upon savings institutions as proper places to hold liquid assets, on the assumption that their money will be rapidly available in case of emergency.

The management of liquidity takes several paths. It goes beyond the relatively simple decisions as to what percentage of the firm's liabilities should be held in cash or quick assets. Four different possibilities arise in planning for liquidity.

1. Liquidity can be protected by forecasts and controls over the normal flow of funds which arises as a result of individual deposits and withdrawals, normal loan amortization and re- payments, and the need to pay out moneys on existing com- mitments.
2. Liquidity can be obtained by borrowing cash.
3. Money can be made available by shifting loans to other lenders. What would be the cost of transferring or selling a mortgage in case of need? Such costs, differing among types of loans, must be considered in estimating each one's risk and net yield.
4. The costs of liquidity can be lowered by protecting against so- called income risk. There is the danger that even though a loan may be easily marketable, it will have to be sold at a financial sacrifice because of changes in the money market. Because mortgage loans are made at fixed rates, their value shifts with changes in the going rate of interest. While losses may be con- siderable, gains are less likely. The lender cannot call the loan if interest rates rise, but because most loans specify that they can be refinanced or paid off (frequently with some penalty), the borrower may return the money if rates fall.

### Cash Flow Analysis

Most lending institutions are devoting more time to protecting their liquidity by forecasts of their flow of cash. Depending on the type of institution, such forecasts are made daily, weekly, or monthly. They cover different periods such as tomorrow, the next week or month, or periods up to two years in length.

In these forecasts, factors affecting cash flow which are analyzed and projected may be divided into as few as 5 or 6 or expanded to 20 or more, on both the gain and loss side. The number of items predicted depends on the type of institution, the complexity of its operations, and the excellence of its management.

A most important set of items in the estimates are those related to the flow of savings. Deposits turn over steadily. Thus time de- posits in commercial banks turn over slightly more than once in two years, on the average. In savings banks and savings associations,

the average length of deposit lies between three and four years. In
insurance companies the individual policy reserves remain still longer.

In an expanding economy inflows of savings exceed outflows.
This holds true for most institutions in most months. However,
even in expanding periods, important seasonal factors may exist.
Seasonal movements depend on the area and kinds of funds in the
institution. Proper estimation of seasonal factors saves many head-
aches for the firm by ensuring that it does not suddenly encounter an
unexpected need for cash.

Even with customary growth, periods of sharp withdrawals can
occur. Such losses have followed local economic distress and major
periods of scare buying (like that accompanying the Korean incident), and have also resulted from the competition of other saving
media. For example, several years ago some institutions lost between
5 and 10 per cent of their resources to the bond market in a week
or less when great publicity was given to the market availability of
United States government notes at 5 per cent interest rate (the so-
called magic fives). This flow of funds to governments demonstrated
that savers may suddenly change their form of saving when the
discrepancies among various institutions' rates of return become
obvious and important. Knowledgeable investors watch returns and
shift their savings accordingly.

For a particular firm the extent and impact of such losses depend
on the degree of diversification among the institution's depositors.
What share is owned by large, knowledgeable depositors? What share
is held by employees in a cyclical industry? The individual making
cash forecasts must know his own firm, its market peculiarities,
and the pressures upon it. Many forces can create a concentrated
cash drain. Risks are multiplied because the same forces which
cause faster withdrawals are likely to slow deposits. One cannot
depend on normal inflows to offset outflows occurring because of
these special factors.

Cash flows are also influenced by rates of amortization, interest
earnings, and interest payments. Although they have a heavy
seasonal component, these factors form the more stable part of
the cash flow estimate. The amount of amortization depends upon
the structure of the loan portfolio. Usually it does not change

sharply in short periods. Under level-payment plans for interest and amortization, the per cent of payment going to amortization rises with the age of the loan. High payments against principal may give significant stability to the total flow.

Advance payments on mortgages are another source of funds that varies greatly. They depend on the rate at which houses are resold. Sales in turn are dependent on economic conditions. In periods of tight money or rising interest rates, when firms would like to get their money back faster, an opposite movement is probable. Tight money and high rates make it worthwhile for borrowers not to refinance. In addition, properties are sold subject to existing mortgages, thus cutting off a normal flow of advance repayments.

The outflow of mortgage loans against previous commitments is another difficult area of forecasting which, however, can be much improved through careful analysis. The backlog of outstanding commitments may suddenly cause a firm a good deal of distress. The percentage of commitments taken up by borrowers varies with changing interest rates. The fluctuating rate at which commitments are used can work to the lender's disadvantage. If the money market eases or if he is offered better terms elsewhere, the borrower will not use the commitment. On the other hand, with a tightening market and rising rates, the percentage of commitments actually used increases. Lenders can avoid some of these difficulties by charging for advance commitments. To be profitable, the rate they charge must more than offset the risk of losing because of shifts in interest rates.

### Borrowing on Mortgages

One of the methods through which lenders obtain additional liquidity is by borrowing against the mortgage portfolio. Such borrowing may be done to meet day-to-day requirements for operating capital or to cover emergency requirements for funds which arise through errors in the projection of cash flows or unforeseen withdrawals. Still other borrowing, on either a temporary or permanent basis, aims at meeting heavy demands in certain markets by bringing in funds from elsewhere.

We have already noted the Federal Home Loan Banks as one major source of such borrowing. Saving associations have found the FHLB System a major source of liquidity. It has been a significant source of funds to meet seasonal requirements. In order to increase the amount they could lend over and above their own resources, many associations have remained steadily in debt to the FHL Banks. Finally, most firms plan to use the banks as a rapid source of liquidity in case of sudden need. While not too many have had to borrow for that purpose, the existence of this backing plays an enormous role in day-to-day operations. Without it the individual institutions would have to carry much greater liquidity.

## Mortgage Warehousing

Most other lenders have not borrowed to the same extent on their mortgage portfolios. When they have, their chief method has been through so-called mortgage warehousing at commercial banks. In warehousing arrangements, a commercial bank extends short-term credits to a mortgage company or savings bank on a note, with a group of mortgages serving as general security for the note. In another technique, the original lender sells individual loans to a commercial bank with an agreement to repurchase the mortgages within a stated time period.

Most warehousing is used by mortgage companies to obtain working capital for their day-to-day operations. These organizations make construction and individual mortgage loans to their clients. However, the ultimate lenders, usually an insurance company or mutual savings bank, delay payment to the mortgage company until a fully satisfactory mortgage issued to a final house purchaser can be delivered, most frequently after receipt of the FHA insurance or VA guarantee.

During the period in which money has been paid to the builder or seller but before the mortgage company has received its payment from the final lender, it requires interim financing. Commercial banks lend mortgage companies operating capital on notes against their total assets, which primarily include the partially completed loans in their portfolios. When correspondents take final delivery of the individual mortgages, the payments they make to the mortgage companies are used to liquidate the bank loans.

The specific techniques of warehousing require the mortgage companies to pledge particular assets behind their notes. Such questions as transfer of title, escrow accounts, and checking of construction by the banks depend upon a company's financial stability, its past record, and the experience of the commercial banks with it and with other mortgage lenders.

Warehousing of mortgages to meet unusual cash drains or in anticipation of future cash flows is not as common, but it does occur. At times, mutual savings banks and insurance companies have miscalculated their cash flow because of an uneven takedown of commitments or because of a sudden demand for cash. Rather than sell permanently some assets, they have preferred to borrow on part of their portfolio. Such techniques have also been adopted by some savings banks as the normal procedure for meeting seasonal surges in their fund requirements.

Normally warehousing takes place through the pledging of individual mortgages against a note. Sales of specific loans to commercial banks with a repurchase agreement are not as common but have some definite advantages. In such cases, the borrower's balance sheet need not show a debt to the bank even though his repurchase contract has the same effect.

In all warehousing, the commercial bank attempts to retain the maximum degree of security by obtaining the right to foreclose on the final property if necessary. In the vast majority of cases, however, it expects that the loan will be repaid through the normal operation of the mortgage company. Individual loans need be taken over only if the mortgage company runs into difficulties.

## Sales of Participations

A final technique of borrowing against a mortgage portfolio is through the use of mortgage participations, by which is meant the sale of a share of an individual loan to another lender. The buyer pays the seller for his share and becomes the legal owner of whatever share he purchased. Again the objective may be to obtain.

either working capital or long-term funds. The principal type of short-period participation occurs when a savings bank sells 80 or 90 per cent participation in mortgages in its portfolio to a commercial bank. Usually there is an agreement to repurchase, and frequently the right of recourse is granted; that is, the seller remains responsible for all losses.

Normally in these cases, the servicing remains with the original lender. The commercial banks are paid fees in accordance with commercial loans rather than mortgage rates. The lines of credit are extinguished either seasonally or when the brief period of need has passed.

In contrast, savings associations sell large numbers of participations on a permanent basis in order to increase the lending they can do in their own market. As an example, a California association may agree to sell a 50 per cent participation in each of 100 mortgages to an Ohio association. Each firm is a legal owner of one-half of each loan. They share the risks. Because California has needed more savings than are available, mortgage interest rates have been higher there than in Ohio. The participation agreement leads to increased interest for the Ohio firm, more money to lend in California, and more diversification for both associations.

Typically in such agreements, the originating association keeps all or most of the initial fees received for making the loan. It also retains part of the interest payment as a fee, say ½ per cent of the outstanding balance, for servicing the loan. Both associations share equally in amortization, repayments, and any losses.

### A Secondary Market

Sales of assets are another major source of liquidity. Most institutions hold governments or other liquid assets as a first source of additional funds. Such assets are normally short-term assets, to avoid the problem of having to take capital losses which arise when interest rates shift in the long-term market. If, however, more funds are required than can be made available from these first lines of defense, mortgages may have to be sold.

The market in which existing mortgages are bought and sold

is the secondary mortgage market.[1] It is a place where lenders desiring increased cash can sell loans already in their portfolio, hopefully at close to their true value. The transactions in this market must be differentiated from other transactions which are occasionally spoken of as secondary-market operations. Such other acts already discussed include the insuring or guaranteeing of mortgages and the sale of mortgages by agents to correspondents, which is the typical mortgage company operation of making loans against commitments from the ultimate source of funds.

In actuality, except for FHA-VA loans, a true secondary market remains primarily a hope rather than a fact. While the market in government-insured and government-guaranteed loans is far from efficient, they are traded nationally. In addition, as we saw in Chapter 4, liquidity for insured loans has been considerably enhanced by the Federal National Mortgage Association. Fanny May has furnished sizable funds by buying government-underwritten loans at critical market periods. In contrast, a secondary market for conventional loans remains primarily an embryo. It is very difficult for a lender to find buyers for any number of conventional mortgages in his portfolio.

Because the growth of such a market would be so significant, it is worth examining the reasons for its failure to expand as well as the advantages to be expected if it were to grow.

The major difficulty is that mortgages remain primarily local devices. Even the actual loan instruments differ tremendously among areas. No basic procedure exists for transmitting information on a national scale as to what is happening in a local market or how it is performing. This is true both for loans as a whole and for individual loans. Differentiation due to this lack of knowledge is increased by laws and regulations which curtail the rights of lenders to operate in other localities.

The growth of a true secondary market depends on both legal and institutional changes. Legal changes required include the repeal of regulations limiting the area within which lenders can own mortgages. Also necessary would be the standardization of mortgage

[1] Cf. Oliver Jones and Leo Grebler, *The Secondary Mortgage Market*, University of California, Los Angeles, 1961.

instruments, more similar rules of foreclosures, and the ability of foreign corporations to foreclose or otherwise operate in local markets.

In the area of institutional changes, the ability to trade mortgages over a distance depends upon more exact methods of appraising and risk rating. The fact that the FHA and VA standardized the instruments, gave a known risk, and made it legal to operate over the whole country led to the establishment of a secondary market and the relative success of the FHA-VA programs.

The existence of a true secondary market for conventional loans would go far toward solving the individual lender's problem of mortgage liquidity. An institution would know that if it needed cash, it could sell conventional mortgages from its portfolio with far smaller losses than at the present.

A well-operating market would adjust the prices of existing mortgages to other forms of loans. It would give a better determination of mortgage prices and yields, and the allocation of resources to different investments would consequently improve. Because of the poor secondary market, the costs of selling mortgages are high. At present, lenders find it difficult to sell mortgages out of their portfolios when offered new lending opportunities with greater yields. As a result, only major gaps between different types of credit will make it worthwhile to sell existing holdings.

A better secondary market would lower the liquidity risk and increase competition among mortgage lenders. The costs of mortgages would fall. Although some institutions would experience lower gross yields because of this increased competition, their net yields might be higher because their costs of safety and of operations would fall.

Existing mortgages carry high gross yields because of their lack of liquidity and because many sources of potential funds are barred from all or part of the market. Increased liquidity would attract more lenders, such as pension funds. It would also increase the share that mortgages could form of most portfolios.

The flow of funds among regions would improve. Without a secondary market, rapidly expanding localities find their interest charges rise above those in localities with more stable or stagnant conditions. The flow of funds to the mortgage market as a whole would also be better. It would respond more readily to demand and supply, since lenders could adjust their portfolios more easily. Periods of acute tightness like those experienced in the past would be less likely.

Another possibility, is that true secondary-market institutions similar to the European Mortgage Banks could emerge. Such units issue general-market bonds or debentures against their holdings of mortgages. Such institutions or somewhat similar mortgage investment trusts would make it easier for the small saver or investor to tie his funds directly to the mortgage market by establishing new forms of securities.

All the opportunities of a secondary market would be easier to realize if the problem of additional liquidity through simpler sales could be solved. Without a better secondary market, the cost of achieving liquidity through sales of conventional mortgages remains too high. Selling in the secondary market can now be done for government-insured loans, but for other mortgages it is possible only at a high cost.

## PROTECTING AGAINST INCOME RISKS

The fact that mortgage loans last for long periods means that three separate adjustments must be made in the gross interest rates, or yields on mortgages, that do not apply to the interest rate on shorter, more liquid loans. These three factors—the income risk on longer loans, the term of the loan, and the inclusion of rights to repay sums in advance—are all features that the bond and other money markets recognize require higher charges. Since mortgages contain all these features, they should be acknowledged and allowed for in calculating net returns.

### Interest Rate Movements

Figure 9-1 shows the prices at which a standard mortgage would have sold as a result of changes in current market interest rates. These movements in value may be considered as typical of the quarter-to-quarter changes which affected an average existing mortgage portfolio because of interest movements. The figure does not consider the impact of seasoning or similar influences on value. At the height of mortgage interest rates in 1959, a specific mortgage would have had a capital value nearly 15 per cent less than at the peak of its value in 1951. Declines of as much as 3 per cent in value occurred between adjacent quarters.

If existing portfolios had had to be liquidated or if lenders had been required to value their mortgages at actual market worth, many institutions might have been in considerable difficulty. The movements in capital value in some periods would have more than offset operating profits.

The Appendix to Chapter 6 explained in detail why the value of existing mortgages alters when market interest rates change. The current value of any loan is the discounted stream of future interest and amortization payments. When the market shifts, the new interest rate requires that discounting take place at a new rate. This causes a shift in the mortgage's current value. No one will offer more for it than could be obtained by current lending. If the mortgage has to be sold, the price offered will be based upon the current present value, not the face interest payments.

Calculation of the present value of a loan is complicated somewhat by the fact that the date the mortgage may be expected to be paid off will vary depending upon how its face interest rate compares to the current market. Thus Figure 9-1 is based on the assumption that 25-year mortgages will, on the average, be repaid by the end of 12 years. However, the actual fall in value may be greater than assumed. Loans which carry an interest rate below the market and those for long terms have a smaller probability of advance repayment. Experiences of repayments based on rising prices for properties cannot be extrapolated as an estimate of average lengths in other periods. In cases where prices have fallen or not gone up it may be worth paying a higher interest rate in order to get out more funds in cash. Lenders in theory can increase their protection somewhat against loans being assumed by new borrowers simply because they have favorable terms. They can include acceleration clauses to require that loans be repaid if a property is sold.

### The Term Structure of Interest Rates

The term of the loan is another significant factor affecting its true yield. In normal periods, borrowers must pay higher interest or premiums on loans for longer periods. This fact, often neglected in the mortgage market, is a basic part of the structure of the

FIGURE 9-1   *Market Value of a 4½ Per Cent, $12,000 Mortgage* (Assuming total repayment on the average is in 12 years)

SOURCE: Federal Housing Administration, "Average Typical Prices Offered for FHA-insured Loans."

bond market. For example, the municipal bond market has recently had periods when rates for loans rose by an average of 5 basis points, or 0.05 per cent in interest payments, for each year of additional length. Twenty-five-year bonds have carried interest rates that ranged from 25 to 75 per cent higher than those for one-year bonds.

The reason for this rising rate has been analyzed under the title "the term structure of interest rates." The existence of rising rates under normal circumstances is clearer, however, than the reasons for it. One explanation of the increases is the assumption that lenders believe that risk on any loan rises with the length of its maturity. Such a risk premium may exist in fact, but in theory it is not necessary. A more probable reason is that there are more savers who desire to hold near money or very liquid assets than who want to have a guaranteed interest rate on loans extending far into the future.

A desire for liquidity is not universal. Insurance companies, for example, enter into contracts in which they guarantee certain rates of interest on their policy reserves for long periods. As a result, these companies want to ensure a rate on their assets that extends as far into the future as their outstanding commitments. However, while they and some other savers desire long-term assets, statistically more savers seem to want short-period loans. Such a surplus of demand for short-term assets can lead to the familiar term structure of rates characterized by a rise with length to maturity.

Since the existing term structure means borrowers pay more for longer loans, mortgages should also carry a higher interest rate the longer the period of amortization. Mortgages with equal monthly payments will have varying amounts going each month to interest and principal depending upon the amortization period. For a mortgage with a 5 per cent interest rate and payments spread over 20 years, the average period for which the principal is outstanding is about 12 years; that is, it is equivalent to about a 12-year bond. In contrast, in the case of a similar loan amortized over 30 years the funds will be loaned out on an average for about 19 years.

While particular market conditions will cause differences in the rates charged for loans with these two different lengths, a fairly typical condition of the term structure would indicate that the longer loan should be charged about ⅜ per cent more in annual interest rates than the shorter one. The particular amount charged for the longer loan should rise with the average rate of interest and with the likelihood that advance repayments will be delayed.

### Prepayment Privileges

A final consideration affecting the interest yield depends on whether the note of mortgage is closed or open. A closed loan cannot be prepaid without a penalty; an open one can. Most frequently modern mortgages allow prepayments, but only with a prepayment penalty that decreases depending on the length of time the mortgage has been in existence.

The importance of this feature arises from the fact that in the United States, unlike many other countries, the lender cannot require the borrower to pay higher interest rates after the original agreement has been made. On the other hand, with an open mortgage or one with a low prepayment penalty, the borrower can renegotiate or obtain a mortgage at a lower rate elsewhere.

This ability to renegotiate is exactly equivalent to the call feature on a bond. As such it also has a recognized value. A callable, or optional, bond allows the borrower to refinance and save interest if rates fall. Furthermore, the lender risks having to liquidate his investment and find another in a period that may not be as favorable. Uncertainty of maturity added to that of the length of the term increases the uncertainty of most mortgages.

Since the mortgage market has not given proper consideration to this feature, we must turn to the bond market to obtain an estimate of the value of this call privilege.

Studies of the bond market have compared similarly rated bonds with and without call privileges. A bond which could not be paid off for a minimum of five years was worth 15 basis points more than one that could be paid off at any time. A 10-year deferment was worth 25 extra points. In effect this means that an open mortgage, that is, a mortgage without a prepayment penalty, probably should be considered as having a $\frac{1}{4}$ per cent lower interest yield than a closed one.

It can be seen that in comparing the potential yields of different mortgages or of mortgages as compared to bonds, it is necessary to estimate the various income risks, costs of the term structure, and costs of potential calls if a useful comparison is to be possible. Many of these differences might be neglected if it were not for the problem of liquidity. The risks and costs of these features are due to the potential need to sell mortgages or reinvest funds in the future. The better the job an institution can do in estimating its flow of funds, the greater the ease with which it can borrow against its portfolio; and the higher the efficiency of the secondary market, the lower are the risks and costs in these factors which differentiate mortgages.

## RESERVES

The final task of risk management is the establishment of adequate reserves. When reserves are discussed, they are usually thought of as required primarily because of the existence of risky assets. Examinations of institutions that have failed in recent years, however, indicates that embezzlement or defalcation on the part of officers can also be a major cause of failure. Reserves, therefore, are also required in addition to bonding and insurance in order to cover malfeasance and other failures of employees to perform their duties properly.

The discussion in this and the last three chapters should have made clear the shortcomings in the widely held idea that reserves should simply be a fixed share of an institution's assets. The risk that a firm faces varies with many more factors than the mere existence of assets.

In the first place, each type of individual asset has a separate risk attached to it. Loans on raw land or income properties carry two to three times the risk of loans on single-family houses. The risk falls fairly rapidly with the age of the loan. The whole concept of mortgage risk rating, whether done formally or informally, indicates that firms can increase or decrease their potential losses as they see fit.

In risk management, a significant problem arises because an individual firm must recognize that it has to be concerned with the variance of losses in addition to their average. Any individual firm has a certain probability of being above or below the average losses for a group of firms. With respect to the random element in losses, the distribution around this average should be a fairly normal curve. Recognizing this fact, an institution can properly estimate its probable cost of risks and net yields based upon random losses from the averages. To protect itself by reserves, however, it must consider the possibility that its losses will be near the extremes of the normal curve.

In addition to the individual random elements, however, reserves are also required to handle the problem of portfolio risks. The amount of portfolio risk is partly a function of the size of the firm. With proper management, the larger the size of the firm, the smaller the probable variance around the average will be. All other factors being the same, small firms need considerably larger reserves than do large firms.

The risks of the small firm are still greater because it is more likely to suffer from nonrandom risks. Thus any errors in mortgage risk analysis are likely to have a relatively greater impact on a small organization than on a large organization. Diversification is harder to manage, particularly with respect to regional dangers. To protect itself, the small firm must be far more aware of the perils of too much lending in any specific area, to any individual or firm, or on any one type of property.

The additional problems raised by liquidity can partly be handled by reserves, but they can also be managed through planning. Thus government-insured loans have a greater access to the secondary mortgage market than do conventional loans. There are other possible arrangements that can make it easier to sell some mortgages, thereby reducing dependence on liquidity reserves. The need for reserves can also be lowered by a better distribution of loans by amortization period and a better forecasting of the flow of funds.

## SUMMARY

The skill with which risks are managed has been growing steadily, but it still requires the greatest adroitness and judgment on the part of all practitioners. The rapid increase of knowledge makes this judgment far sounder. The spread of standard procedures, the improvement of forms, and the growth in knowledge of credit management and appraising all assure that these better techniques will be available throughout the whole institution. It is vital, however, that the existence of these safeguards not cause individuals to become careless or negligent. The history of past difficulties with mortgages demonstrate that the worst results occur after a period when all has been going brilliantly.

Risks depend on the over-all portfolio composition as well as on the probability of loss on individual loans. Diversification reduces a firm's risk because it decreases the likelihood of many loans going bad simultaneously from the same cause.

Liquidity, or the ability to get cash rapidly, also requires special planning. It is affected by the firm's flow of funds and by the ability to convert existing assets into cash. The ability to raise cash frequently depends on the success of the firm in tapping particular secondary markets.

Other features of mortgages which, together with liquidity, vary with their length and terms include the possibility of loss due to interest rate movements, the amount of yield necessary to compensate for their long life, and the frequently neglected estimation of the cost or value of specific prepayment privileges.

## SELECTED REFERENCES

American Bankers Association: *The Commercial Banking Industry,* Prentice-Hall, Inc., Englewood Cliffs, N.J., 1962.

Conard, J. W.: *Introduction to the Theory of Interest,* University of California Press, Berkeley, Calif., 1959.

Jones, Oliver, and Leo Grebler: *The Secondary Mortgage Market* University of California, Los Angeles, 1961.

Kendall, L. T.: *The Savings and Loan Business,* Prentice-Hall, Inc., Englewood Cliffs, N.J., 1962.

National Association of Mutual Savings Banks: *Mutual Savings Banking,* Prentice-Hall, Inc., Englewood Cliffs, N.J., 1962.

Phelps, C. D.: "The Impact of Tightening Credit on Municipal Capital Expenditures in the United States," *Yale Economic Essays,* vol. 1, no. 2, 1961.

Walter, J. E.: *The Investment Process,* Harvard Business School, Boston, 1962.

Wehrle, L. S.: "Life Insurance Investment," *Yale Economic Essays,* vol. 1, no. 1, 1961.

# Profit Planning————————————————————10

The need for profit planning has expanded along with the size and dynamics of the lending industry. In the past, small firms lacked the skills necessary to analyze their problems accurately. In periods of rapid expansion such as the mortgage market has gone through, individual inefficiencies were masked by the increased earnings flowing from larger volumes. But with more stable, competitive markets, greater attention must be paid to costs, pricing, and marketing.

Financial institutions act as intermediaries between savers and borrowers. Some are profit-making; others may be mutual, cooperative, or some other form of not-for-profit institution. No matter what their type, their ability to attract savers and to pay competitive rates for their money depends upon the efficiency of their operators. Proper profit, or net income planning culminates in increased efficiency, lowered costs, and the making of more funds available for payments on savings, for profits, or for allocations to reserves.

Planning for increased profits requires analysis along several lines. The firm must look closely at its cost structure and establish a proper financial budget. It must also examine its competitive situation and develop a market strategy which will permit it to compete successfully through its rate structure or other services. The decisions with respect to spending, type of asset, and projected volume must also take into account the various possible tax impacts.

All the different parts of the profit-planning process are interrelated. Management must determine the firm's budgeted expenditures. It may act to cut costs or raise income. But whether or not unit costs will actually fall depends only partly upon the management's action. Profit margins and returns will also reflect the volume of business attracted under the particular policies adopted.

The demand for loans for a given institution varies with the market and also with the amount and type of competition among the various lenders. Each firm influences its own demand through the policies it adopts with respect to its interest rates, its terms of loans, and its fee structure. It also alters the number of customers it obtains through the amount of its advertising and its program of community relations, including expenditures for its offices, charities, good will, and similar factors.

Tax problems are extremely complex. They differ according to types of lenders, types of assets, and types of loans. They change from period to period. Their impact on net yields is so tremendous that in many cases they dominate the firm's decision making.

## COST ANALYSIS

The starting point for profit planning is on the side of costs. Firms have better knowledge and control over their costs than over the other parts of their operations. The accounting records which firms must maintain in order to report their capital position and income for tax and regulatory purposes form a base from which cost analysis can take off.

Records used for cost analysis usually must be recast and supplementary ones added. Cost analysis requires the management to choose courses of action based on conditions and alternative actions which will take place in the future. Accounting not oriented to cost analysis usually deals with the past. It measures the acquisition costs of previously purchased assets and resources and then allocates them to particular periods according to standard procedures. While some of these recorded allocations will be useful for future decisions, many will not.

Items such as good will, costs of portfolio acquisitions, depreciation, and changes in market value of mortgages are frequently not included in accounts or are dealt with in such an arbitrary manner that they give little knowledge helpful for future action. As an example, many accounting systems charge off currently all the expenses of obtaining a loan portfolio. Recently, however, sales of mortgage companies and of groups of loans have made it clear that additions to the portfolio have an immediate value which will be realized in many future periods. Loans placed on the books contribute to profits as they continue in existence. Some of these profits can be cashed by selling the loan.

Costs engendered in obtaining these loans should, for the purposes of earnings analysis, be considered as charges against future rather than current income because they will pay off in the future. Such allocations to the future are common in the insurance field. where financial analysts usually show 20 to 50 per cent of the value of unearned premium reserves as part of the firm's value. Current changes in these reserves are taken into income. Increases in a mortgage loan portfolio are equivalent to these unearned premiums. The costs of obtaining them have been paid out, but income from them will flow in during the future.

For purposes of cost analysis, in addition to treating items differently, the firm must restructure a considerable amount of its data. The accounting records must be adjusted to reflect true alternative costs and revenues, not simply those shown on the books. The expense and income accounts must be regrouped so that they will be in a more logical form for necessary decisions. Financial accounting divides costs into those for interest and other payments for money on the one hand, and those for operating expenses, on the other. Cost-volume analysis requires the further division of operating expenses in accordance with the time period over which they can be influenced.

The most common divisions of operating costs for profit planning are as follows:

1. Fixed costs are those which do not change with the volume of lending in a given period. The amount spent for rent, heat, and insurance will usually not alter with the number of loans made.

Whether a cost is fixed or nonfixed will depend on the length of the period under consideration. Thus almost all costs are fixed for a day. For a year many costs can be changed.

2. Controllable, or regulated, costs are those which will be fixed when once determined for a budget period but which can be changed from one period to the next. An advertising budget, once determined, will not vary with the volume of business. However, advertising expenses can be altered drastically from one period to the next. Other costs such as officers' salaries, number of employees, and wage rates again tend to be controllable because they can be altered within fairly short periods. But once fixed they will not change with volume.

3. Variable costs are those costs which move as a result of changes in volume of lending. Some costs, such as payments to a servicing agent or correspondent based purely on the number or amount of loans, may be completely variable. Others may be partially variable. For example the number of clerks required to handle originations—say one clerk per 35 loans per month—will be a function of the number of loans opened per month. However, within short periods, the number of clerks will not vary. A few additional loans will be handled without more personnel. This type of cost is variable in steps. It will rise when a certain volume is reached, then hold nearly constant, then rise again as a new level is attained.

### Resemblance between Lenders' and Retailers' Costs

Lending operations display a cost situation different from that of many industrial and construction firms but not too unlike many retail operations. In analyzing his costs, the lender discovers that most fall into the controllable category. He must decide on their level for the coming quarter or year, but once this decision has been made, their total does not vary much with volume.

Thus, with a given volume of expenditures, the actual unit costs of the firm in the budget period depend primarily on the volume of business that is engendered. The management determines the budget for its controllable costs. The fixed costs have already been incurred for the coming period. Except for the price of money, the other variable costs tend not to be large.

Once the budget is set, the firm stands ready to do as much business as it can attract. With a given budget, the larger the volume of lending, the greater the net yield. If the volume of business is not adequate to support the level of costs picked by the management, it must decide whether to lower prices or try to build volume in other ways.

Decisions are complicated by the difficulties of getting a proper time horizon. As noted, the value of new loans cannot be measured purely in terms of their additions to this year's revenue. Similarly, it is hard to judge the value of good will or the impact of increasing size on the future. Lenders hold widely conflicting views on the value of growth. Is advertising done today a valuable asset for next year, or does its influence disappear rapidly? What are the increased probabilities of getting a future deposit from, or making a future loan to, someone who is a customer today? Over how wide a circle will this good will spread?

**Operating Expenses and Volume**

The problem of cost analysis is further complicated by the fact that many costs are joint; that is, they are paid out for services which apply to both the saving and lending operations or to several types of investment services. Some investment officers supervise both the bond and mortgage portfolios. Some executives administer both deposit and lending services. A new expensive building or a series of community advertisements will attract both depositors and borrowers. The proper allocation of joint costs increases the amount of judgment needed in analyzing costs, but it does not diminish the need or the success to be gained from a well-functioning system. A wasted ad is no less inefficient because half of its cost should be charged to the saving side and half to lending.

Few published reports divide current operating expenses into those related to investment functions and those related to saving functions. For those which do, it is difficult to separate mortgage from other investment expenses. However, the published reports do indicate considerable variation by type and size of institution in the share of gross operating income which goes to current operating expenses.

In recent years the current operating expenses of mutual savings banks have been about 15 per cent of total operating income. But in savings and loan companies with their somewhat higher mortgage portfolio, smaller size, and more rapid growth, operating expenses have taken up a larger share of current income. Savings associatio1s at the end of World War II had expenses which equaled nearly 30 per cent of their operating income. Since that time both income and expenses have risen, and the interest rate level is higher. Under the impact of higher money charges, by 1962 total operating expenses had fallen to 20.3 per cent of gross operating income.

The data also show that up to a point, decided advantages accrue with scale. In 1962, for associations with under $500,000 in assets, total operating expenses were 33.6 per cent of gross income. The percentage fell steadily to 20.7 per cent for institutions with $5 million to $10 million. A slow decrease in relative expenditures continued until institutions with over $100 million in assets showed a ratio of 19.2 per cent.

These statistics are subject to normal qualifications because the firms included have differing geographical mixes and rates of growth. It appears clear, however, that very significant economies of scale do appear when an institution moves from small to moderate size. There are probably also some continuing economies as size continues to grow, for example, increased use of data processing and spreading of overhead.

These reported figures show the final results after the fact of whatever cost analysis these firms used. Studies of what happens to the operating ratios in a dynamic situation when scale increases are still more vivid. Given a budget period of a year, the decrease in unit operating expenses and the corollary increase in net yield is very dramatic as the number of loans expands. Similarly, numerous management experts report that the return on executive time given over to cost analysis is high. Many firms expanding rapidly in the postwar period found their costs had gotten out of hand. Only with the advent of a more competitive money market were they compelled to examine costs more carefully. They were surprised and perhaps appalled at the large cost-savings opportunities they found which had previously been neglected.

For life insurance companies, convention reports carry the total investment expense. It must be recognized that they make somewhat arbitrary allocations of expense, primarily for tax accounting purposes. According to these reports, investment expenses range between 5 and 10 per cent of investment income, with the great majority clustering around the 5 per cent level.

## COST–CONTROL DECISIONS

Some indication of the problems encountered in controlling costs and in the logic of particular decisions may be gained by examining the actual cost-budgeting process which firms go through. The decisions they reach show the logic of profit planning and the type of knowledge which lending officials require to make the decisions that will contribute most to their lending yields.

Even a rather simple classification of expense accounts will include 50 or more. All must be scrutinized in the control of costs. Data for comparative purposes group them into a few main accounts. The FHLBB reports for savings and loans divide expenses into compensation, advertising, occupancy, supervisory, audit, and insurance, and all other expenses. In 1962, total operating expenses averaged 20.3 per cent of gross operating income. The subtotals were 8.9 per cent for compensation, 2.3 per cent for advertising, 2.3 per cent for occupancy, 1.7 per cent for Federal insurance, etc., and 5.1 per cent for all others.

Costs of these magnitudes are those with which the manager must work. In his cost analysis, the executive must find the answers to numerous questions. What should the budget for lending expenses be for next year? What are necessary expenses if the volume of lending stays where it is, rises somewhat, or falls somewhat? How should the variations of expenses with volume influence his decisions as to the best level of loans to budget for? He makes certain new allocations based on his analysis. He also obtains information on probable cost variations at levels of lending at, above, and below recent experience. These costs then become given data which he uses in devising his pricing and marketing strategies.

In the executive's initial analysis, while many costs are virtually fixed for the next year, other costs are controllable. It is the expenditure level for the latter that he establishes in his budget. He knows that variances will occur around his budgeted items, but he also knows that the budget gives him a base. He will be able to analyze and check any variations from it as they occur to see whether they are necessary or are due to errors or carelessness.

Finally, he recognizes that some costs vary partly with the amount of loans outstanding, partly with the amount of new loans made, and partly with the size and type of the new loans. Their type and amount are a critical part of his cost decisions. Most important of the variable costs is the actual amount he must pay for the money on loan. For example, in 1962 savings and loan associations paid out 62 per cent of their gross income as dividends (interest) on their accounts.

### Fixed Costs

Fixed costs have been defined as those over which the company has little or no control during the course of the year and which do not vary with the volume of lending. A major item in this category is occupancy expenses. The amounts paid for maintenance, light, heat, and rent or taxes do not alter much in the course of a year. The same is true of depreciation and other charges related to furniture and office equipment. Minimum legal fees, auditing, accounting, bank examinations, and account insurance are all relatively fixed.

Other categories, particularly the compensation, fringe benefits, and expenses of a minimum number of officers and staff, also will be fixed. It usually does not pay to fire personnel because of moderate changes in volume, especially if the movements are assumed to be temporary. Postage, telephone, and a whole host of other costs fall into this same quasi-fixed category.

When the firm plans its strategy over a period longer than a year, many of these costs no longer are fixed. Overhead can be reduced in many ways. Much of management can be fired. Offices can be closed. Cars and other equipment may not be replaced.

Still more common is a strategy which avoids adding to fixed expenses until the firm is certain that a new and larger volume is stable. In this sphere, insurance companies and savings and loans seem to have followed nearly diametrically opposed policies. Insurance companies have tried to keep costs as variable as possible. They have used much rented space and equipment. They have contracted for correspondents, fee appraisers, and consultant services to avoid adding personnel and space to their own overhead.

Many savings and loans, on the other hand, have attempted to keep their costs in line by expanding as rapidly as possible. New buildings and new branches are expected to create the additional volume necessary to pay for themselves. Existing fixed costs plus those newly contracted for can, it is hoped, be spread over the additional volume.

## Controllable Costs

For many lending institutions, the line between fixed and controllable costs is hard to draw. Many accounts, such as compensation, fringe benefits, and entertainment expenses, appear under both headings. The executive must use his own judgment to determine how much staff could be reduced if volume fell or how much it should be expanded assuming a 5 or 10 or some other per cent increase in the volume of lending.

Items which are more clearly controllable include advertising, travel and entertainment accounts, auto and other equipment, charitable contributions, and dues and subscriptions. Many of these items are difficult to allocate between savings and investment. Many more are controllable but, as in the case of dues and subscriptions, tend to become automatic unless a special jolt hits the firm.

Advertising is the largest controllable cost. Because it is so difficult to prove the specific worth of any piece or amount of advertising, it tends to be under constant scrutiny. On the other hand, it is also frequently treated with a "don't rock the boat" attitude. If a firm is making money and all seems to be going well, many executives are loath to take a chance on experimenting with the effect of changed advertising expenditures.

## Cost of Money to Be Loaned

Lenders' major variable cost is the amount paid for the money which the firm lends out. This may run two-thirds of gross operating income or more. Two factors influence the firm's cost of money.

First, the movements of total demand, supply, and government policy in the over-all money market determine the average interest rate on such money-market items as treasury notes, long-term governments, corporates, and municipal bonds. (See Chapter 4.) The returns on such items set the opportunity costs for mortgages. Most institutions can buy other assets or lend in the other money markets. As a result, the going rate in all lending markets is competitive with mortgages and must enter into the analysis of the variable costs of money.

Second, however, most financial institutions have a more direct control over their money costs through their own policies in paying for, and attracting, savings. The analysis of the cost of savings is similar to that of lending. Institutions have certain fixed and variable costs in their saving operations. They also face a competitive situation in the savings market. They can alter both the rates they offer for funds and the advertising and other expenditures they make to attract them.

As noted above, lenders need not consider the cost of money fixed. However, in determining what their costs of lending will be, they do have to consider the possible results of their policies to attract savings. At a minimum, their cost of money is its worth in alternative uses. Above that minimum, their cost of money depends on how much the firm has to spend to attract each additional amount of money. A cost schedule exists for funds. Its shape depends upon the rate at which fixed costs per unit fall as they are spread over additional units compared to the increasing amounts of variable costs that may be needed to bring in savings. Particularly important are the amounts paid out in interest on new and old accounts as a result of any change in interest or dividend rates.

Therefore it is clear that the savings and lending budgets are not independent but are mutually determined. Given certain market rates of interest, bond prices, other lenders' payments on savings, and other lenders' quotations for mortgages, the executive planning his policy and budget has an opportunity to alter his actions and expenditures simultaneously along some or all of the paths discussed in this chapter. Numerous observers have called attention to the awakening realization of this fact by progressive financial institutions. A learning process spreads new techniques from the better to the less informed firms. Lenders recognize that a profitable solution to their earnings problems may be made by moving along any of the various possible alternative paths. They may change the charges for loans, the payments for savings, or the expenditures for either or both.

### Other Variable Costs

Numerous other costs vary directly with the amount of lending. Many are payments supplied on a contract or fee basis, such as appraisals, credit reports, and individual legal opinions. Costs such as clerical expenditures and supplies are semivariable. At any given time an institution may have a good deal of excess capacity. A single additional loan does not require new personnel, and up to a point additional business leads to more efficient use of the same staff. But finally, as portfolios grow, new personnel must be hired. At critical points, however, savings may be possible. When expansions occur, new techniques can sometimes be substituted for new or even existing personnel. The rapid spread of electronic data processing is a clear example. Even before a size is reached at which computers become efficient, significant advances in the use of other office machinery become possible.

Some variable costs are a function of the number of loans rather than of their amount or magnitude. As a result, the cost per dollar falls with the amount of money loaned. Efficient servicing agencies estimate that it costs from $20 to $25 a year to service an average home loan. This works out to a cost of 2 per cent to service a loan with an outstanding balance of $1,000, while it is less than $\frac{1}{20}$ per cent with an outstanding balance of $50,000.

This size economy has been one of the traditional reasons why large loans on commercial or other buildings have had slightly lower interest rates than home loans even though their risk was actually greater. The lower cost of servicing such loans has been passed on to the borrower. In addition, however, such rates are lower because they are in a more competitive market. Many small lenders are not equipped to seek out and service all the loans they need or want at a particular time. These larger loans can be brought to them for direct negotiations and acceptance or rejection. As a result, borrowers with large loans may find more competitive bidding for them.

Previous chapters made it clear that risks too are a major type of variable cost. The normal or portfolio risk must be charged against the quoted interest rate as a correction in estimating the net yield. Loans that require extra servicing also lower the final yield. The number of personnel required to handle loans rises with the percentage of delinquencies or other problems. Servicing costs vary with the number, size, and risk of the individual loans.

## MARKETING AND INCOME ANALYSIS

Simultaneously with the examination of costs, the lender must analyze his income accounts and plan his marketing strategy. Income analysis requires that the expenditures for marketing, the theory of competition, and the pricing of services all be considered. Loans may be attracted by advertising and direct solicitation, by special services, including offices and their design, by varying the lending package, or by altering the interest charges and the fee structure. The interest rates and fees charged, corrected for risk premiums and costs, determine the amount of income.

### Marketing and Pricing

The recognition that lenders' marketing and pricing problems are comparable to those of other businesses has been spreading rapidly.

In past times many lending institutions, because of the necessity of treating their depositors' funds conservatively, tended to be unprogressive in their marketing as well. Recently, lenders have paid far more attention to this entire area, and knowledge has increased considerably.

As the economy has become more interested in scientific management, the number of formally trained executives in financial institutions has grown. Trade associations have continued to stress and spread the knowledge of good management practices. The marketing and pricing of the services of mortgage lenders are being scrutinized and improved in ways similar to those of other types of business organizations.

A mortgage lender analyzing the competitive situation in his own market must determine whether to compete by cutting the prices and terms of his loans or by adopting nonprice techniques such as more advertising or improved services. He chooses according to his firm's particular strengths and weaknesses.

The ability of a lender to plan his own strategy is greatly enhanced by the complexity of the mortgage market. Since the legal and portfolio needs of different institutions vary so widely, each lender can plan a multivariable strategy. He must be certain to protect the areas where his competition is greatest while taking advantage of those where his strength lies.

At times questions are raised as to whether it is proper or fair for lenders to vary their charges or services in accordance with the amount of their competition. Can they justify asking at one and the same time 5 per cent for one type of loan and 6 per cent for another? One school of thought holds that the basic theory of our free-enterprise market structure requires discriminatory pricing among different groups—that uniform prices based on some mistaken idea of fairness usually are less good for the community and national welfare than frankly discriminatory prices based on the careful determination of the supply and demand situation for particular loan categories.

When parts of a market fail to cover their true costs, they are being subsidized by other groups which, in turn, obtain less than the true value they should from the market. The individual businessman best performs his function by attempting to analyze the component parts of the market properly and setting his prices accordingly.

At times it may appear that equity can be increased by correcting basic flaws in the market rather than by attempting to exploit them. If a lender feels that some groups are being needlessly penalized, he can take this into account in his pricing policy. It is important, however, that such a policy be determined specifically and with forethought rather than through neglect or failure to understand the market situation.

In the absence of logic and knowledge, a price system will be purely haphazard and unlikely to reflect an efficient or equitable situation. Lenders who make decisions on some mistaken concept of fairness frequently are fair neither to themselves, nor to the community, nor to the individual borrower.

### Price Competition

The pricing of mortgages includes setting the interest rates, fees, and discounts quoted for particular types of loans. Lenders are in an imperfectly competitive market. They face competition from other lenders, but the degree of competition varies greatly with the type of property, its location, and the time.

As an example, in most areas savings and loans find far more competition for FHA- and VA-guaranteed loans than for conventional ones, since they can be bid for by mortgage companies and sold in the national market. Similarly insurance companies may actively solicit loans for higher-priced units and apartment houses but not for smaller or cheaper dwellings. Banks may be actively in or primarily out of the local market depending on available funds. For older homes, competition may exist primarily among savings and loan associations.

The knowledge of what others are doing is an important factor in setting one's own rates. Because national lenders find it harder to shift rates to meet local competition, their rates are a known factor which can be treated as such by others in pricing decisions. Local firms can react more immediately and concretely to changing quotations. Their current situation with respect to funds and need for loans and their probable reactions must be given more weight in setting one's own policy than the situation and reactions of national lenders.

Lenders increase their flexibility by altering their fees, discounts, and services before they change interest rates. Because they may cause reactions among borrowers with outstanding loans, it is frequently easier not to change interest rates. Also, interest rate moves may more easily be met by competitors. Since loans are so different, it is frequently possible to tailor yields through the fee structure without upsetting the market or one's competitors.

Altering services or the use of nonprice competition may also make more sense in many cases than changing rates. Again, experience in other marketing areas makes it clear that some customers can be attracted primarily on a price basis while others respond to a different set of stimuli. It is almost always a mistake, however, to assume that putting all one's efforts into one type of competition will give the best results. Discount houses expanded rapidly because department stores neglected price-conscious families. Lenders cannot afford to neglect any method of competition simply because in the past they have been most successful with one particular approach.

### Nonprice Competition

The strategies of nonprice competition are as varied as the elements they deal with. Institutions attract borrowers and depositors by their advertising, by their locations and offices, by the speed with which they act, by the number of solicitors they hire, by their gifts, by their public image, and by activities in civic and social groups.

Many of these factors must develop over long periods and should not be shifted with market conditions. On the other hand, they may change without being noticed. Many institutions eager to attract loans have found that customers preferred to go elsewhere because of unsatisfactory experiences in a previously tight market when the lender had more business than he wanted. Booming firms must remember the future and guard against a decline in service.

Firms can attract business by spending more for their services. Frequently the rate at which loans are processed can be speeded up, but only through paying for unused resources in many periods. The management must decide specifically on the level of services it wants to furnish. The higher processing costs of faster services should be counted as a definite expenditure to improve the competitive position of the firm. When costs of this type are recognized and estimated, decisions can be made as to whether they earn their way or whether the extra costs could be used more effectively along other lines.

## Income

The bulk of income originates in the interest rate charged on loans and in the fee structure. In firms which sell various services, however, income may be generated through a loan's impact in these other areas rather than directly.

The interest rate cannot be considered by itself. The net yield is the important factor. This means that all the offsets to income already discussed must enter into the analysis. The rate must be adjusted for differential risks, for the effect of the loan's terms on liquidity, and for additional costs that can be related directly to the individual mortgage. Only when all these elements have been taken into account can the true income from a loan be calculated.

Some types of loans have heavy charges directly related to them. For example in construction lending, the firm needs personnel to inspect the plan, check the documents, watch the progress of construction, and make certain that funds paid out go to the individual claimants so that mechanic's liens will not occur. These requirements reduce the potential income from the loan. Similar needs exist for handling property improvement loans, for land development loans, and for alteration and repair loans. The costs differ by type of loan, and so do the potential yields.

One way to attempt to offset these additional costs is through a fee schedule for special loans. Fees may also be charged on regular mortgages to cover the cost of placing the loan on the books. These fees are a significant part of income. Changes in their amounts are important in keeping the firm competitive.

Because the initial costs of originating a loan may be quite high, if no fee is charged, these costs reduce the profitability of the mortgage for its first several years. On the other hand, fees and their related premiums and discounts allow income to shift without the necessity of altering the quoted interest rate. Because interest rates are usually quoted in even $\frac{1}{4}$ or $\frac{1}{2}$ per cents, any change in the rate has a large impact on both the firm's income and the borrower's payments.

For example, an increase of $\frac{1}{4}$ per cent in the interest rate on a $20,000 mortgage for 20 years means that the firm will collect $718 additional during the life of the loan. Even when discounted at 5 per cent, such a rate change has a present value of over $485.

In contrast, a change of 1 per cent in the mortgage fee would alter current income by $200. This means that a firm may be better off shifting its fees or premiums by $2\frac{1}{2}$ per cent than by altering the interest rate by $\frac{1}{4}$ of 1 per cent. Another way to look at this relationship is to note that fee charges of 1 per cent, 2 per cent, and 3 per cent for loans of this length add three additional steps in the interest rate structure in between the usual $\frac{1}{4}$ of 1 per cent steps that most firms quote.

It is also true that changes in fees may be a better way of competing than by interest rate movements. Fee shading is more difficult for competitors to match. Fees also allow the firm to shape its charges more exactly to the individual loan. If risk or cost analysis indicates that a loan is particularly advantageous, the borrower may be offered a premium. On the other hand, if the risks or costs are particularly high, the loan may still be worthwhile if sufficient fees can be collected to equalize the net income.

### Other Sources of Return

While commercial banks frequently recognize that loans and deposits may be interrelated and therefore that a loan may generate business and income elsewhere in the organization, this is less true of other lenders. Such neglect is unfortunate. A loan that otherwise would not pay for itself may be worthwhile in terms of the prestige it brings a firm, good will, community improvement, or gaining a good customer.

As a clear example, a few life insurance companies have related their mortgage loans to the sale of insurance. They recognize that if the mortgage brings in a customer who otherwise would not buy insurance, some of the usual cost of selling can be credited to the mortgage. A lower yield can therefore be accepted than would otherwise be the case. The borrower-customer can get more attractive terms by entering into both bargains.

Other cases exist of lending institutions' engaging in more than one line of business. If problems of conflict of interest and of monopoly pressures can be avoided, certain types of tie-in sales may be profitable. For example, a mortgage company with escrow, title, and insurance affiliates may be able to accept lower fees for the mortgage itself.

Still more frequent is the recognition of the impact of loans on an institution's public image and also on its own welfare through strengthening the community. Mortgages on churches may be a nuisance and unprofitable in and of themselves, but if they attract depositors and borrowers, their advantages may offset their basic intrinsic problems.

Most deposit institutions recognize that they depend for their funds on their locality. As a result, the more they can help local firms and local business activity, the better off they will be. They may therefore lend in their own markets at somewhat lower rates than required for equivalent loans elsewhere. They properly recognize that by helping their community, they are helping themselves.

## TAXES

The final factor entering into income analysis is the influence of the particular tax situation of the institution on its lending policies. Decisions are primarily affected if differential rates of taxation exist for the separate types of investment. When such differences exist, it will pay lenders to alter their investments to take advantage of income which may be taxed at a lower rate.

It is far simpler to note that tax rates have a general impact than it is to discuss their specific effects. The tax laws, particularly with respect to financial institutions, have gone through major revisions in recent years, and further changes may be expected. The actual laws and their impact vary both among types of institutions and among firms in the same industry. Generalizations are difficult and change with time and particular situations.

## Bad-debt Reserves

The specific tax treatments which separate mortgages from other investment lie primarily in the area of accounting for bad-debt reserves and to some degree in the timing of expenses and losses. Previous chapters have discussed the very real risks which mortgages face. Because of them, one must think of current interest receipts as partly a net yield and partly a payment to compensate for future losses. Such a theory leads to the establishment of bad-debt reserves. These reserves contain receipts put aside from income to compensate for possible future losses.

Unfortunately the potential losses can be no more than estimates. No way exists of accurately predicting their future levels. This impreciseness of estimates, which is of primary concern to management and supervisory agencies, is also of interest to the income tax collector. Money placed in a bad-debt reserve is usually not subject to income taxes unless and until it is transferred out of the reserve. At such a time, it is returned to the current income account and becomes subject to prevailing tax rates.

If the bad-debt reserves exceed actual losses, a firm has two types of potential tax savings. Most importantly, the excess amount in the reserve establishes what is loosely called a tax-free loan from the government. Earnings subject to tax are cut in half (assuming a 50 per cent tax rate) when they must be declared as current income and placed in surplus or undistributed profits. The government takes its taxable share from these sums. For every $1,000 earned only $500 remains after taxes to reinvest in the firm where it can work for future earnings. In contrast, income transferred to the bad-debt reserve pays no tax. All of it is available for reinvestment. A company desiring to build up its available funds is saved taxes on that part of income credited to an authorized bad-debt reserve. However, if this credit to the reserve exceeds actual future requirements, it is really part of current earnings or income. The existence of the reserve gives a tax saving. The amount of this saving is retained for the present by the firm. Even if it must pay equivalent taxes at some future time, in the interim the sums can be used profitably by the institution.

A second possible saving exists if it is assumed that tax rates will be lower in the future. If the rate is lower at the time when the reserves are carried to earnings and can be paid out in dividends, thus becoming subject to taxes, an additional saving will be realized.

### Authorized Reserves

For many years, because they could reduce any potential earnings by a transfer to loss reserves, mutual savings banks, savings and loans, and insurance companies paid minimal income taxes. This is no longer the case.

Mutual savings banks and savings and loans now work under a complex formula of authorized reserves. In effect, they have to calculate their normal income subject to tax. In this calculation they can take credit for routine expenses, including interest or dividends on share accounts or deposits. These institutions can then transfer 60 per cent of the remaining otherwise taxable income to a bad-debt reserve against their mortgages. This nontaxable transfer is authorized providing that as a result of this transfer, the reserve against mortgages is not over 6 per cent and that total reserves are not above 12 per cent. Where these transfers to reserves are less than 3 per cent of the increase in risk assets, a somewhat greater percentage of current earnings may be transferred without taxes.

For banks, bad-debt reserves may be based upon a 20-year moving average of recent experience or on any 20 years' experience after 1927. They can make tax-free transfers to a bad-debt reserve based upon their per cent of loss experience multiplied by the amount of outstanding loans. Their total reserve may not exceed three times the average experience factor multiplied by their outstanding loans.

Insurance companies now are taxed on a ratio derived from earnings required on their reserves over total earnings. Various adjustments are made for types of earnings and for general expenses. The formulas are extremely complex and vary from firm to firm.

The net effect of these changes in the tax law is to cause the taxability of mortgage earnings to vary from year to year within the same institution, among institutions in the same year, and among assets at separate times. The relative tax rates for mortgages will fluctuate depending on recent losses and on previously accumulated reserves. The calculation of comparative net yields raises still more difficult problems because the variables are so numerous. As a result of the new rules, the net impact of taxes on decisions appears somewhat less than in former periods. However, it still is a factor that must enter into earnings analysis. At times it may still be the decisive factor determining whether or not an institution should expand its mortgage portfolio in comparison with other potential investments.

## SUMMARY

Profit planning is a basic part of the lending process. Firms must consider how their costs will vary with projected volumes of loans. They must budget and control their costs so as to achieve the desired relationships between current and future earnings. They have many choices as to which costs to accept. They can also plan so as to obtain various desired relationships between fixed and variable costs.

In trying to attract savings and loans, financial institutions face traditional marketing problems. They can change their payments and charges. They can alter their fee schedules. They can also vary the services they offer. Which type of competition should be engaged in will depend on their local situation, but it will also vary with conditions in the over-all money market.

Until recently tax considerations were extremely important, particularly in determining the differences in net yields among assets. Although recent tax changes have altered this situation somewhat, the tax factor still remains a critical decision variable.

## SELECTED REFERENCES

Bierman, Harold, Jr.: *Topics in Cost Accounting and Decisions*, McGraw-Hill Book Company, New York, 1963.

Conway, L. V.: *Mortgage Lending,* 2d ed., American Savings and Loan Institute, Chicago, 1962.

Harlan, N. E., et al.: *Managerial Economics,* Richard D. Irwin, Inc., Homewood, Ill., 1962.

McMichael, S. L., and P. T. O'Keefe: *How to Finance Real Estate,* 2d ed., Prentice-Hall, Inc., Englewood Cliffs, N.J., 1953.

Robinson, Roland I.: *The Management of Bank Funds,* 2d ed., McGraw-Hill Book Company, New York, 1962.

Walter, J. E.: *The Investment Process,* Harvard Business School, Boston, 1962.

Wehrle, L. S.: "Life Insurance Investment," *Yale Economic Essays,* vol. 1, no. 1, 1961.

# Portfolio Policy and the
# Supply of Mortgage Funds———————11

The final factors shaping lending decisions are the policies each institution follows in managing its portfolio. Some policies are dictated by legal or regulatory restrictions; other policies may be decided on as a matter of rote. The decisions which we consider here are those that managements make with respect to the proper distribution of their assets, given their current and projected demand for, and supply of, funds.

Each institution determines, on the basis of its lending analysis and its flow of funds, its willingness to lend particular amounts of money on mortgages under specific terms, conditions, and rates. The sum of all of these individual decisions gives the supply schedule for mortgage loans. Lenders in the mortgage market stand willing to advance certain sums of money for each particular set of circumstances. The actual amount lent will depend upon both this supply curve of lenders and the demand which borrowers bring to the market.

## PORTFOLIO POLICIES

Management decisions as to the distribution of total holdings among various types and maturities of loans and investments constitute portfolio policy. Frequently this policy is implicit rather than ex-

267

plicit. Many institutions have paid little attention to the need for a portfolio policy and the reasons for adopting one. Instead, they base lending policies on institutional practices or rules of thumb reaching far back into the past. Any logic or justification which these policies once had may long since have vanished.

In other institutions, particularly in well-managed ones, it is recognized that each change in economic conditions, in the money market, or in the competitive situation requires a reexamination of, and perhaps a shift in, portfolio policy. In still other cases, changes occur almost unnoticed as rules of thumb are altered to agree with market realities. Old shibboleths may still be mouthed, but in actual practice they are not followed.

Each firm's decisions are limited by its charter and supervisory body. Almost all state and Federal regulations put specific bounds on the type and amount of mortgages an institution can hold. In addition, the policy adopted will have to reflect the firm's type, size, and geographical location. How and where a bank or an insurance company invests are conditioned by the amount of funds it receives, where its office is located, and the particular business it is in.

Every fiduciary institution recognizes a special relationship to its depositors, or clients. When it accepts funds from a large number of individuals, a trustee type of relationship results. The managers must pay particular attention to the firm's safety and liquidity. To be successful and fulfill their entire task, however, they must also give considerable weight to the potential returns of different forms of investment.

Each institution evaluates changing conditions. It adopts new policies to meet events as they occur. These policies should be well thought through, logical, and clearly expressed. Lending criteria must result from analysis rather than from a haphazard reaction to unexpected events.

## GOALS AND DECISIONS

Firms have a portfolio policy whether they recognize it formally or not. But unless a program is established which requires that the goals of the policy and methods of implementing it be reviewed periodically, the policy is not likely to be logical. Many firms fail to analyze their needs but instead simply react to market pressures when the forces impinging on them are so great that they can no longer be neglected. Management suddenly realizes that its flow of funds has shifted or that it is having trouble generating loans at current rates. As a result, it alters its lending decisions to meet these changes.

Other firms attempt to alter the conditions and amounts of mortgage lending only as a result of a conscious decision after a careful examination of what is happening. They try to analyze the impact of shifting credit requirements, maturities, and types of loans on their future yields and long-term goals.

### Objectives

Most advisers recommend that the first step in the development of any portfolio policy be a clear statement of the goals to be achieved. Why is the firm making certain types of loans? What does it hope to achieve by changing its mortgage policy? What weight should be given in any change to the needs and desires of depositors, potential borrowers, the management, or stockholders?

After the firm states its goals, procedures must be established for the management of its portfolio to achieve them. These plans specify such matters as how the necessary decisions will be made, who will take the responsibility, and how often the policy will be reconsidered. The program must specify the type of decisions with respect to assets that a policy review must include. It also must establish the criteria for making these decisions.

Many types of criteria might be used to define the firm's goals. It does little good to have too simple a statement of policy, such as that there will be an attempt to maximize profits or net yields. Situations are too complex. A more operational set of criteria is necessary. Those responsible must have guidance as to what types of action the management believes will be of greatest aid in obtaining the over-all goals.

It is necessary in establishing the criteria to recognize the impact on the long-run success of the firm of such factors as rate of growth or leadership in new techniques and markets. Growth, because it increases scale, may lower unit overhead costs, may have tax advantages, and could lead to greater diversification, has often been selected as a goal in and of itself. Another aspect is a consideration of the amount of risks, particularly with respect to possible portfolio losses, that the firm will accept.

When it changes its portfolio, a firm must decide whether to move with the industry average or to strike off by itself and hope to be an innovator and industry leader. On the one hand, the firm may aim to stay near the industry's norm with respect to timing, types of assets, and profitability. The advantage of attempting to steer by the industry's norm is that a management is less likely to incur criticism. If something goes wrong, everyone in the industry will suffer together. The excuse that the management did only what the industry thought proper will usually be accepted as a sufficient explanation. However, following the industry may not avoid bankruptcy or other dire results such as occurred in the 1930s. It also will not allow the management to profit from its own ability.

On the other hand, policy may stress innovations and an attempt to choose the most profitable paths. The firm can carefully examine the market, relative risks and yields, and future prospects. Then the management can use its analytic skills to search out the best solutions. It can hunt for new opportunities, pockets in the yield curves, and better operations. Such a goal may yield high potential profits but also higher risks.

A mixed strategy might call for a policy of constantly searching for more profitable paths but moving only part way down them away from the industry's norms. The firm establishes as its goal that of being a limited innovator. It will use its skills but not take unusual risks. In terms of current practice, even limited innovations and modest changes are likely to make the firm among the most progressive and successful.

## Types of Policy Decisions

Having determined its goals, the lender must adopt a specific program to select the policies which will achieve its objectives. Both the goals and the program should be in writing so that they will be logical and clear to all in responsible positions. The programs should be described in broad general terms, but they must also show in detail which decisions must be made and how often each specific decision criterion should be reviewed.

The decisions should consist of agreements to expand or contract particular classes of assets. After the general lines of movement have been established, the program's implementation will be up to the individual lending officers. Which assets will be purchased at any time will depend upon several different factors.

First consideration should be given to the type of asset. How much money should the firm place in mortgages, bonds, consumer loans, stocks, or other assets? Within each of these categories how much should go to particular subcategories? For example, how much of the money allotted to mortgages should go into one-family residences, multifamily residences, income property, or raw land?

Another important determination relates to the quality distribution of assets. In times of easy money, mortgage portfolios show a tendency to fill with lower-quality loans. Offers that would be rejected in normal circumstances are taken because money is so available. A policy statement with respect to quality should point out to lending officers the likelihood that such tendencies may occur. It should specify how far the firm is willing to go to generate additional business and what compensating advantages should be sought.

Another significant dimension is that of maturity. The average length of the portfolio determines its liquidity risks and the probability of income losses or gains that can result from shifting interest rates. If interest rates are low, every long-term mortgage carries a heavy risk of a market loss. The maturity distribution of the mortgage portfolio is traditionally hard to control, but it is not impossible. More emphasis can be put on construction or short-term financing. Differentials might be charged loans of longer maturities. Existing mortgages with shorter lengths could be bought from Fanny May.

Diversification is another major portfolio policy. Diversification is possible with respect to type of loan, type of mortgage, timing or origination, and geographical dispersal. Unless the firm's written policy sets up certain criteria for these factors, it cannot expect lending officers to develop a properly balanced portfolio.

## Portfolio Management

Other considerations enter into portfolio management in addition to the establishment of goals and a program. One question is how rapidly a firm should attempt to adjust its portfolio. Should it buy and sell mortgages in the market to speed up adjustments, or should it alter its assets only in accordance with its flow of new funds and repayments on old? Some firms have a policy of reinvesting repayments in the same sphere from which they flowed, with changes in policy thus affecting only the spending of new funds. A hierarchy of rates of change can be drawn up depending on whether a company sells some of its present assets, shifts its gross flow of funds to new activities, moves its net flow, or is only willing to redirect part of its net flow.

Another basic requirement for good choices is that there be adequate information on true costs. Unless the firm has a program of earning analysis that generates appropriate estimates of alternative costs, it cannot make logical portfolio decisions. It is clear that these cost estimates will never be exact. The firm must gather as much information as it can, order it logically, and then use its best judgment. However, without some estimates of difference in net yields, any possibility of making good decisions disappears.

The knowledge of what flow of funds to expect is also critical. Such information is expanding rapidly. Without an estimate of what money will be available, the firm has trouble with commitments. It cannot measure the impact of one set of decisions in contrast to others.

Another management policy question is how far to go with decisions based on forecasts of probable cyclical movements in the money market. Most large-sized lenders find that some forecasts are necessary. It is therefore profitable to develop skills in this sphere. Frequently they will not radically alter portfolios on the basis of forecasts only, but they will lean in the direction indicated. If the forecast implies that they should avoid present commitments and stay in cash, they will not stop lending entirely, but they will try to increase their short-term liquidity.

For example, some savings and loan associations project the future money and mortgage markets in determining when to borrow and when to repay supplemental funds from the Federal Home Loan Bank. Some lenders make similar decisions with respect to selling FHA-VA loans. Other firms, however, never give a thought to how the present should be adjusted to prepare for the future. They think mainly in terms of the borrowers that approach them in any period. If their customers demand more money, they borrow. If potential borrowers do not appear, they pay off their debts.

The use of short-cut, rule-of-thumb policies for portfolio decisions frequently makes it impossible to follow more sophisticated judgments and procedures. Consider a firm which aims at maintaining its level of mortgages as a constant percentage of its assets. In such a case, the market and not the management will determine what the firm does. The firm must alter its lending criteria in response to its competition and the flow of funds. If it fails, it does not obtain the proper number of loans to keep its mortgage ratio constant. Since the amount of money and competition for mortgages alter, such a criterion means a firm must tighten terms as the money market tightens and ease them when more money is available. The institution goes through a cyclical process of shifting the risks it assumes without examining the why and wherefore of such a policy. The actual yields are likely to vary sharply from period to period.

## LEGAL REQUIREMENTS

The most striking fact about legal requirements is their tremendous variation. They have developed separately for each type of institution. Often there has been a complete neglect even of related regulations in neighboring fields. For commercial banks and savings and loan associations, a dual system of chartering and supervision by state and Federal authorities exists. State units follow local laws, while national banks and Federal savings and loans operate in accordance with their Federal charters. Both Federal and state units conform to regulations of the Federal insuring authorities.

State regulations are especially varied. General statements can be made concerning the regulations which apply to Federal units, but each state may establish almost unique regulations in its own jurisdiction. In many states, however, general provisions have been adopted which permit the state's institutions to make any loan allowed to a Federal institution doing business in the state. Some state laws are specific, but legislatures attempt to keep them current with the Federal acts. However, lags frequently develop as a result of infrequent meetings of state legislatures and the lack of urgency with which they may consider changes. In other cases, the state's rules may be far more liberal than those of the Federal authorities. Therefore, while in general it is true that rules similar to the Federal regulations apply throughout the country, in actuality any particular state may differ vastly from the norm. Rules are in constant flux. Savings and loan associations and mutual savings banks have been pushing for major changes in Federal legislation.

Mutual savings banks and life insurance companies are chartered only by states, although the mutual savings banks have had laws introduced which would allow Federal charters. Again wide variations in regulations exist, depending upon each firm's home state. Life insurance companies' rules have an additional complexity. While primarily regulated by their home state, life insurance companies must comply substantially with the investment requirement and limitations imposed on local or domestic insurers in any other state where they desire to do business.

Substantial compliance is a technical problem. How restrictive any state's regulations are for an outside firm frequently depends upon the individual company's surplus and the forms of liability it assumes. For most firms, New York State law is paramount. New York State insurance companies hold more than a third of all life insurance assets. Those companies licensed to do business in New York hold more than 80 per cent of the total. In addition, since New York has traditionally been outstanding in the high quality of its insurance legislation, many other states follow New York's lead in establishing specific requirements.

### Savings and Loan Associations

Regulations affecting savings and loan associations tend to be most liberal with respect to loans on single-family houses. In comparison with other lenders, savings and loans are somewhat more restricted in other mortgage lending, quite restricted in geographical area, and most highly curtailed in their ability to lend on or invest in assets other than mortgages.

In general, lending is restricted to within a 100-mile radius of the office of the firm. This limit does not apply to FHA-VA loans or to mortgages participated in with associations elsewhere. Loans on apartment units are allowed, but their share of total assets is limited. Still smaller sums may be loaned on raw land or on land improvements.

Except for mortgages, possible investments are extremely limited. In effect, associations could purchase only United States government securities or short-term notes of government agencies such as the Federal Home Loan Banks and the Federal National Mortgage Association. Under changed regulations in 1964, they were authorized to add municipal bonds and loans for expenses of college students to their portfolios. They also can and do hold real estate either for their own offices or that taken over as security on a loan.

Under the pressure of a high inflow of savings and the successful experience of the FHA and VA with low-down-payment and long-amortization loans, the mortgage lending requirements have been steadily liberalized. As an example, directors of Federal associations can authorize loans of up to 90 per cent of the first $20,000 of the actual purchase price plus 80 per cent of the next $5,000. This means that a $22,000 loan can be made on a $25,000 house provided that it is amortized monthly over a maximum period of 25 years and that tax and insurance escrows are collected. FHA and VA loans can be made in accordance with the most liberal regulations of those agencies.

The amount that can be lent on a mortgage depends in general on the length of the amortization period and the type of property. Homes require the smallest down payments. Mortgages on multifamily units can cover loans of from 50 to 75 per cent of value, depending on the size of the loan and its amortization period. Business properties require a 50 per cent down payment on 25-year loans but only 40 per cent on 20-year loans. Recently associations have been allowed to lend for sites and land acquisitions. Such loans are limited to three years, to 60 or 70 per cent of value, and to a limited share of the association's total assets.

These various regulations taken together severely circumscribe the portfolio decisions of management. Within limits, the officers can determine the type of loans and their terms. They encounter greater difficulties if they try to diversify. They lack the choice that other institutions have of selecting other types of loans and securities. If management feels that the time is not right for increasing its mortgage loan portfolio, it can only expand its cash or governments. Because on the surface the potential yield of mortgages seems so much greater than that of bonds, managements have frequently neglected the finer points of portfolio policy.

### Mutual Savings Banks

Mutual savings banks as a group come closest to the savings and loan associations in their portfolio policies. Since they are entirely state institutions, their regulations differ widely. Their mortgage restrictions are more liberal. They also have a wider choice of other assets.

The single-family-home mortgage can have the highest loan-to-value ratio. Its limit tends to 80 per cent. Because of their location in built-up central cities, the savings banks make many more loans on apartment houses and commercial buildings. In fact, they are the largest lenders on apartment units of all groups.

Until approximately 1950, most mutual savings banks were restricted in their mortgage loans to a 50-mile radius or to their home state. Since then they have been able to make or purchase federally insured or guaranteed loans throughout the country. In many cases they have used this privilege to buy blocks of mortgages already outstanding. With insurance companies, they form the main base of the national mortgage market.

Mutual savings banks have much greater freedom than savings and loans in purchasing bonds and making small loans. In certain states they may purchase small amounts of stock or other securities. In most cases, however, their investments are carefully circumscribed, usually depending upon the legal list of the state's supervisory authority.

These regulations allow the savings banks a rather active portfolio policy. Still, since 1954, virtually all their net increases in funds have gone in the mortgage market. The flexibility of savings banks, however, has been sufficient so that in some years they have committed only 70 or 75 per cent of new money to mortgages. In other years new mortgage loans have exceeded their net inflow. Bonds have been sold or allowed to run off, with the proceeds placed in mortgages.

### Life Insurance Companies

The life insurance companies have the most portfolio flexibility of any of the major savings institutions. The larger companies in particular pay a great deal of attention to shifts in their portfolios. Since these companies sell insurance on a national basis, they are usually allowed or even forced to lend over wide areas.

Some states place a maximum limit on the total amount of mortgage holdings, usually 40 per cent of assets but sometimes more. In addition, as with all other lenders, limits are established on the size of individual mortgages and the amount that can be granted to a given borrower. Such limits are usually related to the total assets or capital of the lender.

A maximum 66⅔ per cent loan-to-value ratio has been traditional with insurance companies. In recent years, this ratio increased to 75 per cent and in some cases to 80 per cent for single- or two-family houses. None of the limits applies to government-insured or government-guaranteed loans. The insurance companies are the largest lenders on commercial and income properties.

Although the laws of most states give broad lending powers, they do establish various limitations requiring that certain classes of investments or loans not exceed a given ratio to total assets. These ratios are more liberal than those for other financial intermediaries. Common stocks and ownership of real estate for income are examples of authorized investments usually forbidden others. In addition, most states have general leeway provisions which enable each

company to take loans otherwise forbidden up to a specified percentage of its assets or capital.

Because their lending powers are so broad, the life insurance
firms must pay a great deal of attention to portfolio policy. They
cannot assume that existing ratios are proper. While they have
tended to put 40 to 45 per cent of their net flow into mortgages,
their annual investment rates have varied from 35 to over 75 per cent.

## Commercial Banks

Although commercial banks have the widest discretion in lending
and investing, their mortgage regulations tend to be stricter than
their own requirements in other lending areas and also among the
strictest for any financial institution. Because money-market movements are so important to them and because of their need to maintain
liquidity, the portfolio policy of commercial banks tends to fluctuate
far more rapidly than that of other lenders.

The regulations severely limiting national banks in their mortgage
lending stemmed from the idea that banks should primarily do commercial lending. The aftereffects of this concept still remain. The
original Federal Reserve Act made no provision for urban mortgages. In 1916, mortgages of 50 per cent could be made for one
year, and in 1927 this was liberalized to five years. In 1935, national
banks were authorized to make government-insured loans up to
the limits established by the FHA. They could also make 60 per
cent loans lasting 10 years, providing some amortization provisions
were included. Full amortization was not necessary, since a so-called
balloon payment was authorized at the end of the 10-year period.
In 1964, conventional loans of 80 per cent were allowed providing
they were fully amortized over 25 years.

In addition to limitations on terms, banks are strictly limited
with respect to the amount of their total funds they can place in
conventional mortgages. They may lend only up to an amount equal
to their capital and surplus or up to 60 per cent of their time
and savings deposits, whichever is greater. While many large banks
do not approach their allowance, this limit is the critical factor
in determining the mortgage portfolio of many individual banks.

The maximum does not apply to commercial or industrial loans where real estate is offered as an additional security. Mortgages for such purposes are very common. The maximum also does not apply to FHA-VA loans. The fact that government-insured loans can be made outside of the commercial banks' limits of mortgage lending is one of the factors which put these loans at the margin and cause the banks to vary their lending on these securities far more than on conventional mortgages.

The portfolios of the banks are so complex and pressures upon them are so great that constant shifts in policy are not surprising. Banks find large variations both in their flow of available funds and in the relative yields of separate classes of earnings. They react by shifting their investment policies sharply, even in very short periods.

## THE SUPPLY OF MORTGAGE FUNDS

Taken together, the examples in this book show that the amount of money available for mortgages has fluctuated widely and interest rates charged have also moved, but not as violently. We have examined in detail the different forces at work which cause these phenomena. Now we want to put them together and summarize them.

The amount of funds available for mortgages depends on the level of savings, the amount of money created, and the willingness of savers and financial institutions to lend on mortgages in contrast to other loans or investments. The yields or prices of mortgages depend partly on the amount of money available in the mortgage market but also on the demand for it. Borrowers want money but not in unlimited amounts or at any price. It is the interaction of the suppliers of funds and the potential borrowers that determines the prices that prevail in the market and the amounts loaned at those prices.

First we consider the supply factors for money. How much will lenders make available at each potential interest rate? Every reader who recalls any book in elementary economics will recognize that what we are discussing is the concept of a supply curve. He will also recognize that in this discussion we must handle separately two questions that are often confused.

First comes the relationship between the interest charges and the amounts loaned at a given time (the shape of the curve). As an illustration of a schedule or curve of potential lending at one time but at different rates, lenders might make available on mortgages, in any one year, $25 billion if prevailing interest rates were 5 per cent, $28 billion if they could receive $5\frac{1}{2}$ per cent on the average, and $30 billion if the average new mortgage was written at 6 per cent. Whether or not such a shape is likely for the supply curve is discussed in the next section.

The second question of the supply curve is how it shifts from one period or year to the next because of alterations in monetary policy, savers' desires, or lenders' portfolio policies. These variables cause changes in the supply curve's position and explain its year-to-year shifts. What would happen if the market made $28 billion available at $5\frac{1}{2}$ per cent interest in one year and then far more money was created the next? We might find that as a result of this creation of money, institutions would be willing to lend the same $28 billion on mortgages at only 5 per cent. In contrast, if money were very tight, mortgage borrowers as a whole might have to pay an average rate of $6\frac{1}{4}$ per cent in order to borrow $28 billion.

Analysis of this problem is complicated by the fact that the prevailing rates and the actual amounts transferred in the market measure changes in both the shape of the supply curve and its position together with similar movements on the demand side. What we see in the statistics are the points of equilibrium where both curves come together. We can only attempt through logic to separate the different movements reflected in these changes in equilibrium.

### The Shape of the Curve: The Elasticity of Supply

The shape of the mortgage supply curve, or in economic terms, its elasticity, determines how much the interest rate charged on mortgages will rise and fall as the demand for money and amounts of money available in the mortgage market shift. Can a sudden increased demand for mortgages be met without a major rise in the interest rate? Supply will depend on how much money can be attracted away from other uses and into the mortgage market. Results will differ depending upon whether mortgage demand is expanding by itself or along with all other requirements for funds. The answer is significant because it will influence both the possible levels of construction and the amounts each borrower will pay for his own shelter.

The opposite side of the coin is what happens when the demand for mortgages falls. Will this lead to a decrease in interest rates, or will there simply be fewer funds for mortgages and more elsewhere, with only minor adjustments of rates? We are interested in how dependent or independent the mortgage market is in comparison with other credit markets. What is the interest elasticity of mortgage lending? Will the increases in interest charges be large or small when the demand for mortgages rises or when a contraction occurs in the amount of money available?

The interest rate we would like to measure and analyze is the market yield on current commitments. It will be an average of the rates charged for all the sums loaned on mortgages at one time. The rates charged should be corrected for differential risks and for loans made against commitments from previous periods. Important variations exist in the rates in different parts of the country depending upon demand and competition in specific localities, but in examining over-all trends they are averaged out.

### Factors Influencing Elasticity

The elasticity of mortgage lending with respect to interest rates is a fact, but one which is hard to measure. It depends on whether or not individual lenders are willing to shift the amount of money they put into mortgages when interest rates change relative to other markets. While at any time lenders can shift their flow of funds among their assets, it is harder legally for some to substitute assets than others. Each is faced with a somewhat different choice.

Whether or not lenders do avail themselves of their opportunities to shift portfolios is far from clear. Some analysts argue that because mortgages are so specialized, the competition is dampened and the mortgage market remains somewhat insulated from others, with lenders failing to adjust amounts loaned as much as one would expect. This group assumes that the flow of mortgage funds has a rather low interest elasticity. Sharp changes in interest rates have only minor impacts on the amount of money available to the mortgage market.

This view mirrors statements frequently made by those lenders who speak as if they attempt to lend all their available funds at whatever rate prevails in the market. They do not change their willingness to lend if the interest rate rises or falls. They claim, in effect, that changes in interest rates and amounts loaned depend entirely on shifts in the demand for mortgages and the availability of money (the position of the supply curve) rather than on interest elasticity (shape of the supply curve).

The strongest point made to support the idea that lenders do not change the amount they lend very much as interest rates rise is based on the argument that lenders follow a portfolio policy which neglects interest. Some observers believe that most lenders simply commit a fixed percentage of their assets to mortgages under all circumstances. If savings and loans believe that they must lend on mortgages all the money they receive or if insurance companies follow an automatic policy of investing 40 per cent of their growth in assets in mortgages, then reactions to interest rate changes will be inelastic. Firms whose portfolio goal is a fixed ratio of mortgages to assets will not alter lending much when interest rates change.

Additional arguments are put forth for the idea that lenders pay little attention to interest rates in deciding how much to lend. Lenders have mainly fixed costs. Therefore, making loans under diverse yield situations may be more profitable than a failure to lend, since as long as loans more than cover their direct costs, they will make some contribution to income. Another idea is that growth is so profitable that it always pays to expand as fast as possible. If this is true, loans would be made as fast as funds to lend out became available and differences in yields on the loans would be of secondary importance.

While these arguments that mortgage lending is inelastic are frequently made, many observers feel that the opposite is true. Many institutions do make mortgage lending decisions based on the net yield available in the different credit markets. Even if some institutions follow a shortsighted or incorrect portfolio policy, there are enough others to give the whole supply curve considerable elasticity. Commercial banks do enter and leave the mortgage market. Life insurance companies do increase their purchases of bonds and make more loans when rates on these other investments exceed their estimated return from mortgages. These lenders also come back to the mortgage market when relative yields rise.

Many lenders also shift their holdings of cash and liquid assets, withdrawing from the mortgage market if they feel interest rates are too low or are likely to rise. Even savings and loans vary their borrowings and repayments from the Federal Home Loan Banks as interest rates shift. Firms curtail their lending increasingly when they feel that the mortgage market has become too competitive and that maintaining volume is possible only through accepting more and more marginal loans. At such times, they rethink their marketing problems and may decide they are better off not trying to win as many loans of types that have a high degree of competition.

Another situation that may cause more elasticity than is frequently recognized occurs when lenders vary their risks and therefore their net yields in an attempt to maintain volume. Lenders may maintain their charges and their contract interest rates, but if this can be accomplished only through a deterioration of quality, then supply is more interest-elastic than is frequently recognized.

A final factor which may increase the interest elasticity of the market is the ability to attract individuals as lenders if rates get high enough. Individuals frequently play an unimportant part in mortgage lending, but this is far less true during periods of high interest rates. They add their supply of funds to that of other lenders as a direct result of the increased yields offered by mortgages.

### The Amount of Money Supplied

Chapter 2 and Tables 2-1 and 2-2 furnish information on the supply of funds made available through saving and through financial institutions and others. The striking fact evident in these tables is the marked changes in the amount of funds flowing into the credit markets at different times. We note from Table 2-2 that year-to-year changes in the availability of total funds average about 30 per cent. The sharpest shifts occur in the creation of money at commercial banks and in the amount of money individuals save and invest directly or entrust to financial institutions.

The total change in funds, however, is only one of the factors influencing the position of the supply curve for mortgages. It also shifts with the demand from other borrowers. Business, government, and consumers alter their bids for credit depending on whether they want to increase expenditures on plant and equipment, buy more cars, raise inventories, or finance a government deficit.

The shifting total supply of money and the varying demands of other forces are the main causes of fluctuations in the supply curve for mortgage loans. The mortgage total in Table 2-3 shows sharp movements, caused by the net decisions of all lenders as to how they will lend. They have to consider the amount of money made available to them, the bids from other borrowers, and the bids from those who want to borrow in the mortgage market.

A special factor affecting the mortgage market should be emphasized again: when money is unusually tight, two separate sources of funds become available which have the effect of short-circuiting the traditional lending decisions of financial intermediaries. These two sources are the Federal National Mortgage Association and the direct loans of individuals. Both have expanded markedly in critical periods in the past, and their movements are portents for the future.

Fanny May operates to add funds to the mortgage market through its issues for debentures. When all institutions have reached their desired portfolios with respect to mortgages, they are still willing to purchase short-term notes. The FNMA is able to sell these notes and buy mortgages with the receipts, thus increasing the funds available for mortgages more than would otherwise be the case.

The expansion of individual lending occurs primarily through an increase in the amount of second-mortgage loans. The majority of these are probably purchase-money mortgages. In periods when the supply of mortgage funds is ample, sellers of houses receive cash for their equities. Lenders lend the new owners considerably more on their purchase than the previous owner owed on his partially amortized mortgage. The seller can use this cash above his previous debt to invest or deposit where he sees fit.

When funds are not as available, lenders lower the amount they will furnish. If the seller wants to receive the same price, he has to agree to accept part of the sale proceeds in the form of a second mortgage rather than cash. In effect, he is forced to lend part of his accumulated equity directly to the mortgage market instead of being able to take it out in cash.

Frequently the second-mortgage holder finds that he needs cash. As we have noted, the market for second mortgages is poorly organized. It is risky because the holder usually cannot afford to make payments on the first mortgage in case the borrower defaults. Administrative costs are high because the mortgages are frequently small. For all these reasons, when second mortgages trade, it is usually at a high discount from their face value.

## The Resulting Mortgage Flows

Table 11-1 shows the final impact of all the shifting of supply and demand, the willingness to vary lending with interest rates, and the changing portfolio policy of each type of lender. It illustrates both the changes in the amount of mortgage loans and how such changes compare with the institutions' total movements of funds.

A major difficulty in drawing conclusions from the table arises from the fact that the mortgages actually issued in a period may reflect lending against commitments made considerably in advance. This is clearest for 1956, when both life insurance companies and mutual savings banks maintained their levels of mortgage lending for several months, much against their wills. In order to meet their commitments they had to resort to warehousing and other practices not previously employed.

Even with the problems of lags, it still is clear from Table 11-1 that lenders do change their portfolios. The amounts of fluctuation are related to the importance of mortgages in their portfolios and to the rates of change in their over-all receipts of funds. Thus savings and loans have almost always invested between 90 and 95

TABLE 11-1  *Net Lending on Mortgages by Types of Financial Institutions and Comparison to Net Increase in Total Assets, 1952–1963* (Net lending in billions of dollars)

| | 1952 | 1953 | 1954 | 1955 | 1956 | 1957 | 1958 | 1959 | 1960 | 1961 | 1962 | 1963* |
|---|---|---|---|---|---|---|---|---|---|---|---|---|
| **Savings and loans** | | | | | | | | | | | | |
| (1) Net mortgage lending | 2.8 | 3.6 | 4.1 | 5.3 | 4.3 | 4.3 | 5.6 | 7.5 | 6.9 | 8.8 | 9.9 | 12.0 |
| (2) % of change in assets | 93.3 | 94.6 | 97.6 | 92.9 | 87.8 | 87.8 | 90.3 | 90.4 | 97.2 | 94.6 | 97.1 | 93.0 |
| **Commercial banks** | | | | | | | | | | | | |
| (1) Net mortgage lending | 1.1 | 1.0 | 1.7 | 2.4 | 1.7 | 0.6 | 2.2 | 2.5 | 0.7 | 1.6 | 4.0 | 5.3 |
| (2) % of change in assets | 12.2 | 25.0 | 16.5 | 48.0 | 39.5 | 12.0 | 14.5 | 59.5 | 75.3 | 10.1 | 20.6 | 27.7 |
| **Life insurance companies** | | | | | | | | | | | | |
| (1) Net mortgage lending | 1.9 | 2.1 | 2.7 | 3.5 | 3.5 | 2.2 | 1.8 | 2.1 | 2.6 | 2.4 | 2.7 | 3.6 |
| (2) % of change in assets | 42.2 | 43.7 | 52.9 | 67.3 | 68.6 | 44.9 | 35.3 | 40.4 | 48.1 | 42.9 | 42.2 | 54.5 |
| **Mutual savings banks** | | | | | | | | | | | | |
| (1) Net mortgage lending | 1.5 | 1.6 | 2.1 | 2.4 | 2.3 | 1.4 | 2.1 | 1.9 | 1.9 | 2.2 | 3.2 | 3.9 |
| (2) % of change in assets | 88.2 | 88.9 | 100.0 | 120.0 | 115.0 | 73.7 | 84.0 | 135.7 | 126.7 | 104.8 | 103.2 | 111.4 |
| **Other financial†** | | | | | | | | | | | | |
| (1) Net mortgage lending | … | … | … | 0.1 | 0.2 | 0.1 | 0.2 | 0.3 | 0.2 | 0.2 | 0.3 | 0.5 |
| (2) % of change in assets | … | … | … | 4.0 | 5.1 | 2.2 | 3.7 | 4.5 | 3.4 | 3.2 | 4.5 | 11.4 |
| **Government‡** | | | | | | | | | | | | |
| (1) Net mortgage lending | 0.6 | 0.4 | 0.1 | 0.5 | 0.7 | 1.3 | 0.3 | 2.4 | 1.8 | 1.0 | 0.6 | −0.5 |
| (2) % of change in assets | 33.3 | 36.4 | 11.1 | 29.4 | 31.8 | 43.3 | 15.0 | 55.8 | 46.2 | 34.5 | 17.1 | −27.8 |
| **Other nonfinancial** | | | | | | | | | | | | |
| (1) Net mortgage lending | 1.1 | 1.2 | 1.7 | 2.0 | 1.8 | 2.0 | 2.1 | 2.4 | 1.9 | 2.4 | 4.6 | 4.9 |
| (2) % of change in assets | 14.3 | 17.9 | 33.3 | 12.3 | 45.9 | 20.7 | 25.0 | 11.0 | 27.1 | 40.0 | 42.4 | 42.2 |

* Estimate.

† Corporate pension funds and credit unions.

per cent of the money they have supplied to the credit market in mortgages. Loans have ranged from 87.8 per cent to 97.6 per cent of their total funds. The movements in the ratio cannot be clearly related to expansions or contractions in their flow of funds or their investments. One period when inflow fell saw a still sharper curtailment of mortgage lending. In another, both fell, but lending fell by less than the inflow. Similarly there is no clear indication of a relationship between changes in interest rates and lending.

Mutual savings banks, with the next highest percentage of lending on mortgages, show far larger percentage shifts. A clear indication exists that the amount of mortgage lending reacts more slowly than movements in funds. Savings banks frequently show cutbacks of mortgage loans as funds increase and extensions of loans as funds decrease.

Insurance companies seem to have a more clearly defined portfolio policy than do the two previous types of institutions. They have far more flexibility, both because their cash inflow is more regular and because they have more obvious areas into which to shift their loans. The movements in their mortgage lending have been sharp and appear to reflect the differential yields of mortgages versus other loans. In 1958, for example, when their lending was comparatively low, the differential between market rates on FHA mortgages and on bonds was one of the lowest in the post war period. (See Figure 4-1.)

The major shifts have been by commercial banks. The chief factor here has been the availability of money and the competitive rates on short-term treasury bills. The amount of mortgage lending and its share of current new funds have been much larger when short-term rates were cheap. The principal exception came at the end of the period when short-term rates were held up by Operation Twist, while at the same time banks experienced a large inflow of savings deposits which, by law, they could use to increase their mortgage portfolios.

The data in Figure 4-1 indicate that mortgage interest rates are somewhat more sluggish than other money rates. Of course, this difference is obvious and is to be expected in comparison with short-term rates. It also, however, seems to be true with respect to bonds. The differential closes when rates are rising and expands when markets ease. This implies that many lenders continue to place money in mortgages even when their yields become somewhat less attractive in relative terms. On the other hand, enough follow a flexible portfolio policy that the amounts made available to mortgages do shift by more than movements in the market's total resources.

All these various facts can be summarized rapidly. The ability of financial institutions to lend varies as savings and money creation alter from period to period. There are also sharp shifts in the demands of different classes of borrowers. As a result, yields on securities fluctuate. They do not move together, but rather there is a ranking of changes, with the top position held by treasury bills, then on to bonds, and finally to mortgages.

The shifts in funds and in relative interest rates cause lenders to alter their policies and to change the amounts they make available for mortgages. In periods of rising interest rates, the upward movement in mortgage rates has not been sufficient to cause lenders to increase the mortgage market's share of total lending. In fact, the opposite happens. The increases in interest rates on mortgages have not been as large as in other credit instruments.

Mortgage borrowers as a whole face a difficult problem. If, as many believe, the elasticity of supply of mortgage money is not great, even fairly small additions to mortgage loans may be available only at much higher interest rates for all. Under the present system, some potential borrowers simply do not get the money they want. Either they stay out of the market, or sellers are forced to place funds in mortgages through second liens. The present system causes adjustments to be made through a rationing of demand for funds rather than through the supply or price of mortgage money.

## THE DEMAND FOR CREDIT

The influences determining the demand for mortgage money are far more complex than is frequently recognized. Press and magazine discussions of demand often paint completely conflicting pictures. In some cases, observers act as if the only critical lending variable is the available supply of credit. They talk of an unlimited demand which supply fails to meet for some obscure reason. These discussions are closely related to those which hold that there is a very small interest elasticity in the supply of credit.

Sometimes within one such article and frequently in other articles the opposite point of view prevails. It claims that the interest elasticity for mortgage borrowing is great. Small changes of interest rates or of amortization periods cause large volumes of demand to appear or disappear. The problem is not simply one of finding mortgage funds but one of finding them at specified prices and terms.

Analysis makes it difficult to maintain either extreme position. Some of the basic demand for borrowing clearly depends upon its price. Some construction and some turnover of properties will be delayed if money is tight or if its price rises. The amount of refinancing is also related to interest rates and general credit availability.

If the supply schedule for mortgage funds is rather inelastic and if the interest elasticity on the demand side is great, then large movements in the amount loaned occur primarily because even small shifts in the amounts made available lead to some increases in mortgage interest rates, and these in turn cause the sums demanded to decrease. If, on the other hand, demand is not elastic, the sharp changes in lending must be due to a rationing of credit, since otherwise borrowers would still seek money, even at the higher rates. Lenders determine how much they are willing to lend and its price. They cut off their loans at a given point even though they could lend more at the prevailing interest rates. This also means they could lend the same amount at higher rates. Borrowers would be willing to pay more if they could get more money, but the lenders do not offer them the opportunity.

## SUMMARY

Whereas some lenders follow fairly automatic lending policies, other lenders alter the amounts made available to the mortgage market through making deliberate changes in portfolio policy. This means that, as a matter of policy, they periodically reexamine their lending criteria and decide whether to increase or decrease their loans in particular categories. The factors that they consider include type of asset, quality, length of maturity, and geographical and other methods of diversification.

The elements entering into their decision are knowledge of the existing asset distribution, forecasts of the flow of funds, and projections of possible interest rate movements. At all times the strict legal requirements must be complied with.

As a result of changing portfolio policies and also of movements in funds and in relative yields, lenders alter the amount of money and the share of their assets that they make available to the mortgage market. While some lenders follow fairly automatic lending policies, enough do alter their portfolios to cause considerable movements in interest rates. The changed interest rates and the easier availability of credit or its opposite, the rationing of credit, bring marginal lenders into the market.

While some demands for credit are heavily influenced by its price, there is little evidence to indicate how much of demand falls into this category. The following chapters, which deal with the demand side, show what factors are important.

## SELECTED REFERENCES

American Bankers Association: *The Commercial Banking Industry,* Prentice-Hall, Inc., Englewood Cliffs, N.J., 1962.

Brigham, E.: Financial Intermediaries in the Residential Mortgage Market," unpublished Ph.D. thesis, University of California, Berkeley, California, 1962.

Kendall, L. T.: *The Savings and Loan Business,* Prentice-Hall, Inc., Englewood Cliffs, N.J., 1962.

National Association of Mutual Savings Banks: *Mutual Savings Banking,* Prentice-Hall, Inc., Englewood Cliffs, N.J., 1962.

Robinson, Roland I.: The Management of Bank Funds, 2d ed., McGraw-Hill Book Company, New York, 1962.

Walter, J. E.: *The Investment Process,* Harvard Business School, Boston, 1962.

Wehrle, L. S.: "Life Insurance Investment," *Yale Economic Essays,* vol. 1, no. 1.

# The Financing of Single-family
## Houses————————————————————————12

Previous chapters have discussed financing of real estate from an over-all point of view and from that of lenders supplying the money. Now we examine the problems of those who want to borrow money. We are interested in how they go about finding the money they need, how they determine the amount to try for, and what problems arise in fitting their demands to the institutions' supply.

The largest and most important share of real estate credit finances the construction, ownership, transfer, and repair of houses for occupancy by individual families. While the vast majority of these structures hold only one family, a few duplexes, triplexes, and fourplexes, exist.

In the market for residential loans borrowers may meet some variations in terms and conditions among lenders, but usually a particular institution will offer only slight flexibility. Some, but not very much, give-and-take exists in the amount lent and even in the interest rate. A borrower turned down by one lender usually cannot negotiate, but must search out another whose terms he can meet.

Mortgages in the single-family market finance four distinct types of transactions. First comes construction financing, which includes money for land, land development, and the building of the house from the time the first earth is turned until it is completed and sold and title is taken by the first owner-occupier. The second major sphere is the financing of purchases of new houses. In some cases the construction and sale financing are merged in a unified trans-action, most frequently when the house is built to order for the first occupier.

A third category comprises mortgages issued to finance sales of existing houses. In the United States, houses are sold or transferred every 8 to 10 years on an average. Their sums and effect on the economy are vast. From the point of view of mortgage laws and instruments, there is no difference between mortgages issued for the ownership of new houses and those for the transfer of ownership to second and successive owners. However, major differences exist in the manner in which the mortgages arise, in how lenders treat them, and in their impact on the economy.

The final category of single-family lending is for refinancing or advancing additional sums to homeowners. Funds are required for repairs, alterations, or maintenance of the units. Money may be advanced for nonhousing purposes. Since the mortgage market is more highly developed and has better security than markets for consumer or small-business loans, many families find that their cheapest source of money is the withdrawal of some of the equity built up in their homes. They refinance with a new mortgage, add to their existing mortgage, or sign a junior mortgage to obtain funds for other purposes.

## LENDING AND THE PURCHASE OF HOUSES

The financing of single-family units and the rates and availability of money in this market have wide-reaching influences on our entire economy and on each of us as individuals. They affect the level of investment and capital formation, the standard of housing, the amounts available for other consumption purposes, the methods of design and production of houses, and the entire urban environment.

Most discussions of real estate credit examine its impact on cur-rent rates of building. Builders, construction workers, and real estate men are particularly concerned with the extreme instability of new construction. Fluctuations in housing production rank among the largest in the economy. The effects they have had on those who make their living in this sphere have been most unfortunate. The impact on the rest of the economy has been multiplied as the income generated in the industry has fluctuated. Most observers believe the credit situation has been an important cause for these construction movements.

The availability and terms of construction mortgages do more than influence the level of building. They also determine to some extent the quality, choices offered, and units built. The question of what types of units are built must be analyzed separately from the question of how many units are started.

The type and amount of financing also have major impacts on homeownership and consumption of housing services. The number of homeowners has increased steadily as mortgage terms have eased. This increased ownership has affected significantly many economic and sociological decisions. Where a family lives, how it votes, how much it spends on its house, how often it moves—all are influenced by homeownership.

The mortgage does more than change ownership. It also determines how a family splits its income among real housing expenditures, money spent for other goods, and saving. The real costs of housing can differ considerably from the current financial payments made for mortgages and other housing expenses. These differences are determined by the size and terms of a home's mortgage.

Finally, mortgage terms affect the value of the housing stock and the prices at which individual houses sell. The amount of mortgage credit is an important determinant of whether houses sell at profits or losses. The amount of turnover is influenced by prices. Many families have made sizable gains as the capital value of their houses has risen. They have come to expect such gains as a normal part of homeowning.

Comprehending how mortgage money influences each one of these areas is a major part of understanding real estate finance. What happens to building and construction, how house prices rise and fall, and why it is harder to turn over units in some periods than in others are all critical factors for those concerned with real estate.

A house constitutes the largest single purchase ever made by

most families. Buying a house has been greatly simplified, yet it
remains a complicated transaction, probably more complex than
is frequently recognized. The complexity lies not only in the legal
and financial steps involved but also in the variety of choices which
must be made simultaneously.

Since services are provided only at fixed locations, the choice
of a house also determines a package of environmental factors.
House sites include a mixture of status, access, convenience, municipal services, and job opportunities. A house in the central core
may mean saving the cost of an extra car. The social reputation of
some areas is higher than that of others. The schools in various
locations may differ strongly. Services such as water, police and
fire protection, and sewers also vary widely, even in a single metropolitan area.

The type and availability of financing determine the quality, size,
and price of houses purchased. They also have a significant impact
on tenure. Few households can purchase a house from their accumulated savings. Without financing, most families must obtain their
housing in the rental market.

Contrary to common impressions, large numbers of houses are
owned free and clear of debt. In fact, nearly half of all homes
carry no current mortgage. Such is not the case at the time of
purchase. Only 10 to 15 per cent of houses lack loans when first
bought. Even for these, mortgages may have played an earlier part.
A number of them are bought with funds realized from the sale
of a house on which the mortgage had been paid up.

The choice of a house and method of financing it influence the
spending and saving from future incomes. The house is not only
the family's largest financial undertaking; if the mortgage is paid
off, the house will be its most valuable asset. The average family
has few financial possessions over and above the equity in its house.

## OWNERSHIP OR RENTAL

To try to decide primarily on economic grounds whether it is better
to own or rent is an incomplete and unsatisfactory approach. Analysis can give only an incomplete idea of relative costs. It usually

shows that at either end of the spectrum cases exist where the economic advantages and savings of one decision or the other are so clear that they should determine the outcome. In the majority of cases, however, economic analysis yields less clear results. Whether ownership will cost more or less than rental will depend on the future of the housing market. A large share of costs depends upon the amount a house depreciates or appreciates between its purchase and eventual sale.

Furthermore, decisions tend not to be made purely on economic grounds because real freedom of choice is lacking. The rental and ownership markets are too dissimilar. Rental units are concentrated in multifamily apartments or in older single-family houses in run-down areas. Rarely are new, individual dwellings built for rent. Individual dwellings in the rental market are found there only because of unusual circumstances. A family that wants a freestanding house with surrounding space in a newer section of town usually must purchase. On the other hand, if a family wants to avoid maintenance, if it wants a unit close to downtown in almost any major city, if it is tired of grass cutting and garden maintenance, renting is almost the only choice.

People who buy houses raise their housing standards. Owned homes are larger, are more expensive, and cost more to maintain. In every group, owners occupy better housing and probably pay a larger share of their income than do renters. When they choose homeownership and a mortgage, families on the average step up housing's share of their current budgets by 20 per cent or more. However, those whose mortgages are paid off have somewhat lower financial costs than do tenants. How financial costs compare with real ones is explored shortly.

## Who Are the Homeowners?

While homeownership is the goal of most American families, many never achieve it. Other families that once owned sell and become renters. The ownership of a house no longer guarantees lifelong stability. Americans have been increasingly mobile even as the ownership rate has skyrocketed.

Some homes turn over because people follow their jobs to other areas. Many are sold as people adjust to new family sizes and incomes. First purchasers may have neither the income nor assets for a house adequate for their entire lifetime. With time, as families can afford better housing, they sell their first houses and move up to the next. In this generation, the average American family will own four or five houses compared to the single home which only a fraction of the previous generation could buy.

Table 12-1 shows three principal factors that determine whether a family is likely to purchase and own a home. Most important is the family's income. The percentage of ownership rises steadily from 50.6 per cent of families with incomes of $3,999 and under to 84.1 per cent of those making $15,000 and over. Owned homes require higher monthly expenditures. They are a luxury more easily afforded as incomes rise. Low-income families usually have no choice. Even if they want to own their home, they are not likely to find a mortgage lender who will advance the necessary funds.

A second key factor in ownership is the age of the head of the family. Census estimates show homeownership rises steadily with age. Table 12-1 shows an ownership rate of 59.4 per cent for normal families in which the head of the household is under 45 years old; the rate rises to approximately 77.5 per cent for families in which the head is 65 or older. Ownership rates increase most rapidly between 25 and 35. In this period, the largest proportion of families can afford to become homeowners and want to do so.

Ownership rates rise from 40.8 per cent for households with only one person to 69.1 per cent for families of five persons. They then fall slightly for still larger families, which frequently can afford only minimal housing. Although family size is strongly related to age of head and both factors are related to income, each of the three factors has an independent effect on ownership. Their combined effects give large differences in ownership rates at the extremes. A single-person household with a head under 35 and a low income is unlikely to purchase or own a home. On the other hand, homes are owned by well over 80 per cent of high-income families with heads over 55 and four or more persons.

At first glance, other single characteristics of families also seem

TABLE 12-1  *Owner Occupancy According to 1960 Census*

**1. Percentage of owner occupancy by income group**

| $3,999 and under | $4,000 to $4,999 | $5,000 to $5,999 | $6,000 to $6,999 | $7,000 to $7,999 | $8,000 to $8,999 | $10,000 to $14,999 | $15,000 and over |
|---|---|---|---|---|---|---|---|
| 50.6 | 54.9 | 62.0 | 67.5 | 71.0 | 74.2 | 78.9 | 84.1 |

**2. Percentage of owner occupancy by type of household and age**

| Normal family | | | Other types | |
|---|---|---|---|---|
| Head under 45 years | Head 45 to 64 years | Head 65 years and over | Head under 65 years | Head 65 years and over |
| 59.4 | 74.4 | 77.5 | 41.9 | 59.9 |

**3. Percentage of owner occupancy by size of family**

| Number of persons | | | | | |
|---|---|---|---|---|---|
| 1 | 2 | 3 | 4 | 5 | 6 |
| 40.8 | 63.5 | 63.5 | 67.5 | 69.1 | 64.2 |

SOURCE: U.S. Bureau of the Census, *U.S. Census of Housing, 1960, Metropolitan Housing,* HC(2), no. 1.

to have considerable influence on homeownership. Variables such as occupation, education, size of city, and area of the country all are related to ownership. Thus owners of businesses and professional people are most likely to own, while unskilled and semiskilled laborers are most likely to rent. Ownership rises with the amount of school completed. Small towns and suburbs in the West have far more homeowners than large cities in the North.

A more careful analysis of the data, however, shows that these latter characteristics are highly correlated to the first three. They add a little but not much to the probabilities of ownership. Income, age of head, and family size alone account for almost the total differences in ownership rates.

These facts accentuate the existence of separate markets for rental units and homes. Builders who have tried to appeal to families by building cooperatives or condominiums of large-sized apartments have been almost entirely disappointed. A family with children and sufficient income is almost certain to choose ownership of a single-family unit. In most areas of the country apartment houses built with efficiency and one-bedroom units have tended to be the most successful because they appeal to the typical non-homeowners.

## REAL COSTS VERSUS FINANCIAL OUTLAYS

While most people decide to buy or rent primarily as a matter of taste, the costs of ownership necessarily enter in. Many families are shocked when they find they must forgo large amounts of other goods because they chose too expensive a house. Others may be pleased or highly dissatisfied when they sell their house and find how far their cost of living in it has diverged from their original ideas.

### Estimating Costs

While it is impossible to tell at the outset exactly how much homeownership will really cost, the factors which determine future financial outlays and real costs are limited and well worth considering in detail. Table 12-2 displays these variables under simplified assumptions. In examining the table, some terms should be understood. (1) The acquisition or capital cost of buying a house is most significant, since its size directly determines many of the real and financial costs. The acquisition cost is the purchase price plus the closing, financing, and other costs which must be paid before title is passed. (2) Real costs of owning reflect the economist's measure of true costs. He includes all out-of-pocket costs. Such charges are those paid at the time of purchase plus current expenses, which exclude amortization payments. To these are added any changes in equity, which can only be determined by the revenue of the sale. To these the economist further adds an imputed, or opportunity, cost for the interest forgone on the equity tied up in the house. (3) Finally there are financial outlays. These include the initial cash payments plus the annual cash payments including interest and amortization. Additional expenses or receipts of cash may occur at the time of sale.

In Table 12-2, the acquisition cost of the house is $20,400. This is the first critical variable. Most housing expenditures rise or fall in accordance with the amount initially invested. However, the relationship between initial cost and expenses is not exact. Houses purchased for the same price will experience different patterns of taxes, maintenance, and resale value. To obtain patterns with the most favorable results, careful shopping at the time of purchase is essential.

In the example, the purchaser obtains a $16,000 mortgage at 5½ per cent interest payable over 25 years. This means that he must put up an initial equity of $4,400 in cash. The first three lines under "annual costs" show where real costs and financial outlays differ. The owner must pay the mortgage holder $1,179 per year for interest and amortization. Of this sum, $779 covers the average annual interest on the mortgage for the first 10 years, and $400 per year goes for amortization. The interest payment is a real cost. It applies in both columns. Amortization, however, is not a real cost. Part of this sum increases the owner's equity, and part covers depreciation.

Real costs include $290 forgone interest on the owner's equity. The sum of this interest depends on the initial payment and the rate at which equity builds up or decreases. How fast the equity changes depends on how much the amortization of the mortgage exceeds or falls short of true depreciation. Table 12-2 assumes that the owner's equity rises at 1¼ per cent a year. In other words, amortization exceeds depreciation by this amount. The table estimates that the owner has an opportunity cost of interest equal to

TABLE 12-2   *Costs of Owning a $20,000 House for 10 Years*

|  | *Real costs* | *Financial outlays* |
|---|---|---|
| Acquisition or capital cost: | | |
| Purchase price.............................. | $20,000 | $20,000 |
| Closing costs (2%)......................... | 400 | 400 |
| Total....................................... | $20,400 | $20,400 |
| Initial expenditures: | | |
| Down payment (20%)....................... | $ 4,000 | $ 4,000 |
| Closing costs (2%)......................... | 400 | 400 |
| Total...................................... | $ 4,400 | $ 4,400 |
| Annual costs (average for 10 years): | | |
| Interest on mortgage (5½%)................. | $   779 | $   779 |
| Interest on equity (5½%; assuming growth of 1¼% per year)........................... | 290 | |
| Amortization (25 years)...................... | | 400 |
| Taxes (1½%)............................... | 300 | 300 |
| Maintenance (1%)......................... | 200 | 200 |
| Insurance, etc. (½%)....................... | 100 | 100 |
| Total...................................... | $ 1,669 | $ 1,779 |
| Less income tax savings (25%).............. | 342 | 270 |
| Adjusted total | $ 1,327 | $ 1,509 |
| Final costs: | | |
| Loss through depreciation (1%).............. | $ 2,000 | |
| Excess amortization over depreciation (reduction in financial outlays).................... | | −$ 2,000 |
| Selling costs (8%)......................... | $ 1,440 | $ 1,440 |
| Average costs per year: | | |
| 1% depreciation: | | |
| Annual costs or outlays.................... | $ 1,327 | $ 1,509 |
| Average loss in equity, from depreciation, and closing and selling costs............. | 384 | −    16 |
| Total...................................... | $ 1,711 | $ 1,493 |
| 2% Appreciation........................... | $ 1,292 | $   991 |
| 3% Depreciation........................... | $ 1,942 | $ 1,861 |

the rate he pays the lender on his mortgage. This opportunity cost can be much higher or somewhat lower. Small businessmen or consumers frequently pay 10 to 20 per cent for borrowing on other assets. If they could use their equity in the house in place of loans, it could save them these high rates. The opportunity cost is the sacrifice they make of having an equity in the house while they pay high rates for borrowed money.

The fourth, fifth, and sixth items under "annual costs" are the same in both columns. Property tax payments, maintenance and repairs, and insurance are included in both real and financial costs. Nationally, a figure of 3 per cent of the value of a house is a fairly typical annual expense for these items. Such costs vary greatly, however, among localities and houses. They are the items which can and should be carefully investigated for each particular house prior to the decision to buy.

The final annual cost item, income tax savings, also varies tremendously for individuals. It is an offset rather than an expense. Income tax savings are funds which a borrower does not have to pay to the Bureau of Internal Revenue. They may range from zero to 50 per cent or more of interest (both real and imputed) and of local taxes, depending on the family's tax bracket and whether or not expenses are itemized. With payments at the level shown, it almost always pays to itemize. Real costs show a higher income tax saving than do financial outlays because, while deductions of interest and local taxes occur in both cases, the tax collector does not require payments for the imputed return on equity. Even though it is merely an imputed return that is not taxed, it is a real saving. If the owner paid rent instead of owning and thus could invest his equity elsewhere, he would have to pay income taxes on the income received. These total income tax savings on homes form a sizable subsidy to the homeowner. Every family should be aware of this potentiality in making its decisions.

Finally we note that the annual real costs total $1,327, while annual financial outlays are $1,509. The financial outlays in this case run about 15 per cent higher than real costs. This is normal. The amount of the difference, of course, depends on the size of the mortgage and the rate of amortization. The higher the required monthly mortgage payment, the greater will be the gap between real costs and financial outlays in current budgets.

## Calculating Final Costs

The calculation of annual outlays is not hard. Lending institutions estimate them every day as part of the mortgage process. Most people, in deciding what size and price of home to seek, also calculate them. These annual payments, however, constitute only one segment of the actual expenses of ownership. The final amount it costs to own depends on how much equity is returned when the house is sold. This in turn is contingent on what happens to the housing market and the length of time between the purchase and sale of the house.

Changes in a house's price depend on how good a buy was made originally, on what happens to the specific house and its locality, and on movements in the general price level. For most of the postwar period, homeowners experienced very favorable trends. Increases in the general price level, particularly in land prices, were so large that they offset most structures' physical depreciation and obsolescence. As a result, people who sold houses found their values had appreciated rather than depreciated.

Unfortunately for many, in the early 1960s the rapid price rises came to an end. People who cheered because prices were stable for the goods they purchased were annoyed when much of the profit in homeownership disappeared. The final figures of Table 12-2 show the effect on ownership costs of different rates of depreciation. The estimates cover the impact at the end of 10 years of a 1 per cent depreciation rate (selling price 10 per cent less than purchase), a 3 per cent depreciation rate, and a 2 per cent appreciation rate (selling price 20 per cent above purchase). Even though these changes in the depreciation rates are small, they cause movements in the true costs of ownership of 25 per cent per year or more. In the table, the final financial outlays are lower than the final real costs because they fail to include the imputed cost of equity.

The last major cost a homeowner must pay is that of selling

his property. This charge becomes important if a family moves in a short period. Selling costs plus initial closing costs usually run 8 to 10 per cent or more of the price. Included are agent fees, title and attorney charges, and escrow and stamp fees, plus the risk of having to redecorate or of holding a unit vacant while the sale is being made. These charges will total close to $2,000 on a $20,000 house. If a family has to move within a year, these charges raise the total cost of ownership for the year by over 150 per cent. The family would have to pay $3,300 for a year's occupancy, excluding possible depreciation or appreciation.

Even over a five-year period, these transfer costs equal 2 per cent a year of the initial price. This adds appreciably to the cost of homeownership. In recent years, fortunate families have experienced appreciation of this order of magnitude, which has offset selling costs and rendered unnecessary a final adjustment to their previously calculated annual payments. However, because selling costs are high, a house that turns over in much less than five years must be a very good buy with low taxes and maintenance if this addition to the total costs is not to make the annual costs of occupancy extremely expensive.

From the table it is simple to estimate that for 10-year periods, the average annual cost of owning a home should range between $65 and $100 per $1,000 of original cost. The exact expense will be contingent primarily on depreciation, but it also will be influenced by differences in the out-of-pocket costs of interest, taxes, and maintenance. On the other hand, houses owned only two or three years probably would have real occupancy costs in the range of $80 to $120 per $1,000 of capital costs. For short periods, the transfer and selling charges plus any loss in value would be far more significant than current charges in determining the actual annual expenses.

## THE MORTGAGE LOAN PATTERN

The analysis of the difference between real and financial costs leads directly to a consideration of the importance of the mortgage loan pattern and of the impacts caused by changes in this pattern. The mortgage loan pattern includes the amount of money borrowed, the relationship of the loan to the acquisition cost of the house, the amortization period, and the interest rate. Of these, only movements in the interest rate have a direct influence on real costs. The other parts of the mortgage pattern determine financial costs and payments. While they have no direct relationship, changing financial payments may so influence the house market and prices that their indirect effects on real costs may exceed the direct results of shifting interest rates.

### Assets and Debts

The close relationship between mortgage credit and house purchases is easy to understand. In theory, houses are offered at various prices to a family that has certain tastes and a given income. On the basis of the relationship between desires, income, and prices, it decides which to buy. In fact, however, the problem is more complex. Because the house is so durable and will furnish services over such a long period, it can rarely be purchased from current income. Since it is an asset which will yield future income, to buy it a family must either offer assets saved from previous income or create an asset (a mortgage) by pledging future income.

For most families, the amount of house desired far surpasses available assets. They must augment their current assets by borrowing on a mortgage. The amount of loan they can obtain becomes a crucial factor in determining what they can pay for the house.

The difference between the available loan and the price is the down payment. Since this must be met by the prospective purchaser from existing assets, the ratio of the down payment to value determines how far a prospective purchaser can multiply existing resources. If a family has $2,000 in savings and the required down payment is 40 per cent, it can purchase only a $5,000 house. If the down-payment requirements are reduced to 20 per cent, the same assets can support a $10,000 purchase. A loan-to-value ratio of 90 per cent would allow this family to shop for a house costing $20,000.

All surveys show that families do have limited assets. For example, households with incomes under $7,500 have, on the average, less than $1,000 in liquid assets. Unless down payments are 10 per cent or less, such families have to buy houses priced under $10,000.

The recognition of the lack of large assets was a major force behind the steady decrease in the required down payments on FHA loans and their complete disappearance from a large share of the loans guaranteed by the VA. Movements in terms for conventional loans have been in the same direction but not as extreme. At the end of the war, most conventional lenders could lend only 60 or 66⅔ per cent of appraised values. Now savings and loans can go to 90 per cent, and others are not far behind.

The actual drop in down payments has not been as sharp as authorized. For the outstanding mortgages in 1960, the average conventional loan had been 70 per cent of price. One out of ten of the houses carried junior mortgages. For these, both loans together averaged 90 per cent of values. In 1963, the average down payments on new houses financed conventionally by savings and loans were 24 per cent; for mutual savings banks the figure was 30 per cent, for insurance companies 32 per cent, and for commercial banks 39 per cent. The equivalent percentages for existing homes were 26 per cent, 33 per cent, 32 per cent, and 38 per cent respectively.

Table 12-2 shows that the required down payments may be increased by closing costs at the time of purchase. Title fees, transfer costs, and recording fees have always existed. However, recent increases in mortgage fees, discounts, and similar charges have done much to offset the impact of the lower down payment. For FHA loans on new houses, closing costs in 1963 averaged about 2 per cent of value. They equaled about 40 per cent of the average down payment. For FHA houses with prices under $15,000, closing costs were almost as large as the required down payment.

**Monthly Payments**

The down payment puts one limit on the ability of a family to purchase a given value of housing. The required monthly payment is a second limiting factor. The monthly payment depends on how much is borrowed, the interest rate, and the rapidity with which the loan is repaid. Here, too, the borrower does not have complete freedom of choice. Chapter 7 showed that lenders, on extremely logical grounds, limit the authorized monthly payment on the basis of the income of borrowers.

Table 5-2 shows the various determinants of the monthly payment. The required payment rises directly with the size of the loan. Other proportions are not as simple. Under the level-payment procedure, the ratio of interest to amortization shifts with the length of the loan and the interest rates. As noted, the required monthly payment does not respond evenly to increases in the amortization period. For example, at 6 per cent interest, we can find what happens to monthly payments for each 5-year increase in the period over which amortization occurs. We start with a payoff period of 5 years and go to one of 30 years. The required monthly payments are decreased by 42 per cent when the amortization period goes from 5 to 10 years. They fall 25 per cent, then 15 per cent, then 11 per cent, and then 6 per cent for the successive 5-year additions. The longer the loan period, the less impact is felt from each further 5-year increase in length. The interest ratio in each payment is much higher in the larger loans.

One frequently hears arguments that a borrower should pay as much down and select as short an amortization period as he can manage. Those who offer this advice seem to be confused as to what is good for the lender and what is good for the borrower. We saw that the lender's risks may rise perceptibly if the borrower's equity is too small. This risk primarily applies to the down payment, however. The impact of longer amortization periods is not as clear, although it is probably true that risks increase for loans beyond 25 years in length. If the borrower is forced to default with a low equity, the lender is likely to suffer a larger loss. The borrower's risks and dangers may be the opposite of the lender's. If some unfortunate event occurs or if a house turns out to be a bad buy, the lower his equity, the less will be the borrower's loss.

A second argument used to urge borrowers not to lengthen the term of their mortgage is still weaker: it is that the longer the term of the mortgage, the higher will be the percentage of interest in the total payments. Thus, a constant-payment loan of $1,000 at 6 per cent interest amortized over 30 years will include about $1,160 in interest payments, whereas the same loan paid off in 15 years will include only $520 in interest charges. The two interest payments are compared, and it is assumed that the smaller interest payments are clearly preferable.

This argument misses the whole concept of lending and borrowing. It should never be used by a lender because the same logic would lead to the conclusion that no household should ever borrow. A cash payment avoids all interest charges. People borrow because they can use the money and feel the satisfaction gained from the loan is greater than its cost. Interest is the cost of borrowing. No one should waste the services of other people's money if it is not needed. On the other hand, if the larger loan greatly improves a family's housing standards or the money is needed for other purposes, the larger the loan, the better off the family will be.

The family's real costs include a return on its equity. Building up equity reduces interest paid but at the cost of interest forgone. Most consumer advisers believe that families should borrow on mortgages rather than elsewhere. Clearly no advantage is gained from saving $5\frac{1}{2}$ per cent interest by larger monthly payments on a mortgage if it means paying 16 per cent on an auto loan. Since the house is the best security most families own, their interest costs will be lower through borrowing on a mortgage than in any other way.

## Saving and Investment

The average family should think of the proper size and length of the mortgage loan as a critical question in budgeting and investing. When a family chooses the amount of its mortgage loan and its monthly payments, it determines both the rate of saving it will perform and the amount of housing services it will consume. It also determines the leverage on its housing investment.

The acquisition cost of a house is directly related to the services it renders. In a well-operating market, the choice of a price bracket determines the housing standard the family will maintain. Many families find that they can achieve the standard they want only by using all their assets and assuming a maximum loan. They must multiply their assets as far as possible by using a lending scheme with the lowest down-payment ratio. Having selected as high a standard as assets available for down payments will allow, they must reduce the necessary monthly payments as far as possible by extending the amortization period.

Attempts to obtain maximum mortgages with respect to both amount and amortization make a great deal of sense in relation to the family life and income cycle, the proper allocations of savings and consumption, and considerations of the house as an investment.

Houses are lived in for long periods. People selecting a house today should consider not only their current income but also its likely pattern during the entire period they will remain in the house. Most families buying a house can look forward to rising incomes. If they pick a house which fits their present income well, they may want to move when they progress to a higher income level and have a wider sphere of choice. On the other hand, if they overspend and make a maximum effort in terms of their present incomes, the relationship will improve when their wages and salaries rise. They will want to remain in the house longer. Their average standard of living in the house will be closer to their average income for the entire period they occupy it.

This same reasoning makes sense because the longer payment period gives a more logical saving and consumption pattern. Part of the monthly payment goes for current real costs and part for amortization which forms a potential savings. Table 12-2 showed that real costs are not affected by the speed of amortization. Larger payments simply increase the amount by which equity rises; i.e., they increase the family's rate of saving. When a family considers various payment patterns, it must ask itself whether it prefers to increase its saving rate or not. Some families want higher savings. Many, particularly young ones, will feel that they need to spend as much of current income as possible for consumption. They will want to do their saving later when their incomes are higher and family expenses less. Longer amortization periods cut the amount of forced current saving.

## Liquidity and Leverage

Another aspect of borrowing a maximum sum on good security is that of liquidity, which applies to many individual investments in addition to houses. The argument is sometimes advanced in favor of higher down payments that you decrease your monthly payments and therefore your risk. The truth of the contention depends on whether compulsory saving is necessary. What would the individual do with the money not put into down payment? If he dissipated it foolishly, his payments would be higher and he would have little to show for them. If he invested the amount not put into down payment in his business or in some other enterprise, he might run a high risk with the hope of a large gain.

On the other hand, if he kept this sum as a liquid reserve, he would decrease his risks while incurring only low or negative costs, depending on the money value to him. Risks would be less for in most families, the danger in mortgage payments is not of falling slightly below the amount needed each month but rather of an inability to pay anything for some interval. A man who lost his job would find that the difference in monthly payments resulting from a 20-year instead of a 30-year amortization period would not help much in meeting his payment needs.

A mortgage has another advantage to the average family. It is usually a debt which can be extinguished at will, and is therefore another form of liquidity. Most modern mortgages are drawn up with the interest rate fixed for their entire period. Usually the debtor can repay them without a penalty or with only a negligible one. (Warning: some carry heavy prepayment penalties.) Although the debt can be retired, the debtor cannot, as a rule, be forced to pay it off in advance.

If the interest rate rises, the borrower has a bargain; he is paying less than the going rate on his debt. If the interest rate falls, he may be able to refinance his mortgage and start again at the new, lower rate. This is one of the few circumstances where an individual can gain as a debtor. Many profited in this manner by the swings in the interest rate in both the 1940s and the 1950s. In a similar way, an unwary individual may lose on bonds. Corporations often have the right, either completely or within stated limits, to determine when a bond should be paid off. The holder of the bond loses if interest rates rise. If they fall, the corporation can gain by calling and paying off the bond.

The homeowner with a large mortgage is also employing leverage. His down payment gives him the ability to control a very large asset—his house. He may give up $1,000 in bonds, deposits, or stocks for ownership of a $15,000 asset. Whether he gains from his leverage depends on the length of time he holds his asset and what happens to housing prices in the interim. His investment may work out well or poorly. The average family, however, can in this manner buy an asset which will protect a large part of its housing expenses from inflation. This has been an important factor in making homeownership so popular.

## PRICES AND VALUES IN HOUSING

At any single time in an active market, prices are a fair measure of the intrinsic value of a house. Changes in prices over time, however, may not be a measure of actual movements in real values. Families with different taste patterns shop and buy houses. The amounts they offer and receive indicate the current values placed on particular housing packages. The types of houses sold at the same price may vary greatly. Houses have numerous value dimensions. They differ in location, in size, in age, in design, and in quality of construction. Each family decides how it trades off one dimension against another until it finds the particular package which suits it.

When houses are examined over time, large increases in prices are evident. The average one-family, owner-occupied house was worth about $4,400 in 1940, about $7,400 in 1950, and about $11,900 in 1960. Increases in average values are partly caused by higher prices for the newly constructed units added to the stock, but they also reflect sharp rises in the average prices of units in existence at the start of each decade. Money values of existing houses have risen rather than declined over time since the 1930s.

Part of this rise for existing units was due to real changes in the quantity of services rendered by this stock. The worst units were pulled down, thus raising the average. Other units were altered so as to improve their values. However, a large share of the rise simply reflected higher prices. The amounts charged for houses with a given value of real services went up steadily. The rise in housing prices was faster than that for goods in the rest of the economy.

## Mortgage Lending and Values

These higher prices have frequently been used to attack the liberalization of mortgage terms. It is claimed that instead of having brought about improved physical standards of housing for the new owners, most of the increased ability of a family to buy higher-valued houses has been dissipated through price rises. The net effect of the liberalized terms, it is claimed, is simply to force home buyers to pay out more money to former owners or to builders, construction workers, and material suppliers. They get little additional space or quality or other dimensions of value in their newly purchased units even though their prices have gone up.

Can such charges be substantiated? Who has been kidding whom in the constant battle for lower down payments and longer amortization periods?

People who argue that most of the impact has gone into price increases believe there is little elasticity in the housing supply. They have conflicting opinions as to where the lack of elasticity is to be found, some believing it is in the existing inventory, some in new construction, and some in both.

When mortgage terms are eased, some people who previously rented houses can afford to buy. If all houses for ownership were filled and no new ones came into the market, new potential owners would bid against each other and existing owners. Prices of houses would rise until some of the new potential would be forced out of the bidding, while some owners would sell, preferring to take a profit and occupy the vacated rental units. All prices would be higher. Some shifts in tenure would have occurred. The former owners would be better off. The easier credit would have enabled the new owners to change from renting to ownership but at the expense of higher prices,

Similar events would occur in terms of quality. Relaxed terms would, in theory, enable people to buy better houses, but most of their increased expenditures would go for higher prices. These effects follow from the assumption that no new houses will be built and no existing ones improved or altered.

As soon as the possibility of construction is allowed, it becomes clear that some or all of the increased demand can be met by new building. The impact on prices will depend on the rapidity with which new units are built and on how their prices change as production expands. Those who feel that credit increases go mainly into prices believe that the building industry is very inflexible. Increases in demand automatically engender sharp price rises.

The facts are unclear. Housebuilding can expand rapidly. On the other hand, periods of rapid expansion see faster than normal price increases. This is particularly true for land. Housing prices have been going up faster than others. However, this may not be due to increased demand. Logical reasons exist for construction costs to rise faster than costs in the rest of the economy. Without the increased demand from easier mortgage terms, they might have risen at a still more rapid rate.

A balanced view would probably hold that in periods of rapid increases in the demand for better houses, and when extra families try to shift rapidly from a rental to an ownership status, housing prices do rise faster than is normal. On the other hand, in most periods, easier credit enables many families to become owners. They gain advantages they otherwise would not have. Other families can afford to purchase better houses. The average level of housing prices over periods characterized by both strong and normal demand may be no higher than it would have been without the easier credit.

## SUMMARY

The relationship of mortgage terms and their effects is not simple. The mortgage agreement influences simultaneously the risks of the lender, the costs of the borrower, and the amount of production. Mortgage terms also affect the amount of money available to the mortgage market and the amount saved both by homeowners and by depositors in savings institutions. Frequently actions to ease or tighten credit have conflicting impacts on the different interests in the market.

These broader problems need not, however, influence the person seeking a loan. His problems are far simpler. He shops the housing market to find the values it offers. He must then decide whether he believes these values will continue to prevail in the future or will rise or fall. He must also determine his chances of remaining in the house for at least four or five years. On the basis of this analysis and the relative values in the ownership and rental markets, he can decide whether to rent or buy.

If he buys, he must shop for available terms. The smaller the down payment, the lower the interest, and the longer the amortization period, the more house he can purchase. His real costs will rise with the amount he pays for the house and with the interest rate for which he contracts. It is worth shopping for a good buy in both the house and in financing terms. He may easily achieve savings of 10 or 20 per cent in his real housing costs.

If he is in a position to choose between higher or lower down payments and longer or shorter amortization periods, he must consider an entirely different set of consequences. He must assess the value of cash in contrast to a high equity tied up in his house. He must decide whether his tastes and personality are such that he needs a forced savings program through rapid amortization payments or will make good use of the money which he can keep as a result of lower monthly payments. There are no simple rules of action. Each family must tailor its savings and investment program to its own needs.

## SELECTED REFERENCES

Case, F. E.: *The Costs of Home Ownership,* Real Estate Research Program, University of California, Los Angeles, 1956.

Fisher, E. M., and R. M. Fisher: *Urban Real Estate,* Holt, Rinehart and Winston, Inc., New York, 1954.

Maisel, S. J., and L. Winnick: *Family Housing Expenditures,* Reprint 25, Center for Real Estate and Urban Economics, University of California, Berkeley, California, 1961.

Martin, P.: *Real Estate Principles and Practices,* The Macmillan Company, New York, 1959.

Ratcliff, Richard U.: *Real Estate Analysis,* McGraw-Hill Book Company, New York, 1961.

# Construction Financing and
# Fluctuations in Housebuilding————————13

The financing of construction is a specialized part of mortgage lending. It has been at the same time among the most lucrative and most risky of the lending markets. In some areas, construction lending is physically separated from final lending. It may be concentrated in the hands of the commercial and mortgage bankers. In other cases, construction lending is engaged in by most of the lenders who make the final loans.

One of the factors which increase the risks of such lending is the instability that characterizes the new-house market. The fluctuations in new housing starts, however, have causes and effects which go far beyond the construction-lending sphere. This instability remains a major problem for all connected with mortgage lending and real estate, as well as for the economy as a whole.

## CONSTRUCTION FINANCING

Construction financing furnishes the necessary capital while houses move from the stage of raw land toward completion, sale, and receipt of money from the ultimate purchaser. Usually, three types of financing are involved. First comes equity capital. Equity funds may be furnished by separate companies which specialize in the subdivision of land, in the planning and selling of the house, or in its construction; or all of these functions may be performed by a single firm. Second, borrowed funds are often required specifically for the subdividing, that is, the process of land development. Money which is not made available on the construction mortgage is required to pay for the land and the improvements made on it. Finally, money for the material and labor in the house itself must be available during the building process.

### Equity Capital

All phases of the construction process tend to be equity-poor. The great majority of firms in the industry are compelled to stretch their capital to the utmost. Typically, the leverage in the industry is large. In theory, lending contracts for construction oblige the builder to furnish equity to 20 per cent of the finished value. In practice, by careful timing and judicious scheduling of work and bills, contractors can cut their equity requirement by more than half. Large tract builders can obtain sufficient leverage to turn over their capital ten times a year or more. With such rates of turnover, profits on equity of over 100 per cent a year have not been uncommon.

Subcontractors, material suppliers, and labor may all furnish credit to the builder. At any point in time the builder's investment in the construction job includes his capital, funds borrowed against the construction loan, and open-book credit from the suppliers. He frequently plans his deliveries and work schedule so as to maximize the amount of unpaid bills not yet overdue.

These unpaid bills create potential mechanic's liens. In many states, if care is not exercised, they may be superior to the loans on the mortgage. Lenders must therefore be careful in determining how far to go in making advances when unpaid bills exist. How far they go depends on the legal situation and on the individual builder's general credit standing. In general, the credit from suppliers accounts for half or more of the investment required to supplement the lender's construction loan.

The relative shortage of capital and high leverage result from the large cost of each construction unit. The factors that force owners to borrow a large share of the necessary capital apply in the con-

struction process as well. A builder who finances all his own work
has of necessity a very low capital turnover rate. Conversely, the
higher his borrowing, the more work he can perform and the greater
his potential profits. Most builders attempt to maximize turnover.
While these are the compelling forces behind the desire to borrow,
the availability of the property for security enables large loans to
be made. An old saying claims that many builders can borrow
$20,000 to build a house who could not borrow $50 to buy a
suit.

The high risks due to heavy leverage plus instability and many
possibilities of errors in each project mean that security markets and
other similar sources of equity are virtually closed to builders. Only
a few firms have issued stock publicly. This is usually possible only
after many years of operations. Even then the record of success has
not been great. Equity is obtained primarily from those active in
the firm plus, occasionally, one or two silent partners motivated
to invest by the promise of possibly high returns.

### Land Development and Subdividing

After the builder's equity, the most risky area of construction
financing is paying for the land and developing it with streets and
utilities. Experiences with loans in this sphere were disastrous in
the 1920s and 1930s. Most financial institutions have been severely
restricted in the amounts they can lend on raw or developed land.
While these restrictions have been relaxed somewhat, they remain
formidable.

The builder who is equity-poor to start with is frequently hard
pressed in obtaining the money to finance the land development
process. Many financing forms have developed in an attempt to
meet this need. Basically most methods depend upon some form
of partnership between the builder and an owner or a lender on
land. The creditor is given somewhat more protection than the
builder, but risks remain great. Payments of 20 per cent or more
are common for money in this field. Because of these high rates,
builders with adequate capital may act primarily as land dealers
and speculators. Land prices have increased so rapidly in many

areas that builders have tied up much of their capital in land purchases.

In typical situations, when builders cannot afford to buy the land, they attempt to obtain credit from the landowner. One method of financing is to purchase one section outright, with options to purchase other sections as needed. This requires less capital, but landowners have hiked the option prices out of the reach of many.

In another procedure, the owner retains title while the land is being developed. He may even furnish part of the capital for improvements. As individual lots are sold, the owner transfers title to the purchaser. Part of the income from the sale is paid to him for his land and risk, while part goes as a return to the developer.

In still another method, the builder buys the land, but the original owner retains a large purchase-money mortgage against the property. The lien is usually a blanket mortgage covering all the land. When an individual lot is sold, the mortgage holder receives his payment for the amount of land involved. To this is added an additional sum so that the mortgage becomes an ever smaller percentage of the value of the still unsold land. Upon receipt of payment, the mortgage holder releases his claim and the purchaser gets a clear title.

As an example, assume that you purchase 25 acres of land for $8,000 an acre, paying 10 per cent down. The total land is worth $200,000 and you put up $20,000, with the remainder financed by a blanket mortgage of $180,000. The land is divided into 100 lots. Each time a lot is sold, you pay the mortgage holder $2,100, and he releases the lot to the new owner. The amount owed on the mortgage becomes a decreasing percentage of the value of the unsold land. The $180,000 mortage will have been completely paid off when 86 lots have been sold, so the developer retains all sums after that point.

If the land is to be built upon or improved before sale, the firm making a construction loan usually requires a subordination agreement. Under such an agreement, the holder of the blanket mortgage agrees to allow his claim to be junior, or second, to the construction loan even though it was recorded first in time. The conditions of such subordination clauses and the release clause which specifies the conditions for transferring titles on individual lots are an important part of the bargaining in land sales. Such conditions, as well as the use of options and developing on others' land, are usually paid for through the fact that the price of the land becomes higher than it would be in a cash sale. For example, in the case of land purchased for $200,000 including a subordinated mortgage, the cash price might be only $150,000.

Credit for construction of land improvements is expensive but not quite as hard to obtain as for purchasing raw land. If the developer has used his own capital to buy the land or has received financing through the owner or other land investor, he will frequently be able to borrow the money needed for streets, lights, and other improvements from a combination of financial institutions, material suppliers, and subcontractors, in a system similar to that used for the construction of the house. In fact, in much tract development the construction of the house and land improvements proceed and are financed together.

## CONSTRUCTION LOANS

The main source of credit for the building process consists of actual construction loans. These are sums lent to the builder or owner for the improvement or construction of properties. In contrast to ordinary lump-sum mortgages, money is advanced in increments only as building progresses. Typically the loans are secured by a mortgage and note pledging the property under construction as security. Firms with excellent credit ratings are sometimes able to borrow on their own notes without the mortgages.

### Additional Risks

The construction loan contains all risks typical of the final mortgage plus certain major additional ones. The builder may not bring the house or tract to completion. Errors in judgment as to costs may occur. Unforeseen events, such as strikes, bad weather, and deaths, may halt production. Losses on other properties or ventures may cause the builder to default. In any such eventuality, the lender will be left with an unfinished structure which will have to be completed if he is to get his money out. In some cases performance bonds are used to insure against losses arising from noncompletion. In most cases and especially in housebuilding, however, the lender depends on his credit analysis and assumes the added risks of noncompletion.

If the building is finished, other risks may still develop. In many states, mechanic's liens may be a problem. Those who work on the building and furnish materials to it may have the right to be paid from the proceeds of its sale prior to any rights of the mortgage holder. If the builder finishes the building but bills remain outstanding, they may have to be paid by the lender. Despite the careful safeguards contained in lending procedures which attempt to protect againt this eventuality, it continues to crop up not infrequently.

Finally, it may be difficult to sell the completed house. The construction loan typically continues until the unit is sold. If delays are long, the builder will have difficulty meeting taxes and interest payments. Some buildings may only be marketed at prices below the amounts advanced on the construction loan. If the builder's equity has been wiped out, the lender may lose.

## Types of Loans

Some construction loans consist only of interim financing, with the assumption that a separate final loan will be made to the ultimate purchaser. In other situations, lending for the interim construction process and the permanent loan to the eventual owner may be tied together in one instrument.

1. Loans may be made against typical permanent mortgages. The note is signed and the mortgage recorded, but money is advanced only as the building progresses. The amortization and interest provisions frequently are not effective until the house is completed. Such mortgages are particularly common for income properties and for single-family homes when the owner has his unit built by a contractor. In these cases, the lender has already approved the ultimate borrower who has signed the note. Frequently the lender protects himself by turning the progress payments over to the owner, who in turn pays the builder. The owner is responsible and must assure

himself that the building will be finished according to specifications. He frequently demands a bond for this purpose.

2. In other cases the lender may agree to do the construction lending and to carry the final mortgage, but he wants to approve the credit worthiness of the ultimate purchaser. Mortgages are drawn which can be assumed by the final purchaser if the lender agrees. Very often the lender advances only a major fraction of the potential loan to the builder, with the last advance made only when the final sale takes place. For example, assume that the lender has agreed to make an FHA loan of $10,000, or 90 per cent of the value, to an ultimate borrower. He may advance only $9,000 to the builder, making the last $1,000 available in the escrow procedure at the time the builder delivers title to an approved buyer.

3. Many loans are made purely on an interim basis. Many institutions that make permanent or final loans will not do construction lending even against mortgages they will ultimately accept. Some institutions are legally forbidden to do construction lending, while others are not equipped to handle this type of business. Still others are too far away. Insurance companies, for example, would find it difficult to supervise construction lending in all the markets within which they operate.

In these cases the builder obtains a construction loan from a local lender based upon the final mortgage commitment of the second institution. Such mortgages and notes may differ greatly from the more usual long-term amortized loan. Frequently they are of a relatively short duration. Many institutions cannot make nonamortized loans for more than nine months or 18 months. The terms and provisions are drawn specifically to secure the construction advances. These specialized interim loans contrast with the first two types or combination loans. In those cases, the mortgages tend to be of the standard type, but they contain provisions for periodic advances as construction progresses.

## Lenders

In each part of the country, different types of lenders dominate the construction-loan market. Local practice depends partly on the legal situation and partly on habit. In most areas mortgage companies are very important in construction lending, particularly when they are large originators of loans to out-of-state insurance companies and mutual savings banks. In these cases the mortgage companies buy final commitments. They then do the construction lending to the builders in order to obtain the right to make the permanent loan when the houses are sold. They use their own capital but supplement it to a large extent by warehousing advances from the local banks secured by their notes and the partially completed mortgages.

In other areas, the construction-loan market is dominated by banks, particularly those with state charters. Construction credit forms part of their normal commercial credit operations. In some areas, however, commercial banks avoid such lending almost entirely. Savings and loans and mutual savings banks do a great deal of construction lending on mortgages which they will hold permanently. In fact some specialize in this type of transaction because high fees and discounts on the construction loan may be a primary source of their profits.

In some areas insurance companies are forbidden to make construction loans. Because they find it difficult almost everywhere to handle this business, they are the least important lenders in this sphere. Their absence offers opportunities to local lenders to specialize in the construction-loan market even when they are not interested in the permanent loans.

### Terms and Rates

Construction loans tend to have terms of 6, 9, and 12 months, with the greatest number in the lowest category. In many of these cases, of course, the loan will be extended. The short term increases the lender's control, since he can take action to avoid prolonged failures to sell.

Because of their risks and considerable administrative requirements, the rates charged on construction loans tend to be high. Interest rates are normally at or close to those on the permanent loan, but heavy charges are imposed in required fees or discounts.

The rate of return to the lender depends on the speed of turnover of the loan. For example, consider a loan on a house in which the period from the initial recording of the construction mortgage to sale is six months. If the money is advanced evenly over the entire period, the average amount of funds outstanding for the entire period is only half the face value of the loan. A $10,000 construction loan advanced evenly in $2,000 increments over 6 months would have an average outstanding loan balance of only $5,000.

Under typical terms, the borrower might be charged 6 per cent interest on the outstanding balance, but he would be required to pay loan fees of from 3 to 5 points, that is, from $30 to $50 per $1,000 loan. On a $10,000 loan advanced over 6 months, the average outstanding money of $5,000 for six months is equivalent to $2,500 loaned for a year. If 3 points were charged, the fee would be $300. This by itself would be equal to 12 per cent simple interest. Added to the 6 per cent actual interest charge, it amounts to a gross interest charge of 18 per cent on an annual basis.

Of course a good portion of this return may be required to cover the added risk and supervision. On the other hand, fees or discounts may run considerably higher in some parts of the country and in certain periods. The fee schedules on construction loans tend to be volatile, rising and falling as money eases and tightens. These shifting costs and the availability of construction credit appear to be most important in causing the rate of building starts to fluctuate.

### The Loan Application

Developers may apply to lenders for a commitment for both the permanent and interim financing, or they may seek only a construction loan. In the latter case they are almost always required to have a firm commitment from a lender who agrees to make the permanent loan when an eligible purchaser has been found. In either case, lenders require the submission of the plans for the completed property, credit statements, and records of previous work.

A careful review of the plans is necessary because the building is part of the security and the ability to sell it at the projected price will determine how soon the construction lender will get his funds back. If the plan is poor and prices have to be reduced, the final sale may not produce sufficient funds for the builder to pay off his loan. The acceptance of the plans by a final lender who issues a permanent commitment on a conventional loan or the granting by the FHA of a commitment to insure is frequently construed by the construction lender as proof that the plans as submitted are appropriate.

As noted above, construction loans are hard to obtain without a permanent commitment. Even when one exists, the lender may feel, on the basis of his own analysis, that costs appear to have been overestimated and the builder seems to be trying to obtain a construction loan that will minimize his own financial commitment. In the opposite direction, the lender may decide that the builder has underestimated costs and lacks sufficient capital to finish the job. The lender may also question the builder's market analysis and his ability to sell the completed units. All of these would be reasons for rejecting the application.

The loan application and its review not only must lead to a decision that the property can be sold at the indicated price, but also must be concerned with the ability of the builder to complete the project. This requires a careful credit analysis of the builder. The loan application must be accompanied by financial statements of assets and liabilities and of previous income, frequently a signed statement of anticipated costs in considerable detail, and a projection of the availability of the funds required to finish the project.

The lender's review will be based in addition on a credit report on the builder to determine his previous financial integrity, his attitude toward his obligations, and his ability to pay his debts promptly. The amount of funds required for the entire operation must be projected. The lender wants to make certain that the builder has sufficient working capital to pay the bills as they arise. He also wants to assure himself that enough equity is available to absorb risks of underestimated costs or overestimated selling prices.

The final processing of the loan under the application includes checks on various technical and legal matters. There must be an agreement as to how the funds will be advanced and repaid. Other agreements give the lender the right to step in and correct or complete the job. Problems of titles, of subordination agreements, of avoiding possibilities of prior liens must all be checked. The builder is required to carry insurance and bonds so as to make completion possible even if various untoward events occur. All possible steps are taken to avoid those risks which can be reduced through careful processing and analysis.

## Disbursement of Funds

The usual procedure for paying out construction loans is through a system of progress payments made at certain stages of the building process. These systems of advances, or draws as they are commonly called, have the purpose of making capital available to the builder to replenish most of the amount he has had to pay from his own capital or borrow from suppliers to bring the building to a certain stage of completion. The lender attempts to ensure that the amount of the loan is less at all times than the amount of value included in the property which serves to secure the advances. He wants to be certain that if he has to take over construction, the funds he has to pay out will not total more than the market value of the completed unit.

The construction mortgage is recorded prior to the start of building. The note specifies the manner in which advances will be made. Many possible payment methods and rates of advance exist. In contracts to build houses for individuals, it is common to require a deposit by the owners of sufficient funds to cover the difference between the contract and the loan. The lender or his agent then reimburses the builder for receipted bills as they are presented. In other cases, the owner may certify the bills, which are then paid directly by the lender.

Far more common, and particularly applicable to operative building, are agreements by the lender to furnish funds when certain amounts of work have been completed or certain stages of construction have been reached. In the most flexible system, but one commonly used only on large construction projects, the lender advances each month a percentage of the total work cost which he and the builder agree went into the structure during the previous period. More usual, particularly for housebuilding, is an agreement to pay a certain percentage of the loan at particular stages of construction.

Schedules for disbursements are negotiated between the builder and lender. Many different forms of agreement are employed, calling for anywhere from three to fifteen payments as the work progresses. A typical agreement based on five advances calls for the bank to pay the builder 20 per cent of the contract price at each of five stages of construction: (1) at completion of foundation and rough flooring, (2) at completion of roofing, (3) at completion of plastering, (4) at completion and acceptance of job, and (5) after the end of the mechanic's lien period.

Under systems such as this, the builder usually calls the lender to report that a particular stage has been reached. The lender then sends an inspector to the site to see that the work has been accomplished. The inspector checks both the quantity and the quality of the work. He ascertains that the plans are being followed, and he sometimes asks to see receipted bills for the materials included in the work. The degree of care used in checking depends on the builder's credit standing, on the lien laws, and on the general health of the construction market.

In theory, under this five-stage system, the builder may be required to invest personal capital in the project up to 20 per cent of the value of the building. When his investment reaches that amount, he reaches the next stage and should be able to draw against the mortgage. His work in progress should be limited to five times his working capital; otherwise there will be periods when he cannot meet his bills because his investments in work in progress exceed his available capital. He may be solvent but illiquid. He should, of course, have some additional, but not necessarily liquid, capital to pay for unpredictable setbacks which could cause losses on the property.

The available amount of working capital, however, is often less. As noted previously, the builder is the beneficiary of an average of two or three weeks' credit from his workers, trade contractors, and material dealers. At any stage there is likely to be considerable completed work for which he gets an advance from the lender but for which he has not paid his suppliers. While this enables him to double the work he can undertake with a given amount of capital, it is one of the factors which make construction lending so risky.

## FLUCTUATIONS IN NEW CONSTRUCTION

The construction rate of new houses is among the most volatile parts of the economy. Builders and real estate men go through periods of feast and famine in rapid succession. This fact is obvious in Figure 13-1, the top line of which shows the number of houses started in each quarter from 1950 through 1963. Housing fluctuated from quarters with starts of over 1,700,000 units at annual rates to quarters with starts of under 1,120,000. On an annual basis, movements of 30 to 40 per cent from peaks to troughs occurred three times. Every person concerned with real estate financing needs a thorough understanding of why these movements occur so he can predict them and avoid their unfortunate consequences.

In addition to changes in the number of housing units (family accommodations) built, important movements occur in the average size, quality, and value of each unit. Since mortgage financing influences and is influenced by both types of changes, we want to consider each dimension—the number of units started and their average value—separately.

Orders to construct new houses come from three basic groups: (1) individuals who contract for, or build, houses for their own use, (2) builders or developers who start rental units, and (3) builders who start houses that they expect to sell to new owner-occupiers. While the percentages in these various groups have varied widely in different periods, for the first three years of the 1960s they appear roughly to have divided the market one-quarter, one-quarter, and one-half respectively.

What determines the number of dwelling units entrepreneurs order in any period? Over any moderately long time span, such as 5 to 10 years, the number of dwellings built is closely related to the basic demand for new units. This demand comes primarily from the formation of new households. Every increase of a household requires an additional house in our total stock. Another and in-

FIGURE 13-1   *Housing Starts, Final Demand, and Changes in Housing Inventories in the United States, Annual Rates, 1950–1963*

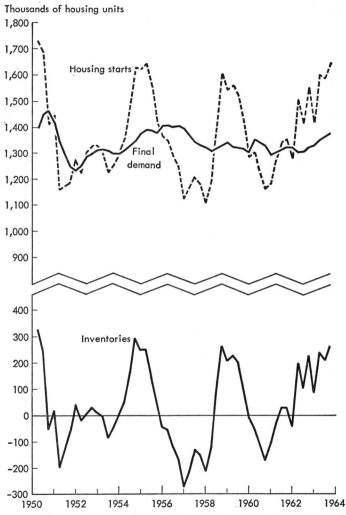

SOURCE: Sherman J. Maisel, "A Theory of Fluctuations in Residential Construction Starts," *American Economic Review*, June, 1963.

creasingly important part of basic demand is the need for new units to replace dwellings removed from the stock because they are old, worn, or destroyed by fire or flood or for a myriad of other reasons. The requirements for replacements run from a third to a half of new household formation.

Finally, houses may be started which increase the inventory of units under construction or of finished but unoccupied units. Clearly, entrepreneurs are not likely to build up this inventory of vacancies willingly, but their actions frequently have this effect. The dashed lines on Figure 13-1 show the actual destinations of the houses started in each quarter. While they account for over 90 per cent of the total demand for the decade, the fluctuations of units needed for household formation and removals have constituted only a small share of the over-all fluctuations measured on a quarterly basis. In fact, they account for less than 15 per cent of the quarter-to-quarter alterations in starts. In contrast, the movements in starts destined for inventories have accounted for over 85 per cent of the quarterly variance, even though for the period as a whole inventory increases account for less than 10 per cent of starts.

## THE BASIC DEMAND FOR NEW DWELLINGS

Table 13-1 shows in detail the uses to which housing starts were put during the decade of the 1950s and the early 1960s. The tables and the figures in this chapter are only approximate because statistical variations in this sphere of housing data are large. To understand what determines the rate of housebuilding, one must know what sets the level of basic demand for households and for removals shown in these figures as well as how and why builders over- and undershoot this level, thus causing major movements in inventories and construction starts.

### Household Formation

Increases in the number of households form the largest part of building demand. Builders plan on being able to sell or rent their new units either to newly formed households or to those whom they may attract from existing units. In turn, emptied dwellings attract new households, are filled with families from other units, or perhaps are removed from the market. Any housing unit which fails to attract customers remains vacant.

One cannot assume that new families fill new houses. In fact, the opposite is true. New sales units primarily attract already existing households. Movements within the total stock of houses are complex. It is not possible to relate the need for specific buildings to new or old families. However, when all shifting is completed, one additional dwelling is needed for each added household.

A second common error in picturing households and housing demand is to think in terms of the typical family of mother, dad, and two or three children. It is simply wrong. Between the 1950 and 1960 censuses, of the total of 9,800,000 new households, only 5,600,000 consisted of married couples (and only 3,600,000 of these households had children). The remaining 4,200,000 new households, were headed by single persons or by other non-typical family types. The widowed grandmother or the pair of young schoolteachers were as significant in increasing the need for dwellings as was the typical family with children.

What primary factors determine the number of households formed in a period? Basic is the increasing size of the adult population. Changes in social attitudes and tastes have also increased desires for private dwellings. As population has grown, there has been a gradual tendency for people and families to demand their own rather than shared quarters. The growth of this desire for privacy has speeded up in the past 20 years.

Some of the increased demand for greater privacy must be related to higher incomes. In the opposite direction, low or falling incomes delay the time at which people marry and cause more to double up (share space). In depressions, more young couples live with their in-laws. As income rises, the number or individuals who can afford to maintain a separate household also expands.

Other factors which influence household formation in unusual periods are comparatively unimportant in normal times. Some households were not formed because of the wartime shortage of space. In theory people may not get married or may not form households if credit is tight or if rents and the prices of houses are high. However, moderate movements in these variables appear not to have much impact on household formation.

The importance of population on household formation is clear from Figure 13-2. From 1900 to 1940, the line relating the adult population and the number of households is almost straight. From 1890

FIGURE 13-2    *Household Projections*

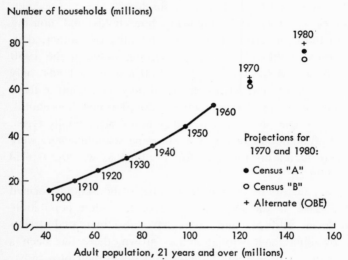

Number of households (millions)

Adult population, 21 years and over (millions)

SOURCE: *Survey of Current Business*, November, 1963.

to 1947 over 95 per cent of household growth can be attributed directly to the population factor. After 1947, other forces caused a rapid increase in households, as is evident from the way the line slopes upward. From 1947 to 1963 additional households not based on population numbered over 5,000,000. This was about 30 per cent of all new households.

In the period from 1940 to 1950, the nonpopulation factors increasing households were very different from those from 1950 to 1963. In the earlier period, the number of married couples shot up. The formation of other types of households actually fell below

TABLE *13-1*  *Dispositions of Total Estimated Starts of Private Housing Units in the United States, April 1, 1950–1960 and 1960–1964*

| | Annual Rates | |
| --- | --- | --- |
| | *1950–1960* | *1960–1964* |
| Net additions to households.............. | 978,000 | 815,000 |
| Net losses to available stock............. | 398,000 | 478,000 |
| Net change in inventory under construction.. | −20,000 | 75,000 |
| Net change in available vacancies........ | 124,000 | 50,000 |
| Total private housing starts............. | 1,480,000 | 1,418,000 |
| Breakdown of net losses to available stock: | | |
| Demolitions, other losses and gains net.. | 406,000 | 485,000 |
| Conversions and mergers............... | 1,000 | |
| Not available vacancies: | | |
| Seasonal......................... | 63,200 | 78,000 |
| Other............................ | 26,300 | 10,000 |
| Subtotal........................ | 89,500 | 88,000 |
| Less offsetting gains, or negative removals: | | |
| Public housing....................... | 42,500 | 40,000 |
| Trailers, group quarters, etc............. | 56,000 | 55,000 |
| Subtotal......................... | 98,500 | 95,000 |
| Total................................. | 398,000 | 478,000 |

SOURCE: Personal estimates based upon various census publications.

the number expected from population factors alone. The bulk of the increase was due to a higher per cent getting married in the age brackets below 35. The war and the postwar period saw many Americans marrying at a much younger age. No one can tell how much of this change was due to the war and the draft, how much to higher incomes, and how much to the increased domesticity of youth wanting a home and children at earlier ages.

After 1950, the rush to earlier marriages slowed down and almost halted. Increased marriages of those under 35 accounted for only slightly over 10 per cent of new household formation not based upon the population factor. The big increase in this later period came primarily from widows. With higher incomes, social security, and similar factors, elderly women could afford to maintain their own homes. Women over 55 accounted for over a third of extra household formation, or well over 1,000,000 units. The other additional households were divided fairly evenly among individual men of all ages, younger women, and older couples.

Figure 13-2 also shows projections of possible households to 1970 and 1980. Three sets of projections are included. In each case from the low circles of Census B to the high cross of the alternate OBE estimate, the expected rate of increase considerably surpasses recent levels of growth. For the period from 1965 to 1975, the lowest (B) projection shows households increasing at an average rate of 1,050,000 per year, while the alternate rate averages 1,340,000. The lowest estimate assumes that the forces which for the previous 20 years caused household formation to increase faster than population growth will slow down and virtually stop. The high estimate assumes that these forces will actually speed up.

Year-to-year movements in rates of household formation seem to depend primarily on income levels. In a depression younger people postpone marriage, and new couples and older people tend to share space with relatives or to move into group quarters. Income changes do not appear to have altered demand for houses by more than 50,000 per year in the postwar period up to 1964. On the other hand, a major depression like that of 1932 would cause a much sharper fall in the demand for houses. There were 300,000 to 400,000 fewer dwelling units required per year as a result of the low incomes of the Great Depression.

## Net Removals

In addition to units needed to shelter additional households, the economy must produce houses to replace those removed from the available stock. Final demand for new construction consists of net household formation plus the extremely varied types of forces operating on the housing stock which we define as net losses to available stock. Table 13-1 lists the different forces which add dwellings to, or which subtract dwellings from, the available stock apart from those dwellings reported as new building in the government figures on private housing starts. In the decade of the 1950s, an estimated 398,000 new dwellings were required each year on the average to replace net losses. This was in sharp contrast to the situation during the Depression, when the forces listed added so many units that no new housebuilding was necessary.

What is likely to happen in these categories in the future, and will they be influenced by real estate financing?

The first category, "demolitions and other losses and gains net," includes losses from fire, floods, and other disasters, units moved from sites, and dwellings converted to nonresidential uses. These losses are offset by related gains of houses moved to new sites and of dwellings formed in previously nonresidential structures, such as hotels or motels.

Demolitions form the most obvious basis for replacements. They occur because of road building, slum clearance, and the tearing down of units to furnish space for more modern structures. Other dwellings are demolished because they are located outside the main housing stream. For example, when people move from farms or leave small villages deserted, the houses they leave behind stand vacant for a while and are eventually demolished.

During the 1950s, the net annual rate of loss from these sources averaged about 0.7 per cent of the housing stock in existence at the beginning of each year. Some evidence indicates that this rate has been increasing slightly. It may have reached an annual level of about 0.8 per cent of each year's beginning stock. Most demolitions are directly related to the size of the housing inventory. A small bulge occurs, however, when new construction is unusually heavy. More rapid movements from rural regions also increase the rate of losses.

The category "conversions and mergers" covers those units formed when existing structures are split to house more families and the contrasting movement when an extra family moves out. These shifts in use may reflect physical alterations of the structure, but more frequently they are purely bookkeeping transactions which record events such as the rental of some rooms in a house to nonrelatives. Prior to 1950, conversions, or additions, far surpassed mergers. In recent years, the two seem to have about offset each other.

The category labeled "not available vacancies" can be analyzed either as a part of net losses to available stock or with total vacancies. The most important subgroup is that made up of seasonal units—vacation homes or those occupied temporarily by households with main residences elsewhere. Seasonal units are second homes. As such they are not available to meet the primary needs of households even though they serve a definite function in our standing stock. "Other" units are off the market because they have been rented or sold, they are held in estates, demolition is pending, or for similar reasons.

Not available units form between 6.5 and 7.0 per cent of the total housing stock. They have expanded at a rate about equal to the growth in dwelling units. This relationship, based upon a constant share of the stock, appears reasonable for those held off the market. We might expect, however, that increasing income and leisure will cause the rate of production of seasonal units to rise faster than households grow in the future.

The final category under net losses, "offsetting gains, or negative removals" might as readily be treated under a discussion of production. It includes new dwellings added to the stock outside of the normal channels of private housing construction. Some are paid for by the government. Others consist of trailers, living quarters in institutions and in plants, and similar quarters. All of these serve to house some of the added families. They reduce the new demand, and therefore must be taken into account. Since most public and press discussions of housing construction concern themselves with the rate of starts of new private houses, it seems easier to handle these miscellaneous categories as an offset against losses than as a part of production.

Unfortunately, very little information exists as to why or how the various categories of net losses alter over time. Some are related to the size of the stock and some to the number of new families. The amount of net removals should be higher in boom periods and much lower in severe depressions. There is no indication that the amounts are influenced by the availability of mortgage credit. Cheaper financing will increase some types of removals while it holds down others. For purposes of analyzing current demand, the categories of net losses must all be balanced against each other. An expected annual rate of net losses to the available stock of about 0.8 per cent of the units existing at the beginning of each year seems reasonable.

## VACANCIES

Most of the large year-to-year fluctuations in housing starts are caused by rapid changes in the number of vacancies. Figure 13-1 shows how sharp and erratic these movements have been. In certain quarters, inventory changes have taken place at an annual rate of over 400,000 units. Included in the housing inventories are units under construction and those held vacant and available for sale or rent.

Inventories of goods in process are required because of the lag between starts and completions. The number of uncompleted units is determined by the length of the production processes and by the changing rate of new starts.

A normal stock of vacant units is needed for new sales and population mobility. An insufficient supply, as in the postwar period, creates a nearly intolerable situation for those requiring different accommodations or wishing to migrate. While individual owners desire no vacancies, the aggregate need is met through prices or rents which make it worthwhile for each to hold his share of vacancies in turn. Normal available vacancies should equal between 3.5 and 4.0 per cent of the stock.

Movements of vacancies around this level have been important. Desired and actual vacancies need not be equal. Because of builders' and sellers' errors of optimism and pessimism, additions to the housing stock diverge from final demand. The resulting shortages or overages influence future starts. The reaction of builders to these vacancies depends on the market's organization. There is strong evidence that changes in mortgage availability or terms are among the basic factors causing these unwanted vacancies to fluctuate as they do.

## Types of Vacancies

Four major housing submarkets exist: (1) newly constructed single-family houses not yet sold or occupied, (2) previously occupied units being offered for resale, (3) new rental units, and (4) previously occupied units offered for rent.

The level of vacancies in one sector may fall temporarily as that in another rises. Builders of new houses attract a surge of buyers by easier credit or price changes. New rental units entice tenants from older ones with lures of status or amenities. Then adjustments occur through the price mechanism and the type of new construction started. A feedback causes starts to fall when vacancies rise, and vice versa. Its timing will vary. Vacancies in new houses that are for sale will have an impact on new starts with only a short delay. On the other hand, vacancies in older rental units may not be reflected in lowered starts for several years.

## Sales-type Vacancies

Although information on both total vacancies and their components is increasing rapidly, it is still inadequate. Since 1955, vacancy rates for all sales-type units have varied between 0.5 and 1 per cent of all units, or from approximately 250,000 to 650,000 dwellings. For-sale vacancies have increased by as much as 10 per cent of starts in critical years.

New sales-type vacancies are the smallest and, under normal circumstances, have the most rapid impact on new starts. Because of carrying costs, any lengthening of the period of sale rapidly erodes the builder's profits. Furthermore, the volume of unsold new units is controlled by limited builders' capital and by the unwillingness of lending agencies to finance additional starts when the builder has a backlog of unsold units.

Vacancies for sale are also found among existing units. Again owners attempt to keep them at a minimum. Most vacancies are due primarily to emergencies, death, foreclosures, or migration. Real estate men advise against vacating a unit prior to its sale because an owner's expenses continue for the empty unit, placing him at a disadvantage in bargaining with prospective purchasers.

While vacancies in existing units slow sales and lower prices of competing units, their impact on starts is less immediate than that of vacancies in newly constructed houses. Similarly, any particular area may experience a local economic disaster, with accompanying high vacancies that will have little or no influence on starts elsewhere. As a result, the spatial separation of markets leads to higher total vacancies for the country.

### Empty Rental Units

The probability of sizable increases in unwanted vacancies is greater for rental than for sales-type units. The quarterly Census Surveys indicate that rental vacancies nearly doubled between 1955 and 1961. Moreover, even though rental vacancies rose nearly as fast as new construction, starts continued to expand. In 1961, apartment starts surpassed their previous (1925) peak, while a new postwar peak for rental vacancies was also established. The rate of rental starts still continued upward in the following years. Total rental vacancies equaled a four- to five-year production level for multifamily units. In recent years, about a quarter to a third of vacant rental units have appeared to be located in buildings less than three years old. This is equivalent to a 30 to 40 per cent vacancy rate for new structures.

Rental vacancies are nearly three times as numerous as vacancies in sales-type units. There are several explanations for these higher vacancy rates: (1) Since payments would fall on his occupied units also, an owner may maximize his returns by allowing vacancies to increase rather than by cutting rents. (2) In a market so complex and diverse as rentals, the scarcity of reliable information tends to breed inaction and hence an increase in vacancies. (3) During the first two years of operation, delays in renting are normal. The total period for new construction between start and full occupancy covers a three- to four-year time span, and thus a long period elapses before the vacancies feed back and cause a curtailment of new starts.

## Financing and Vacancies

Credit is a major variable influencing the margin by which starts exceed or fall short of final demand. Tightening of credit affects the terms and prices of construction loans, as well as the discounts that builders of single-family units must pay for financing. Movements in terms have been sufficient to wipe out all potential profits. For promoters of apartments, availability of credit rather than price has been a critical factor because most often their main concern is to minimize required equities. Relative changes in credit availability and terms may also bring about vacancy disequilibria if they cause households to move from one sector of the market to another, because their vacating of old units will have only a lagging impact on starts.

Because of all these influences, the fact that mortgage terms have changed rapidly has been one of the main factors causing housing starts to fluctuate as they do. When money is easy, builders rush starts. They have more money available and they pay less for it. With easier terms, they can attract families from existing units. All these forces increase inventories. Finally the pressure of vacancies builds up. Houses cannot be sold. Apartments cannot be rented. Prices fall. Foreclosures rise. Lenders are more careful. Less money is available, and the number of starts falls.

## THE PRICE AND QUALITY OF NEW CONSTRUCTION

Real estate financing also has a great impact on the size, quality, and price of units constructed.

Most units started today more than meet the basic housing needs of families. They include extra space, extra refinements, extra bathrooms, garages, appliances, and all the other items considered so necessary in our standard of living. The space and quality built into houses have advanced fairly regularly. Values have expanded as households have striven to meet unfilled desires. Prices have expanded even faster. The cost per item in houses increased at the same time as the number and quality of items rose. While our level of housing is high compared to other countries and the past, it is still not as high as the average family would like it to be.

It has been possible to expand the amount we pay and to fill some of these desires because family incomes and assets have gone up and because the mortgage market, through easier terms, has enabled persons with given incomes to expand the amount of house they can purchase. With both forces operating, capital expenditures have risen rapidly.

The average amount of expenditure per housing start fluctuates with the level of household income, with mortgage terms, and with changes in tastes. Increased tastes for housing raise the amount of income families allocate to their mortgage payments. While in the postwar period small fluctuations have occasionally caused these factors to fall and expenditures to drop temporarily, their general trend has been upward.

As incomes rise, families have more money to spend on discretionary items. Because housing is a necessity, its share of additional income should be expected to be somewhat smaller than current percentages. (Technically its income elasticity is less than 1.) Since housing needs are met directly after food and clothing needs, minimum housing requirements are taken care of at low incomes. Additional housing expenditures have to compete with demands for all other goods. Accordingly, most past studies have shown that as incomes rise, the amounts spent on housing rise only 60 to 80 per cent as rapidly as other expenditures.

The postwar period witnessed somewhat of a shift in these relationships. Tastes for housing rose at the same time as incomes increased. The shift in tastes has been attributed to suburban living, higher homeownership rates, a more family-oriented life, and many other factors. Whatever its cause, it resulted in increasing the amount spent on housing faster than expected. The amount of spending per family for new houses has risen about as fast as income.

When a family allocates a given sum to housing payments, the amount of house it can buy depends upon the available terms it finds in the mortgage market. The easier the terms, the more mortgage it can carry and the more valuable or larger house it can purchase. The amount of expenditure per housing unit has moved closely in line with shifting mortgage terms. Longer amortization periods and lower down payments have brought about the purchase of expensive units. Fluctuating interest rates have caused equivalent rises and falls in the amount of housing purchased.

## SUMMARY

Construction financing is a specialized part of total real estate financing. Prior to the construction loan, numerous arrangements have to be worked out to make equity capital and funds for land development available. When land financing has been arranged, traditional lenders step in to finance the construction process. These loans are risky because so many things can go wrong. The cost can rise above the initial estimates. The market may be lower than projected. Funds can be diverted to other projects.

Because the problems are great, the payments for construction money have been relatively high. The high yields have attracted lenders who specialize in this sphere. They attempt, through their careful handling of applications and of progress payments, to keep their risks within manageable limits.

The terms of construction financing and the availability of the final loan seem to be significant forces in determining both the number of units started and their average values. Fluctuations in housing starts in the postwar period have probably increased rather than decreased. On the other hand, there has been a steady growth in the share of income devoted to housing at given income levels.

The role of real estate finance in fluctuations appears to take somewhat the following path: Easy credit increases a builder's profits. Buyers spend more. Builders sell or rent more expensive units. Costs of financing fall. The total amount of construction rises. As the movement continues, however, risks also rise. Unwanted vacancies accumulate and lead to falling prices and rents. Starts are curtailed. The size of fluctuations tends to be much greater for rental units than for single-family houses, since the rate of reaction is slower. Lenders and developers must recognize why all these fluctuations occur, and they must keep constantly in mind the probability that a reaction will set in. Otherwise they are likely to find themselves heavily over-committed in a falling market.

## SELECTED REFERENCES

Atkinson, L. J.: "Long-term Influences Affecting the Volume of New Housing Units," *Survey of Current Business,* November, 1963.

Bryant, Willis R.: *Mortgage Lending,* 2d ed., McGraw-Hill Book Company, New York, 1962.

Herzog, J. P.: *The Dynamics of Large-scale Housebuilding,* Research Report 22, Center for Real Estate and Urban Economics, University of California, Berkeley, Calif., 1963.

Maisel, S. J.: "A Theory of Fluctuations in Residential Construction Starts," *American Economic Review,* June, 1963.

————: *Housebuilding in Transition,* University of California Press, Berkeley, Calif., 1953.

Martin, P.: *Real Estate Principles and Practice,* The Macmillan Company, New York, 1959.

U.S. Housing and Home Finance Agency: *Financing of House Construction in the Northwest,* Washington, 1951.

# Investment Analysis in Real Estate————14

Both borrowers and lenders are vitally interested in how to analyze the risks and potential gains in the purchase and financing of investment real estate. The sums of money that change hands are great. Actual gains and losses have been large. Significant questions arise as to how the potential risks should be split among the interested parties. In theory lenders have attempted to accept only safe loans and have charged fixed rates. In practice the situation is very different. The mere existence of some equity over and above the loan has not guaranteed the lender's safety. Many mortgages are actually risk instruments. Such possibilities must be discovered by careful analysis. All those who share in an enterprise ought to attempt to obtain net yields (after risk reserves) that will make their loans or investments worthwhile.

## BORROWING ON INCOME PROPERTY

Loans on income properties and loans on residential properties are made in very different situations. In the income sphere, negotiation or bargaining concerning amounts and terms is the rule, not the exception. The borrower is in business to make money. His net income, or the amount for which he can sell a property, is heavily

342

determined by the conditions of the loan. It is well worth his while to negotiate with one or several firms to get the best possible terms. He rarely expects to be granted all he asks for.

One factor that makes bargaining possible is that certain conditions have different values to the borrower and the lender. Their tax situations may be entirely dissimilar. The length of their time horizons may differ radically. As an example, if a borrower is primarily interested in his cash flow rather than his accounting costs or eventual equity, he may find it well worthwhile to accept a higher interest rate in trade for lower amortization payments. The lender may be in exactly the opposite position. Thus a bargain becomes possible.

Critical to most lending decisions on income properties are the income statement and the capitalization rate. Both are estimates of the future. For existing buildings there is some historical basis for these estimates. For proposed construction, both projections are derived from only the scantiest data. It is therefore not strange that a good deal of personal negotiation must take place to determine a proper capitalization rate before a meeting of the minds occurs on what future income and expenses will be and what risks exist. When agreement has been reached as to the probable value of the property, the amount that can be lent and the necessary payments can be settled much more rapidly.

The factors that enter into borrowing on income properties are rarely set out in a logical manner. The reasons for this neglect are not clear. Possibly the development of analytic techniques for analyzing real estate investments was delayed because the construction of income properties was so greatly restricted after the debacle of 1929. Probably the general spread and lack of organization of the market for income properties have restricted studies of it. Few large firms invest in real estate. The market was primarily left to individual entrepreneurs and speculators who were too busy making money to develop any uniform concepts or theories of what they were doing.

When larger firms did develop after 1960, they tended to follow the hit-and-miss practices that had characterized the individual investors. The slight shock that hit the financial markets in 1962

caused sufficiently large losses among these firms to show that their
basic concepts and procedures left much to be desired. The death
toll of real estate firms and the losses suffered in their stocks were
much greater than for other sectors of the market.

The handicaps to successful analysis of income properties, from
both the buyers' and the lenders' points of view, are numerous.
An extreme scarcity of data prevails. Accounting rules and precepts
are still in the process of development. Statements of even the most
reputable of accounting firms must be examined with extreme care.
Frequently a study of the footnotes to the statement leads to an
interpretation completely different from that gained from the values
listed in the balance sheet. The discrepancies among the accounts
for tax, financial, and investment purposes are tremendous. It is
frequently not obvious which purposes the accounting statements
attempt to serve.

Furthermore, future prospects rather than the past are of prime
significance. The ability and integrity of those making the projections
are extremely important. It is very difficult for a lender or outside
appraiser to judge the relevance of many projections. For an amateur
or hopeful investor, the odds against a reliable estimate are tremendous.

The situation is discouraging but not hopeless. Numerous major
advantages accrue to real estate investment. Many of the country's
largest fortunes have been made in this sphere. Probably more postwar millionaires arose from the real estate development industry
than from any other part of the economy. The stakes are high.
Real estate investment is a game that can be entered with a lower
outlay than most others. What are the key factors which create
the opportunities, risks, and profits in real property investment?
How are they related to the problems of the mortgage lender and
borrower?

## THE KEY FACTORS IN INVESTMENT ANALYSIS

Several key factors make real estate investment what it is. We show
their importance and then explain each in the more detail. The five
critical points for analysis are:

1. The rent-roll, or gross income
2. Operating expenses and net income
3. Risks and errors in estimates
4. Leverage
5. Tax factors

First and foremost, each site and property are unique. Income, or rent, varies as much with market acceptance as with costs or varies more with market acceptance. As a result, slight differences in planning, a new insight into use, or improvements in the market cause large differences in the gross income received. Second, the share of income going to current operating costs is far less than is typical of most industrial or retailing operations, but its percentage may change radically. While, on the whole, returns to the property average a larger share of total income, the actual ratio of operating costs depends on the type of property. The share of operating costs runs from zero for a net-net lease on a single-tenant property, to a third or so on shopping centers or other retail property, to a half on office buildings and minimal-service apartments, up to two-thirds or more on apartment houses with large expenditures for service.

The third point is that these returns in most cases are not certain. They depend on future costs and conditions in the market. The demand for income properties suffers major fluctuations of over- and underoptimism. The planning and building period is long. Knowledge is imperfect. Too many or too few units may come to the market in any period. The time from the start of planning to final rental for a new income property may run from three to five years. High unrented inventories may accumulate because many units are being worked on simultaneously. Excess inventories in small markets can exceed annual growth rates many times. As a result, the unwanted inventory may not disappear for several years or more.

In addition to problems in estimating demand, uncertainty arises in the projection of expenses. Price and wage changes plus movements in the property tax throw off initial guesses. Experience demonstrates that these costs frequently move out of phase with income, thus putting great pressure on estimated net returns.

Potential returns and risks are magnified by the existence of high leverage in real property markets. While most developed properties are large and costly, the typical developer or owner invests only a small share of the needed capital. The system of lending on income properties places most of its dependence for safety on the property. The borrower is frequently a paper corporation whose only financial resource is the equity in the property. In addition to primary lenders who furnish two-thirds of the capital or more, other lenders will add necessary sums if they are promised high rates of return. A typical owner may have an equity of only 10 or 15 per cent. Since he guarantees fixed payments to the mortgage holders, his returns fluctuate sharply with even small movements in gross and net income.

Finally, real estate has had special advantages as a tax shelter. Taxes may be delayed and ultimately avoided or paid for at a lower rate. Real estate has been favored (although the Treasury has objected and makes constant attempts to have Congress change the law) because most of the cash received has been treated as a return of capital and not current income. Heavy depreciation allowances are authorized under the income tax laws. The cash flow is offset by depreciation credits. The owner pays a smaller current income tax. If he sells at a later date and shows a profit, he will have to pay some taxes, but they will have been delayed and, in addition, may be at a lower capital gains rate.

## A Typical Investment Statement

Figure 14-1 presents a typical investment statement which illustrates each of these five factors critical in the analysis of income properties. The statement covers the proposed construction of a 100-unit apartment house in a suburb. The land is offered at a purchase price of $30,000. This is the initial investment. The proposal shows that the cost of development, excluding the land, will be $910,000.

The appraised value of the development, based on an income of $86,000 and a capitalization rate of 8.6 per cent, is $1,000,000. When the development is completed, the land which cost $30,000 will have a value of $90,000. This is typical of the developmental

FIGURE 14-1   *A Typical Investment Statement*

*Investment Schedule*

| | |
|---|---:|
| Cost of land.......................................... | $    30,000 |
| Cost of development and building........................ | 910,000 |
| Increased value of developed land...................... | 60,000 |
| Total value of project................................. | $1,000,000 |
| From first mortgage (5½% interest)...................... | $ 660,000 |
| From second mortgage (8% interest)..................... | 200,000 |
| From cash equity...................................... | 80,000 |
| Total cash required................................... | $ 940,000 |

*Annual Income Statement*

| | |
|---|---:|
| Gross rent............................................ | $ 165,000 |
| Less vacancy factor (5%)............................... | 8,250 |
| Effective gross income................................. | $ 156,750 |
| Less operating expenses................................ | 70,750 |
| Net cash income....................................... | $   86,000 |
| Less average annual depreciation........................ | 36,500 |
| Less average interest.................................. | 42,301 |
| Net taxable income.................................... | $    7,199 |

*Cash Flow Analysis*

| | |
|---|---:|
| Net cash income....................................... | $   86,000 |
| Less payment on first mortgage (8.25%)................. | 54,483 |
| Less payment on second mortgage (12%)................. | 24,000 |
| Net cash flow......................................... | $    7,517 |

*Tax-free Cash Flow (average, first 10 years)*

| | |
|---|---:|
| Depreciation (double declining balance, 4.01%)............ | $   36,500 |
| Average amortization................................... | 36,182 |
| Difference........................................... | $      318 |

process. Land can carry anywhere from 3 to 100 or more dwellings per acre. The ultimate value depends on the capitalized return in a particular development scheme. While in theory land sells at a price based upon its highest potential use, most of the value accrues to the developer and not to the original owner.

The process of development is risky and requires hard work and skill. The amount of land far exceeds the number of knowledgeable developers. As a result, the promoter can usually buy land in a market well below its value in a finished project. If this difference did not exist, only a small amount of development would take place.

The cost and value estimate is the promoter's breakdown of where the money for the total investment will come from. An insurance company has issued a commitment for a first mortgage for 66 per cent of the value, or $660,000, at 5½ per cent interest payable with constant payments over 20 years. Another commitment for a second mortgage exists for $200,000. It includes constant payments of 12 per cent of the initial balance, including 8 per cent interest. The required equity is $80,000, or the difference between the actual developmental costs of $910,000 plus 30,000 for the land and the two mortgages, which total $860,000.

The next section of the figure shows the basic information required for cash flow and income tax analysis. On the basis of his examination of the market and comparable rents being received elsewhere, the developer estimates that rents will average $1,650 per apartment per year, or that the total rent-roll will be $165,000. After subtracting a vacancy factor of $8,250 to cover an estimated 5 per cent loss in rents, the effective gross income is $156,750. The promoter's schedule of assumed operating costs is $70,750. This includes property taxes but not interest, amortization, depreciation, or income taxes. Subtracting his operating expenses from his gross income, he arrives at a net income estimate of $86,000 per year.

For tax purposes the net taxable income shows an average gain of $7,199 per year during the first 10 years. This is based on the use of a double declining-balance method of depreciation for an estimated 40-year life. It allows an average of 4.01 per cent depreciation against the $910,000 cost of development, or an average of $36,500. The tax advantage is actually somewhat greater than the average for the period, since the heaviest depreciation can be taken at the start. It is $45,500 for the first year. The interest payments are also higher at the start than the average for the period because under a constant-payment plan, amortization payments increase and interest payments decrease as time goes on. Interest is charged against a smaller outstanding balance of principal in each new period.

The cash flow analysis shows related data. The net cash which the property throws off is $7,517 per year under the assumed conditions. This figure is obtained from the net cash income of $86,000 before mortgage payments or income taxes, minus the two mortgage payments totaling $78,483. The resulting difference of $7,517 is a cash return of 9.4 per cent on the required equity of $80,000. This might be too small for many investors to find it an interesting proposal.

It should be recognized that the relationship of the net cash flow to the required equity is probably the basis of the decisions of most investors. Sophisticated investors, however, take many other factors into account. The experienced investor with capital will consider the expected change in the value of the property and the possibilities that future movements will increase profitability rather than cause losses in the net income. (The final section of this chapter shows a more complete analysis.) For example, if the investor assumes that no real depreciation will take place in the property, his profit would be increased above the net cash flow by over $36,000 per year. While no depreciation in 10 years might be deemed excessive optimism, any amount below $360,000 would mean that his real profits would exceed his net cash return.

## INVESTMENT ANALYSIS

Some analysis required by these five key factors in real estate is straightforward, but much of it is extremely complex. Techniques of analysis have improved over the years as a result of individual experience in the real estate business. In several areas short cuts, or so-called rules of thumb, have developed. As in any investment procedure, an investor with the time, skill, and energy to dig beneath the accepted short cuts finds that he can greatly improve the basis of decisions and their probable outcomes. Short cuts are suitable for a very preliminary screening process, but they should not be depended upon for final action.

### The Rent-roll, or Gross Income

The obvious first step in any investment analysis is to calculate the anticipated future income. This income depends directly upon the rents which can be charged. The total potential rents for a fully occupied building equal the gross rent, or income, estimate. This total, less an allowance for vacancies and uncollected items, furnishes the effective gross income. Gross rent is the largest and most important estimate in the entire analytic process. Small errors in the gross are multiplied in the net income.

Estimates of future income for both existing and proposed buildings call for an exercise in imagination and creativity. Income results from meeting an unfulfilled demand in the market. The largest increases in value arise from seeing new potentials and creating the property to meet them. Many of the large profits in income properties result from such foresighted actions. The promoter builds a new type of apartment or one in a new location. He sees the need for a shopping center or office building where none existed before.

For existing buildings, the present rent-roll is one, but only one, of the factors serving as a basis of the future rent estimate. Current leases may have been written under entirely different demand conditions. They may be far above or far below the present or anticipated market. The date on which they must be renewed may be the key to estimating future success. The new owner may recognize demands for use previously unexplored. Productive use of wasted space may sharply raise the rent-roll.

The estimating problem differs considerably for each type of property. For a single-tenant building, the present lease and prospects of renewal may be critical. For commercial property, the amount of business which can be expected under given percentage leases will be most significant. For apartments and office buildings, an analysis of future competition is required. In each case, it is necessary to recognize that estimates are only that. They have a probability of coming true, but may diverge considerably from reality.

It is common and useful to base estimates on standard units of measure and upon data that can be gathered from similar properties. Thus, at any time, competitive office buildings rent at so much a square foot. Apartments rent per unit or per room. Stores are expected to sell a certain volume per front foot or per square foot of selling space. These estimates of income per unit gathered in the local market are extended to the number of units in the property under consideration in order to get the total rent projection.

The units must, however, be adjusted for qualitative differences. Rents depend on location. The status, size, differences in services, and age of properties will all affect the amount that can be charged. A particular property might be able to charge 50 per cent more or less than the average market rent, depending on how its quality differs from the average.

The expected duration of the estimated rents must be specified. Does any special factor so affect quality that some of the rents may not hold up? The latest style in buildings may command a temporary premium, but in five years other, newer units may receive the premium instead. Neighborhoods that are in the process of decline may indicate a much lower potential rent in 10 years. Frequently a beginning rent-roll and one 10 and 20 years in the future will be estimated, with the investment statement based upon their average.

Finally, the rents that will be lost through normal vacancies and failures to collect must be estimated and subtracted. These losses also depend on the type of building. A vacancy of more than a few months in a property with one or a few tenants means a disaster under most financing schemes. On the other hand, in apartments or office buildings, losses of from 3 to 10 per cent are normal. Vacancies will vary by type and style of building, depending on the kinds of tenants expected. An apartment on Wilshire Boulevard in Los Angeles may have a turnover of tenants as high as ten times a year. Other, more stable areas may average turnovers of only one in two or three years. The difference between gross rents and effective gross income will be much greater in one case than the others.

## Operating Expenses and Net Income

The second step in the investment analysis is to project operating expenses and to subtract them from the estimated effective gross income in order to obtain a calculation of net income. This concept of net income as utilized in real property differs considerably from that found in most financial and investment analyses. An examination of Standard and Poor's or Moody's will show for most companies net income which has interest, depreciation, and income taxes subtracted out.

For real property, net income is normally calculated before amortization, interest, depreciation and income taxes. These items play such an important role in the final value of a real estate investment that they must be calculated separately. They vary tremendously from investor to investor on a personal basis and are not a true attribute of the property. They depend on the individual's own cash, his tax bracket, and the mortgage he can negotiate. The net income as stated is a more objective fact. It is the free and clear income which would be received without financing if the property were owned outright. Using it as a base, each investor can calculate the other factors for himself.

The kind and amount of operating expenses vary tremendously with type of property and kind of lease. Many single-tenant leases are on a so-called net-net basis. They require the tenant to pay all operating expenses including realty taxes. In other cases, the tenant may agree to pay all expenses except certain unexpected costs, such as those for a new roof or boiler. In leases for gasoline stations, it is common for the tenant to assume all costs except those for increases in tax assessments. This is to forestall attempts of local assessors to soak the big "foreign" companies.

In contrast to net leases, owner-operated properties frequently have heavy operating expenses. When they run as high as 50 per cent of gross income or more, errors in estimates may cause a sharp decline in net income. The level and quality of the services rendered and the type and age of the property influence the costs of operation. Particularly on proposed buildings, standard costs of similar structures can be used as a basis for the projections. For existing buildings, the investor's knowledge of standard costs elsewhere will be used to recompute or reconstruct the previous expense experience of the particular property. Thus, if the expense schedule shows no painting, the prospective investor will add an annual charge of $12 per room or whatever the normal expenditures in the area may be. Other adjustments will also be made where the expense account appears too high or low. On the other hand, for certain items like water and heat bills, the actual records give a better indication of future costs than standard costs estimated from elsewhere.

The three basic kinds of operating expenses are general costs, replacement costs or reserves, and taxes and insurance. General costs are those expended in each period. They include items such as wages and salaries, leasing costs, utility services, repairs and maintenance, and miscellaneous. Replacements of items such as stoves, elevators, roofs, and furnaces occur only at longer intervals. Proper procedures establish an annual expense charge credited to a reserve so that expenses are spread evenly rather than concentrated in the year replacement actually occurs. Taxes and insurance are normally calculated on an annual basis.

Estimates of expenses require a calculation of their probable frequency, and this in turn depends on the quality of service. Painting may be necessary anywhere from once a year to once every five years or more. The number of employees will vary with the level of maintenance, requirements for guards, operators, etc. Replacements may be anticipated from general experience. The amount of utilities depends on how they are metered and on previous experience.

It is not enough to estimate the potential requirements for each item. They must be put in cost terms by calculating probable movements in wage rates and prices. The trend for these items has been upward. A decision must be made as to whether or not to extend this trend for the future period. Clearly the inclusion of some type of adjustment should give better estimates than the simple-minded assumption that the *status quo* for wages and prices will continue.

Such adjustments are particularly necessary for taxes and insurance. The trend of rates in both these areas has been rising.

The possibility of a change in assessments should be checked. In some areas, there is a regular cycle of reassessment in which the amount is revised every five to seven years. In other cases, the sale of a property and a new mortgage are likely to lead to an automatic reassessment.

All these calculations add up to the total estimated operating expenses. They are subtracted from the gross income to give the estimated net income. The final net projection results from two separate judgments, of gross income and expenses. Any errors in either side will carry through and may cause major difficulties with the final anticipated net income.

## Risks and Errors in Estimating

The probabilities of errors in estimating net income and the future value of the property increase the risks of ownership and decrease the present value of an investment. If the anticipated income is overestimated, a capital loss will follow. If it is underestimated, profits will be higher. The factors influencing the riskiness of future returns can be found discussed in most appraisal books under the heading of "capitalization rate."

Earlier analysis of risk showed that losses experienced in the Depression by income properties were, on the whole, above average. The nearly complete failure of mortgage bonds to meet their promised payments is also evidence of the serious miscalculations that can be made. A major share of the losses was due to failure to anticipate demand properly. Some of the underestimates occurred because the Depression was unusually deep. Similarily in the future, any loss in national income will cause a drop in demand. Marginal properties or those in the process of construction or leasing will be hard hit.

Even when economic conditions do not change, errors in judgment are common. Projected investment statements are based on the experience of other buildings. The analogy may be faulty, or other errors in market analysis may occur. Even when an idea is sound, the amount of competition may not be gauged correctly. Many firms may see the same opportunity and jump in to meet it simultaneously. Because the construction process is long, a large oversupply may not become apparent until many new buildings are completed. It may take a long time to work off the oversupply. In the interim, the net income will be reduced by vacancies and the necessity of offering rent concessions.

While errors in demand are most probable, cost estimates may also be wrong. Failures to anticipate tax increases, unexpected repairs, and sharp rises in wages or other costs are all common.

Both income and expense calculations may also go wrong because of inflation. It is frequently assumed that inflation works to the benefit of property owners. Certainly many poor investments have been bailed out by price rises. However, whether properties benefit depends on whether inflation causes income to rise faster than costs. When a large part of costs are fixed payments for interest and amortization, this may occur. But if rents are fixed by lease or controls and expenses are not, inflation can cause a drop in net income and in values.

Inflation works in another way. The investment schedule in Figure 14-1 did not attempt to estimate future changes in the value of the property. However, this is often a critical element in investment decisions. The present value of a property depends not only on the net income but also on future capital gains or losses. Ownership of a property gives the right to a future stream of income. Included in this stream is the final price to be received when the property is sold. The entire future stream must be discounted back to the present to get the current value.

### Capitalization

Frequently it is assumed that no change in the capital value will occur by the time of sale. When that is true, the annual net income can be capitalized to get the present value. Thus, for Figure 14-1, the net income of $86,000 per year was capitalized at a rate of 8.6 per cent to give the estimated value of $1,000,000.

$$V = \frac{I}{R}$$

where $V$ = capital value
$I$ = net income
$R$ = capitalization rate

This calculation assumes that the 8.6 per cent rate is high enough to cover the risks that a capital loss may occur rather than a capital gain.

The chances of capital changes depend on such factors as true depreciation, inflation, and liquidity considerations, that is, the need to sell in a depressed market. Thus if obsolescence or neighborhood deterioration sets in, incomes in future years may be lower. On the other hand, if prices rise, costs of new buildings may go up. More expensive new buildings will require higher future rents. Even if the present building commands lower rents than new ones at that time, the building's income will still be at or above current levels. The depreciation of the existing building and inflation will have offset each other so that net incomes will remain at present levels.

Discussions of capitalization rates deal with various ways to estimate the risks which will affect the income streams. One method assumes that the income stream can be divided into parts, each with different risks. Thus the 8.6 per cent rate might be derived as follows: Assume that the $660,000 mortgage should be capitalized at the rate charged for interest, 5.5 per cent, which is the equivalent of 3.7 per cent for the whole property. To this could be added 4.9 per cent derived from applying a 14 per cent rate to the remaining $340,000. This gives a total rate of $3.7 + 4.9 = 8.6$ per cent. The 14 per cent rate used for the equity would cover the risks of a fall in the value of the property over the 10 years for calculation.

The same rate could have been derived by adding a potential depreciation estimate, say 1.5 per cent per year, to the 5.5 per cent rate (or 3.7 on the total) for the mortgage and an assumed rate of 10 per cent on the equity (3.4 on the total). Thus there would have been $3.7 + 3.4 + 1.5 = 8.6$. Other systems would include using different rates for each mortgage and the equity. Some make the heroic assumption (wrong except in extreme cases) that the amortization payments equal the proper depreciation rate and thus capitalize on the basis of the total mortgage payments plus a return on equity. Others use a summation technique that adds interest rates for bonds, liquidity risks, management costs, depreciation, and additional risks.

It should be recognized that each of these techniques has little to offer in and of itself. Good estimates of the true risk depend on the skill and judgments of the person making the computations. The various techniques which have been derived are simply crutches to help the analyst in his task. None can be better than the skill of the user. At times the market as a whole uses rates which a skilled observer believes to be too high or too low. This gives him an opportunity to trade. Everyone in making a purchase should believe that he has calculated net income and the capitalization rate properly and that he knows the price is right and the purchase worthwhile. If he assumes that the market has overvalued the property and the price is too high and he still buys, he must believe than another sucker will come along who will make equivalent errors in his estimates and so will buy from him at the going price, or higher.

## LEVERAGE

One of the crucial factors present in most real estate investments is leverage, or the ability to control a large investment with only a small outlay of equity capital. The prospects of both gains and losses are enhanced. Changes based on the average return to the entire investment accrue to the equity holder. Because of the highly developed mortgage system, the owner has to put up only a small percentage of the total price as equity. The remainder of the required funds are furnished by lenders who receive only a fixed return but have the right to take over the property if the owner fails to make his payments.

### Income Variations

The statement in Figure 14-1 is a good example of leverage. The owner, for $80,000 in cash plus $60,000 in created land values, is able to own and control a property worth $1,000,000. Lenders have furnished 86 per cent of the total value and 91.5 per cent of the cash needed for the development. This ratio is not unusual in many markets.

The ownership of the property contains opportunities for large percentage gains but also for disastrous losses. Whether leverage brings gains depends on the accuracy of the net income estimate and the share of net income which the owner has to pledge to the mortgage holders. Let us examine how leverage works in practice, with Figures 14-1 and 14-2 as examples. Let us assume that the actual cost of land and development is $940,000 and the net return is $86,000. The average cash return on the total investment is 9.15 per cent. The owner's return will depend on how much he borrows and on whether he has to pay more or less than this average rate of return for the money he borrows.

Consider three possibilities. In the first case the estimates are correct, in the second rent projections are 5 per cent too low, and in the third they are 5 per cent too high. There are no changes in operating costs. An error of 5 per cent in demand estimates is quite small. It could result simply from changes in vacancies even if the unit rent estimates were correct. We examine separately the impact of these 5 per cent errors on cash returns (first three columns of Figure 14-2) and also on the real, or economic, income (last three columns of Figure 14-2). This true return, figured after 10 years, is based on an assumption that the property is sold and the true depreciation, or loss in value, averages 2 per cent per year. We do not consider the effects on real income that arise because the cash returns are spread over the whole 10 years or because of separate tax implications.

Looking down the first column in Figure 14-2 we see that the amounts the owner must pay in interest and amortization on either one or two mortgages are not far from the cash yield on the entire property. If the initial projections are correct, leverage makes only a slight difference in the yield on the equity. The next two columns show, however, that even small movements of cash flow, causing it to be more or less than the required mortgage payments, create a clear impact of leverage. Thus when the average cash return on the total investment goes from 9.15 to 10 per cent, the yield on the equity when two mortgages are in existence more than doubles. The net cash income rises by only 0.85 per cent of the total investment, but leverage causes an increase of 10 per cent in the return on the equity because it is now such a small part of the total.

The effects of leverage are still clearer when income falls. As

FIGURE 14-2  *A Comparison of the Effects of Leverage*

| | Net cash income | | | Economic income after average depreciation of $20,000 per year | | |
|---|---|---|---|---|---|---|
| | *Gross rents* | | | *Gross rents* | | |
| | *change* | *+5%* | *−5%* | *change* | *+5%* | *−5%* |
| Net rental income...... | $86,000 | $94,000 | $78,000 | $86,000 | $94,000 | $78,000 |
| All cash (free and clear): | | | | | | |
| Cash flow.......... | $86,000 | $94,000 | $78,000 | | | |
| Economic income..... | | | | $66,000 | $74,000 | $58,000 |
| Return on equity..... | 9.15% | 10.00% | 8.30% | 7.05% | 7.88% | 6.17% |
| With first mortgage of $660,000 (annual payment $54,483, average amortization $24,182): | | | | | | |
| Cash flow.......... | $31,517 | $39,517 | $23,517 | | | |
| Economic income.... | | | | $35,699 | $43,699 | $27,699 |
| Return on equity..... | 11.25% | 14.11% | 8.40% | 12.74% | 15.60% | 9.90% |
| With two mortgages of $860,000 (annual payments $78,483, amortization $36,182): | | | | | | |
| Cash flow.......... | $ 7,517 | $15,517 | $ −483 | | | |
| Economic income..... | | | | $23,699 | $31,699 | $15,699 |
| Return on equity..... | 9.40% | 19.45% | −0.61% | 29.62% | 39.62% | 19.62% |

the cash flow falls below the required rate of payments on the mortgage, the erosion of return on the equity becomes rapid. A small drop in net income means, in this case, that the owner must put up additional cash. Any additional decreases in rent or underestimate of expense would have to be made up entirely from his pocket. With a 10 per cent vacancy factor, the property does not throw off enough income to meet the fixed payments on the two mortgages.

**True Depreciation**

In the last three columns of Figure 14-2 we see the potential gains to be realized when the true depreciation differs from the amount of amortization. These columns show the economic income resulting from assumed changes in capital, neglecting, however, the time patterns of the cash and interest flows. In the time pattern, equity is being built up through amortization. The interest payments become less each year. The owner does not get his equity out until the property is sold. The final three columns assume an actual depreciation in the initial $1,000,000 capital value of 2 per cent, or $20,000 per year.

We note that for a free and clear property, the yields with depreciation taken into account are lower than are the estimated cash flows. If the property value is depreciating, part of the total cash flow is actually a return of capital. If no depreciation reserve were established, the owner would be overestimating the true income of his property.

In the second group of figures—those based on a single mortgage—the yields on equity, taking depreciation into account, exceed the cash flow estimates. This occurs because the amortization is greater than the true depreciation. The cash flow left after amortization is less than the true economic return.

The differences become extremely large in the last case. In this situation, while the amortization on the second mortgage reduces the cash flow, it does not change the rate at which the value of the property moves. The added amortization reduces the debt and increases the owner's equity. Here, we note the clearest example of leverage at work. The expected economic yield on the $80,000 equity becomes extremely large. Even small movements in net income or in depreciation cause the rate of return to shift rapidly.

It is important to recognize that these additional potential rates of return become possible because the owner assumes added risks. This can be seen from his altered ability to continue to meet his required payments and keep control of the property under the various situations.

Sizable shifts in income would cause only minor swings in the rate of return for a person who put up all cash for the building. Even if gross income fell over 50 per cent, the owner could still meet his expenses.

When lending occurs, the owner's ability to meet payments is rapidly reduced. The first-mortgage holder takes the least risky part of the investment. Mortgage amortization payments could still be met even if gross income fell 20 per cent below anticipation. Interest payments could continue if gross income fell nearly 40 per cent. For his money, the first-mortgage holder gets paid 5½ per cent interest. The equity holder behind the first mortgage assumes some risk of leverage. If gross income fell 20 per cent, he would lose his investment. As a result, he demands slightly over 9 per cent in cash, and over 10 per cent in real income on his investment.

The second-mortgage holder takes more risk than the first lender. If the expected gross rents decrease by only 5 per cent, the property will not pay enough for his interest and amortization. His interest will be cut into if rents are overestimated by 13 per cent. For taking this risk, he gets paid 8 per cent interest, and his loan is paid off in less than 15 years.

The risks and the opportunities of the equity holder stand out in Figure 14-2. The leverage raises his potential returns rapidly, but it also means that if the estimate of net income is too high, by even 5 per cent, he will lose his entire investment. Another point becomes clear from a comparison of the bottom figures in the third and sixth columns. If amortization is too rapid, the owner may find that he is earning a potential real profit but that he does not have enough cash to meet his mortgage payments. This is not an unusual situation in highly leveraged positions.

## TAXATION

The final critical factor for investment analysis is the tax situation. Because real property is subject to accelerated depreciation, it is common for the book value to be reduced for tax purposes at a more rapid rate than the market value falls. The depreciation allowance is subtracted from the current net income in order to determine the income subject to tax. The amount by which tax depreciation exceeds real depreciation is income which accrues to the owner currently but is not subject to normal income taxation. The immediate tax advantage arises from the postponement of any tax on this income. The owner has the use of the funds which do not have to be paid currently to the tax collector. In addition, there are possibilities that future taxes will be reduced or that they may even be avoided completely.

The tax advantage depends primarily on any differences between depreciation allowable for tax purposes and the true depreciation. Tax considerations do not guarantee any profit in and of themselves. The existence of authorized depreciation per se may cause errors in judgment. Many investors have been intrigued by the mathematics of buying a tax loss which could save them current income, only to find that they had bought a real loss. They did not save taxes because no income was earned.

### Cash Flows

The data in Figures 14-1 and 14-2 illustrate the workings of the tax shelter. The net cash flow is $86,000 before interest, amortization, and depreciation. Taxable income is reduced by any payments for interest and by authorized depreciation, but it is unaffected by amortization payments. In this case, with a base for depreciation of $910,000, expected life of 40 years, and a double declining-balance method of depreciation, the authorized deduction for depreciation will be $45,500 in the first year and $28,700 in the tenth, averaging $36,500 for the entire period. (See Table 6-7.)

If we now examine the first column of Figure 14-2, we can calculate the impact of this authorized deduction in the case of an $86,000 net income. With no mortgage, the owner will receive $86,000 in cash and will, on the average, have to pay taxes on $49,500 income. With a first mortgage of the indicated size, his average interest payments will be $30,301 per year over the first 10 years. His tax deductions from net income will be $30,301 + $36,500 = $66,801; he will have to pay taxes on an average of $19,199 income per year. In the first year, the tax deductions will be $81,332, so he will have to pay taxes on only $4,668. (See Figure 14-3.) For the whole period, his actual cash receipts will be $31,517 per year, and $12,318 of this total will not be subject to current income taxes. This is the amount by which his average depreciation allowance exceeds his average amortization payments. With two mortgages, his tax considerations are as shown in Figure 14-1. On the average, over the first 10 years, his total deductions of interest plus depreciation are $78,801. He receives an average of $7,517 in cash, a small part of which is not taxable. In the first year he shows a tax loss of over $11,000, which can be used as an offset against other current income.

## Tax Advantages

The calculations in the previous section were based on the amount of taxable depreciation. The extent of the tax advantage depends on the amount of true depreciation. For example, if no depreciation occurs, then at the end of 10 years the property can be sold for its full $1,000,000. The owner will now have made a capital gain to the amount by which the sales price exceeds his book value. His books will show a land cost of $30,000 and a book value for the buildings of $544,726, or the original cost of $910,000 less the accumulated depreciation of $365,274. He will have made a capital gain of $425,274, or $1,000,000 — $544,726 + $30,000.

What have the total gains been to the investor from the tax advantages of this situation? In this case there was no real depreciation. The authorized tax depreciation meant that in each year the owner's true current income was understated by an average of $36,500. If the tax rate on his highest income bracket averaged 50 per cent, he had nearly $18,250 extra to spend or invest each

FIGURE 14-3 *Calculation of Rate of Return.* (Based on $280,000 equity investment over a $660,000 mortgage at 5½ per cent interest amortized with constant payments in 20 years)

|  | First year | Tenth year |
|---|---|---|
| **Current income:** | | |
| Gross income............................. | $156,750 | $156,750 |
| Less operating expenses................. | 70,750 | 70,750 |
| Net Cash Income....................... | $ 86,000 | $ 86,000 |
| Less Interest........................ | 35,832 | 21,053 |
| Less Tax Depreciation................. | 45,500 | 28,665 |
| Net Taxable Income.................... | $ 4,668 | $ 36,282 |
| **Cash flow after taxes:** | | |
| Net Cash Income......................... | $ 86,000 | $ 86,000 |
| Less Mortgage Payment................... | 54,483 | 54,483 |
| Less Taxes (50% of net taxable income).... | 2,334 | 18,141 |
| Net Cash Flow........................... | $ 29,183 | $ 13,376 |

Cash received at sale (reversion):

Selling price (assuming 2% depreciation)................. $800,000

Less repayment of outstanding mortgage................. 418,627

Less capital gains tax (25% of $225,874)................. 56,468

Final cash receipt.................................... $324,905

Calculation of rate of return:

$$280,000 = \frac{29,183}{(1+r)^1} + \cdots + \frac{13,376}{(1+r)^{10}} + \frac{324,905}{(1+r)^{10}}$$

year which would have had to be paid in taxes if he had been required to calculate his true current income. On the other hand, if the building finally sells for only its depreciated value as shown on his books, there will have been no tax advantage. The calculation of taxable income will have been an accurate estimate of true income.

The tax depreciation can, but need not, be related to the rate of amortization on the mortgages. The amortization rate less true depreciation determines how fast the owner builds up his equity in the property. The depreciation for tax purposes less the amortization payment determines how much cash the owner receives on which he need not pay current income taxes—his so-called tax-free cash flow. All sorts of possibilities exist for gains, losses, and related cash flows. For example, if the amortization rate and the true depreciation rate are equal, the owner is not building up an equity. The cash flow should be tax-free, since it is a return of capital. On the other hand, if there is no true depreciation, the owner's current income is increased as indicated in the previous paragraph. Part of his real income is being received in cash for other uses and part is going back into the building by increasing his equity. The actual situation will usually be a combination of these various possibilities.

Let us return to the case where there was no loss through depreciation so the building sold for its original value. Even if the owner now had to pay a tax at the same rate as he would have had to pay on current income, he would still be ahead. He would have avoided paying current taxes on most of his income from the property for between 1 and 10 years. The fact that he could use the money in the interim has a value. In investment analysis this value is found by comparing the present value of the tax paid at the end of 10 years to the present value of the taxes not paid in each interim year.

Further advantages will accrue if the ultimate tax is paid at lower rates or if it is not paid at all. Under the 1964 tax laws, the owner need pay a maximum rate of only 25 per cent on his gain of $425,274 instead of the 50 per cent rate he would have had to pay if the gain had been received as current income. Obviously this is a sizable difference. It is one that the Treasury wants to avoid. Under the new legislation, some of the capital gain resulting from excess depreciation is liable to taxation at current rates. The formula for recapture is complex, with less and less being paid the longer the holding period.

Included in the general theory of differential timing and rates of taxes on real property are several fine points which serve to give the investor added advantages. Most of these, however, are under attack by the Bureau of Internal Revenue, so they should be assigned quite high risks in investment analysis. The authorized rate of depreciation which can be applied to a property may be increased in the early years to give a higher tax shelter. The rates vary depending on the type and age of the property and on current tax legislation and rulings, which are in constant flux. The general principle has been that the investor wants to maximize current deductions. Properties with a high ratio of land value to buildings usually have a lower over-all depreciation rate because land cannot be depreciated. In contrast, properties with a high percentage of stoves, furnishings, or other personal property have a higher over-all rate because such property is authorized a faster write-off.

Other important factors affecting the taxes paid are the timing and method of final disposition of the property. Many sales are made primarily for tax advantages when the rate of authorized depreciation of the property becomes low. The method of disposition has an important impact on the amount of taxes. Death may mean that the capital gains tax will not have to be paid. The same may be true of a gift to a charitable institution, even though the actual market value may be counted as a deduction for tax purposes. Exchanges also can transfer the tax burden from men or organizations in a high tax bracket to those in lower ones. For this reason, exchanges are a very complex and specialized area of investment analysis.

Because the risks and returns differ so greatly depending on leverage and taxes, a system of sales and financing has been developed whereby investments can be divided up in many ways. Each participant in an agreement can take the part which suits his needs. On large investments the various property rights can be sliced into as many as 10 or more segments. Each participant shapes the section he takes to his own needs. Institutions lend on only the safest parts at the lowest rates. Some equity holders may have so much leverage that their chances of receiving any income are slight; but if they succeed, their gains may be tremendous. Others take shares which tend to minimize tax burdens. Each further division offers extremely interesting problems for investment analysis, as well as possibilities of gain for the promoter who can slice a property in the optimum manner.

## SUMMARY

### Rate-of-return Calculations

While it is still not common practice, many progressive investors are applying to real estate investments the methods of analysis which have been developed in financial analysis and the investment decisions of business firms. These methods enable the analyst to calculate the present value of the expected future yields.[1] The techniques allow the investor to put all the information discussed previously in this book into a single yield estimate which can then be compared with the prospective cost of the real estate and with other competitive investments.

The Appendix to Chapter 6 showed that to calculate the present value of an investment, we must estimate the cash flow in each future period and discount this flow back to the present. The annual cash flow depends upon the gross income, the operating expenses and net income, the method of financing, and effective tax rates. In addition there will be a capital amount (the reversion) to be obtained when the property is sold. The sum to be received back will depend on the depreciation or appreciation of the property and also on the method of financing, or on amortization arrangements. (See Figure 14-3.)

The discount rate used will reflect the degree of risk involved in the particular investment. Thus each slice of the investment will have different risks, separate leverages, and unique claims on the cash flow. A separate calculation is therefore required to estimate the expected rate of return to each potential lender and to the equity holder.

In our illustrations of the effects of leverage and taxation, we used a similar technique; but instead of attempting to estimate the amount of risk and therefore the proper discount rate, we estimated the

[1] For a technical description of these techniques, see R. B. Ricks, *Recent Trends in Institutional Real Estate Investment*, Research Report 23, Center for Real Estate and Urban Economics, University of California, Berkeley, Calif., 1964, especially chap. 6.

potential return and asked the question, "Would this be sufficient, given the risk, to justify the investment?" The two techniques produce similar results, except in special circumstances. The previous discussion pointed out, but did not estimate, the differences in the flow of income in each year caused by declining depreciation amounts and lower total interest payments.

Figure 14-3 shows the type of calculations necessary to find the rate of return. It contains only the data necessary for calculating the net cash flow expected in years 1 and 10. In practice the years between would have to be calculated in a similar manner. The two years included differ, as would each of those in between, depending upon how much in taxes must be paid in each year.

The figure also shows the calculation of the amount of cash which will be received at the time of the sale. This depends on the selling price (which in turn depends on what real depreciation or appreciation has occurred), on the amount of the mortgage which is still owed, and on the capital gains tax. The tax will be based on the difference between the depreciated value of the property shown on the books and the selling price. The expected rate of return r is the discount rate which will cause the present value of the future returns to exactly equal the proposed investment of $280,000. Having found this rate of return, the investor would then have to decide whether such a rate of return was satisfactory, given all the risks involved.

Instead of solving for the expected rate of return, the investor could use an alternative technique. He could first attempt to estimate the proper capitalization rate for such an investment, given the possibilities of errors in estimating future returns. He could then find the present value of the estimated cash flows based on the desired discount rate. If the value was greater than the necessary expenditure of $280,000, it would be worth making the investment.

In either process, it is clear that the acceptable rate of return will vary with the risks which arise from the leverage, the potential errors in the market analysis, and the possibilities of unexpected increases in operating expenses. The danger of a complete loss of the investment will vary also with the terms of the financing. If the required mortgage payments exceed the net cash increase in any period, the total investment may be lost. The borrower and the lender must both evaluate their separate and joint risks to determine whether proposed terms are suitable or should be modified in some way.

## SELECTED REFERENCES

Casey, W. J.: Various books and pamphlets published by the Institute for Business Planning, New York.

Kahn, S. A., et al.: *Real Estate Appraisal and Investment,* The Ronald Press Company, New York, 1963.

McMichael, S. L., and P. T. O'Keefe: *How to Finance Real Estate,* 2d ed., Prentice-Hall, Inc., Englewood Cliffs, N.J., 1953.

Martin, P.: *Real Estate Principles and Practices,* The Macmillan Company, New York, 1959.

Ricks, R. B.: *Recent Trends in Institutional Real Estate Investment,* Research Report 23, Center for Real Estate and Urban Economics, University of California, Berkeley, Calif., 1964.

# Financing Income Properties——————15

The previous chapter discussed the major concepts of investment analysis for real property. This and the final chapter show how promoters, brokers, and lenders apply these general principles to the financing of income properties. Real estate practitioners must concern themselves with sources of funds, methods of organizing projects, ways to obtain money, and the specific techniques of market analysis required by particular properties.

Properties in the income field may be classified according to any one of several systems. One major method is by type of use. In attempting to estimate probable success or failure of projects, one can most usefully compare them to other units that serve similar functions and needs. Five major types of use exist:

1. **Multifamily housing, or apartment houses.** These form the largest segment of income properties, totaling about a third of all investment structures. Their analysis closely follows that of the general housing market.

2. **Commercial properties,** such as retail stores, shopping centers, garages, and gasoline and service stations. The income of these units depends upon their ability to attract customers, the amounts those customers will spend, and the costs of sales.

3. **Office buildings.** Some are large, general-purpose buildings rented on a competitive basis to numerous tenants. Others may house doctors or other trade and professional groups in a special-use building. Many large or small office structures are occupied by a single firm. The demand for these buildings depends upon the amount of business, governmental, or other services being rendered.

4. **Industrial units and warehouses.** Many are planned initially for a single user who knows exactly what functions he requires in the available space. Other users may find it nearly impossible to fit their needs into the same complex. In contrast, some buildings of this type serve a more general purpose. In many, future success is completely tied to the fortunes of the company for which it was initially designed.

5. **Miscellaneous specialized properties,** including hotels, motels, theaters, bowling alleys, hospitals, nursing homes, clubs, and innumerable others.

Each of these groups can be cross-classified in other ways. One system divides buildings into those that will be owner-occupied, in contrast to those that will be buffeted by the competition of the market. Another considers whether they will be for general, limited, or specific uses.

General-use properties can be rented by a wide variety of users. They may have frequent tenant turnover, and they require a fair amount of day-to-day administration. Limited-use properties serve only a single use and occupancy. Their value depends upon the firm renting them. Their income flows partly from the property but more from the success with which the individual renter conducts his business. Specific-use properties include specialized industrial plants and institutions such as hospitals. If the company to whose use such a property is specialized fails, it may be extremely difficult to find another tenant.

## SOURCES OF FUNDS

While large sums of money are required to finance investment properties, exact data as to where it comes from are lacking. Because of the government's concern with housing, much information has been gathered on residential property and lending. Exactly the opposite is true of nonresidential properties. No censuses exist for nonresidential structures. Mortgage data are primarily weak guesses or residuals.

New construction of income properties in 1963 totaled about $16 billion. Mortgage lending, including construction loans, financing of new units and refinancing, aggregated $30 billion.

Commercial banks are the largest construction lenders. They are also an important source for permanent loans. National banks can lend two-thirds of the appraised value of income properties for a maximum of 20 years. State banks lend in accordance with each jurisdiction's own regulations.

For permanent financing of both new and existing income properties, insurance companies are by far the most significant source of funds. They can lend from two-thirds to three-quarters of the appraised value. Their loans can extend for longer periods than the other lenders'. They can purchase the land under a structure or buy the entire property. They are interested in lending, sales and leasebacks, and outright ownership.

Pension, foundation, endowment, and similar funds are also significant in the market. Because of their exemption from taxes on profits, these institutions find ownership particularly advantageous. They and the insurance companies welcome large transactions that can be handled directly from their headquarters. These factors lead to their greater participation in the financing of income properties.

In their home areas, mutual savings banks do considerable lending. They lend more funds on apartment houses than any other type of institution. This reflects the concentration of both their money and a large share of apartment building in New York. Savings and loans hold a much smaller share of the income market than of that for residential properties. They are more restricted in their ability to lend on income properties. While regulations vary from state to state, most limit the share of portfolios which can be loaned on properties other than single-family homes. Depending on the state, loans on income property by savings and loans may be restricted to 15, to 20, or to 25 years and not allowed to rise above 50 to 70 per cent of value.

Individuals are also a major source of funds. They usually furnish the equity funds required for specific projects. Other devices such as bonds and syndications also exist whereby individuals' funds are brought in to supplement those normally available to the promoter.

## DEVELOPMENT PROCEDURES

The techniques of financing income property are not simple. The period for planning and negotiations is long. The number of firms and individuals involved may be great. Similar procedures are used for financing existing buildings to be sold or refinanced and structures proposed for construction. Since the latter are more complicated, we describe their procedures. The methods used for existing buildings are simply contractions of the more complete process.

The initial step in the construction of an income property is the recognition by a developer that a need exists. Because of this demand, a parcel of land can be improved. When development is completed, the value of the improved land will be greater than the sum of the costs of acquiring the land plus costs of constructing the building. The developer's profit depends primarily on this difference. It is, however, also influenced by the costs and terms of financing, by the amount of leverage, and by taxation.

Having recognized a need, the developer must perform some market analysis in order to estimate the demand. He may at times be interested in the true, basic, long-run demand. In many cases, he only wants to be certain a buyer will be available at some point in the process to ensure him a profit. His market analysis may vary from a rough "back of the envelope" estimate to a complete consulting report running 100 pages or more.

Having assured himself of sufficient demand, he next plans the development. If not already a landowner, he will have to buy or option a parcel. The costs of the property and the financing arrangements that the landowner makes available are likely to be crucial elements.

The developer needs to make preliminary plans for the buildings, in sufficient detail for quite accurate cost estimates. They will also be used in leasing and for his initial financing application.

Following his plans, the developer can draw up an investment analysis of the project similar to that in Figure 14-1. The project must promise an adequate return to the various fund suppliers. On the basis of these estimates, he must decide how much to attempt to raise through loans and how much from equity funds. How it will be gathered must also be determined. The developer must consider the number of partners or investors he will need in order to raise the necessary cash. This in turn will help determine the corporate or noncorporate structure of the ownership unit.

The leasing and financial negotiations proceed together. The developer needs to know the general terms under which financing will be available. On the other hand, financing usually will not be available until he can show sufficient leases or indications of demand for the lender to feel safe.

His actual application for the loan may be extremely complex, as shown by the list of application exhibits on page 200. He must convince the lender that the projected income and expense estimates are accurate. The lender will check his plans, his market analysis, and his projected operating costs and income. The lender will capitalize the net return to determine the value of the development and the size loan it can carry.

The primary lender will usually be restricted to a loan for two-thirds of the appraised value. Fortunately for the developer, this may be much more than two-thirds of his actual costs. He can, and usually does, plan to hold his own cash contributions to 10 per cent or less. Because the lender depends so much on the income statement, he will, for many types of property, insist on seeing enough AA-A1 leases at least to guarantee the mortgage payments. If the developer cannot produce the proper names, he will have to get a larger share of his financing from secondary sources. The size and conditions of the loan may be the subject of extensive bargaining. The lender and the developer have separate problems which make agreements possible. On the other hand, in tight-money periods many developments are postponed because no bargain can be reached.

Once the promoter receives his final loan commitment, he can proceed with construction. He may use a building contractor or do the contracting himself. He may plan to keep the development as an investment or at least to manage it. In other cases he may develop property for sale to an owner-occupier or to another investor.

The remainder of this chapter considers some general problems in financing considerations. Chapter 16 takes up problems of analysis related to each of the different types of income property.

## THE FORM OF OWNERSHIP

Several rather crucial problems arise in deciding what legal form ownership of income property should take. Liability for the mortgage, for other debts, and for injuries or other public damages attributable to the property is important in many cases. Corporations usually have limited liability. Other ownership forms frequently do not. Corporations have other advantages. They make centralized control simpler. They also have easily transferable shares that can be split into any denominations. For persons in high income brackets, the rate of corporate tax may be lower than their personal income tax.

On the other hand, corporations have to pay an income tax themselves. As their income is paid out, it will be subject to taxes again. Furthermore, corporations may have trouble passing through losses to be used for tax-offsetting purposes.

Attempts to merge tax advantages, limited liability, control, and ease of transferability have led to the establishment of many mixed forms of ownership in the real estate field. Anyone concerned with real estate should be aware of the advantages and disadvantages of the various forms.

### Individual Ownership, Joint Tenancy, and Tenancy in Common

The simplest and most common way of holding property is through individual ownership. For tax purposes, the owner reports the profits or losses from the property as part of his income. The owner is, however, liable without limit for any debts contracted by him as a result of his property ownership. He is liable for personal injury or similar claims of persons damaged through the property. Furthermore, the property will be subject to liens for any of his other debts.

Joint tenancies and tenancies in common are similar to individual ownership but relate to two or more persons. They differ primarily with respect to the share of ownership and the rights of survivorship. In a joint tenancy, the ownership interests are equal, and the survivor owns the property. In a tenancy in common, there may be unequal shares, and the deceased's interest becomes part of his estate. Taxes and liability basically follow the rules of individual ownership. Difficulty with tenancies in common arises when there is disagreement as to management or sale. The owners must agree to all the terms and conditions before a sale is possible.

### Partnerships and Joint Ventures

Partnerships are the usual form of holding property among several individuals if there is a wish to remain unincorporated. Partnership problems also arise primarily in the sphere of liability. Each partner can normally bind the group. In addition, each is usually liable individually for the entire debt and personal liabilities created by the property owned by the partnership. The advantage in holding property in a partnership is that it pays no income tax in and of itself. The partnership files its own return, but it pays no taxes. Instead each partner picks up his share of the total return and includes it on his own report.

Because of the problems of liability and control, various methods are used to adjust the partnership while retaining its tax advantages.

A limited partnership means that control and liability for some partners are curtailed. The partnership is divided into general and limited partners. The general partners are subject to the usual rules of liability and have a voice in management and control. The limited partners may have no voice in management. Their liability may be limited to their initial capital contribution. The partnership need not dissolve because of the death of a limited partner, whereas it is terminated by the death of a general partner.

A joint venture is a partnership formed for a single purpose. It is most common in real estate and construction, where the purpose is usually the purchase, development, or ownership of a single property. The joint venture is frequently a limited partnership and gives management and control to one individual or a few individuals.

### Corporations

When a business grows to any size, the corporation becomes the most widely used ownership form. This applies in real estate as in other fields. Corporations are creatures of the state and must be chartered by them. What a corporation can or cannot do is limited by its charter. Many states have special rules and taxes applying to real estate corporations.

The disadvantages of corporations are found primarily in the sphere of taxation and record keeping. The corporation pays the state special fees for its charter. It also requires extra legal advice and expenses. Certain taxes must be paid simply to continue in existence whether the firm is profitable or not. The records of major actions requiring approval by directors must be kept in a specified form. Taxes must be paid to transfer stock. A still more important influence on decisions is the corporate profit tax. All these taxes can be very burdensome. Finally, losses or depreciation allowances accruing to the corporation in the course of its business cannot be passed on to the owners.

The considerable advantages of the corporation frequently outweigh the drawbacks. The corporation is a legal entity distinct from its stockholders and management. It holds property in its own name. It can sue and be sued. Limited liability exists. The owner of stock contributes a certain capital sum. His liability is confined to that amount. If the property goes bad or an unexpected accident and damages occur, the stockholder will lose only his investment.

The corporation has a life of its own. It can continue even if its owners or officers die. Its decisions are subject to regular rules and procedures, not to the whims of individual partners. The corporation shares are transferable. If someone does not like what is happening, he may sell out.

## Syndicates

In the postwar period "syndication" has swung from being an almost magic name to becoming almost a dirty word. This transition did not apply to the syndicate as a form of business, but was caused by the abuses performed in its name.

A syndicate is usually a group of investors gathered together to invest in one or more properties. They may own through a partnership, corporation, or trust. Frequently joint ventures with a few general and many limited partners have been set up. Real estate ownership through this normally burdensome form is possible because the management problems are small, income distribution simple, and liability coverable by insurance. Lenders looking mainly to the property for security have been willing to lend to partnerships of this type.

Syndication has attracted numerous potential investors to individual properties. Real estate development's major problem has traditionally been that of finding equity capital. A logical solution was to interest several people—friends, clients, or acquaintances—in the joint purchase of a property. The investment analysis could be explained to a few key people, who would then frequently bring in additional money from friends and relatives. This type of partnership has been traditional throughout the real estate industry.

In the 1950s, however, the concept of syndication expanded beyond the informal groupings of friends and neighbors. It was recognized that this system of holding property had the potentialities of attracting large new sums of money to the real estate market. Funds came from individuals attracted by the advantages of property ownership but without sufficient capital to purchase a property by themselves. Another advantage to syndicators was the fact that since investments were fairly small, investors did not feel the necessity for the intricate financial and market analysis required for successful real estate investment.

Syndicators or promoters take the responsibility of finding attractive real estate investments. They option properties or purchase them for resale to a syndicate. The investment is established as a limited partnership or corporation. The equity is divided so that each share can be sold for $1,000 to $10,000. This technique of split ownership greatly multiplied the number of real estate investors.

Syndicates take many forms. In New York many of the largest income properties have been purchased and resold in this manner. While some syndicates include thousands of holders, many remain closer to the original concept, with shares being sold to only 10 or 20 professional men or part-time investors. The syndicate offers the developer a market for his property. He frequently retains the management of the property, paying out income as it is received.

Sales have also been made to unsophisticated investors, the emphasis being placed on form of ownership and ability to own real estate, rather than on the necessary financial analysis. Instead of being briefed by an analysis of the market and of its potential, the prospective investor was shown an income statement promising a 10 per cent return and decided tax advantages. Selling emphasized possible sharp rises in real estate values which could lead to large residual values. A high current yield and tax advantages were stressed, while the traditional risks in real property investments were played down.

Results have varied tremendously. Initially many syndicates were extremely successful. Because real estate required such large sums of equity, returns on many properties were higher than in other spheres. Splitting of investments to small purchasers gave an added market. There was a sufficient gap between the traditional real estate returns and what small investors could earn elsewhere so that all gained. However, as interest in syndicates and in real estate investment in general increased, the number of really excellent investments dwindled. The amount of money seeking good properties rose faster than the number of properties. These problems led to others. The market for the syndicate shares was illiquid. Only limited trading was possible, frequently through the office of the original syndicator. To give more liquidity, some of the largest syndicators pooled many of their property holdings into public corporations, the stocks of which were traded over the counter and in some cases on major exchanges.

As a result of the problems besetting the industry, the quoted prices of many of the public companies fell between 50 and 80 per cent from 1962 to 1963. Shares in individual syndicates showed similar losses.

## Mechanics of Syndicates

Syndicates can be classified in many ways. They may be limited partnerships or corporations. They may be small private undertakings or large public offerings. The promoters may be investors or brokers. Those interested in forming or joining a syndicate must be clear in their own mind as to its purpose.

Typically the idea of the syndicate originates with the promoter. He sees an existing property which he feels is a good buy. He puts together a development proposal requiring more capital than he has available. He must then decide what his relationship should be to the ultimate syndicate. In many cases, promoters think of the syndicate primarily as a way of selling a property. For a new development, the syndicate will make construction possible, and it will ensure the promoter's profit.

For existing buildings, the syndicator in effect buys a large property at wholesale and sells at retail. For example, he may find that a structure costs or can be built for $1,000,000 and requires $200,000 of equity above the mortgage. Analysis reveals that at a price of $1,100,000 with an equity of $300,000, each equity dollar can be promised a 10 per cent return. He divides the ownership into 30 units of $10,000 each and sells them. If successful, he has $100,000 to pay for his effort. He also may retain a management contract by which he earns a continuing share of rents and income.

In other cases, the syndicator may feel that the investment is so good that he wants to retain a maximum share. He sells off only enough shares to raise the necessary cash equity, retaining the remaining shares as payment for his effort. His ultimate profit depends on the success of the syndication.

In a related technique, he establishes a separate syndicate to own the property but gives a corporation he controls a 20- or 30-year lease at a fixed rate. The rent is fixed to pay the syndicate its promised return. His profits depend upon his success in managing the building. Any income above the guaranteed rental will accrue to him. This system has the advantage of giving the equity investors an apparent guaranteed return. If they pay only the real cost of the building, he will have to earn his profits in the future. His profits will not result simply from an initial markup in price, which the market may not support. The disadvantage is that the owners will not share in any increased value except through their residual rights at the end of the lease. If the lease does not succeed, they will take the loss. Their situation may be extremely dangerous if the syndicator takes both a large initial profit and also retains the lease.

Many syndications were initially planned as limited partnerships, thus avoiding the corporation income tax and giving the owners the advantages of rapid depreciation. When authorized depreciation exceeds the cash flow, the partners receive the entire flow in non-taxable cash and in addition can decrease their income from other sources by the amount of unused depreciation. When the property's income exceeds its depreciation, the profits go directly to the investor. They are not decreased by the corporate profit tax.

In a typical limited partnership, the management may be vested in three to five general partners, who remain liable for losses and have full rights of control. Because the partnership will be dissolved if one dies, necessary planning for such events must take place. Limited partners subscribe for specific amounts of the total capital. Their liability is limited to the amount each furnishes. Normally their shares are transferable. Where a partnership of this type contains too many attributes of a corporation, the Bureau of Internal Revenue will tax it as a corporation. Avoiding this difficulty requires careful planning and tax advice.

Recently most syndications have been offered through stock in corporations. The rise of allowable depreciation and the consolidation of properties with various rates of depreciation have added to the traditional advantages of the corporate form. These syndicates frequently plan for nearly the entire cash flow to be offset by allowable depreciation. The corporation pays only a small income tax. In addition, a large proportion of the payments to the shareowners is considered return of capital and not taxable as personal income

until or if these repayments surpass the amount paid for the stock.
They reduce the owner's basis of cost. When the shares are sold,
the amount, if any, by which the price exceeds the reduced cost
basis is a capital gain.

Tax complications of management are great. To retain tax advantages, properties must be sold when their allowable depreciation
gets too small; the corporation may then have a potentially taxable
capital gain. Various techniques serve to reduce the tax impact.
It is frequently problematical whether the relative costs of attempting
to avoid taxes exceed the costs of the tax payment.

The control over syndicates varies from state to state depending
on the stock and corporation act of the state. In addition, if shares
are sold on an interstate rather than intrastate basis, if there are
more than 25 investors, and if the offerings total $300,000 or more,
the offerings are subject to the Securities Exchange Act. The problem of ensuring fairness among the promoters and purchasers of
shares is difficult. A great deal depends upon the accuracy of the
market analysis and on future trends. Some states attempt to be
certain that the promoter accepts his full share of the risks. They
also may require that he not receive a return until those who put
up the cash have received a fair profit on their investments.

### Real Estate Investment Trusts

In 1960, the tax laws authorized the formation of real estate
investment trusts. By 1964, over 40 major trusts have been formed.
An analogy is usually drawn between real estate investment trusts
and closed-end mutual funds. The owner buys a share in a trust
to obtain diversification and professional management. Providing it
pays out 90 per cent of its income, the trust is not a taxable entity.

The trust must be one in fact as well as name. The property
must be owned and controlled by independent trustees. In a clear
attempt to avoid conflicts of interest, the trustees cannot be officers
or employees of firms servicing the properties of the trust. The
trust cannot carry on an active business. It must be primarily an
investment vehicle. At least 75 per cent of its investments must
be in property or mortgages.

Real estate investment trusts must have over 100 owners. No five of them may control as much as 50 per cent of the shares. The stock must be completely transferable. Recipients of the trusts' payments treat their receipts for tax purposes in accordance with the manner that they accrue to the trust. Thus payments may be a return of capital not taxable to the individual. They may include ordinary income. They may also include capital gains. The shareholder receives a statement showing the percentage falling in each category and reports accordingly for his tax purposes.

Real estate investment trusts have primarily been used to purchase or hold a diversified group of properties. Some have also been established to spread the risks in mortgage ownership. In their initial stage, trusts have been somewhat less speculative than syndicates. Their promotions have stressed real estate as a sphere for investment with above average returns and an inflationary hedge. They have not promised high speculative profits.

### Cooperatives and Condominiums

Cooperatives and condominiums have become major sources of equity capital for apartment houses. Cooperatives were frequent in the 1920s, but they had a disastrous experience. After the war they were reintroduced as part of the FHA program. Their advocates were primarily interested in the cooperative idea and cheaper housing. They gained their chief impetus when developers discovered that because of their tax advantages, they were a method of reopening the market for luxury apartments.

Builders and promoters have sold cooperatives primarily through four claims: (1) There is a large tax saving compared to renting. The cooperative qualifies for the tax saving as if it were an individually owned home. (2) An inflationary hedge exists, since the owner holds an equity. (3) Costs of management and operation are less. Each cooperator will handle his own maintenance and, if necessary, will rent out his own unit. (4) The purchaser of a cooperative can live in an apartment house rather than a single-family unit, yet he has all the status and attributes of home-ownership.

Most sales have been made to those who preferred apartment living but felt that ownership gives lower costs (for tax or other reasons) than renting. The boom was intensified by a shortage of new luxury apartments, since few investors were willing to build such units. People wanting large apartments frequently had little choice. In the case of medium-priced apartment units carrying FHA-insured mortgages, low down payments and costs less than rent were the principal attraction. Another push came from owners who wanted to sell units which rent control prevented them from renting profitably during the postwar boom.

Typically, cooperatives have been promoted by builders or developers or owners of an existing structure. The promoter agrees to sell the apartment structure to a newly formed cooperative corporation which he organized and whose stock he sells. This corporation borrows money on a mortgage. The equity is raised by selling shares to the future cooperator-tenants. The number of shares each purchaser must buy is proportional to the value of the dwelling unit he will occupy. The cooperative corporation's charter specifies the establishment of a board of directors and their method of election, rights, and duties. Each purchase of stock gives the buyer a proprietary lease. In this lease, the stockholder agrees to pay his share of the joint costs, including heat, maintenance, taxes, and mortgage payments. Controls are usually specified over subletting and resale.

The value of a cooperative to an individual depends, as in other property ownership, on how good a buy was made initially. Many buyers have failed to investigate and have paid the owner too high a profit. This raises their costs and foreshadows the likelihood of a loss rather than a gain on a resale. Nothing in the cooperative form per se guarantees that this type of homeownership will be any more or less successful financially than the more traditional type.

In fact, one major disadvantage of cooperatives should be stressed. Operating costs and mortgage payments are shared mutually. If some owners cannot meet their payments and so default on their shares, the burden carried by the remaining owners will go up. They may attempt to lease the units on which defaults have occurred as ordinary rental units, but the rent received may be too small to cover all costs. In such a case, the remaining owners' costs rise. The higher each remaining owner's share becomes because of others' defaults, the more probable are additional defaults. The point may be reached where all the remaining owners will be forced to default on the mortgage. That was the typical experience of the 1930s.

The condominium is a form of cooperative which attempts to avoid this problem. It is a common method of ownership in Western Europe and has come into increasing use in the United States. The condominium consists of a joint ownership of common property, such as halls and entries, but individual ownership of each family's dwelling unit. The form of establishing the condominium varies among states. Some require approval as a subdivision and the filing of a master deed. Each apartment owner receives a deed to his own property. He can borrow on it as he sees fit. He pays directly his own taxes and mortgage payments.

He also agrees to pay his share of the common costs. Sums not paid under this obligation can be made a lien against his title. He can sell or transfer his individual unit as he sees fit. However, restrictive agreements requiring that the right of first refusal be granted to the others in the condominium are common.

The big advantage of condominiums is the protection against rising charges to meet mortgage payments on empty apartments. Resale may also be simpler because new mortgage terms can be arranged, whereas the traditional co-op has a problem in financing any new buyer if the seller has accumulated a considerable equity either through debt amortization or increased prices. A disadvantage has been the difficulty of establishing the legal rights and forms of this type of ownership in many states. New laws have been required to spell out the individual rights and to establish the basis of tax collections. The promoters of traditional cooperatives have also claimed that because in cooperatives transfers of stock are controlled by the board of directors, it is easier to maintain discriminatory policies.

## NONMORTGAGE, NONEQUITY FINANCING

In addition to mortgages and equity financing, at least two other major methods of obtaining funds for real property are significant

386 CHAPTER 15

for borrowers and lenders. The first technique uses transfers of property accompanied by leases. The second consists of bonds or debentures.

### Leases: Sale-and-Leaseback

The term "sale-and-leaseback" refers to the purchase of a property and the simultaneous lease of it back to the seller at a previously agreed-upon price. Usually the purchase and lease cover whole properties, but in several well-known cases only the land has been sold. The leases are normally net-net and run for long periods; 20- to 30-year leases with a series of options to renew at lower rents for another 20 or 30 years are common.

The major reasons for using sale-leasebacks rather than mortgages include the amount of money that can be borrowed, different tax benefits, and possible improvements in a firm's balance sheet. Which advantage is predominant depends on the particular firm, but in some cases all occur simultaneously.

1. In typical cases, a company can borrow only two-thirds of the value of a property and must furnish equity for the remainder. In contrast, on a sale, the lender (purchaser) may pay up to 100 per cent of the value. The firm gets more capital at near the relatively low mortgage interest rate. A small interest bonus is normal because of the lender's increased risk. To a capital-short company or a real estate promoter, these additional funds may be extremely valuable.

2. The tax benefits arise from the differential tax rates which apply to normal corporations in comparison to tax-exempt colleges or foundations and insurance companies. While the latter have varying rates of taxation, they are almost always well below the amounts paid by a typical successful corporation. The tax benefit depends primarily on the amount of authorized depreciation. This will be low when the proportion of land to structure is high. Sale-leasebacks are more common on central-city properties where such land ratios apply. They are also used when the selling company has a low tax base because of rapid depreciation or a long history of ownership of the building.

Although the original owner or seller in such cases is able to take only a small depreciation deduction against taxes, he can deduct the whole rent payment on the lease for tax purposes. The new owners are not concerned with the depreciation rate because they typically pay little or no income taxes anyway. This difference may boost net income after taxes to the original seller by a large amount. An added advantage is that any subsequent improvements may be depreciated over the life of the lease rather than over the improvements' normal life.

3. The balance sheet improves for two reasons. If the property has been heavily depreciated, its sale will yield a capital gain. The amount of gain less its tax becomes an addition to the firm's capital. Second, the lease appears only indirectly as a liability. It will normally be reported as a footnote to the balance sheet. In contrast, a mortgage is a normal debt. The mortgage's existence influences the firm's debt ratio and can cause restrictions in a firm's lending agreements to take effect.

The lender also sees advantages in the sale-leaseback market. His return is usually somewhat higher than on a regular mortgage, with about equivalent risks. Residual values may accrue to the lender after the lease is up. Because they have a much lower discounting rate, the present value of such residuals tends to be higher for lenders than borrowers. Many lenders not equipped to handle small mortgages welcome the large size and comparative investment ease of these sale-leaseback packages.

Terms for sale-and-leasebacks depend upon the type of properties and the seller's credit rating. Leases of major firms, such as Sears Roebuck or Woolworth, are judged on the company's credit standing. Charges are based upon the amount they would have to pay in the bond market plus a sum to amortize some or all of the loan plus a small premium. Typical payments run from 6 to 8 per cent. On the other hand, when a lease covers a specialized property, such as a bowling alley or a motel rented by a firm with little or no capital, the rate may be extremely high. The lender (owner and lessor) increases his risk because the percentage of value covered is higher. He must be compensated for this added danger.

As already noted, in addition to the usual sale-leaseback, leases may cover only the land. Building on leaseholds is traditional for all properties in some parts of the country. In other sectors, a large amount of income property may be built on leased ground.

In these cases, the land is lent rather than money. The building's owner requires less capital because, instead of having to purchase the land, he pays for it through an annual rental payment on a lease which frequently lasts 50 or 99 years.

Some extremely interesting syndicates have been based upon special lease provisions. Their objective has been to tailor large capital requirements to the needs of different groups of lenders and investors. As an example, the money needed to purchase a large office building might be obtained in four or more ways. The land might be sold to a nonprofit organization that did not require depreciation for tax purposes. A syndicate might own the building with a large conventional mortgage from an insurance company or bank. The syndicate might attempt to guarantee a large tax-free cash flow to its small participants. The owner syndicate might get its return from a sublease to a management firm with guaranteed payments. The managers would furnish some capital. They in turn would depend for their profits on a successful operation of the building.

### Bonds and Debentures

Real estate bonds have a long and undistinguished record. They came into prominence as part of the speculative boom of the 1920s but almost disappeared under a wave of defaults during the 1930s. Originally bonds were used to attract additional mortgage money to the real estate market. The bonds looked like those issued by industrial or utility companies. They were backed by a mortgage on individual properties.

Most bonds were backed by first mortgages, but second- and third-mortgage bonds also existed. The concept was similar to mortgage borrowing. The property owner promised to meet his bond payments. If he failed, the trustee for the bondholder foreclosed and became the owner of the property. Problems arose both because of the great deflation in real estate values and because many firms underwriting and issuing bonds used unduly optimistic appraisals of current and future values. Their profits arose from developing properties and selling the bonds. While successfully tapping a new source of financing, they were not sufficiently careful in evaluating the real worth of their properties. The value of the building used for security fell far below the amounts paid by most subscribers. The problems of operating buildings by bondholders' committees were great. The investments were not liquid. To raise cash, many buildings had to be sold at well below their real value.

The reappearance of real estate bonds in the postwar period has been on a somewhat different basis. Many have been issued by capital-short but promising industrial or merchandising corporations. They have been able to increase the amount of money they could borrow on a property above that possible on a mortgage. Small chain stores, drugstores, and discount houses have difficulty raising capital to purchase properties. By issuing debentures backed by both their general credit and a mortgage, they can borrow more than through a mortgage alone. In many cases debentures have made 100 per cent loans possible.

In some cases convertible debentures have been used. In others, the bonds have had stock warrents attached. Some lenders believe that since they put up a large share of the capital, they should have an opportunity to share in any potential growth. Such arrangements have been particularly common for new shopping centers when the major leases are not AA-Al.

In other cases debentures have been used in syndicate operations either as a form of tax saving or to differentiate risk. Where the syndicate is a corporation, interest on bonds is an expense, not a profit. The limits to which bonds instead of stock can be used in financing depend upon complex tax rulings. Ratios of stocks to bonds have to be carefully planned. They differ for each situation.

As an example of risk differentiation, some syndicates use bonds plus stock for the investors who put up the cash, while the promoters receive only stock. In this manner, those who furnish the equity have the right to the initial return. They also own the entire property if the bond payments cannot be met. Similar arrangements can be handled through different classes of stock. Whether bonds are used instead of stock frequently is determined by the tax consequences.

Recently, special issues of real estate bonds have been made based on mortgages issued by the FHA. The idea is to give small investors a safer instrument than they could normally obtain. The borrower gets a better rate from the bonds than he would from a large mortgage.

## SUMMARY

A wider group of lenders is active in the market for income properties than in the market for homes. Insurance companies, banks, and pension funds all play a more significant role. The amount lent depends primarily on the valuation of the individual property. This valuation usually reflects the capitalization of the expected income.

A large number of methods have been devised for raising equity capital. Each of these techniques gives a different mixture of risks, potential liabilities, and control. In addition, this chapter has constantly called attention to tax consequences in discussing the usefulness of a particular financing device. This is a reflection of the current real estate market and high taxes. Which method of raising capital will be used is determined by the manner in which it influences management and control, the safety of the investment, the individual liabilities of the participants, and the net return after taxes.

## SELECTED REFERENCES

Bryant, Willis R.: *Mortgage Lending,* 2d ed., McGraw-Hill Book Company, New York, 1962.

Casey, W. J.: Various books and pamphlets published by the Institute for Business Planning, New York.

Hoagland, H. E., and L. D. Stone: *Real Estate Finance,* rev. ed., Richard D. Irwin, Inc., Homewood, Ill., 1961.

Kahn, S. A., et al.: *Real Estate Appraisal and Investment,* The Ronald Company, New York, 1963.

McMichael, S. L., and P. T. O'Keefe: *How to Finance Real Estate,* 2d ed., Prentice-Hall, Inc., Englewood Cliffs, N.J., 1953.

Pease, Robert H., and Homer V. Cherrington: *Mortgage Banking,* McGraw-Hill Book Company, New York, 1953.

Ricks, R. B.: *Recent Trends in Institutional Real Estate Investment,* Research Report 23, Center for Real Estate and Urban Economics, University of California, Berkeley, Calif., 1964.

# Analysis of Types of Income

# Properties————————————————————16

        In this chapter, the major features of financing income properties, discussed previously, are applied to specific types of property. General principles, which with only a few exceptions need not be repeated, apply to all. Decisions with respect to type of ownership, amount of leverage, tax treatments, mortgage applications, need for negotiation, and value of analysis apply in all cases. Also generally applicable in determining the desirability of investment in income properties are such factors as whether they will provide an inflationary hedge or create new values; or, on the contrary, whether the lack of liquidity or the required magnitude of the average investment will diminish their attractiveness.

Property characteristics and individual features which differ and which must be considered include market analysis, the buildings and their tenants, typical investment analysis, and the source and amounts of available credit. Every property differs from every other. Adjustments must be made to conform to the unit's specific type, its state, and its locality. Although the number of perfect textbook cases is few, the general principles of analysis still apply. Experts get help from these principles every day. Knowledge of the past and of new developments together with personal judgment will make today's novices into tomorrow's experts. Judgment can be gained only through practice in the application of the principles to specific properties.

## APARTMENT HOUSES

Apartment houses are the most important of income properties The market contains millions of existing structures. It is also the area of greatest current activity. Almost any investor or small group can handle some type of apartment development. Size ranges from structures with four or five units to developments containing thousands.

The late 1930s and the early postwar period rang the death knell for many apartment houses. The tremendous overbuilding of the 1920s caused havoc in the 1930s. The market was just beginning to readjust when the war brought rent control. At the end of the war, units were filled, but income was too low to enable competitive construction to take place. In addition, the easy terms available appeared to make individual houses too attractive for apartments to be built. The small amount of apartment construction in the early 1950s took place mainly as a result of special FHA financing. The upsurge of the 1960s was a surprise to many, but had been predicted by careful observers of rising basic demand.

### General Characteristics

Apartment houses are residential units containing four or more individual dwellings, each with its own cooking and bathing facilities. They may run from a single room to 10 or more. The individual units may be completely bare, or they may be furnished by the management. While some appeal primarily to transients, renting for only a week or month, others rent to semipermanent tenants on minimum leases of three years or upward.

Traditionally, apartments were thought of as high-rise, semifireproof or fireproof structures in the central city. They had elevators and often services such as operators, central switchboards, and doormen. With increases in service costs, these features have tended to disappear. New apartment structures may be in a suburb or outlying section as often as in the central city. They are more likely to be walk-ups. Their construction technique may differ only slightly from that of the single-family home.

The apartment house building boom follows the rapid expansion in recent years of households without children. Married couples without school-age children form a major market for apartments. Single individuals or two or three unmarried persons sharing a unit are as important. Young schoolteachers, secretaries, and salespeople frequently establish their own households. Widows and widowers are also likely to move from single-family houses to apartments.

In a few cities, apartments are rented to families with children. Except for these few locations and public housing, the average American chooses the single house for family living. Few recent apartments have contained as many as three bedrooms. Even so, in many locations, the larger units are harder to rent because of the absence of families in the apartment market.

### Market and Structure Analysis

Because apartment demand is so diverse, considerable effort must be given to market analysis. A large structure of 100 units might be a great success in the center of a city but a complete flop on its border. An identical structure might fail completely in another city of the same size 300 miles away. Each city and neighborhood tends to be unique in its attitude toward apartment living.

Because of the past experience of wild overbuilding, any prospective investor should check carefully the current rental market. Have numerous apartments been built recently? Such a fact is by itself no sure indication of danger, but it may be a warning. Many cities had a high backlog of apartment demand, made evident by new construction. New needs tend to expand at a far slower pace once past needs are met. Danger signals exist when new structures remain 20 per cent vacant at the end of six months or have over 5 per cent vacancies after a year. Another warning is vacancies which show up through for-rent signs on older buildings. Concessions and general price cutting on these units may increase their attractiveness compared to newer units.

Location and neighborhood are important influences on demand

and also on the type of structure built and its units. Different areas appeal to different types of people. A college or a university may create a demand from both married and unmarried students. Office buildings have many younger people who like to live nearby. Large industrial parks increase the need for apartments containing lower-priced units for working men.

The type of structure, the size of its units, and their price range should be planned in relation to the locality. Single people and young couples frequently are satisfied with efficiency or one-bedroom units. They may put more stress on the rent level than on space and design. On the other hand, older couples, used to more space and less noise, may be strongly influenced by design. In many areas parking facilities, both for occupants and visitors, may be critical in retaining tenants.

The characteristics of the structure also largely determine operating and maintenance costs. Waste in the public spaces may be expensive to clean, light, and heat. New, jerry-built units may require more frequent painting and maintenance. In older structures the state of the equipment and its maintenance may cause high or low expenditures. An apartment house that needs a new elevator, new carpets, new ranges, and similar items may yield no cash income for several years.

### Investment Analysis

To project income and expenses for the future, investment analysis must utilize all past and current information concerning both the property in question and similar structures in the city. This income analysis must then be combined with a knowledge of risks and of funds available through mortgages and equities to determine whether or not an investment will pay off.

For existing buildings, actual rent-rolls and expense statements should be available. For projected structures, income must be estimated. In both cases, investors must check to measure the accuracy of the projected net income and relate the assumed average operating experience to that of other buildings in the neighborhood. Figure 16-1 shows an investment analysis for a typical apartment house.

Most important is the projected rent. In any area, sizable variations exist in rents charged for each size of dwelling unit. The range decreases sharply when the comparison is limited to apartments in similar locations and with comparable designs.

FIGURE 16-1   *Apartment House Investment Analysis*

**52 apartments containing 133 rooms.**

*Investment Schedule*

| | |
|---|---|
| Cost | $484,200 |
| Mortgage (70%) | 338,940 |
| Equity | 145,260 |

*Income Schedule*

| | |
|---|---|
| Gross rent | $ 63,800 |
| Less 5% vacancies | 3,190 |
| Effective rental income | $ 60,610 |

*Operating Expenses*

| | |
|---|---|
| Labor | $  2,424 |
| Utilities | 1,200 |
| Maintenance and repair | 4,546 |
| Management | 3,395 |
| Total | $ 11,565 |
| Taxes and insurance | 7,880 |
| Total expenses | $ 19,445 |
| Net income | $ 41,165 |
| Less annual mortgage payment (6% at 20 years) | 29,139 |
| Annual return to equity (8.28%) | $ 12,026 |

Projections must include future rents. These depend on what is happening to the location, the relationship of current rents to costs, and whether the building is expected to depreciate relative to others because of its age, design, or construction. Well-located apartments of excellent design and with rents close to the units' reproduction costs may expect to maintain current rents into the future. On the assumption that land and construction costs will continue to rise, the difference between present and future costs of construction would allow a unit, even as it aged, to maintain its current charges because higher costs would drive up the rents on newer units. On the other hand, if the location were expected to deteriorate or if basic flaws existed in the design, projections of substantially lower rents would be realistic for the future.

Estimates of rent losses and vacancies are likely to be arbitrary. They should, however, reflect the type of units involved. Unless the demand has been badly overestimated, units for rental on long leases will have lower vacancy ratios than apartments for transients. Units built for students or other seasonal groups will have to plan for higher seasonal vacancies. These vacancies subtracted from the estimated gross rent-roll give effective gross income.

Expenses for fixed charges, for operations, and for maintenance are also built up from previous experience, other related information, and projections of the future. Real estate taxes are likely to be the largest single item. They vary from area to area, in some cases averaging under 2 per cent per year of value, in others exceeding 5 per cent. Under our present distribution of services and tax burden among localities, tax rates have been rising steadily. Increases of 2 to 4 per cent for each of the past 10 years are not unusual. Whether it is logical to assume similar increases for the future will depend on the laws of each local area.

Similarly, operating and maintenance expenses must be projected. Repairs, decorating, and replacements depend on the state of current maintenance and on the age of the structure. A backlog of overdue maintenance work may lead to costs far above the average. On the other hand, new buildings, after their first year or two, can expect below average expense. In all cases, the required physical work will have to be corrected for possible increases in wages and other costs.

The effective gross income less expenses gives the estimated net. This must be capitalized to arrive at a current investment value. The rate of capitalization will be affected by the type of structure and its relative risks. It will also be influenced by available financing terms. As an example, a recent study of the San Francisco area showed capitalization rates varying from 5.2 to 14.7 per cent. These were considerably lower than 10 years earlier. At these rates, an apartment house of the type shown in Figure 16-1 would sell for approximately $484,200.

The investor should check the price against the cost of the building and the land. With selling prices much above the amount at which similar units can be built and sold, construction will expand. Projected rents are likely to fall to those necessary to support only the true cost level.

### Financing the Apartment House

Having decided that an apartment is a worthwhile venture, a prospective owner or developer is then faced with the necessity of obtaining financing. He needs an equity plan and a lender's commitment.

Apartment house loans are made by savings and loans, mutual savings banks, insurance companies, and commercial banks. Their willingness to lend varies with types of property, the state of the money market, and their own demands for funds. Prospective investors and brokers must keep constantly aware of the current market situation and the type of loans each lender is making.

The application and loan request should be tailored to each institution's particular requirements. The borrower must decide which loan terms he feels are most critical. He may have an opportunity to bargain about fees, interest rates, amount of amortization, or amount of loan. How much can he afford to give up in one area to get what he needs in another? He may be concerned with lack of equity, need for a high cash flow, or real costs. He must negotiate with the lender to shape the loan to his needs.

The request for a tentative commitment may be based only on a rough indication of price and the form of equity financing. With a commitment the promoter will have to firm up his complete proposal. He will have to form a corporation, syndicate, partnership, or other entity for holding the property. With sufficient working capital he can make a final offer, obtain an agreement to sell, and get his firm lending commitment. After the sale is closed, the market and the skill of his analysis will determine his future results.

## OFFICE BUILDINGS

The term "office building" usually brings to mind an image of the Empire State Building or Chrysler Building or the equivalent skyscraper (usually the First National Bank) in one's hometown. Such structures are competitive office buildings, planned with space to rent to a succession of large or small tenants. But office buildings include many other types. There are the numerous single-occupancy buildings, owned and occupied by a single firm or by a unit of the government. Most business districts have a telephone building, a utility building, and one or more insurance companies with large downtown headquarters.

Single-occupancy units are even more frequent in the outskirts. They may be at a company's plant, in an industrial park, or simply off by themselves with plenty of parking. Similar structures are built on a competitive basis. Most common are professional buildings, often built by two or three doctors for their own use. Some are larger structures housing the offices of a number of doctors and dentists. Small competitive buildings for salesmen, business services, or numerous other groups are also found.

The original big office building boom took place in the 1920s. Overbuilding was rampant. When the Depression ended, more than half these units were in receivership. The postwar boom was slow in coming, but when it hit, it tended to exceed the earlier one. This more recent surge, however, was more concentrated in New York than the previous one. Most other large cities have had only small additions to their downtown space. The most common large, new buildings have been those constructed for a major firm's headquarters or regional office needs.

### General Characteristics

Office space demand arises from the ever-growing importance of services and paper work in the American economy. There are more white-collar workers who must be housed. The amount of space needed per worker has also grown. For many purposes, workers must cluster with other workers in similar jobs. Another chief need is for parking space for their cars.

Most construction has been based on prior commitments. The promoter with control over land draws up preliminary plans. He then attempts to obtain commitments for future leases, on the basis of which he can get the necessary financing. That achieved, he can start construction. Only a small minority of builders have had enough equity to proceed without prior leases.

A critical problem of office buildings is their high proportion of operating costs. Numerous services must be rendered which vary only slightly with the occupancy rate. If space is not fully occupied, income falls much more rapidly than costs. The net is squeezed. The tax problems of office buildings may also exceed those of other income properties. The percentage of value in land tends to be high. Local taxes are heavy. Land cannot be depreciated.

### Market and Structure Analysis

The market and the structure are of unusual importance in office buildings. The amount of rent they can charge and their ease of leasing are closely related to their competitors. Most cities have only one or two prime office areas. People want only these locations because they are where the propinquity exists that is the basic need of office buildings. Two or three blocks can make a difference in rents of 25 to 50 per cent for space differing only in location.

Market analysis requires a study of both the location and amount of space required. Information is frequently available on the percentage of vacancies in existing units. Data may also be found on the rate at which space needs have been growing. In most cities existing companies have been expanding. In addition, the influx of new corporations has exceeded the number leaving.

Analysis of specific locations must consider trends in transportation, availability of employee conveniences, existence of new competitors, and new complementary buildings. Since office building clients deal with each other, certain types of growth may greatly enhance a location, while others will harm it. In suburban areas, the chief factor is likely to be cheap space close to good trans-portation. The location should not be impossibly far from eating places, shopping centers, and other employee needs.

Structures must be carefully analyzed with respect to design and operating costs. Newer buildings have air conditioning, faster ele-vators, automatic elevators, and more flexible interior space. Some buildings have outmoded floor plans, making some space less de-sirable. They may leave large, unrentable public spaces that are expensive to maintain. The ratios of rentable space to gross space and to land area have a heavy influence on net income. They affect the relationships of rentable space to property taxes and other costs.

The quality of construction and the current state of maintenance determine how rapidly maintenance costs will rise and whether or not major replacements will be needed. Many prewar buildings have been completely modernized and renovated. Others with tenants tied down by long leases have neglected to stay abreast of the market.

The analysis of the building must also include a careful study of the tenants and their leases. The typical competitive building houses a variety of tenants whose leases expire throughout the next 10 years. What probabilities exist that they will want to renew and at what rents? A major factor will be the movements in rent levels since leases were initially signed. Investigation may also reveal such indications of lowered demand as the subleasing of space to others by present tenants or tenancy by businesses that have tended to concentrate in another part of town.

Such tenants will almost certainly be lost. On the other hand, some firms may need more space. Other firms may be on the verge of being forced out of owner-occupied buildings as owners expand. These and similar factors must be part of the basic market analysis.

### Investment Analysis

The information necessary for investment analysis is found in Figure 16-2. Basically, it contains the same type of information as that for the apartment house. In many cities expense ratios for existing buildings can be obtained through the National Associ-ation of Building Owners and Managers. Using a standard accounting

FIGURE 16-2   *Office Building Investment Analysis*

225,000 square feet rentable office space.

*Investment Schedule*

| | |
|---|---|
| Cost...................................................... | $4,115,000 |
| Mortgage................................................ | 2,880,000 |
| Equity................................................... | 1,235,000 |

*Income Schedule*

| | |
|---|---|
| Gross rent ($4.50 per square foot)....................... | $1,012,500 |
| Less 5% vacancies..................................... | 50,256 |
| Effective rental income.............................. | $ 961,875 |

*Operating Expenses*

| | |
|---|---|
| Cleaning............................................... | $ 136,080 |
| Utilities................................................ | 96,390 |
| Elevators.............................................. | 62,370 |
| General expense....................................... | 85,050 |
| Total.............................................. | $ 379,890 |
| Repair and tenant maintenance........................ | $ 73,710 |

*Fixed Charges*

| | |
|---|---|
| Insurance.............................................. | $ 11,340 |
| Taxes.................................................. | 102,060 |
| Total.............................................. | $ 113,400 |
| Total expenses......................................... | $ 567,000 |
| Effective rental income............................... | $ 961,875 |
| Less total expenses................................... | 567,000 |
| Free and clear return................................ | $ 394,875 |
| Less annual mortgage payment (6½% at 20 years)......... | 257,670 |
| Annual return to equity (11.1% yield)................... | $ 137,205 |

system, they publish results for different types of buildings. Their data include information on vacancy trends.

Income analysis is usually based on the number of square feet of rentable area. Typical annual rents run from $3 to $6 per square foot. Probable changes require an analysis of present leases and the competitive situation. Vacancy and collection losses must be estimated also.

Operating statements for office buildings show higher cost ratios than do most other income properties. Wages to cover cleaning, management, and in less modern buildings, elevator operations all add to expenses. More service is usually rendered. A building's future appeal depends upon how good the service is. Difficulties in estimating repairs, maintenance, and future taxes are identical to those for apartments. In typical buildings, costs including taxes and insurance run from 45 to 65 per cent of net rents. In older buildings they run higher.

In estimating the capitalization rate or its inverse, the expected free and clear return, a good deal depends upon the tenants and available financing. The better the tenants and the longer their leases, the higher the mortgage and the lower the risks. Free and clear returns are expected to run from 9 to 12 per cent a year. That means, as in the example, that the property will be worth from 8 to 11 times its free and clear return. It will, in this case, be valued at 4.1 times its expected rent-roll. Other properties might vary in value from 4 to 7 times the rent-roll, depending on the expense ratio and the quality of the tenants.

A check against land and construction costs is necessary, particularly in the case of small outlying buildings. In these cases, there are plenty of promoters and lots of space. No firm needs to pay more than a reasonable profit on actual cost to any building owner. More may be paid in a temporary shortage, but this type of space can be created too readily for the market not to be competitive.

### Financing the Office Building

Money sources for office building mortgages will depend partly upon size. Large buildings have been almost entirely the preserve of larger or more aggressive life insurance companies. Smaller ones are financed, in addition, by savings associations and banks. Interest rates tend to be higher and terms poorer for competitive office buildings than for other income properties. If a building is built for a single company or leased by it for the mortgage period, the terms depend upon the company's credit. Between the extremes, the terms are influenced by the percentage of the mortgage payments covered by AA-A1 leases.

Typical loans run from 60 to 66⅔ per cent of appraised value and from 10 to 20 years. For the shorter-period loans, amortization will not be complete. A balloon payment is left at the end, and it is assumed that the owner will be able to refinance. The shorter period gives the lender more control over future rates.

## STORES AND SHOPPING CENTERS

Commercial buildings for consumer sales have traditionally been the backbone of most cities. The 100 per cent locations where people have congregated and sales have been largest have had the highest land values. In the postwar period tastes shifted. Thousands of new outlying shopping centers were constructed. The values of many existing stores declined precipitously. Recently, even the values of some newer units have declined.

The key to the analysis of stores and shopping centers is the fact that their value depends upon the volume of sales they can generate and the cost of attracting their customers. The postwar market has witnessed important shifts in the ability of particular locations to attract customers. These changes have been closely related to the growth of the automobile and population decentralization—the movement into the outlying suburbs.

While the United States has seen the most rapid growth in metropolitan areas, the expansion has been almost entirely concentrated in the fringes. The majority of the largest central cities have lost population. While actual losses in retail volume have been less common, the rate of expansion in central-city sales has been minimal compared to that of the outskirts. Shopping centers have been both an effect and a cause of these changes.

Sales depend upon the number of customers and their incomes. The population growth in the suburbs has meant that the customers are there. The growth of income and the use of the automobile caused a decided alteration in shopping habits. Women no longer walk to their neighborhood shops or take public transit downtown. They drive to shop. As a result, sales depend upon the

ability to handle the parking problem. As people shifted from public
transit to autos, downtowns became congested. Parking was difficult,
and was not to be found at every store's door. For most purposes,
customers came to prefer stores with parking.

Along with parking, shopping centers seemed to offer other advantages. They were more informal, pleasanter, open longer hours,
and did more unified promotions. Offsetting disadvantages in lack
of choice and higher expenses were not sufficient to detract from
their general utility for most customers.

The shopping center boom was based on growing population,
higher incomes, greater parking, easier access, and changed merchandising techniques.

### General Characteristics

Conventional stores form shopping districts equivalent in many
ways to more recent shopping centers. On the other hand, each
district grew by action of many individual owners. Competition
was rife, in contrast to the unified planning of later developments.
Since so large a part of postwar promotions and sales has been
concerned with the shopping center, it is simpler to analyze its
features and then apply the same reasoning to the investment
analysis of existing stores.

A shopping center is frequently defined as a group of 10 to 100
or more retail stores on a single site, usually owned, developed,
and managed as a unit. It may also have various related service
and recreational units such as banks, restaurants, movies, and professional and business offices.

The center has certain other typical characteristics. Most important are the large parking areas which occupy most of the site.
Centers are planned as unified wholes. Common features include
architectural design, connections through malls, and special service
facilities for unloading and other transportation. Stores are selected
to complement rather than compete with each other. Frequently
they are required to join a merchants' association for joint promotion
efforts.

Centers are usually divided into three types according to their size and the market to which they appeal:

1. **Neighborhood centers** are the smallest, ranging from 5 to 15 stores. They serve a market of from 500 to 2,000 families. Their sizes vary from 10,000 to 60,000 square feet. A supermarket is usually their key tenant, with a drugstore the next most likely to appear, followed by variety or hardware units, dry cleaners, laundromats, and similar service enterprises.

2. **Community centers** are the middle group. They range in size from 20 to 40 stores and serve markets of 4,000 to 15,000 families. Their space varies from 40,000 to 140,000 square feet. Their key tenant is usually a junior department store or major variety store. They may include more than one supermarket, several apparel shops, and a wide variety of stores selling convenience goods.

3. **Regional centers** are competitive with the traditional downtown. They contain from 40 to well over 100 stores and, hopefully, serve markets of 100,000 to 250,000 customers. They are usually anchored by one or more major department stores. They offer a considerable choice of goods through several variety stores, major apparel chains, specialty stores, and a wide variety of other services.

Vast numbers of individual stores may be found in the built-up areas of cities and on numerous string streets, which in many areas are as typical of the suburbs as are shopping centers. Single units also stand alone in the midst of their own parking spaces. This type of development is particularly common for supermarkets in built-up areas.

### Market and Structure Analysis

Location is the critical factor in the valuation of stores. Their value depends upon their ability to attract customers, which in turn is a function of their location. Unfortunately, good location is not an absolute matter. What seems good today may be poor tomorrow as a result of new competition or changes in traffic patterns.

Most men who promote and finance stores depend heavily upon market surveys for an evaluation of the location and its future.

These projections are usually based on adjustments of current results when the building has an operating experience. When no prior experience exists, the market analysis aims at determining a logical trading area. This area contains the people who can be expected to purchase particular types of goods in the center.

The trading area depends upon the type of center, its location, and its competition. Neighborhood units based on supermarkets draw customers primarily from their immediate surroundings. Grocery shoppers are unlikely to drive by many stores to seek out a particular one. Exceptions occur only when a market differs sharply in its character and prices from the intervening ones. Larger centers may serve overlapping districts. The amount of business they get depends on their ability to merchandise as well as on their ease of access.

Trading areas are frequently mapped as a series of concentric circles. It is assumed that the shopping center will draw decreasing percentages of customers as distances increase. More careful surveys base their circles on driving times. A good freeway may enable customers to reach a certain store in the same time it takes to reach another store only half the distance via crowded or minor roads. Locations on or near major highways are critical for larger centers.

The market survey must also include estimates of the share of each circle that will shop at the center. That, in turn, depends upon the amount of competition. Many shopping centers run into difficulties because available land invites future competition. A shopping center may be doing extremely well; then a new center 2 miles or so down the highway may cut off most of the traffic from one side, and the original center may experience a sharp drop in sales.

The amount of sales obtained from each surrounding circle, adjusted for distance and competition, depends upon the number of households, their incomes, and their spending habits. Such information can be developed for most areas. Expected sales on items such as food and clothing follow regular patterns. To estimate the total income of each area, analysts multiply the number of families by average income. From available budget studies they can then estimate how much will be spent for food. The amount a particular store can get of such estimated expenditures depends on its competition.

The size of the center, its design, mix of stores, and type of tenant must be planned together. The market analysis shows what competition can be expected from various types of stores. The amount of potential sales available in individual categories is also estimated. Standard lists show which types of stores are most likely to enter centers of different sizes. They also indicate the number of customers and the projected sales they need to support them on an economic basis.

The physical design of the unit depends upon the size of the center, the shape of the site, and the area of the country. Designs vary widely. They have to be attractive yet inexpensive to build. Customers should find it easy to move from store to store to maximize their complementary pulling power. Questions of sun or snow protection are very different in Texas and Massachusetts. There should be sufficient variety in size of stores to fit the needs of many different tenants. Some need width but not depth, while others require the opposite.

Parking is always a problem. There must be plenty of it. This means the parking area will be three to four or even more times as large as the store area. Some designs stress front parking, others side or rear. Again, a great deal depends on the locality and the size of the center.

Getting the tenants is the critical issue in most developments. Leases are signed on the basis of the market survey and preliminary plans. Usually a few key tenants are the heart of the operation. Without them the other tenants cannot be attracted, nor can the project succeed. Still more crucial is the fact that without them no mortgage money will be forthcoming. The result is that key tenants are frequently in the driver's seat. This is particularly true when plenty of land is available so that the tenants can choose from among a large number of offers.

In many cases the key tenants have insisted upon becoming partners in the development. In others, they have been given free land on which to build their own units. Other inducements may include low rents or no set minimum until the success of the property is established. A few key tenants in most projects will do a majority of the total volume of business.

## Investment Analysis

The investment analysis of shopping centers is tied in very closely to the amount of sales the property will generate. Most leases provide

FIGURE 16-3   *Shopping Center Investment Analysis*

**200,000 square feet store area.**

*Investment Schedule*

| | |
|---|---:|
| Land (28 acres at $20,000 per acre)...................... | $  560,000 |
| Parking lot paving (700,000 square feet at 40¢ per square foot) | 280,000 |
| Building (200,000 square feet at $13.60 per square foot)..... | 2,720,000 |
| Cost............................................... | $3,560,000 |
| Mortgage............................................ | 2,400,000 |
| Equity.............................................. | 1,160,000 |

*Income Schedule*

| | |
|---|---:|
| Fixed minimum rentals (at $1.75 average)................. | $  350,000 |
| Estimated overages ($10,800,000 volume at 4% average = | |
| $432,000 less $350,000 minimums)...................... | 82,000 |
| Total rent........................................ | $  432,000 |
| Less operating expense............................... | 55,000 |
| Less taxes........................................... | 65,000 |
| Net free and clear return............................ | $  312,000 |
| Less annual mortgage payment (6½% at 20 years)......... | 214,725 |
| Annual return to equity (8.4%)........................ | $   97,275 |

for minimum payments which will cover only mortgage and tax requirements plus a large share of expected operating costs. Returns to the equity holders depend upon the center's generating enough sales to permit the tenants to pay overages. A case example of an investment analysis is contained in Figure 16-3.

Most information is obtained on a square-foot basis. Thus the center in this case has 200,000 square feet of selling area. It is on a site of 28 acres purchased for $20,000 an acre, or a total of $560,000. The remainder of the site is primarily parking space. It costs an additional $280,000 to prepare. The building costs $13.60 per square foot. The total cost of the project is thus $3,560,000, or $17.80 per foot of selling space. This is in the range of competitive costs for many centers.

In this case, fixed minimum rental payments average $1.75 per foot. Actual minimums vary from $1.25 per foot for a junior department store up to $5.00 a foot for a candy or jewelry store. The rental agreements specify that the various stores will pay from 3 to 9 per cent of whatever volume of sales they make in the year or the minimum amount, whichever is greater. The property's value will depend on how much the rents based on the percentages of sales exceed the minimum. According to the market analysis using stabilized estimates of the future, the stores should have sales of from $40 to $80 per square foot per year. The percentage rents for all stores are expected to average 4.0 per year. Total volume is estimated at $10,800,000, or $54 of sales per foot. At this volume, the rent would total $432,000. The sum of $350,000 is the guaranteed minimum. The larger amount is derived from the projection that there will be $82,000 of rent overages based on the percentages of sales.

Taxes and other operating expenses are estimated at $120,000. This amount includes funds for maintaining the common areas and for some joint promotion. Most leases contain clauses specifying that the tenants' minimum rents will rise proportionately with increases in all the costs except for management.

The free and clear return in the figure is $312,000. In this case the mortgage payments total $214,725. Based on the estimates, this offer is not too attractive to the equity investor. The mortgage covers only 70 per cent of the total cost. The estimated cash flow gives a return to the equity of slightly under 8.5 per cent. On the other hand, the minimum guaranteed rents more than cover all expenses. Risk of loss will depend on whether any tenants are so poor that they are likely to go bankrupt.

The prospects of gain depend partly on the tax situation and partly on hopes for increased volume. The volume might rise because of a more rapid market growth than projected or if inflation caused a rise in the average price of each unit sold. In either case, the owner's leverage would work to increase his profits rapidly. A 20 per cent increase in the volume of sales would cause rents to rise by an equivalent amount. The owner's return would nearly double.

## Financing the Shopping Center

The equities for shopping centers usually come from individuals, syndicates, corporations that are tenants, real estate corporations, real estate trusts, and insurance companies. In other words, in recent years, most types of real estate investors have been interested in purchasing shopping centers. Their interest has been heightened by the great success of many of the early centers. Returns were high because of the high leverage and the fact that unexpected overages occurred. As competition has expanded, however, the average amount of rental overages received by each project has been falling.

The major lenders in this sphere have been insurance companies. Smaller centers, however, have also been financed by local lenders.

Insurance companies have established rules of thumb which they frequently use as the basis of their negotiations in each separate situation. Most such rules make the size of the mortgage depend upon the quality of the tenants. In one system, the value of an AA-A1 tenant is considered twice that of small neighborhood firms. The amount of mortgage would be 7 times the guaranteed rent from the larger tenant plus 3.5 times the guaranteed rents of the smaller firms.

A similar system considers the actual required mortgage payments plus estimated operating costs. The national tenants' minimum leases must cover the required mortgage payments. The national tenants' minimums plus minimums of one-half the tenants left must cover all necessary payments. Related requirements are based on costs. For example, some lenders insist that the mortgage not exceed $10 to $14 per square foot of floor space. The amount loaned per foot varies with location and the type of development.

The type of tenants and their leases also determine the loan-to-value ratio and the interest and amortization payments. Loans are usually limited to two-thirds of appraised value, but they may run from 65 to 80 per cent of actual cost. The interest rates range from 5½ to 7 per cent. Total payments including amortization vary between 9 and 11 per cent per year. The length of the mortgage is frequently 10 to 15 years. This means that a balloon payment is required when the note is due.

As in other areas, shifting requirements of lenders with respect to necessary equities and rates of payment on the loan have been important in determining the number of shopping centers started in any period. Numerous projects have been brought almost to the point of starting construction, only to find that movements in the going rates for loans made it impossible to get a large enough mortgage based upon the existing leases. New negotiations with tenants, waiting for better mortgage terms, or new plans became necessary.

## INDUSTRIAL AND SPECIAL–PURPOSE PROPERTIES

Among the many other types of property that require financing, most fall in the special-purpose class. Special-purpose properties, because of their design and construction, have but little use for, or would be very expensive to revamp for, purposes other than those for which they are built. In most such cases, the success of the building depends upon the success of the business operated within it. It is difficult to separate the analysis of the property from the firm operating it.

Examples of special-purpose buildings are motels, hotels, bowling alleys, hospitals, nursing homes, banks, and specialized industrial plants. It is clear from the list that a constant need exists for properties of these types. On the other hand, it is also clear that many of them seem to have gone through periods of drastic overbuilding.

In all such cases, risks were initially recognized as high. Financing was hard to get. But because an underlying demand existed, successfully completed projects paid large returns. Developers and lenders assumed, because some were successful, that risks were less than they had previously judged. Lenders and promoters had some data to go on. It became easier to raise the necessary capital. Soon an oversupply became evident. Risks were reevaluated. This type of cycle has been common in many of the special-purpose markets.

The number of possible special-purpose properties is too large to deal with each individually. The general lines of analysis laid out for the previous cases apply to them also. There must be a careful projection of the market plus a specific estimate of income and operating costs. This can then be translated into an effective net income. Based upon knowledge of mortgage terms available for these properties, tax consequences, and risks, these projected returns can be capitalized into an estimate of value.

The estimate of value becomes the basis for attempting to get the necessary financing. If money can be raised, the project can proceed. As in all such cases, two types of success are possible. The first is based on convincing prospects that a line of reasoning is sound, that a demand exists, and that a profit will be forthcoming if the project is built. If investors are available, a promoter will make a profit. The second type of success is measured by the actual market results after the project is in operation. The possibilities of true profits, as opposed to merely promoter's profits, will depend upon how good a job of analysis and risk estimation has been performed.

## SUMMARY

Each type of income property requires a separate investment analysis. Frequently much of the analysis is done with rules of thumb stressing such factors as multiples of gross rents, costs per square foot, and percentages of gross income. While these short cuts are useful for initial analysis, they turn out to be faulty and dangerous for final decisions. The careful investor recognizes the vast differences in expected returns and risks which arise from the financing agreement. The investment analysis must consider the pattern of expected cash flows both because their time path is an important determinant of the true yield and because their relationship to the promised mortgage payments controls the risk.

The methods by which gross rents and costs are projected will also have an important impact on the reliability of the value estimate. The maintenance or improvement of the rent-roll is far more probable in some situations than in others. Cities are changing at a rapid rate. Extremely valuable downtown properties have dropped in value 50 to 75 per cent in only a few years. Others have experienced equivalent gains. A simple assumption that what is will continue to be is likely to be wrong as often as right.

Similar problems arise with respect to costs and expenses. They will be strongly influenced by the design, construction, and previous maintenance of the structure. They will also be affected by shifting wage rates and taxes. Many buildings have required large additional expenditures in an only partially successful attempt to lower wage costs.

Fluctuating tendencies to lower estimates of the risks involved on the strength of examples of recent successes have been as significant as the actual net revenue estimates are in determining the future of purchases and loans. The fact that some enterprising promoters have taken chances and have uncovered very successful markets does not mean, as frequently happens, that the risks assumed to exist in such markets should be substantially lowered. A tendency exists for the successful leader to attract too many followers. Risks may actually rise after an initial success because of failures to recognize how many people are attempting to exploit the new market.

The history of the past few years gives little indication that the real estate market has become a simpler or more stable object of analysis. Periods of inflation and rising prices have covered over many errors and have enabled many poor developments to turn in large or even tremendous profits. As soon as the market has stabilized, however, marginal investments that in inflationary periods would have worked out successfully have turned bad.

The future promises to be one of further growth and change. Widespread opportunities for investment will continue to appear. On the other hand, the postwar backlog of accumulated demand has disappeared. The number of investors and promoters actively engaged in seeking real estate investments has expanded tremendously. Those who fail to use careful investment analysis and whose failure is not compensated for by a generous amount of luck will have a much more difficult time than in the recent past. Those who learn to use a sharp pencil and to think through the complicated problems involved in investment decisions will improve their probabilities of success.

## SELECTED REFERENCES

Bryant, Willis R.: *Mortgage Lending,* 2d ed., McGraw-Hill, New York, 1962.

Casey, W. J.: Various books and pamphlets published by the Institute for Business Planning, New York.

Hoagland, H. E., and L. D. Stone: *Real Estate Finance,* rev. ed., Richard D. Irwin, Inc., Homewood, Ill., 1961.

Kahn, S. A., et al.: *Real Estate Appraisal and Investment.* The Ronald Company, New York, 1963.

Martin, P.: *Real Estate Principles and Practices,* The Macmillan Company, New York, 1959.

McMichael, S. L., and P. T. O'Keefe: *How to Finance Real Estate,* 2d ed., Prentice-Hall, Inc., Englewood Cliffs, N.J., 1953.

Pease, Robert H., and Homer V. Cherrington: *Mortgage Banking,* McGraw-Hill Book Company, New York, 1953.

# Glossary of Real Estate Financing Terms*

Abstract of Title   A summary or digest of the conveyances, transfers, and any other facts relied on as evidence of title, together with any other elements of record which may impair the title.

Acceleration Clause   A clause in a trust deed or mortgage giving the lender the right to call all sums owing him to be immediately due upon the happening of a certain event.

Acknowledgment   A formal declaration before a duly authorized officer by a person who has executed an instrument that such execution is his act and deed.

Administrator   A person appointed by the probate court to administer the estate of a person deceased.

Ad valorem   Latin for according to value.

Adverse Possession   The open and notorious possession and occupancy under an evident claim or right, in denial of, or opposition to, the title of another claimant.

Agent   One who represents another from whom he has derived authority.

Agreement of Sale   A written agreement or contract between seller and purchaser in which they reach a meeting of minds on the terms and conditions of a sale.

Amenity   That which contributes satisfaction rather than money income to its owner.

Amortization   The liquidation of a financial obligation on an installment basis.

Appraisal   An estimate and opinion of value.

Assessed Value   A valuation placed upon property by a public officer or board as a basis for taxation.

---

* Acknowledgment is made to the *Savings and Loan Fact Book* and the State of California Division of Real Estate *Reference Book*.

**Assessment**   The valuation of property for the purpose of levying a tax or the amount of the tax levied.

**Assignee**   One to whom property is transferred.

**Assignor**   One who assigns or transfers property.

**Assumption of Mortgage**   The taking of title to property by a grantee, wherein he assumes liability for payment of an existing note secured by a mortgage or deed of trust against the property, becoming a coguarantor for the payment of a mortgage or deed-of-trust note.

**Attachment**   Seizure of property by court order, usually done to have it available in event a judgment is obtained in a pending suit.

**Balloon Payment**   The final installment payment on a note when that payment is greater than the preceding installment payments and pays the note in full.

**Beneficiary**   (1) One entitled to the benefit of a trust; (2) one who receives profit from an estate, the title of which is vested in a trustee; (3) the lender on the security of a note and deed of trust.

**Blanket Mortgage**   A single mortgage which covers more than one piece of real estate.

**Borrower**   One who receives a loan with the intention of repaying.

**Broker**   One who for a commission or fee brings parties together and assists in negotiating contracts between them.

**Capitalization**   In appraising, determining value of property by considering net income and percentage of reasonable return on the investment.

**Capitalization Rate**   The rate of interest which is considered a reasonable return on the investment and is used in the process of determining value based upon net income.

**Collateral**   Stocks, bonds, evidence of deposit, and other marketable properties which a borrower pledges as security for a loan. In mortgage lending, the collateral is the specific real property which the borrower pledges as security.

**Commission**   An agent's compensation for performing the duties of his agency; in real estate practice, a percentage of the selling price of property, percentage of rentals, etc.

**Commitment**   A pledge or a promise or firm agreement to make a loan.

**Compound Interest**   Interest paid on original principal and also on the accrued and unpaid interest which has accumulated.

**Conditional Sale Contract**   A contract for the sale of property stating that delivery is to be made to the buyer, title to remain vested in the seller until the conditions of the contract have been fulfilled.

**Condominium**   A system of direct ownership of a single unit in a multi-unit structure. The individual owns the unit in much the same manner as if it were a single-family dwelling; he holds direct legal title to the unit and a proportionate interest in the common areas and the underlying ground. (See Cooperative.)

**Constant rate**   A level payment on a mortgage which includes both interest and principal payments.

**Construction Loan**   A loan which is made to finance the actual construction of improvements on land.

**Contract**   An agreement, either written or oral, to do or not to do certain things.

**Contract of Sale**   An agreement to transfer title after certain payments or conditions have been met.

**Conventional Loan**   A mortgage loan made by a financial institution without insurance or guarantee by the FHA or VA. It is called a conventional loan because it conforms to accepted standards, modified within legal bounds by mutual consent of the borrower and lender.

**Conveyance**   The transfer of the title of land from one to another. An instrument which carries from one person to another an interest in land.

**Cooperative**   A system of indirect ownership of a single unit in a multi-unit structure. The individual owns shares in a nonprofit corporation which holds title to the building; the corporation in turn gives the owner a long-term proprietary lease on the unit.

**Corporation**   A group or body of persons established and treated by law as an individual or unit with both rights and liabilities distinct and apart from those of the persons composing it.

**Debentures**   A form of bond or note.

**Debt**   A sum of money due by certain and express agreement.

**Deed** A written instrument which, when properly executed and delivered, conveys title.

**Deed of Trust** A conveyance of the title to land to a trustee as collateral security for the payment of a debt with the condition that the trustee shall reconvey the title upon the payment of the debt, and with power of the trustee to sell the land and pay the debt in the event of a default on the part of the debtor.

**Default** Failure to fulfill a duty or promise or to discharge an obligation.

**Deficiency Judgment** A judgment given when the security pledge for a loan does not satisfy the debt upon its default.

**Demand Mortgage** A mortgage which is payable on demand of the holder of the evidence of the debt.

**Depreciation** Loss of value in real property brought about by age, physical deterioration, or functional or economic obsolescence. Broadly, a loss in value from any cause.

**Discount** Interest or a fee deducted from loan at time it is made or sold.

**Easement** The right, privilege, or interest which one party has in the land of another.

**Economic Life** The period over which a building will yield a return on its investment.

**Eminent Domain** The right of the government to acquire property for necessary public or quasi-public use by condemnation; the owner must be fairly compensated.

**Encumbrance** Anything which affects or limits the fee simple title to property, such as a mortgage, an easement, or a restriction of any kind. Liens are special encumbrances which make the property security for the payment of a debt or obligation, such as a mortgage or taxes.

**Equity** The interest or value which an owner has in real estate over and above the liens against it.

**Equity of Redemption** The right to redeem property during the foreclosure period, such as a mortgagor's right to redeem within a year after foreclosure sale.

**Escrow** The deposit of instruments and funds with instructions to a third neutral party to carry out the provisions of an agreement or contract.

**Estate**   The degree, quantity, nature, and extent of interest which a person has in real property.

**Execute**   To complete, to make, to perform, to do, to follow out; to execute a deed is to make a deed, including especially signing, sealing, and delivery; to execute a contract is to perform the contract, to follow out to the end, to complete.

**Federal Home Loan Bank (FHLB)**   One of the 12 federally chartered regional banks of the Federal Home Loan Bank System. A bank's primary function is to supply credit to member institutions.

**Federal National Mortgage Association (FNMA, also called Fanny May)**   A quasi-governmental corporation which supplements private mortgage funds by buying and selling FHA and VA loans.

**Federal Savings and Loan Insurance Corporation (FSLIC)**   An instrumentality of the Federal government which insures the savings accounts in member institutions.

**Fee**   The highest type of interest a person can have in land. Absolute ownership (subject to laws) with the right to dispose of it or pass it on to his heirs as he sees fit. The term "fee" is of Old English derivation.

**Fee Simple**   In modern estates, the terms "fee" and "fee simple" are substantially synonymous.

**Fiduciary**   A person in a position of trust and confidence.

**Financial Intermediary**   A financial institution which acts as an intermediary between savers and borrowers by selling its own obligations for money and, in turn, lending the accumulated funds to borrowers. The classification includes savings associations, mutual savings banks, life insurance companies, credit unions, and investment companies.

**Foreclosure**   A procedure whereby property pledged as security for a debt is sold to pay the debt in event of default in payments or terms.

**Forfeiture**   Loss of money or anything of value due to failure to perform, for instance under an agreement to purchase.

**Garnishee**   To attach a specified sum from wages to satisfy a creditor.

**Graduated Lease**   A lease which provides for a varying rental rate, often based upon future determination; sometimes rent is based upon the result of periodic appraisals; used largely in long-term leases.

**Grantee**   The purchaser of property; a person to whom a grant is made.

**Grantor**   The seller of property; one who signs a deed.

**Gross Income**   The total income from property before any expenses are deducted.

**Hundred Per Cent Location**   A city retail-business location which is considered the best available for attracting business.

**Hypothecate**   To give a thing as security without the necessity of giving up possession of it.

**Income Property**   A property which produces a money income to the owner.

**Installment Note**   A note which provides that payments of a certain sum be made on the dates specified in the instrument.

**Interest Rate**   The percentage of a sum of money charged for its use.

**Involuntary Lien**   A lien imposed against property without consent of an owner.

**Joint Tenancy**   Joint ownership by two or more persons with right of survivorship; all joint tenants own equal interest and have equal rights in the property.

**Judgment**   The final determination of a court of competent jurisdiction of a matter presented to it; money judgments provide for the payment of claims presented to the court or are awarded as damages.

**Junior Mortgage**   A lien that is subsequent to the claims of the holder of a prior mortgage.

**Land Contract**   A contract ordinarily used in connection with the sale of property in cases where the seller does not wish to convey title until all or a certain part of the purchase price is paid by the buyer; often used when property is sold on small down payment.

**Lease**   A contract between owner and tenant, setting forth conditions upon which the tenant may occupy and use the property and the term of the occupancy.

**Leasehold**   The estate held by virtue of a lease.

**Lessee**   One who contracts to rent property under a lease contract.

**Lessor**   An owner who enters into a lease with a tenant.

**Lien**   A form of encumbrance which usually makes property security for the payment of a debt or discharge of an obligation. Examples: judgments, taxes, mortgages, deeds of trust.

**Liquidity**   The cash position of an association measured by the cash on hand and securities quickly convertible into cash.

**Loan**   A sum of money lent at interest to be repaid.

**Loan Fee**   The charge made at the granting of a loan in addition to required interest.

**Market Value**   (1) The price at which a willing seller would sell and a willing buyer would buy, neither being under abnormal pressure; (2) as defined by the courts, the highest price estimated in terms of money which a property will bring if exposed for sale in the open market, allowing a reasonable time to find a purchaser with knowledge of property's use and capabilities for use.

**Mechanic's Lien**   A claim, created by statutory law in most states, existing in favor of mechanics or other persons who have performed work in, or furnished materials for, the erection or repair of a building.

**Moratorium**   The temporary suspension, usually by statute, of the enforcement of liability for debt.

**Mortgage**   An instrument recognized by law by which property is hypothecated to secure the payment of a debt or obligation; procedure for foreclosure in event of default is established by statute.

**Mortgage Company**   A private corporation whose principal activity is the origination and servicing of mortgage loans which are sold to financial institutions.

**Mortgagee**   One to whom a mortgagor gives a mortgage; a lender.

**Mortgage Insurance Premium**   The amount paid by the borrower for insurance by the FHA of a loan.

**Mortgagor**   One who gives a mortgage on his property to secure a loan or assure performance of an obligation; a borrower.

**Net Income**   That part of the gross income which remains after the deduction of all charges or costs.

**Net Yield**   That part of the gross yield which remains after the deduction of all charges or costs including necessary reserves.

**Nominal Interest Rate**   The interest rate stated in the loan agreement.

**Note**   A signed written instrument acknowledging a debt and promising payment.

**Obsolescence**   Loss in value due to reduced desirability and usefulness of a structure when its design and construction become old-fashioned and not in keeping with modern needs.

**Open-end Mortgage**   A mortgage which states the intention of the borrower and of the lender that the mortgage shall stand as security not only for the original loan but also for future advances that the lender may be willing to make.

**Option**   A right given for a consideration to purchase or lease a property upon specified terms within a specified time.

**Participation Loan**   A mortgage loan in which more than one association has an interest. One association makes the loan, and one or more associations purchase an interest in the loan.

**Partnership**   As between partners themselves, a contract of two or more persons to unite their property, labor, or skill or some of these, in prosecution of some joint and lawful business, and to share the profits in certain proportions.

**Percentage Lease**   A lease on property the rental for which is determined by the amount of business done by the lessee; usually the rental is a percentage of gross receipts from the business, and there is a provision for a minimum rental.

**Personal Property**   Any property which is not real property.

**Points**   The amount of a discount stated as a percentage.

**Prepayment Penalty**   A penalty for the payment of a debt before it actually becomes due.

**Present Value**   The current value of an amount to be received in the future.

**Principal**   The amount of debt.

**Proration of Taxes**   The division of taxes equally or proportionately to time of use.

**Purchase-money Mortgage or Trust Deed**   A trust deed or mortgage given as part or all of the purchase consideration for property.

**Quitclaim Deed**   A deed to relinquish any interest in property which the grantor may have.

**Reconveyance**   The transfer of the title of land from one person to the immediately preceding owner. This particular instrument is commonly used when the performance or debt is satisfied under the terms of a deed of trust and the trustee conveys the title he has held on condition back to the owner.

**Recourse**   The right to claim against a prior owner of a property or note.

**Redemption**   Buying back one's property after a judicial sale.

**Release Clause**   A stipulation that upon the payment of a specific sum of money to the holder of a trust deed or mortgage, the lien on a specific described lot or area shall be removed from the blanket lien on the whole area involved.

**Reserves**   Those portions of earnings which have been set aside to take care of possible losses in the conduct of business; listed in the balance sheet as a liability item.

**Right of Way**   A privilege operating as an easement upon land, whereby the owner, by grant or by agreement, gives to another the right to pass over his land, to construct a roadway, or to use as a roadway a specific part of his land, or gives the right to construct through and over his land telephone, telegraph, or electric power lines, or gives the right to place underground water mains, gas mains, or sewer mains.

**Risk**   The probability of future loss.

**Risk Rating**   A process by which various risks are evaluated, usually employing grids to develop precise and relative figures for the purpose of determining the over-all soundness of a loan.

**Sales Contract**   A contract by which buyer and seller agree to terms of a sale.

**Savings and Loan Association**   A financial intermediary which receives savings and invests these savings mainly in mortgage loans. Always a corporation, it may be either a mutual or a capital stock institution and may be either state chartered or federally chartered.

**Savings Bank**   A financial intermediary which receives savings in the form of deposits and invests these deposits in mortgages and other securities allowed by law. The banks, with the exception of a few in New Hampshire, are mutual institutions and are governed by self-perpetuating boards of trustees.

**Secondary Financing**    A loan secured by a second mortgage or deed of trust on real property.

**Security**    Something given, deposited, or pledged to make secure the fulfillment of an obligation or the payment of a debt.

**Servicing**    The collection of payments on a mortgage. Servicing by the lender also consists of operational procedures covering accounting, bookkeeping, insurance, tax records, loan-payment follow-up, delinquent-loan follow-up, and loan analysis.

**Sheriff's Deed**    A deed given by court order in connection with the sale of property to satisfy a judgment.

**Sinking Fund**    A fund set aside from the income from property which, with accrued interest, will eventually pay for replacement of the improvements.

**Statute of Frauds**    A state law which provides that certain contracts must be in writing in order to be enforceable at law. Examples: real property lease for more than one year; agent's authorization to sell real estate.

**Subject to Mortgage**    When a grantee takes title to real property subject to mortgage, he is not responsible to the holder of the promissory note for the payment of any portion of the amount due. The most that he can lose in the event of a foreclosure is his equity in the property.

**Subordination Clause**    (1) A clause in a junior lien permitting retention of priority for other liens; (2) a clause in a first deed of trust, permitting it to be subordinated to subsequent liens, for example, the liens of construction loans.

**Tenancy in Common**    Ownership by two or more persons who hold undivided interest, without right of survivorship; interests need not be equal.

**Title**    Evidence that the owner of land is in lawful possession of it; an instrument evidencing such ownership.

**Title Insurance**    Insurance written by a title company to protect a property owner against loss if title is imperfect.

**Trust Deed**    *see* Deed of Trust.

**Trustee**    One who holds property in trust for another to secure the performance of an obligation.

**Trustor**  One who deeds his property to a trustee to be held as security until he has performed his obligation to a lender under terms of a deed of trust.

**Usury**  On a loan, claiming a rate of interest greater than that permitted by law.

**Valuation**  Estimated worth or price; the act of valuing by appraisal.

**Vendee**  A purchaser, or buyer.

**Vendor**  A seller, or one who disposes of a thing in consideration of money.

**Waste**  Damage to property by neglect or otherwise.

**Zoning**  Specification by city or county authorities of the type of use to which property may be put in specific areas.

# Index